# CHILTON BOOK COMPANY

MW00355875

## REPAIR & TUNE-UP GUIDE

# MAZDA 1971 to 1987

All U.S. and Canadian models of RX-2 • RX-3 • RX-4 •
808 (1300, 1600) • Cosmo • GLC • 323 • 626

Vice President and General Manager **JOHN P. KUSHNERICK**
Editor-in-Chief **KERRY A. FREEMAN, S.A.E.**
Managing Editor **DEAN F. MORGANTINI, S.A.E.**
Senior Editor **RICHARD J. RIVELE, S.A.E.**
Senior Editor **W. CALVIN SETTLE, JR., S.A.E.**
Editor **JOHN M. BAXTER, S.A.E.**

**CHILTON BOOK COMPANY**
**Radnor, Pennsylvania**
**19089**

## SAFETY NOTICE

Proper service and repair procedures are vital to the safe, reliable operation of all motor vehicles, as well as the personal safety of those performing repairs. This book outlines procedures for servicing and repairing vehicles using safe, effective methods. The procedures contain many NOTES, CAUTIONS and WARNINGS which should be followed along with standard safety procedures to eliminate the possibility of personal injury or improper service which could damage the vehicle or compromise its safety.

It is important to note that repair procedures and techniques, tools and parts for servicing motor vehicles, as well as the skill and experience of the individual performing the work vary widely. It is not possible to anticipate all of the conceivable ways or conditions under which vehicles may be services, or to provide cautions as to all of the possible hazards that may result. Standard and accepted safety precautions and equipment should be used during cutting, grinding, chiseling, prying, or any other process that can cause material removal or projectiles.

Some procedures require the use of tools specially designed for a specific purpose. Before substituting another tool or procedure, you must be completely satisfied that neither your personal safety, nor the performance of the vehicle will be endangered.

Although the information in this guide is based on industry sources and is as complete as possible at the time of publication, the possibility exists that the manufacturer made later changes which could not be included here. While striving for total accuracy. Chilton Book Company cannot assume responsibility for any errors, changes, or omissions that may occur in the compilation of this data.

## PART NUMBERS

Part numbers listed in this reference are not recommendations by Chilton for any product by brand name. They are references that can be used with interchange manuals and aftermarket supplier catalogs to locate each brand supplier's discrete part number.

## SPECIAL TOOLS

Special tools are recommended by the vehicle manufacturer to perform their specific job. Use has been kept to a minimum, but where absolutely necessary, they are referred to the text by the part number of the tool manufacturer. These tools can be purchased, under the appropriate part number, from your Mazda dealer or regional distributor or an equivalent tool can be purchased locally from a tool supplier or parts outlet. Before substituting any tool for the one recommended, read the SAFETY NOTICE at the top of this page.

## ACKNOWLEDGMENTS

The Chilton Book Company expresses its appreciation to the Mazda Technical Center, Inc., Irvine, California 92714; YBH Mazda, Inc., Edgemount, Pennsylvania 19028; Mazda Motors of America (East), Inc., Jacksonville, Florida; and Toyo Kogyo Co., Ltd., Hiroshima, Japan.

Chilton's Repair & Tune-Up Guide: Mazda 1971–87
ISBN 0-8019-7752-5 pbk.
Library of Congress Catalog Card No. 86-47774

# CONTENTS

# Quick Reference Specifications For Your Vehicle

Fill in this chart with the most commonly used specifications for your vehicle. Specifications can be found in Chapters 1 through 3 or on the tune-up decal under the hood of the vehicle.

 ## Tune-Up

Firing Order_____

Spark Plugs:

    Type_____

    Gap (in.)_____

Torque (ft. lbs.)_____

Idle Speed (rpm)_____

Ignition Timing (°)_____

    Vacuum or Electronic Advance (Connected/Disconnected)_____

Valve Clearance (in.)

    Intake_____        Exhaust_____

 ## Capacities

Engine Oil Type (API Rating)_____

    With Filter Change (qts)_____

    Without Filter Change (qts)_____

Cooling System (qts)_____

Manual Transmission (pts)_____

    Type_____

Automatic Transmission (pts)_____

    Type_____

Front Differential (pts)_____

    Type_____

Rear Differential (pts)_____

    Type_____

Transfer Case (pts)_____

    Type_____

## FREQUENTLY REPLACED PARTS

Use these spaces to record the part numbers of frequently replaced parts.

| PCV VALVE | OIL FILTER | AIR FILTER | FUEL FILTER |
|-----------|------------|------------|-------------|
| Type_____ | Type_____ | Type_____ | Type_____ |
| Part No._____ | Part No._____ | Part No._____ | Part No._____ |

# General Information and Maintenance

## HOW TO USE THIS BOOK

Chilton's Repair & Tune-Up Guide for the Mazda is intended to help you learn more about the inner workings of your vehicle and save you money on its upkeep and operation. It is designed to aid the owner of both rotary powered and piston powered Mazdas to perform service operations on his or her automobile.

The first two chapters will be the most used, since they contain maintenance and tune-up information and procedures. Studies have shown that a properly tuned and maintained car can get at least 10% better gas mileage than an out-of-tune car. The other chapters deal with the more complex systems of your car. Operating systems from engine through brakes are covered to extent that the average do-it-yourselfer becomes mechanically involved. This book will not explain such items as rebuilding the differential for the simple reason the the expertise required and the investment in special tools make this task uneconomical. It will give you detailed instructions to help you change your own brake pads and shoes, replace points and plugs, and do many more jobs that will save you money, give you personal satisfaction, and help you avoid expensive problems.

A secondary purpose of this book is as a reference for owners who want to better understand their car and/or what their mechanic has to say. In this case, no tools at all are required.

Before starting disassembly read through the entire procedure. This will give you the overall view of what tools and supplies will be required. There is nothing more frustrating than having to walk to the bus stop on Monday morning because you were short one bolt on Sunday afternoon. So read ahead and plan ahead. Each operation should be approached logically and all procedures thoroughly understood before attempting any work.

All chapters contain adjustments, maintenance, removal and installation procedures, and repair or overhaul procedures. When repair is not considered practical, we tell you how to remove the part and then how to install the new or rebuilt replacement. In this way, you at least save the labor costs. Backyard repair of such components as the alternator is just not practical.

Two basic mechanic's rules should be mentioned here. One, whenever the left side of the car or engine is referred to, it is meant to specify the driver's side of the car. Conversely, the right side of the car means the passenger's side. Secondly, most screws and bolts are removed by turning clockwise.

Safety is always the most important rule. Constantly be aware of the dangers involved in working on an automobile and take the proper precautions. (See the section in this chapter Servicing Your Vehicle Safely and the SAFETY NOTICE on the acknowledgment page.)

Pay attention to the instructions provided. There are 3 common mistakes in mechanical work:

1. Incorrect order of assembly, disassembly or adjustment. When taking something apart or putting it together, doing things in the wrong order usually just costs you extra time; however, it CAN break something. Read the entire procedure before beginning disassembly. Do everything in the order in which the instructions say you should do it, even if you can't immediately see a reason for it. When you're taking apart something that is very intricate (for example, a carburetor), you might want to draw a picture of how it looks when assembled at one point in order to make sure you get everything back in its proper position. (We will supply exploded views whenever possible.) When making adjustments, especially tune-up adjustments, do them in order; often, one adjustment affects another, and you cannot ex-

pect even satisfactory results unless each adjustment is made only when it cannot be changed by any other.

2. Overtorquing (or undertorquing). While it is more common for overtorquing to cause damage, undertorquing can cause a fastener to vibrate loose causing serious damage. Especially when dealing with aluminum parts, pay attention to torque specifications and utilize a torque wrench in assembly. If a torque figure is not available, remember that if you are using the right tool to do the job, you will probably not have to strain yourself to get a fastener tight enough. The pitch of most threads is so slight that the tension you put on the wrench will be multiplied many, many times in actual force on what you are tightening. A good example of how critical torque is can be seen in the case of spark plug installation, especially where you are putting the plug into and aluminum cylinder head. Too little torque can fail to crush the gasket, causing leakage of combustion gases and consequent overheating of the plug and engine parts. Too much torque can damage the threads, or distort the plug, which changes the spark gap.

There are many commercial products available for ensuring that fasteners won't come loose, even if they are not torqued just right (a very common brand is Loctite®).

If you're worried about getting something together tight enough to hold, but loose enough to avoid mechanical damage during assembly, one of these products might offer substantial insurance. Read the label on the package and make sure the product is compatible with the materials, fluids, etc. involved before choosing one.

3. Crossthreading. This occurs when a part such as a bolt is screwed into a nut or casting at the wrong angle and forced. Cross threading is more likely to occur if access is difficult. It helps to clean and lubricate fasteners and to start threading with the part to be installed going straight in. Then, start the bolt, spark plug, etc., with your fingers. If you encounter resistance, unscrew the part and start over again at a different angle until it can be inserted and turned several turns without much effort. Keep in mind that many parts, especially spark plugs, use tampered threads so that gentle turning will automatically bring the part you're threading to the proper angle if you don't force it or resist a change in angle. Don't put a wrench on the part until it's been turned a couple of turns by hand. If you suddenly encounter resistance, and the part has not seated fully, don't force it. Pull it back out and make sure it's clean and threading properly.

Always take your time and be patient; once you have some experience, working on your car will become an enjoyable hobby.

## TOOLS AND EQUIPMENT

Naturally, without the proper tools and equipment it is impossible to properly service your vehicle. It would be impossible to catalog each tool that you would need to perform each or any operation in this book. It would also be unwise for the amateur to rush out and buy an expensive set of tools on the theory that he may need one or more of them at some time.

The best approach is to proceed slowly, gathering together a good quality set of those tools that are used most frequently. Don't be misled by the low cost of bargain tools. It is far better to spend a little more for better quality. Forged wrenches, 10 or 12 point sockets and fine tooth ratchets are by far preferable to their less expensive counterparts. As any good mechanic can tell you, there are few worse experiences than trying to work on a car or truck with bad tools. Your monetary savings will be far outweighed by frustration and mangled knuckles.

Begin accumulating those tools that are used most frequently; those associated with routine maintenance and tune-up.

In addition to the normal assortment of screwdrivers and pliers you should have the following tools for routine maintenance and tune-up:

1. Metric wrenches or SAE/Metric wrenches and sockets and combination open end/box end wrenches in sizes from $\frac{1}{8}''$ (3mm) to $\frac{3}{4}''$ (19mm); and a spark plug socket ($\frac{13}{16}''$ or $\frac{5}{8}''$ depending on plug type).

If possible, buy various length socket drive extensions. One break in this department is that the metric sockets available in the U.S. will all fit the ratchet handles and extensions you may already have ($\frac{1}{4}$, $\frac{3}{8}$, and $\frac{1}{2}''$ drive).

2. Jackstands for support;
3. Oil filter wrench;
4. Oil filler spout for pouring oil;
5. Grease gun for chassis lubrication;
6. Hydrometer for checking the battery;
7. A container for draining oil;
8. Many rags for wiping up the inevitable mess.

In addition to the above items there are several others that are not absolutely necessary, but handy to have around. These include oil dry, a transmission funnel and the usual supply of lubricants, antifreeze and fluids, although these can be purchased as needed. This is a basic list for routine maintenance, but only your personal needs and desires can accurately determine your list of tools.

The second list of tools is for tune-ups. While the tools involved here are slightly more sophisticated, they need not be outrageously expensive. There are several inexpensive tach/dwell meters on the market that are every bit as good for the average mechanic as a $100.00 professional model. Just be sure that it goes to least 1,200–1,500 rpm on the tach scale and that it works on 4, 6 or 8 cylinder engines. A basic list of tune-up equipment could include:

1. Tach/dwell meter;
2. Spark plug wrench;
3. Timing light (a DC light that works from the car's battery is best, although an AC light that plugs into 110V house current will suffice at some sacrifice in brightness);
4. Wire spark plug gauge/adjusting tools;
5. Set of feeler blades.

Here again, be guided by your own needs. A feeler blade will set the points as easily as a dwell meter, but slightly less accurately. And since you will need a tachometer anyway... well, make your own decision.

In addition to these basic tools, there are several other tools and gauges you may find useful. These include:

1. A compression gauge. The screw-in type is slower to use, but eliminates the possibility of a faulty reading due to escaping pressure.
2. A manifold vacuum gauge.
3. A test light.
4. An induction meter. This is used for determining whether or not there is current in the wire. These are handy for use if a wire is broken somewhere in a wiring harness.
5. A simple, hand-held vacuum pump. Useful for finding vacuum leaks or inspecting and testing many emission control systems.

As a final note, you will probably find a torque wrench necessary for all but the most basic work. The beam type models are perfectly adequate, although the newer click type are more precise.

## Special Tools

Normally, the use of special factory tools is avoided for repair procedures, since these are not readily available for the do-it-yourself mechanic. When it is possible to perform the job with more commonly available tools, it will be pointed out, but occasionally, a special tool was designed to perform a specific function and should be used. Before substituting another tool, you should be convinced that neither your safety nor the performance of the vehicle will be compromised.

Some special tools are available commercially from major tool manufacturers. Others can be purchased from your car dealer. In most cases where a tool is designed for a particular

job on a particular car model and therefore made available through the dealer network, you can also purchase a similar tool at an automotive parts store or elsewhere. You might want to give the factory part number to not only your dealer but to other sources and shop competitively for the item you need.

NOTE: *Special tools are occasionally necessary to perform a specific job or are recommended to make a job easier. Their use has been kept to a minimum. When a special tool is indicated, it will be referred to by manufacturer's part number, and, where possible, an illustration of the tool will be provided so that an equivalent tool may be used.*

## SERVICING YOUR VEHICLE SAFELY

It is virtually impossible to anticipate all of the hazards involved with automotive maintenance and service but care and common sense will prevent most accidents.

The rules of safety for mechanics range from, don't smoke around gasoline, to, use the proper tool for the job. The trick to avoiding injuries is to develop safe work habits and take every possible precaution.

## Do's

• DO keep a fire extinguisher and first aid kit within easy reach.
• DO wear safety glasses or goggles when cutting, drilling, grinding or prying, even if you have 20/20 vision. If you wear glasses for the sake of vision, then they should be made of hardened glass that can serve also as safety glasses, or wear safety goggles over your regular glasses.
• DO shield your eyes whenever you work around the battery. Batteries contain sulphuric acid; in case of contact with the eyes or skin, flush the area with water or a mixture of water and baking soda and get medical attention immediately.
• DO use safety stands for any undercar service. Jacks are for raising vehicles; safety stands are for making sure the vehicle stay raised until you want it to come down. Whenever the vehicle is raised, block the wheels remaining on the ground and set the parking brake.
• DO use adequate ventilation when working with any chemicals. Like carbon monoxide, the asbestos dust resulting from brake lining wear can be poisonous in sufficient quantities.
• DO disconnect the negative battery cable when working on the electrical system. The primary ignition system can contain up to 40,000 volts.
• DO follow manufacturer's directions whenever working with potentially hazardous

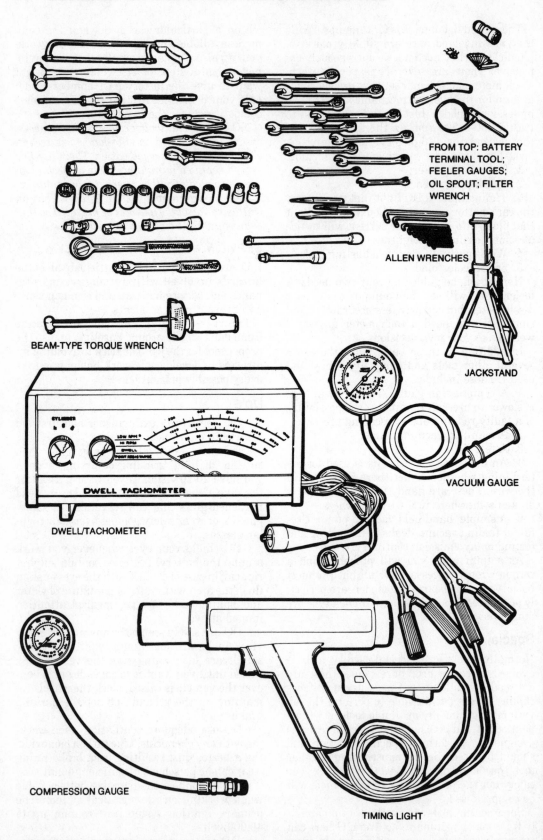

FROM TOP: BATTERY TERMINAL TOOL; FEELER GAUGES; OIL SPOUT; FILTER WRENCH

ALLEN WRENCHES

JACKSTAND

BEAM-TYPE TORQUE WRENCH

DWELL TACHOMETER

DWELL/TACHOMETER

VACUUM GAUGE

COMPRESSION GAUGE

TIMING LIGHT

**You need only a basic assortment of hand tools and test instruments for most maintenance and repair jobs**

materials. Both brake fluid and antifreeze are poisonous if taken internally.

• DO properly maintain your tools. Loose hammerheads, mushroomed punches and chisels, frayed or poorly grounded electrical cords, excessively worn screwdrivers, spread wrenches (open end), cracked sockets, slipping ratchets, or faulty droplight sockets can cause accidents.

• DO use the proper size and type of tool for the job being done.

• DO when possible, pull on a wrench handle rather than push on it, and adjust your stance to prevent a fall.

• DO be sure that adjustable wrenches are tightly adjusted on the nut or bolt and pulled so that the face is on the side of the fixed jaw.

• DO select a wrench or socket that fits the nut or bolt. The wrench or socket should sit straight, not cocked.

• DO strike squarely with a hammer; avoid glancing blows.

• DO set the parking brake and block the drive wheels if the work requires that the engine be running.

• DO turn the ignition switch off on late model cars with an electric cooling fan. With the ignition turned on, the fan can start with no warning!

## Don'ts

• DON'T run an engine in a garage or anywhere else without proper ventilation — EVER! Carbon monoxide is poisonous; it takes a long time to leave the human body and you can build up a deadly supply of it in your system by simply breathing in a little every day. You may not realize you are slowly poisoning yourself. Always use power vents, windows, fans or open the garage doors.

• DON'T work around moving parts while wearing necktie or other loose clothing. Short sleeves are much safer than long, loose sleeves and hard-toed shoes with neoprene soles protect your toes and give a better grip on slippery surfaces. Jewelry such as watches, fancy belt buckles, beads or body adornment or any kind is not safe working around a car. Long hair should be hidden under a hat or cap.

• DON'T use pockets for toolboxes. A fall or bump can drive a screwdriver deep into your body. Even a wiping cloth hanging from the back pocket can wrap around a spinning shaft or fan.

• DON'T smoke when working around gasoline, cleaning solvent or other flammable material.

• DON'T smoke when working around the battery. When the battery is being charged, it gives off explosive hydrogen gas.

• DON'T use gasoline to wash your hands; there are excellent soaps available. Gasoline may contain lead, and lead can enter the body through a cut, accumulating in the body until you are very ill. Gasoline also removes all the natural oils from the skin so that bone dry hands will suck up oil and grease.

• DON'T service the air conditioning system unless you are equipped with the necessary tools and training. The refrigerant, R-12 becomes a deadly poisonous gas in the presence of an open flame. One good whiff of the vapors from burning refrigerant can be fatal.

• DON'T hurry. This means avoiding getting yourself into a time trap because you didn't allow enough time to do the job or because you're working outside and the weather is changing. Working at a sensible pace, you're more likely to anticipate safety problems by thinking ahead and by using tools more effectively.

## HISTORY

Toyo Kogyo Co., Ltd., Mazda's parent company, began manufacturing cork products over fifty years ago. In 1927, the company expanded into the machinery and tool business; by 1930 they were producing motorcycles under the Mazda name.

The first three wheeled trucks appeared in 1931. The first automobile prototype was built in 1940, but it was not until twenty years later that a production car, the Mazda R-360 coupe, was sold.

In the interim, Toyo Kogyo produced light three wheeled trucks, reaching, in 1957, a peak annual production of 20,000 units.

Shortly after automobile production began in 1960, Toyo Kogyo obtained a license from NSU-Wankel to develop and produce the rotary engine.

The first prototype car powered by this engine was the Mazda 110S, a two passenger sports car which appeared in August 1963. The car did not go on sale until it had been thoroughly tested. The first units were offered for sale in May 1967. The 110S was soon joined by a smaller, cheaper model which put the rotary engine within the reach of the average consumer. Various models powered by the rotary engine were produced for the Japanese home market.

In 1970, Toyo Kogyo began importing Mazda cars (both rotary engined and conventional) into the United States. At first they were available only in the Pacific Northwest, but they have rapidly expanded their market to include almost all of the U.S.

## Development of the Rotary Engine

Toyo Kogyo was the first auto manufacturer to apply rotary engine technology to successful, mass produced automobiles. This required an unusual degree of courage, but that wasn't enough. The development engineers had to apply a tremendous amount of creative energy to create an engine that would not only perform well, but would be easy to manufacture. This required a greatly accelerated research and development effort almost unequalled in the annals of mass production autodom. Toyo Kogyo engineers had to produce, in five years, and engine which would compete with a seventy year old cousin. While it can hardly be said that the modern Wankel is as highly refined as the piston engine, the engineers did, indeed, produce a viable competitor, in spite of having only one fourteenth the development time. Having learned about the Wankel engine at a German rotary engine symposium, the Toyo Kogyo engineering staff reached the point, in early 1960, where they could visualize the Wankel rotary in practical automotive use. An initial visit to the NSU works in Germany occurred in October of that year (NSU was the initial Wankel engine developer).

The first prototype engine was built using drawings supplied by NSU. The engine had serious vibration, wear, and oil consumption problems.

And so, the first year was spent studying the fundamentals: basic behavior and problems of the rotary engine. Then, two years were spent actually mapping these characteristics in detail. Early in 1962, an engine was mounted in a test car to get more practical experience in just how a successful engine should be designed. For example, this work led very soon to a decision to develop a twin rotor engine in order to overcome vibration occurring at low speeds when the throttle was closed. The fourth and fifth years were spent studying means of further improving in-vehicle performance, the basics having been resolved by the end of the third year.

Toyo Kogyo committed itself in dramatic fashion to rotary engine development. Initial investment in a rotary test center was $750,000. Yet in 1964, a completely new test laboratory was built incorporating both basic and endurance test cells. Perhaps even more indicative of the devotion to unqualified success in design of the rotary was the decision to apply the same severe standard applied to the 70 year old piston to the fledgling rotary engine.

The development project's most exciting aspect was the coverage of absolutely new ground. The design of the apex seals on the rotary engine is difficult because of an inherent lubrication problem. The rings in a piston engine separate a combustion space from a lubricated area. Thus, the rings can be coated with oil supplied from below. The apex seal separates two adjacent combustion spaces, and thus can be lubricated only via the mixing of a trace of oil with the fuel. The ultimate solution of the problem of minimizing the amount of oil consumed by the engine was the use of a self lubrication material on the seals. This material (initially carbon impregnated with aluminum) had to be compatible with the working surface on the inside of the rotor housing. That coating, in turn, had to be of a material which could be readily plated onto the aluminum housing.

Other problems that had to be solved included achieving a port design which gave high speed performance with stable combustion at low speeds and stabilizing rotor housing temperatures. The latter problem required finning the water passages selectively so that varying amounts of heat were carried from various portions of the housing, even though housing temperature was almost uniform.

## SERIAL NUMBER IDENTIFICATION

### Vehicle

#### All except RX-2

The serial number on these models is on a plate located on the driver's side windshield pillar and is visible through the glass.

A vehicle identification number (VIN) plate, bearing the serial number and other data, is attached to the cowl.

#### RX-2

The VIN plate location and composition of the serial number for RX-2 models is the same as for RX-3 models, above. The only difference between models is the location of the RX-2 serial number plate which is attached to the upper left hand side of the instrument panel. The plate is visible through the windshield.

### Engine

On piston engines up to 1981, the serial number and type code is located on a plate mounted at the right/front/top of the block, except on the GLC type TC engine, which has the plate on the front of the cylinder head. On 1982 and later models, the engine number is located on the cylinder head just below No. 1 sparkplug.

On rotary engines, the type code is located either on the front or rear housing, on the top surface of the housing, left side. The serial number is stamped on the intermediate hous-

## Model Identification

| Year | Model | Body Type | Code |
|------|-------|-----------|------|
| 1971 | RX-2 | Sedan | — |
|  | RX-2 | Coupe | — |
| 1972 | RX-3 | Sedan | S124 BL |
|  | RX-3 | Coupe | M124 B6 |
|  | RX-3 | Wagon | S124 WL |
|  | RX-2 | Sedan | SN1224A-S |
|  | RX-2 | Coupe | SN122A-SCA |
| 1973 | RX-3 | Sedan | 2RS 124A |
|  | RX-3 | Coupe | 2RS 124A |
|  | RX-3 | Wagon | 2RS 124W |
|  | RX-2 | Sedan | 2RS 122A |
|  | RX-2 | Coupe | 2RS 122A |
| 1974 | 808 | Coupe/Sedan | SN3A |
|  | 808 | Wagon | SN3AV |
|  | RX-2 | Coupe/Sedan | S122A |
|  | RX-3 | Coupe/Sedan | S124A |
|  | RX-3 | Wagon | S124W |
|  | RX-4 | Hardtop/Sedan | LA23S |
|  | RX-4 | Wagon | LA23W |
| 1975 | RX-2 | Coupe/Sedan | SS122A |
|  | RX-3 | Coupe | SS124A |
|  | RX-3 | Wagon | SS124W |
|  | RX-4 | Hardtop/Sedan | SLA23S |
|  | RX-4 | Wagon | SLA23W |
|  | 808 | Coupe | SSN3A |
|  | 808 | Wagon | SSN3AV |
| 1976 | RX-3 | Coupe | S124A |
|  | RX-3 | Wagon | S124W |
|  | RX-4 | Hardtop/Sedan | LA23S |
|  | RX-4 | Wagon | LA23W |
|  | Cosmo | — | CD23C |
|  | 808 | 1600 Coupe/ Sedan | SN3A |
|  | 808 | 1600 Wagon | SN3AV |
|  | 808 | 1300 Coupe/ Sedan | STC |
|  | 808 | 1300 Wagon | STCV |
| 1977–78 | RX-3 | Coupe/Sedan | S124A |
|  | RX-4 | Hardtop/Sedan | LA23S |
|  | RX-4 | Wagon | LA23W |
|  | Cosmo | — | CD23C |
|  | 808 | 1600 Coupe/ Sedan | SN3A |
|  | 808 | 1600 Wagon | SN3AV |
|  | 808 | 1300 Coupe/ Sedan | STC |
|  | 808 | 1300 Wagon | STCV |
|  | GLC | Hatchback 3 dr. | FA4TS-3,3P,3T |
| 1978 | GLC | Hatchback 5 dr. | FA4TS-5,5P,5T |
| 1979–80 | GLC | Hatchback 3 dr. | FA4US-3,3T,3P |
|  | GLC | Hatchback 5 dr. | FA4US-5,5T,5P |
|  | GLC | Station Wagon | FA4UV-5,5T,5P |
| 1979–80 | 626 | Sedan | CB2MS-P,T |
|  | 626 | Hardtop | CP2MS-CP,CT |
| 1981–82 | GLC | Station Wagon | BB62,63,64 |
|  | GLC | Sedan | BD221 |
|  | GLC | Hatchback 3 dr. | BD231 |
|  | GLC | Hatchback 5 dr. | BD241 |
| 1981–82 | 626 | Sedan | GB211 |
|  | 626 | Hardtop | GB411 |

## Model Identification (cont.)

| Year | Model | Body Type | Code |
|------|-------|-----------|------|
| 1983–84 | GLC | Sedan | BD221 |
|  | GLC | Hatchback 2 dr. | BD231 |
|  | GLC | Hatchback 4 dr. | BD241 |
|  | GLC | Wagon | BD521 |
| 1983–86 | 626 | Sedan | GC221 |
|  | 626 | Diesel | GC222 |
|  | 626 | Coupe 2 dr. | GC311 |
|  | 626 | Hatchback | GC241 |
| 1986 | 323 | Sedan | BF81 |
|  |  | Hatchback 3 dr. | BF82 |
|  |  | Hatchback 5 dr. | BF91 |

## Engine Identification

| Year | Model | Code | Engine Displacement Cu In. (CC) |
|------|-------|------|---------------------------------|
| 1971–76 | RX-2, RX-3 | 12A | 70/1156 |
| 1974–78 | RX-3SP, RX-4 | 13B | 80/1308 |
|  | 808 | — | 96.8/1586 |
| 1976–78 | 808 | — | 77.6/1272 |
| 1977–78 | Cosmo | 13B | 80/1308 |
|  | GLC | TC | 77.6/1272 |
| 1979–80 | GLC | — | 86.4/1415 |
|  | 626 | — | 120.2/1970 |
| 1981–82 | GLC | — | 90.9/1490 |
|  | 626 | — | 120.2/1970 |
| 1984–85 | GLC | E5 | 90.9/1490 |
|  | GLC Wagon | D5 | 90.9/1490 |
|  | 626 | FE | 121.9/1998 |
|  | 626 (Diesel) | RF | 121.9/1998 |
| 1986 | 323 | B6 | 97.4/1597 |
|  | 626 | FE | 121.9/1998 |

ing on engines built before March, 1972, and on the front housing after that date.

## ROUTINE MAINTENANCE

### Air Cleaner

The air cleaner uses a disposable paper element. The filter can be cleaned by blowing low pressure compressed air through it from the inside out. The air filter should be replaced at least every two years or 24,000–30,000 miles. If the car is driven in a dry, dusty atmosphere clean or replace the air filter twice as often.

**Replacing the air cleaner element**

## REMOVAL AND INSTALLATION

Replacing the air cleaner element is a simple, routine maintenance operation. You should be careful, however, to keep dust and dirt out of the air cleaner housing, as they accelerate engine wear. If the outside of the air cleaner housing is dusty, wipe it with a clean rag before beginning work.

On carburetor equipped engines, you typically have to remove only the top cover of the air cleaner. Remove the wingnut at the center of the housing and then unclip the three clips situated around the sides. Then, pull the top cover off and remove the air cleaner element. When installing the new element, make sure it seats squarely around the bulge in the center of the lower air cleaner housing. Install the housing top, turning it until the wingnut mounting stud lines up with the hole in the top (it's usually off center). Note that the top cover should seat tightly all around. Install the wingnut and reclip the clips.

On fuel injection equipped models, loosen the clamp on the air intake hose and pull the hose off the housing. Then, disconnect the airflow sensor electrical connector. Finally, unbolt and remove the housing. Note the direction in which the element is installed and install the new element in the same way (it may be marked **TOP**). Install the top of the housing in reverse order.

## Fuel Filter

The fuel filter on all 1971–77 coupes and sedans except the GLC is located behind the trim panel in the luggage compartment. On wagons, except the GLC it is inside the left rear quarter panel. On the GLC models it is located on the right side of the engine compartment. On the model 626 up to 1982 and late GLC wagons, it is located under the floor in front of the fuel tank. On 1983–85 626 models, it is located on the right of the engine compartment. On the 1986 626, which has fuel injection, it is located on the right side of the engine compartment near the firewall. Replace every 8,000 miles on 1971–73 vehicles, at 10,000 miles and every 12,000 miles on 1976–1982 vehicles. On 1983–86 vehicles, replace at 30,000 mile intervals. The filter should be replaced immediately if dirty fuel has gotten into the gas tank. To replace the filter on all but the fuel injected 626, proceed in the following manner:

1. Remove the trim panel by unfastening its two securing screws, on those models so equipped.

2. Detach both hoses from the filter.

3. Unfasten the filter from its mounting bracket. Install the new filter in the reverse order of removal.

**On the fuel injected 626:**

CAUTION: *Make sure to follow the first step in the procedure below with great care, as failure to do so could result in a fire. Also, if fuel lines must be replaced, make sure to use high pressure fuel hose designed for fuel injection.*

1. Allow the engine to cool as fuel will be expelled when the filter high pressure hose is disconnected! Place a rag around the connection to catch sprayed fuel. Disconnect the battery negative cable.

2. Slide the fuel line clamps back off the connections on the filter. Then, slowly pull one connection off just until fuel begins to seep out. Allow the fuel to seep out until pressure has been eliminated.

3. Pull both fuel hoses off the connectors. Unbolt and remove the filter and bracket.

4. Install in reverse order. Inspect the fuel hoses and replace them, if necessary. Make sure the hoses are pressed fully onto the filter connections, and that the clamps are installed over the bulged portions of the banjo connectors.

### Diesel

1. Using an oil filter wrench, unscrew the fuel filter from its mounting bracket on the cowl and remove it. Make sure the O-ring comes off with the filter.

2. Thoroughly coat the O-ring on the new filter with clean fuel. Install the new filter. Tighten it by hand only, with your hands and the outside of the filter dry clean.

3. Bleed the system by repeated depressing the bleeder handle located on top of the filter mounting bracket until it can no longer be readily depressed.

## PCV Valve

### TESTING

**RX-2 1971–73**
**RX-3 1972–73**

1. Check and clean (or replace) the air filter element, as necessary.

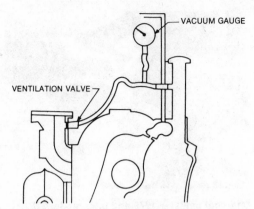

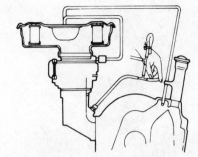

Checking PCV valve—1977–78 Cosmo

Using a vacuum gauge to test the operation of the PCV valve

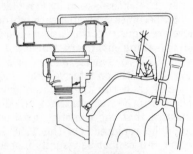

Checking PCV valve—1975 RX-4

2. Connect a vacuum gauge into the PCV valve vacuum line with a T-fitting.

3. Start the engine. Increase engine speed to 2,500–3,000 rpm. The vacuum gauge should read 2.4 in.Hg. If the reading on the vacuum gauge is incorrect, replace the valve.

### 1975 RX-3, RX-4

1. With the engine idling and fully warmed up, disconnect the PCV hose at the oil filler pipe.

2. Squeeze the hose coming from the evaporative canister (at the **X** in the illustration). Engine speed must drop.

3. Close off the open end of the PCV hose. Engine should continue to run.

4. If engine speed does not change when closing off the hose coming from the evaporative canister, or if the engine stalls when closing off the end of the disconnected hose, replace the valve.

### 1975–78 808, 1977–84 GLC, 1979–84 626

1. With the engine idling and fully warmed up, unclamp and remove the hose leading to the PCV valve at the valve.

2. Place your finger over the open end of valve to stop airflow. There should be an audible click and the engine speed should drop noticeably. Otherwise, replace the valve.

### 1976–77 RX-3, RX-4, Cosmo

1. On the Cosmo, pinch off the hose which is teed into the PCV line as shown in the illustration.

2. With the engine idling and fully warmed up, disconnect the PCV hose at the oil filler pipe.

3. Close off the end of the PCV hose with your finger. The engine speed should drop.

4. If the engine speed stays the same, replace the PCV valve.

### REMOVAL AND INSTALLATION

### 1971–73 RX-2
### 1972–73 RX-3

1. Remove the air cleaner and its hoses by unfastening the mounting bolts and wing nut inside it.

2. Remove the fuel return valve and the distributor vacuum lines from the carburetor.

3. Disconnect the hose from the PCV valve.

4. Unfasten the PCV valve and withdraw it from the carburetor.

NOTE: It is difficult to gain access to the PCV valve, to get a wrench on it. It is advisable to either purchase the special factory wrench (49 2113 005) or to use a flexible drive socket wrench.

5. Installation of a new valve is performed in the reverse order of removal.

### All 1974–86 Cars

1. On 808, 626, GLC, and 323 remove the air cleaner.

2. Remove the clip fastening the hose to the outer end of the PCV valve, and pull the hose off the valve.

3. Some models (all rotary engines) use threaded PCV valves with a hex head section incorporating flats so you can use an ordinary open-end wrench, deep well socket, or factory tool 49-1011-120 to remove or install the valve. Unscrew the PCV valve from the manifold on these models, being careful to retain the washer used on some GLCs. On 1982–84 models,

Charcoal filter replacement—1972–73 models

Charcoal canister 1979 and later model 626

simply pull the valve gently while rotating it to remove it from the rubber seal.

4. Installation is the reverse of removal.

## Charcoal Filter

The charcoal filter for the evaporative emission control (EEC) system is located in the top of the air cleaner case on 1972–73 models. It should be checked every 12,000 miles and replaced as necessary.

1. Unfasten the clips and remove the top of the air cleaner case.

2. Inspect the air cleaner element and clean it as necessary.

3. Check the condition of the charcoal filter. If it is saturated with fuel and oil, replace it by unscrewing it from the case. Screw the replacement filter in place.

4. At this time always check the condition of the PCV valve as outlined above.

## Charcoal Canister

### 1971 RX-2

The 1971 RX-2 models use a charcoal canister which is separated from the air cleaner. Check it every 12,000 miles, and replace it as necessary:

1. Be sure that the air cleaner element is not clogged and that the PCV valve is working.

2. Attach a vacuum gauge on the inlet of the PCV valve that connects with the canister, by means of a T-fitting.

3. Increase the engine speed to 2,500–3,000 rpm. The vacuum gauge should read 2.4 in.Hg.

If the vacuum gauge reading is not within specification, the PCV valve is functioning properly, and the hoses are not leaking, replace the charcoal canister.

### 1974–78 Rotary Engines

All rotary engine powered cars except the 1978 RX-4 Wagon built in these years use a charcoal canister which is located in the top of the air cleaner. The entire assembly is replaced if the canister becomes saturated with fuel or oil, or if there are signs that the carbon absorbent material is leaking out. Every 22,000 miles/22 months on 1974–75 vehicles, and every 25,000 miles and 24 months on later vehicles, inspect the unit and then run the vacuum test described below. If the vacuum test is failed, this also indicates that the canister is saturated and should be replaced. On the 1978 RX-4 Wagon, the unit cannot be visually inspected. The vacuum test is the sole basis for replacing the canister on that model.

1. Disconnect the hose leading from the fuel tank and install a vacuum gauge into the Tee in the oil filler-to-PCV valve line.

2. Operate the engine at 2,500 rpm. The vacuum produced should be 2.4 in.Hg. If vacuum is too high, replace the canister.

### 1974–82 Piston Engines

All piston engine cars use a canister located separate from the air cleaner in the engine compartment. It should be checked for leakage of either fuel or activated carbon particles, and lightly tapped to check for looseness of internal parts. If there is leakage or an internal rattle, replace the unit by loosening the hose clamps, pulling of the hoses, unbolting the unit, and reversing this procedure to install a replacement. The inspection should be carried out every 22,000 miles/22 months on 1974–75 cars, and every 25,000 miles/24 months on later cars.

### 1983–85 GLC

1. Check the canister over for signs of leaking charcoal. Tap it lightly with your finger for a rattle, indicating loose charcoal inside. If either type of inspection reveals trouble, replace the unit.

2. Reroute the hoses to port A so manifold vacuum is directly applied. Idle the engine.

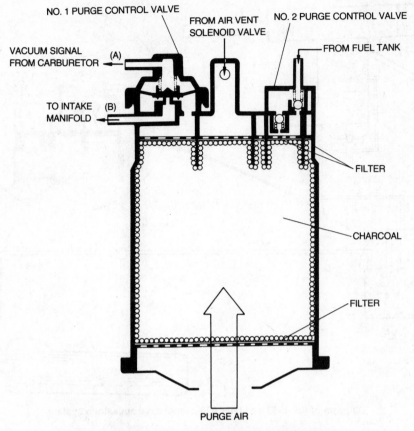

**Canister airflow diagram for '83–'84 GLC**

Then disconnect the hose going to port B and blow through it. Air should pass through freely. Otherwise, replace the canister. Reconnect the hoses if the canister is okay.

### 1983–85 626

1. Remove the air cleaner. Plug the hoses going to the idle compensator, thermosensor, and reed valves. Disconnect the air vent hose coming from the carburetor and plug it.

2. Run the engine until it is warm and leave it idling. Cover the bottom of the canister with your hand in order to feel air being drawn in from underneath. Increase the engine speed slightly. Air should be drawn in. If so, the No. 1 purge valve (and water thermovalve) are working.

3. Should there be no suction at the bottom of the canister, remove the vacuum line going to the No. 1 purge valve and make sure there is vacuum at the end of the hose under all the same conditions. If so, replace the canister, if not check for and repair vacuum hose problems of the water thermovalve.

4. Disconnect the vacuum sensing tube at the pipe coming from the engine. There should

be slight resistance to both blowing and suction. If not, or if you can't make air pass in either direction, replace the canister.

### 1986 323 and 626

These models do not require checking of the canister or related hardware on a routine basis. If your car exhibits fuel leaks, fuel odor, or idling problems, inspect and test these systems as described in Chapter 4.

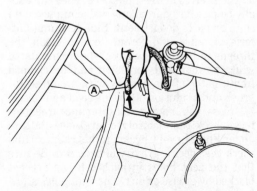

**Disconnect the vacuum sensing tube (A) coming from the engine**

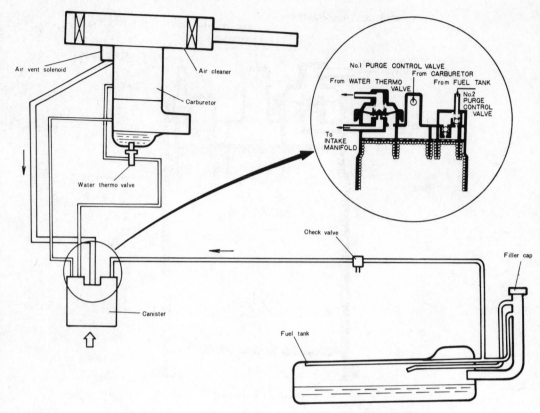

**Diagram of the 1983 and later 626 evaporative emissions system**

## Battery

Loose, dirty, or corroded battery terminals are a major cause of no-start. Every 3 months or so, remove the battery terminals and clean them, giving them a light coating of petroleum jelly when you are finished. This will help to retard corrosion.

Check the battery cables for signs of wear or chafing and replace any cable or terminal that looks marginal. Battery terminals can be easily cleaned and inexpensive terminal cleaning tools are an excellent investment that will pay for themselves many times over. They can usually be purchased from any well equipped auto store or parts department. Side terminal batteries require a different tool to clean the threads in the battery case. The accumulated white powder and corrosion can be cleaned from the top of the battery with an old toothbrush and a solution of baking soda and water.

Unless you have a maintenance-free battery, check the electrolyte level (see Battery under Fluid Level Checks in this chapter) and check the specific gravity of each cell. Be sure that the vent holes in each cell cap are not blocked by grease or dirt. The vent holes allow hydrogen gas, formed by the chemical reaction in the battery, to escape safely.

Late model cars have a battery indicator. Located on the top of the battery, the indicator is blue if there is sufficient electrolyte; if no color is visible, check level and add clean water as necessary.

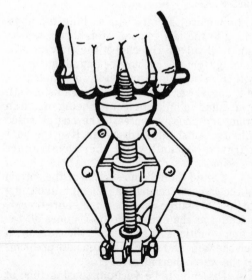

**Battery cable removal tool**

## JUMP STARTING A DEAD BATTERY

The chemical reaction in a battery produces explosive hydrogen gas. This is the safe way to jump start a dead battery, reducing the chances of an accidental spark that could cause an explosion.

### Jump Starting Precautions

1. Be sure both batteries are of the same voltage.
2. Be sure both batteries are of the same polarity (have the same grounded terminal).
3. Be sure the vehicles are not touching.
4. Be sure the vent cap holes are not obstructed.
5. Do not smoke or allow sparks around the battery.
6. In cold weather, check for frozen electrolyte in the battery.
7. Do not allow electrolyte on your skin or clothing.
8. Be sure the electrolyte is not frozen.

### Jump Starting Procedure

1. Determine voltages of the two batteries; they must be the same.
2. Bring the starting vehicle close (they must not touch) so that the batteries can be reached easily.
3. Turn off all accessories and both engines. Put both cars in Neutral or Park and set the handbrake.
4. Cover the cell caps with a rag—do not cover terminals.
5. If the terminals on the run-down battery are heavily corroded, clean them.
6. Identify the positive and negative posts on both batteries and connect the cables in the order shown.
7. Start the engine of the starting vehicle and run it at fast idle. Try to start the car with the dead battery. Crank it for no more than 10 seconds at a time and let it cool off for 20 seconds in between tries.
8. If it doesn't start in 3 tries, there is something else wrong.
9. Disconnect the cables in the reverse order.
10. Replace the cell covers and dispose of the rags.

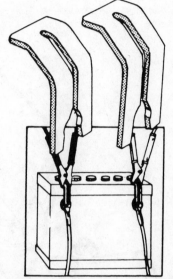

Side terminal batteries occasionally pose a problem when connecting jumper cables. There frequently isn't enough room to clamp the cables without touching sheet metal. Side terminal adaptors are available to alleviate this problem and should be removed after use.

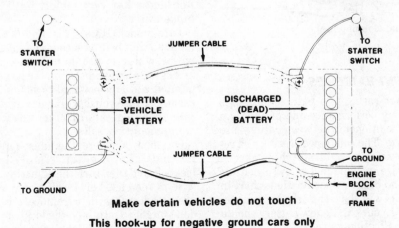

Make certain vehicles do not touch

This hook-up for negative ground cars only

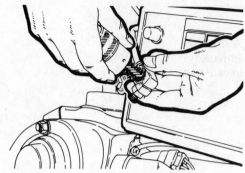

**Battery cable connector cleaning tool**

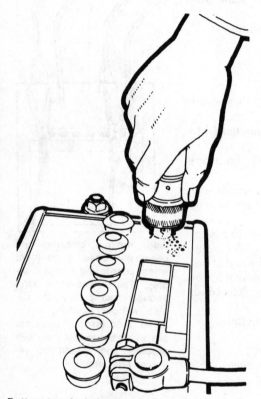

**Battery terminal cleaning tool**

### REPLACEMENT BATTERIES

The cold power rating of a battery measures battery starting performance and provides an approximate relationship between battery size and engine size. The cold power rating of a replacement battery should match or exceed your engine size in cubic inches. Also, consult the Battery and Starter Specifications chart in Chapter 3. This will show the amp/hour capacity required by your car. A new battery should meet this specification as well.

## Belts

### TENSION CHECKING AND ADJUSTING

The belts should be inspected and adjusted at 2,000 miles and then every 4,000 miles. First, inspect the belts for cracks. These usually develop on the inner surface and run back into the backing or outer surface of the belt. Check also for glazing; a completely smooth appearance which indicates slippage. A belt that is in good shape will have a slightly grainy appearance like cloth. Replace belts that show cracks or glazing.

Check belt tension. Applying pressure with your thumb at the mid-point between two pulleys, the belt should stretch or deflect about ½″ (12.7mm). Especially if the belt is loose enough to have actual play, it will require adjustment and should be carefully inspected for signs of slippage.

To adjust belts, first locate the mounting bolt on the air pump or alternator (each has its own belt and adjusts to permit that belt to be tensioned right). This bolt attaches the unit to the engine and has a nut on the back end of it. Put a wrench on either end and loosen the bolt until there is practically no tension on it. Then, loosen the adjusting bolt, which is located on the opposite side of the unit and which passes through a slot. Pull the alternator or air pump away from the engine and tighten the adjusting bolt just enough to hold the unit while you check tension. If possible, it is advisable to avoid the use of a prybar of any kind on the air pump because this can damage the housing. Repeat the adjustment procedure until the belt deflects the right amount, and then fully tighten adjustment and mounting bolts. Avoid too much belt tension or overtightening bolts. A new belt should be tensioned just slightly more (about 0.4″ [10mm] deflection) and checked after several hundred miles of operation to make sure tension is still adequate (tension is lost very rapidly until the belt is broken in).

Late model GLCs, 323s, and 626s may use an adjusting bolt on either the idler pulley (a pulley which is not directly associated with any of the accessories) or on the power steering pump itself. This bolt makes adjustment much easier because you don't have to hold the accessory under a great deal of tension while tightening mounting bolts.

On models where the idler pulley has a lockbolt at its center, simply loosen the lockbolt and then turn the adjusting bolt clockwise to increase belt tension or counterclockwise to decrease it or remove the belt. Just don't forget to retighten the lockbolt when tension is correct, or vibration may cause it be

## HOW TO SPOT WORN V-BELTS

V-Belts are vital to efficient engine operation—they drive the fan, water pump and other accessories. They require little maintenance (occasional tightening) but they will not last forever. Slipping or failure of the V-belt will lead to overheating. If your V-belt looks like any of these, it should be replaced.

**Cracking or weathering**

This belt has deep cracks, which cause it to flex. Too much flexing leads to heat build-up and premature failure. These cracks can be caused by using the belt on a pulley that is too small. Notched belts are available for small diameter pulleys.

**Softening (grease and oil)**

Oil and grease on a belt can cause the belt's rubber compounds to soften and separate from the reinforcing cords that hold the belt together. The belt will first slip, then finally fail altogether.

**Glazing**

Glazing is caused by a belt that is slipping. A slipping belt can cause a run-down battery, erratic power steering, overheating or poor accessory performance. The more the belt slips, the more glazing will be built up on the surface of the belt. The more the belt is glazed, the more it will slip. If the glazing is light, tighten the belt.

**Worn cover**

The cover of this belt is worn off and is peeling away. The reinforcing cords will begin to wear and the belt will shortly break. When the belt cover wears in spots or has a rough jagged appearance, check the pulley grooves for roughness.

**Separation**

This belt is on the verge of breaking and leaving you stranded. The layers of the belt are separating and the reinforcing cords are exposed. It's just a matter of time before it breaks completely.

**Type C**

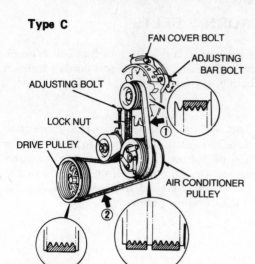

Idler pulley with a lockbolt at the center as used on late model 626s

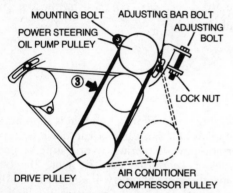

Adjusting bolt and bar associated with the power steering pump pulley—late model GLC

lost. Recheck the tension with the lockbolt tightened and readjust if necessary.

Where the adjusting bolt is associated with the power steering pump pulley on the GLC, loosen the adjusting bar (slotted) bolt, the mounting bolt across from it, and the locknut at the bottom of the adjusting bolt. Turn the adjusting bar bolt counterclockwise to remove the belt or reduce tension, and clockwise to increase it. When tension is correct, tighten the adjusting bolt locknut, adjusting bar bolt, and pump mounting bolt.

On 626s with the grooved type belt driving both the air conditioner and power steering pump, belt tension is much greater. With a used belt, deflection should only be about 0.25" (6mm).

## Hose Replacement

1. Remove the radiator cap.
2. Drain the coolant from the radiator by opening the radiator petcock, if so equipped, or by disconnecting the lower radiator hose. If your car is equipped with a petcock it might be a good idea to squirt a little penetrating oil on it first.

3. To replace the bottom hose, drain all the coolant from the radiator. If only the top hose is to be replaced, drain just enough fluid to bring the level down below the level of the top hose. If the fluid is over a year old discard it.

4. Most hoses are attached with screw type hose clamps. If the old clamps are badly rusted or damaged in any way it is always best to replace them with new ones.

5. When installing the new hose slide the clamps over each end of the hose then slide the hose over the hose connections. Position each clamp about 1/4" (6mm) from the end of the hose and tighten.

CAUTION: *Do not overtighten at the radiator connections as it is very easy to crush the metal.*

6. Close the petcock and refill with the old coolant if it is less than a year old or with a new mixture of 50/50, coolant/water.

7. Start the engine and idle it for 15 minutes with the radiator cap off and check for leaks. Add coolant if necessary and install the radiator cap.

## Air Conditioning

### AIR CONDITIONING SAFETY PRECAUTIONS

There are two particular hazards associated with air conditioning systems and they both relate to the refrigerant gas.

First, the refrigerant gas is an extremely cold substance. When exposed to air, it will instantly freeze any surface it comes in contact with, including your eyes. The other hazard relates to fire. Although normally non-toxic, refrigerant gas becomes highly poisonous in the presence of an open flame. One good whiff of the vapor formed by burning refrigerant can be fatal. Keep all forms of fire (including cigarettes) well clear of the air conditioning system.

Any repair work to an air conditioning system should be left to a professional. Do not, under any circumstances, attempt to loosen or tighten any fittings or perform any work other than that outlined here.

### CHECKING FOR OIL LEAKS

Refrigerant leaks show up as oily areas on the various components because the compressor oil is transported around the entire system along with the refrigerant. Look for oily spots on all the hoses and lines, and especially on the hose and tubing connections. If there are oily

## HOW TO SPOT BAD HOSES

Both the upper and lower radiator hoses are called upon to perform difficult jobs in an inhospitable environment. They are subject to nearly 18 psi at under hood temperatures often over 280°F., and must circulate nearly 7500 gallons of coolant an hour—3 good reasons to have good hoses.

**Swollen hose**

A good test for any hose is to feel it for soft or spongy spots. Frequently these will appear as swollen areas of the hose. The most likely cause is oil soaking. This hose could burst at any time, when hot or under pressure.

**Cracked hose**

Cracked hoses can usually be seen but feel the hoses to be sure they have not hardened; a prime cause of cracking. This hose has cracked down to the reinforcing cords and could split at any of the cracks.

**Frayed hose end (due to weak clamp)**

Weakened clamps frequently are the cause of hose and cooling system failure. The connection between the pipe and hose has deteriorated enough to allow coolant to escape when the engine is hot.

**Debris in cooling system**

Debris, rust and scale in the cooling system can cause the inside of a hose to weaken. This can usually be felt on the outside of the hose as soft or thinner areas.

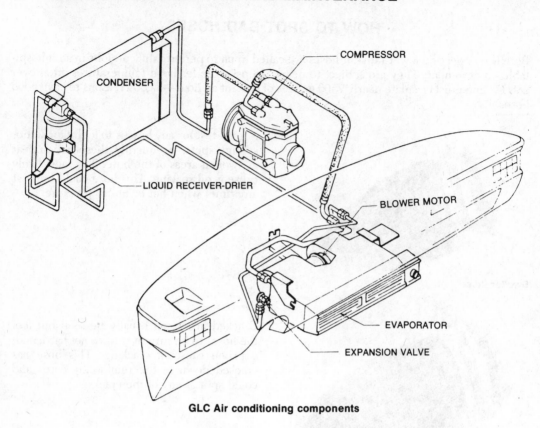

**GLC Air conditioning components**

deposits, the system may have a leak, and you should have it checked by a qualified repairman.

NOTE: *A small area of oil on the front of the compressor is normal and no cause for alarm.*

### CHECK THE COMPRESSOR BELT

Refer to the section in this chapter on Drive Belts.

### KEEP THE CONDENSER CLEAR

Periodically inspect the front of the condenser for bent fins or foreign material (dirt, bugs, leaves, etc.) If any cooling fins are bent, straighten them carefully with needlenose pliers. You can remove any debris with a stiff bristle brush or hose.

### OPERATE THE A/C SYSTEM PERIODICALLY

A lot of A/C problems can be avoided by simply running the air conditioner at least once a week, regardless of the season. Simply let the system run for at least 5 minutes a week (even in the winter), and you'll keep the internal parts lubricated as well as preventing the hoses from hardening. Since this lubricates the compressor seal, which depends on oil to hold

the refrigerant in, running the system is important because it prevents leaks.

### REFRIGERANT LEVEL CHECK

There are two ways to check refrigerant level, depending on how your model is equipped.

#### With Sight Glass

The first order of business when checking the sight glass is to find the sight glass. It will either be in the head of the receiver/drier, or in one of the metal lines leading from the top of the receiver/drier. Once you've found it, wipe it clean and proceed as follows:

1. With the engine and the air conditioning

**Sight glass location—Model 626 shown**

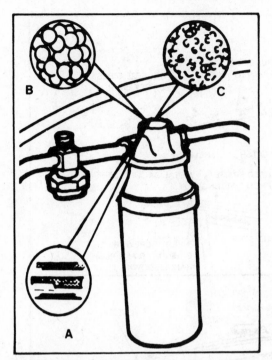

**Oil streaks (A), constant bubbles (B) or foam (C) indicate there is not enough refrigerant in the system. Occasional bubbles during initial operation is normal. A clear sight glass indicates a proper charge of refrigerant or no refrigerant at all, which can be determined by the presence of cold air at the outlets in the car. If the glass is clouded with a milky white substance have the receiver/drier checked professionally**

system running, look for the flow of refrigerant through the sight glass. If the air conditioner is working properly, you'll be able to see a continuous flow of clear refrigerant through the sight glass, with perhaps an occasional bubble at very high temperatures.

2. Cycle the air conditioner on and off to make sure what you are seeing is clear refrigerant. Since the refrigerant is clear, it is possible to mistake a completely discharged system for one that is fully charged. Turn the system off and watch the sight glass. If there is refrigerant in the system, you'll see bubbles during the off cycle. If you observe no bubbles when the system is running, and the air flow from the unit in the car is delivering cold air, everything is OK.

3. If you observe bubbles in the sight glass while the system is operating, the system is low on refrigerant. Have it checked by a professional.

4. Oil streaks in the sight glass are an indication of trouble. Most of the time, if you see oil in the sight glass, it will appear as a series of streaks, although occasionally it may be a solid stream of oil. In either case, it means that part of the charge has been lost.

### Without Sight Glass

On vehicles without a sight glass, the receiver/drier is known as a receiver-drier/accumulator and it's hooked into the system differently. On the standard system with sight glass, the drier is in a high pressure line running from the bottom of the condenser (in front of the radiator) to the expansion valve; a small part shaped a little like a mushroom and mounted on or near the evaporator. On these vehicles (no sight glass) the accumulator is located in a low pressure, large diameter line running from the evaporator to the suction side of the compressor.

This is not to be confused with the Valves In Receiver unit used on late '70s GM cars which does incorporate a sight glass near the top. The receiver drier/accumulator is large and barrel shaped and has only two refrigerant pipe connections and an electrical connection. The VIR has four connections.

Run the air conditioning unit with the vehicle windows open and the fan on high. Feel the temperature of the line going into the evaporator right at the evaporator unit itself, after the orifice tube fitting (where the line should go from warm to cold). Also feel the temperature of the line leaving the evaporator at the top and going into the accumulator. Feel the lower surface of the accumulator.

If the system has enough refrigerant, all these pipes should be at the same temperature. If it is low on refrigerant, the lower accumulator surface and line coming out of the evaporator will be warmer than the line going to the evaporator. If the line to the accumulator is cold but the accumulator surface much warmer, the system may be just slightly undercharged.

If the line leading out of the accumulator and to the compressor is just as cold as the line going in, the system has excessive refrigerant in it. In case of either too little or too much refrigerant, have a professional mechanic who does refrigeration work add or remove refrigerant as necessary.

## Windshield Wipers

Intense heat from the sun, snow and ice, road oils and the chemicals used in windshield washer solvents combine to deteriorate the rubber wiper refills. The refills should be replaced about twice a year or whenever the blades begin to streak or chatter.

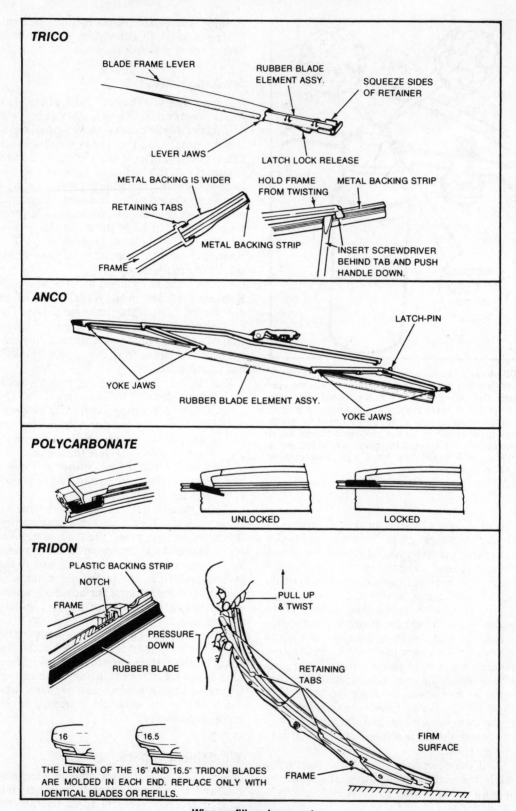

**Wiper refill replacement**

### WIPER REFILL REPLACEMENT

Normally, if the wipers are not cleaning the windshield properly, only the refill has to be replaced. The blade and arm usually require replacement only in the event of damage. It is not necessary (except on new Tridon® refills) to remove the arm or the blade to replace the refill (rubber part), though you may have to position the arm higher on the glass. You can do this turning the ignition switch on and operating the wipers. When they are positioned where they are accessible, turn the ignition switch off.

There are several types of refills and your vehicle could have any kind, since aftermarket blades and arm may not use exactly the same type refill as the original equipment.

Most Trico® styles use a release button that is pushed down to allow the refill to slide out of the yoke jaws. The new refill slides in and locks in place. Some Trico® refills are removed by locating where the metal backing strip or the refill is wider. Insert a small screwdriver blade between the frame and metal backing strip. Press down to release the refill from the retaining tab.

The Anco® style is unlocked at one end by squeezing 2 metal tabs, and the refill is slid out of the frame jaws. When the new refill is installed, the tabs will click into place, locking the refill.

The polycarbonate type is held in place by a locking lever that is pushed downward out of the groove in the arm to free the refill. When the new refill is installed, it will lock in place automatically.

The Tridon® refill has a plastic backing strip with a notch about 1″ (25.4mm) from the end. Hold the blade (frame) on a hard surface so that the frame is tightly bowed. Grip the tip of the backing strip and pull up while twisting counterclockwise. The backing strip will snap out of the retaining tab. Do this for the remaining tabs until the refill is free of the arm. The length of these refills is molded into the end and they should be replaced with identical types.

No matter which type of refill you use, be sure that all of the frame claws engage the refill. Before operating the wipers, be sure that no part of the metal frame is contacting the windshield.

## Tires

### TIRE ROTATION

Tire wear can be equalized by switching the position of the tires about every 6000 miles. Including a conventional spare in the rotation pattern can give up to 20% more tire life.

CAUTION: *Do not include the new SpaceSaver® or temporary spare tires in the rotation pattern.*

There are certain exceptions to tire rotation, however. Studded snow tires should not be rotated, and radials should be kept on the same side of the car (maintain the same direction of rotation). The belts on radial tires get set in a pattern. If the direction of rotation if reversed, it can cause rough ride and vibration.

NOTE: *When radials or studded snows are*

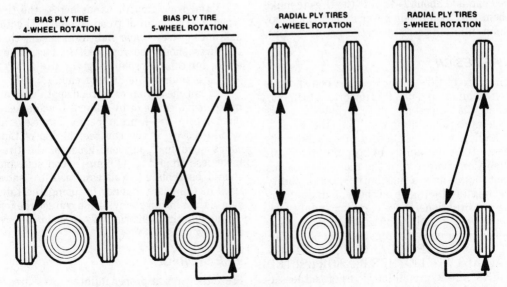

**Tire rotation**

*taken off the car, mark them, so you can maintain the same direction of rotation.*

### TIRE INFLATION

The inflation is the most ignored item of auto maintenance. Gasoline mileage can drop as much 0.8% for every 1 pound per square inch (psi) of under inflation.

Two items should be a permanent fixture in every glove compartment; a tire pressure gauge and a tread depth gauge. Check the tire air pressure (including the spare) regularly with a pocket type gauge. Kicking the tires won't tell you a thing, and the gauge on the service station air hose is notoriously inaccurate.

The tire pressures recommended for your car are usually found on the glove box door, the left side door jamb or in the owners manual. Ideally, inflation pressure should be checked when the tires are cool. When the air becomes heated it expands and the pressure increases. Every 10° rise (or drop) in temperature means a difference of 1 psi, which also explains why the tires appear to lose air on a very cold night. When it is impossible to check the tires cold, allow for pressure build-up due to heat. If the hot pressure exceeds the cold pressure by more than 15 psi, reduce your speed, load or both. Otherwise internal heat is created in the tire. When the heat approaches the temperature at which the tire was cured, during manufacture, the tread can separate from the body.

CAUTION: *Never counteract excessive pressure build-up by bleeding off air pressure (letting some air out). This will only further raise the tire operating temperature.*

Before starting a long trip with lots of luggage, you can add about 2–4 psi to the tires to make them run cooler, but never exceed the maximum inflation pressure on the side of the tire.

### TIRE DESIGN

Tires are of three basic designs: belted, bias-belted, and radial ply. It is important to understand that there are radical differences between the radial design and the others.

Radials were designed to substantially enhance the tire's ability to keep the tread uniformly in contact with the road. This means that radials have a substantially better ability to maintain their grip on the road in tight cornering situations. Since handling stability depends very greatly upon maintaining similar adhesion for both the front and rear of the car, IT IS EXTREMELY DANGEROUS TO MIX RADIALS WITH EITHER BIAS OR BELTED TIRES. Make sure all four tires are either radials or bias or belted tires; the consequences

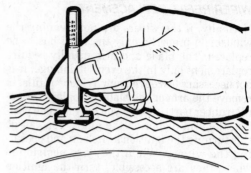

Checking tread depth using a gauge

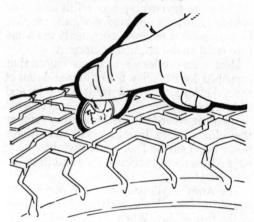

Checking tread depth using a Lincoln head penny

of mixing the two basic types are extremely dangerous!

### TREAD DEPTH

All tires made since 1968, have 8 built-in tread wear indicator bars that show up as ½" (12.7mm) wide smooth bands across the tire when ¹⁄₁₆" (1.6mm) of tread remains. The appearance of tread wear indicators means that the tires should be replaced. In fact, many states have laws prohibiting the use of tires with less than ¹⁄₁₆" (1.6mm) tread.

You can check your own tread depth with an inexpensive gauge or by using a Lincoln head penny. Slip the Lincoln penny into several tread grooves. If you can see the top of Lincoln's head in 2 adjacent grooves, the tires have less than ¹⁄₁₆" (1.6mm) tread left and should be replaced. You can measure snow tires in the same manner by using the tails side of the Lincoln penny. If you can see the top of the Lincoln memorial, it's time to replace the snow tires.

### TIRE STORAGE

Store the tires at proper inflation pressures if they are mounted on wheels. All tires should be kept in a cool, dry place. If they are stored in the garage or basement, do not let them stand on a concrete floor; set them on strips of wood.

## FLUIDS AND LUBRICANTS

### Fuel and Engine Oil Recommendations

All Mazda engines require the use of high quality engine oils labeled SE, SD, or SF. Do not use oil that is unlabeled or which has been reprocessed. Oil viscosity should be chosen on the basis of the range of temperatures you expect during the time the oil will be in the crankcase. You need not change oil because of a short period of unusual temperatures. Temperature ranges and related viscosities for most models are as follows:

- 0° to 85°F (−18° to +29°C): SAE 10W-30
- 0° to 100°F (−18° to +38°C): SAE 10W-40
- 0° to 120°F (−18° to 49°C): SAE 10W-50
- 10° to 100°F (−12° to +38°C): SAE 20W-40
- 10° to 120°F (−12° to 49°C): SAE 20W-50
- Below 25°F (−4°C): SAE 5W-30
- Below 0°F (−18°C): SAE 5W-20

For 1986 models, the viscosity limits have been slightly modified. See the illustration. All engines with catalytic converters require the use of unleaded fuel exclusively, as leaded fuel will almost immediately destroy the effectiveness of the catalytic converter. Unleaded fuel minimizes the accumulation of carbon deposits and corrosion in the engine and exhaust system, thus offering further benefit.

Mazda piston engines not equipped with a catalytic converter should be run only on low lead or no lead fuel (0–0.5 grams of lead per gallon) with a 91 Research octane rating. The use of regular or premium fuels that are fully leaded may cause engine damage.

## Engine

### OIL LEVEL CHECK

Under normal operating conditions, the Mazda rotary engine burns about one quart of oil every 1,000–1,400 miles to lubricate the rotor tip seals. Therefore, the oil level should be checked frequently.

Check the oil level, on all models, with the engine cold or as the last procedure at a fuel stop, to allow the oil time to drain back into the sump, (10 minutes).

The dipstick is located on the driver's side of the engine, next to the oil filler tube. It has either a red or green handle, depending upon the engine/transmission combination. Add the proper viscosity oil, as necessary, through the filler tube.

### OIL AND FILTER CHANGE

On 1971–75 cars, the oil should be changed every 4,000 miles or four months, whichever comes first. On 1971–73 cars, the initial change (with filter) should be performed at 600 miles, while on 1974–75 vehicles, this should be done at 2,000 miles/2 months. On 1976 cars, the initial change (with filter) comes at 2,000 miles/2 months, and changes are made ever 6,000 miles/6 months after that. On 1979 and later models change the oil every 7,500 miles. The car should be driven about 10 miles in order to get the oil hot immediately before draining it.

There is considerable debate in the auto industry about how frequently the oil filter should be changed. Note that the recommendation of both Mazda Motor Corporation and Chilton Book Co. is that the filter be changed at every oil change. This not only ensures adequate filtration even if the car is driven short distances in cold weather, but removes dirty oil from the filter and oil galleries, permitting a more completely effective removal of acids and abrasive materials.

1. Park the car on a level surface. Set the parking brake and block the wheels.

2. Working from underneath the car, remove the oil plug. Have a large, flat container of sufficient capacity ready to catch the oil.

CAUTION: *Be careful not to come into contact with any components of the exhaust system. A serious burn could result.*

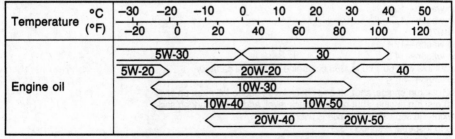

| Temperature | °C | −30 | −20 | −10 | 0 | 10 | 20 | 30 | 40 | 50 |
| | (°F) | −20 | 0 | 20 | 40 | 60 | 80 | 100 | 120 | |
| Engine oil | | | 5W-30 | | | 30 | | | | |
| | | 5W-20 | | 20W-20 | | | | 40 | | |
| | | | 10W-30 | | | | | | | |
| | | | 10W-40 | | 10W-50 | | | | | |
| | | | | 20W-40 | | 20W-50 | | | | |

Engine oil viscosity chart for 1986 models

## Capacities

| Year | Model | Engine Displacement Cu In. (cc) | Engine Crankcase (qts) | | Transmission (pts) | | | Drive Axle (pts) | Fuel Tank (gals) | Cooling System (qts) |
|------|-------|------|------|------|------|------|------|------|------|------|
| | | | With Filter | Without Filter | Manual 4-spd | 5-spd | Automatic | | | |
| 1971–72 | RX-2 | 70/1146 | 5.8 | 4.65 | 3.2 | — | 11.62 | 2.6 | 16.9 | 8.45 |
| 1972–73 | RX-3 | 70/1146 | 5.5 | 4.45 | 3.2 | — | 11.62 | 3.0 | 15.6 ① | 8.45 |
| 1973 | RX-2 | 70/1146 | — | 4.8 | 3.2 | — | 11.6 | 2.6 | 16.9 | 8.5 |
| 1974 | RX-2 | 70/1146 | — | 4.8 | 3.6 | — | 13.2 | 2.6 | 16.9 | 9.9 |
| | 808 | 96.8/1586 | — | 3.8 | 3.2 | — | 13.2 ④ | 2.6 | 11.7 ② | 7.9 |
| 1974–75 | RX-3 | 70/1146 | — | 4.8 | 3.6 | — | 13.2 | 3.0 | 15.6 ① | 10.2 |
| | RX-4 | 80/1308 | 6.8 | 5.3 | 3.6 | — | 13.2 | 2.8 | 17.2 ③ | 10.0 |
| 1975 | 808 | 96.8/1586 | — | 3.8 | 3.2 | — | 11.6 | 3.0 | 11.9 ② | 7.9 |
| 1976 | RX-3 | 70/1146 | 5.5 | 4.4 | 3.6 | 4.6 | 13.2 | 3.0 | 15.6 ⑥ | 9.8 |
| | RX-4 | 80/1308 | — | 3.8 | 3.2 | 4.6 | 13.2 | 2.8 | 16.9 ⑤ | 10.0 |
| 1976–78 | 808 (1600) | 96.8/1586 | 3.8 | — | 3.2 | 3.6 | 11.6 | 3.0 | 11.9 ② | 7.9 |
| | 808 (1300) | 77.6/1272 | 3.2 | — | 2.8 | — | — | 2.2 | 11.7 ② | 5.8 |
| 1977–78 | RX-4, RX-3SP | 80/1308 | 6.8 | 5.3 | 3.6 | 4.6 | 13.2 | 2.8 | 16.9 ⑤ | 10.0 |
| | Cosmo | 80/1308 | 6.8 | 5.3 | — | 3.6 | 13.2 | 2.6 | 17.2 | 10.0 |
| | GLC | 77.6/1272 ⑦ | — | 3.2 | 2.8 | 3.6 | 12.0 | 1.6 | 10.0 | 6.8 |
| 1979–80 | GLC | 86.4/1415 | — | 3.2 | 2.8 | 3.6 | 12.0 | 2.2 | 10.6 ⑧ | 5.8 |
| | 626 | 120.2/1970 | — | 4.1 | 3.0 | 3.6 | 13.2 | 2.6 | 14.5 | 7.9 |
| 1981–82 | GLC | 90.9/1490 | ⑨ | ⑨ | 6.8 | 6.8 | 12.0 | — | 11.1 | 5.8 |
| | GLC Wagon | 90.9/1490 | ⑨ | ⑨ | 2.8 | 3.6 | 12.0 | 1.6 | 11.9 | 5.8 |
| | 626 | 120.2/1970 | ⑩ | ⑩ | — | 3.6 | 13.2 | 2.6 | 14.5 | 7.9 |
| 1983 | GLC | 90.0/1490 | 3.9 | 3.2 | 6.8 | ⑪ | 12.0 ⑪ | — | 11.1 | 5.8 |
| | GLC Wagon | 90.0/1490 | 3.9 | 3.2 | 2.8 | ⑫ | 12.0 | 1.6 | 11.9 | 5.8 |
| | 626 | 121.9/1998 | 4.2 | 4.7 | — | 7.2 | 12.0 | 2.6 | 15.6 | 7.4 |
| 1984 | GLC | 90.0/1490 | 3.5 | 3.2 | 3.4 | 3.4 | 6.0 | — | 11.1 | 5.8 ⑬ |
| | 626 | 121.9/1998 | 4.2 | 3.8 | 3.6 | 3.6 | 6.0 | — | 15.9 | 7.3 |
| 1985 | GLC | 90.9/1490 | 3.9 | 3.2 | — | 7 | 12 | — | 11.1 | 5.8 |
| | 626 Gasoline | 121.9/1998 | 5.1 | 4.8 | — | 7 | 12 | — | 13.2 | 7.4 |
| | 626 Diesel | 121.9/1998 | 7.1 | 6.75 | — | 7 | 12 | — | 13.2 | 9.5 |
| 1986 | 323 | 97.4/1597 | 3.5 | 3.2 | 6.8 | 6.8 | 12 | — | 11.9 | 5.3 ⑭ |
| | 626 | 121.9/1998 | 4.5 | 4.2 | — | 7.2 | 12 | — | 15.9 | 7.4 |

① Station wagon—14.3
② Station wagon—10.4
③ Station wagon—17.7
④ 11.6—1975
⑤ Station wagon—17.4
⑥ Station wagon—14.3
⑦ Also available with 60.1 cu in./985 cc engine—same oil capacity
⑧ Station wagon—11.9
⑨ Add 3.2 qts. run engine, shut off and check level; add to full mark on stick
⑩ Add 3.8 qts. run engine, shut off and check level; add to full mark on stick
⑪ Transaxle—no separate drive axle is used
⑫ Applies to 4-speed, 5-speed—3.6
⑬ 6.3 with automatic
⑭ Applies to manual. Automatic—6.0

3. Allow all of the oil to drain into the container.

The oil filter is easily accessible; it is located on top of the engine, next to the oil filler tube on rotary engine cars. On cars with piston engines, it is located on the right side or rear of the engine.

4. Use a band wrench to remove the oil filter. Note that on the diesel, there are two oil filters, a standard, full-flow oil filter and a bypass oil filter. The bypass filter is replaced at the same interval and in the same way as the standard filter.

NOTE: *Place a container underneath the filter as it will leak oil.*

5. Clean the oil filter mounting flange with a cloth.

6. Lubricate the oil filter O-ring and the mounting surface of the filter with engine oil.

7. Install the filter, being careful not to damage the O-ring.

8. Tighten the filter by hand. Do not use the band-wrench to tighten it. Tighten the diesel bypass oil filter $^2_3$ turn after the gasket contacts the sealing surface, using a band wrench only if necessary.

9. Wipe off and then replace the drain plug, using care not to damage its threads.

10. Working from the top, add the proper viscosity oil through the filler tube which is on the driver's side of the engine. If the filter is being replaced in conjunction with an oil change, be sure the crankcase is refilled with the specified total oil capacity (see the Capacities chart). If, for some reason, only the filter is being replaced, add the difference between the crankcase capacity with filter and without filter. If this figure is not available, add ½ quart.

11. Start the engine without applying throttle and idle it until a few seconds after the oil light goes out. Then, stop the engine and allow it to sit for five minutes or so until all oil has drained back into the crankcase. Then, check the oil level with the dipstick and replenish as necessary.

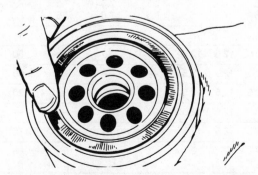

**Lubricate the gasket on the new filter with clean engine oil. A dry gasket may not make a good seal and will allow the the filter to leak**

## Manual Transmission
### FLUID RECOMMENDATIONS

Add SAE 90 EP if the temperature is above 0°F (–18°C) or SAE 80 EP if it is below 0°F (–18°C).

### LEVEL CHECK

Check the transmission oil every 4,000–7,500 miles:

1. Park the car on a level surface.
2. Working from underneath the car, unfasten the filler (upper) plug.
3. Use your finger to check the oil level; it should be up to the bottom of the oil fill hole.
4. Replace the filler plug.

CAUTION: *Be careful if you are working under the car when it is warm; the exhaust system (which is protected by wire mesh) gets extremely hot.*

### DRAIN AND REFILL

The oil should be changed in the manual transmission at 600 miles and then every 12,000 miles or one year on 1971–73 vehicles. On 1974–75 vehicles, transmission oil should be changed at 2,000 miles and then every 12,000 miles or one year. On 1976–78 vehicles, oil is changed at 2,000 miles and then every 24 months/25,000 miles thereafter. On 1979 and later vehicles the oil should be changed at 7,500 miles then at 30,000 mile intervals. Proceed in the following manner.

1. Start with the engine warm. Park on a level surface. Set the parking brake and block the wheels.
2. Remove the drain (lower) plug from underneath the car.

CAUTION: *Be careful not to come in contact with any components of the exhaust system. Severe burns could result.*

3. Allow the oil to drain into a large, flat container of sufficient capacity.
4. Wipe the magnetic drain plug with a clean cloth, until it is free of particles.
5. Install the drain plug.
6. Remove the filler plug and add the recommended lubricant, depending upon temperature.
7. Fill the transmission to capacity (see Capacities chart) until the oil level reaches the bottom of the fill hole.
8. Replace the filler plug.

## Manual Transaxle
### FLUID RECOMMENDATIONS

Add SAE 90 EP if the temperature is above 0°F (–18°C) or SAE 80 EP if it is below 0°F (–18°C).

NOTE: *Checking and replenishing the manual transaxle fluid is accomplished by remov-*

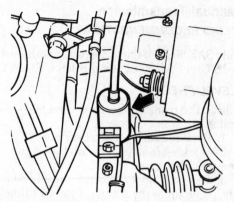

The arrow shows the location of the speedometer cable/driven gear unit of the manual transaxle on late model cars

*ing the speedometer driven gear from the top of the transaxle case. Checking of the transaxle oil is not required as routine maintenance (it is changed at 30,000 mile intervals). However, if you suspect leakage, you might want to check fluid level as a precaution.*
1. Park the vehicle on level ground.
2. Remove the speedometer cable from the

gear assembly by unscrewing the knurled filling.
3. Unbolt and remove the speedometer driven gear.
4. The oil level should cover the gear and gear shoulder.
5. Add gear oil, if necessary, through the speedometer gear mounting hole.
6. Reinstall the speedometer driven gear. Reconnect the speedometer cable.

### DRAIN AND REFILL

Transmission fluid on late model cars with a manual transaxle is to be changed at 30,000 mile intervals. To change the fluid:
1. Unscrew and remove the speedometer cable/driven gear assembly from the top of the transaxle.
2. Place a large, flat container of sufficient capacity under the transaxle drain plug. Remove the plug from underneath the car.
3. After the oil has completely drained install the drain plug and tighten it.
4. Add fluid meeting API specifications GL-4 or GL-5. See the capacities chart for the

## Maintenance Interval Chart

| Operation | 1971–73 | 1974–75 | 1976 | 1977 | 1978 | 1979–80 | 1981–82 | 1983–84 | 1985–86 |
|---|---|---|---|---|---|---|---|---|---|
| **ENGINE** | (Number of months or miles in thousands whichever comes first) | | | | | | | | |
| Air cleaner element—Replace | 24 | 24 | 24 | 24 | 24 | 30 | 30 | 30 | 30 |
| Clean | 2 | 2 | 2 | 2 | 2 | 2 | 2 | — | |
| Charcoal canister filter—Check or replace | — | 22 | 25 | 25 | 25 | 25 | 25 | — | — |
| Fuel filter—Replace | 8 | 12 | 12 | 12 | 12 | 12 | 12 | 30 | 30 |
| Drive belts—Inspect | 4 | 4 | 4 | 4 | 4 | 15 | 15 | 30 | 30 |
| Replace | ② | ② | ② | ② | ② | ② | ② | ② | ② |
| Battery check | 4 | 4 | 4 | 4 | 2 | 7.5 | 7.5 | ⑬ | ⑬ |
| Cooling system—Check | 4 | 4 | 6 | 6 | 6 | 7.5 | 7.5 | 15 | 15 |
| Drain and refill | 24 | 24 | 24 | 24 | 24 | 30 | 30 | 30 | 30 |
| Engine oil—Level check | ① | ① | ① | ① | ① | ① | ① | ① | ① |
| Change oil | 4 | 4 | 6 | 6 | 6 | 7.5 | 7.5 | 7.5 | 7.5 |
| Change filter | 4 | 4 | 6 | 6 | 6 | 7.5 | 7.5 | 7.5 | 7.5 |
| Change bypass filter ⑲ | | | | | | | | | 15 |
| Spark plug replacement | 12 | 12 | 12.5 | 12.5 | 12.5 | 30 | 30 | 30⑭ | 60 |
| Ignition points and condenser | 12 | 12 | 12.5 | 12.5 | 12.5 | — | — | — | 60 |
| Timing adjustment | 12 | 12 | 12.5 | 12.5 | 12.5 | 30 | 30 | 30 | 30 |
| PCV Valve replacement | 12 | 12 | 12.5 | 12.5 | 12.5 | 30 | 30 | — | — |
| Valve clearance adjustment | — | 12.5 | 12.5 | 12.5 | 12.5 | 15 | 15 | 15 | 15 |
| Intake, exhaust and cylinder head bolts adjustment | — | ③ | ③ | ③ | ③ | ③ | ③ | 15⑮ | — |
| Timing belt replacement (miles only) | | | | | | | | 60 | 60⑳ |

## Maintenance Interval Chart (cont.)

| Operation | 1971–73 | 1974–75 | 1976 | 1977 | 1978 | 1979–80 | 1981–82 | 1983–84 | 1985–86 |
|---|---|---|---|---|---|---|---|---|---|
| **CHASSIS** | | | | | | | | | |
| Manual transmission fluid level —Check | 4 ④ | 4 ⑤ | 4 ⑥ | 4 ⑥ | 4 ⑥ | 7.5 ⑦ | 7.5 ⑦ | ⑯ | ㉑ |
| Automatic transmission fluid level check | 4 | 4 | 4 | 4 | 4 | 7.5 | 7.5 | ⑦ | ㉒ |
| Front wheel bearings—Lubricate | 32 | 30 | 24 | 24 | 24 | 30 | 30 | 30 ⑰ | 30 ⑰ |
| Rear axle lubricate check | ③ | ⑤ | ⑥ | ⑥ | ⑥ | ⑦ | ⑦ | — | — |
| Steering gear lubricant check | ⑧ | ⑧ | ⑨ | ⑨ | ⑨ | ⑩ | ⑩ | 15 | 15 ㉓ |
| Tire pressures | ⑪ | ⑪ | ⑪ | ⑪ | ⑪ | ⑪ | ⑪ | ⑪ | ⑪ |
| Tire rotation | 4 | 4 | 4 | 4 | 4 | 7.5 | 7.5 | 4 | 7.5 |
| Ball joint lubrication | 32 | 24 | 24 | 24 | — | — | — | ⑱ | ㉓ |
| Front steering linkage inspection | 24 | 24 | 24 | 24 | 30 | 30 | 30 | 15 | 15 |
| Master cylinder fluid | ⑫ | ⑫ | ⑫ | ⑫ | ⑫ | ⑫ | ⑫ | ⑫ | ㉔ |
| Brake system inspection (lining) | 4 | 4 | 4 | 4 | 4 | 7.5 | 7.5 | 15 | ㉕ |

① Each fuel stop
② Replace as necessary
③ 1st 15,000 miles then every 30,000 miles
④ 1st 600 miles then every 12,000 miles
⑤ 1st 2,000 miles then every 12,000 miles
⑥ 1st 2,000 miles then every 25,000 miles
⑦ 1st 7,500 miles then every 30,000 miles
⑧ 1st 6,000 miles then every 4,000 miles
⑨ 1st 2,000 miles then every 6,000 miles
⑩ 1st 2,000 miles then every 15,000 miles
⑪ Once every month
⑫ Check level at least every 4,000 miles. It is recommended by the manufacturer that the fluid be changed every year (1971–73), every 30,000 miles (1979 and later).
⑬ Check indicator
⑭ Clean and inspect at 15,000 mile intervals
⑮ Torque head bolts only
⑯ Checking not required—replace every 30,000 miles
⑰ Rear wheel bearings also require repacking on 4 WD vehicles
⑱ Inspect at 30,000 mile, 30 month intervals—no lubrication required
⑲ Diesel only
⑳ Diesel—Replace both timing belts at 100,000 miles
㉑ Replace at 30,000 miles
㉒ First 3,000 miles then every 30,000 miles
㉓ Inspect at 30,000 mile, 30 month intervals, no lubrication required. Diesel intervals for inspection only—15,000 miles, 15 months
㉔ Inspect fluid level at 15,000 mile intervals, replace at 30,000 mile intervals
㉕ Inspect drum brakes at 7.5, discs at 15

amount. Check the level by reinserting the speedometer driven gear. The level is correct when the gear is entirely covered with lube, but the level does not exceed the level of the ridge slightly above the top of the gear.

5. Add further fluid if necessary and reinstall the cable/gear unit into the case.

## Automatic Transmission/Transaxle
### FLUID RECOMMENDATIONS

Mazda automatic transmissions and transaxles use Type F fluid only. Do not use Type A or Dexron⁺ type fluid, as the fluid characteristics affect shifting and may cause damage to the transmission clutches.

### LEVEL CHECK

The automatic transmission dipstick is located (rear wheel drive) behind the engine, next to the hood latch, or on the left front side of the engine (front wheel drive with a transaxle). Check fluid level every 4,000–7,500 miles on vehicles through 1982. On later models, check at 7,500 miles and then at 30,000, 60,000, etc.

There are two levels indicated in the dip-

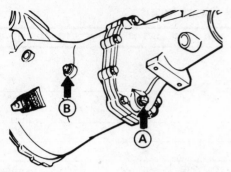

**Manual transmission drain plug "A" and filler plug "B". Typical of rear wheel drive cars**

stick on some models. One is labeled COLD and the other HOT.

To check the fluid level when the transmission is cold, i.e. when the car has been sitting overnight, proceed as follows:

1. Start the engine and allow it to warm up for at least two minutes. Move the selector lever through all the gear positions and then put it in Park.

2. Remove the dipstick and wipe it with a clean cloth.

3. Reinsert the dipstick.

4. Withdraw the dipstick again and note the level on the COLD side. Add Type F fluid as necessary. The difference between L and F is about 0.43 quart (0.41L).

The procedure for checking the fluid level when the transmission is hot is the same as above, except that the reading should be taken on the HOT side of the dipstick.

### DRAIN AND REFILL

1. Raise the car and support it securely on jackstands. Place a large drain pan under the transmission oil pan.

2. Loosen the bolts along the forward edge of the pan, including the ones in the corners at the front, as far as they will go without coming out of the housing. Then, remove all the remaining bolts.

3. Carefully and slowly pull the rear edge of the pan downward to break the seal with the gasket. Tilt the pan downward gradually so you can drain the fluid in a controlled manner.

4. When you have lowered the pan as far as it will go, support it by the center and remove the remaining bolts. Then, lower the pan carefully, and dump the remaining fluid.

**Hot and Cold fluid level markings on the automatic transmission dipstick**

5. Wipe the pan clean of all deposits, and then carefully clean both gasket surfaces.

NOTE: *Do not scrape the gasket surface of the transmission with a sharp scraper; this could scratch the surface and prevent proper seal.*

6. Install a new gasket and the pan. Coat both sides of the gasket with sealer; align the gasket holes with those in the pan. The sealer will help keep the gasket in place on the pan. Align the holes in the pan/gasket assembly with those in the transmission case, install the bolts, and tighten very gently. Then, torque in a criss-cross pattern to 3.5–5 ft.lb.

7. Refill the pan with the amount of fluid specified in the Capacities chart. Recheck the fluid level and replenish as necessary after the transmission has been run until hot and in all gear selector positions.

## REAR AXLE

### FLUID RECOMMENDATIONS

Use the following:
- Above 0°F (–18°C): SAE 90 HP
- Below 0°F (–18°C): SAE 80 HP

### LEVEL CHECK

Check the lubricant level in the rear axle every 4,000 miles on cars built in 1975 and earlier years. Periodic checking of the lubricant level is required at 6,000–7,500 mile intervals on 1976 and later cars. However, if you notice oil seepage from the rear axle, or a change in the sound of the axle, it is a good idea to check the oil level and replenish it if necessary. Any significant leaks should be repaired as soon as possible.

1. Park the car on a level surface and set the parking brake.

2. Remove the filler (upper) plug from the differential.

3. Check the oil level; it should be up to the

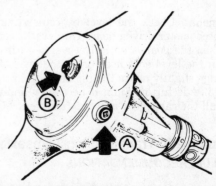

**Typical rear axle housing showing drain plug "A" and filler plug "B"**

bottom of the filler hole. Add lubricant, as necessary.

## DRAIN AND REFILL

The rear axle oil should be changed at 600 miles and then every 12,000 miles or one year on 1971–73 vehicles. On 1974–75 vehicles, it should be change at 2,000 miles and then every 12,000 miles or one year. On 1976–78 vehicles, oil is changed at 2,000 miles and then every 24 months/25,000 miles thereafter. On 1979 and later vehicles the oil should be changed at 7,500 miles then at 30,000 mile intervals. Proceed as described below:

1. Park the car on a level surface. Set the parking brake and block the wheels.

2. Remove the drain (lower) plug and allow the oil to run into a container of adequate capacity.

3. Clean and replace the drain plug.

4. Unscrew the filler (upper) plug and add one of the lubricants specified above, depending upon ambient temperature.

5. Fill to capacity until the level reaches the bottom of the filler hole. See the Capacities chart, above.

6. Replace the filler plug.

## Cooling System

### FLUID RECOMMENDATIONS

Use only a 50/50 solution of water and ethylene glycol antifreeze approved for aluminum engine parts.

### LEVEL CHECK

The coolant level should be checked regularly. Serious engine damage can occur if the engine overheats.

CAUTION: *Check the coolant level when the engine is cold; serious injury could result from escaping steam or hot water if checked when hot. If your car is equipped with an electric cooling fan make sure that the ignition switch is off. The cooling fan will automatically operate if the ignition switch is on and the engine coolant temperature is high or if the wiring connector on the thermostat housing is disconnected.*

**Models Equipped With Expansion Tank**

1. Depress the button on the thermal expansion tank safety cap if there is one. Allow all of the pressure trapped in the system to escape.

CAUTION: *The radiator is not equipped with a safety cap. Do not remove it before removing the expansion tank cap, or when the engine is hot.*

2. Remove the expansion tank cap. The expansion tank should be ½ full on 1971–73 cars,

and ⅓ full on later cars unless Full and Low marks are provided, as on the latest models. The level should be well above the bottom of the tank when the engine is cold.

3. If it is not, carefully remove the cap from the radiator. The radiator should be full.

4. Add a 50/50 solution of ethylene glycol coolant and clean water. If there was no coolant in the expansion tank, fill the radiator all the way, and then replace the radiator cap. Then, fill the expansion tank to the specified level, and replace the expansion tank cap.

NOTE: *Do not use cooling system additives; they may not mix properly with the coolant.*

**Models Without Expansion Tank**

1. Push safety button or turn the radiator cap to the first release point and allow any pressure in the system to escape.

2. Remove the radiator cap. The coolant level (when cold) should be just above the gauge or about 1" (25.4mm) below the filler neck.

3. Add enough of the recommended coolant to maintain the correct level. Do not overfill. If frequent refills are necessary, check the cooling system for leaks.

When checking the coolant level, the pressure cap should be looked at for signs of age or deterioration. Check it for a worn or cracked gasket. If the cap doesn't seal properly, fluid will be lost and the engine will overheat. A worn cap should be replaced with a new one. The fan belt and other drive belts should be inspected and adjusted to the proper tension. (See Checking Belt Tension).

Hose clamps should be tightened, and soft or cracked hoses replaced. Damp spots, or accumulations of rust or dye near hoses, water pump or other areas, indicate possible leakage,

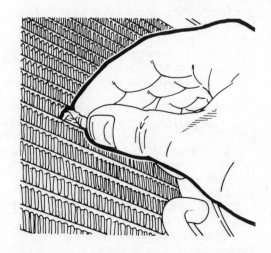

**Remove insects and debris from the radiator fins**

which must be corrected before filling the system with fresh coolant.

Periodically clean any debris, leaves, paper, insects, etc., from the radiator fins. Pick the large pieces off by hand. The smaller pieces can be washed away with water pressure from a hose.

Carefully straighten any bent radiator fins with a pair of needle nose pliers. Be careful as the fins are very soft. Don't wiggle the fins back and forth too much. Straighten them once and try not to move them again.

### DRAIN AND REFILL THE COOLING SYSTEM

The engine coolant should be drained and the system flushed periodically. New coolant mixed with the proper amount of clean water should be used to replace the old, as antifreeze eventually becomes corrosive. This must be done every two years on models up to 1978. Later models require coolant replacement at 30 months or 30,000 miles, whichever occurs first; however, the coolant should be inspected at 15 months/15,000 miles and replaced if it shows signs of rust or corrosion. Coolant that is safe is clear, while coolant that is permitting corrosion will appear cloudy and darker than its original light green or pink color.

Completely draining and refilling the cooling system will remove accumulated rust, scale and other deposits.

1. Drain the existing antifreeze and coolant. Open the radiator and engine drain petcocks, or disconnect the bottom radiator hose, at the radiator outlet.
NOTE: *Before opening the radiator petcock, spray it with some penetrating lubricant.*
2. Close the petcock or reconnect the lower hose and fill the system with water.
3. Add a can of quality radiator flush.
4. Idle the engine until the upper radiator hose gets hot.
5. Drain the system again.
6. Repeat this process until the drained water is clear and free of scale.
7. Close all petcocks and connect all the hoses.
8. If equipped with a coolant recovery system, flush the reservoir with water and leave empty.
9. Determine the capacity of your cooling system (see capacities specifications). Add a 50/50 mix of quality antifreeze (ethylene glycol and water) to provide the desired protection.
10. Run the engine to operating temperature.
11. Stop the engine and check the coolant level.
12. Check the level of protection with an

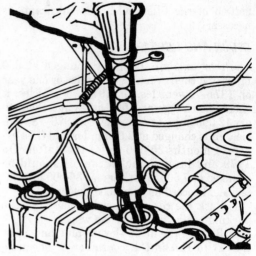

**Testing antifreeze effectiveness**

antifreeze tester, replace the cap and check for leaks.

## Brake/Clutch Master Cylinder
### FLUID RECOMMENDATIONS

Add FMVSS 116, DOT-3 or DOT-4, as necessary.

### LEVEL CHECK

Check the level in the brake and clutch master cylinder reservoirs regularly; at least every 4,000–7,500 miles.
NOTE: *If the brake warning light comes on the brake pedal is depressed and the parking brake is off, stop the vehicle immediately and check the fluid level in the brake master cylinder reservoir.*
Both reservoirs should be kept ⅔ full. Always add fluid slowly, so that bubbles do not form in the hydraulic lines.
CAUTION: *Be careful not to spill brake fluid on painted surfaces, as it is an all-too-effective paint remover.*
Bleed the brake system if bubbles are apparent. See Chapter 8.

### DRAIN AND REFILL

Change the brake fluid in both the brake and clutch hydraulic systems yearly on all 1971–73 vehicles. On later models change the fluid every 30,000 miles or 30 months. However, if your vehicle is driven in a mountainous region continuously or when the brakes are used extensively during continuous hard driving or when the climate is extremely humid all of the time the fluid should be changed annually.

## Steering Gear

### FLUID RECOMMENDATIONS

Use API GL-4 for manual steering boxes. Use ATF Type F for power steering units.

### LEVEL CHECK

#### Manual Steering Except Rack and Pinion

Check the lubricant in the steering gear at 6,000 miles and then every 4,000 miles on 1971–75 cars. Cars from 1976–78 require checking after 2,000 miles, and then every 6,000 miles. Cars from 1979–82 every 15,000 miles.

1. Remove the filler plug.
2. The oil level should be up to the bottom of the fill hole.
3. Add SAE 90 EP gear lubricant, as required.
4. Replace the filler plug.

#### Power Steering

On vehicles with power steering built in years up to 1983, check and replenish the power steering fluid level every 7,500 miles. On 1984–86 vehicles, check and replenish the fluid every 15,000 miles.

## Battery

### FLUID RECOMMENDATIONS

It is ideal to use distilled water in your battery to minimize mineral deposits on the lead plates. However, if the water in your area is reasonably soft, you can simply add clean tap water.

### FLUID LEVEL CHECK

Check the fluid level in the battery at least once a month and more frequently in cold weather. Check the battery first, if the ammeter indicates an abnormality.

The electrolyte level should be 0.4–0.8″ (6–20mm) above the plates in each cell. Add distilled or clean, reasonably soft tap water, if necessary. Do not overfill. If the temperature is below 32°F (0°C), run the engine for five minutes after adding water so the charging action will mix newly added water with the battery acid and prevent freezing.

CAUTION: *Do not smoke around the battery while the caps are removed. Escaping fumes could cause an explosion.*

## Sub-Zero Starter Assist

### FLUID RECOMMENDATIONS

Replenish the antifreeze in the sub-zero starter assist system with a 90% ethylene glycol and 10% water solution, as necessary.

### LEVEL CHECK

Check the antifreeze level in the sub-zero starter assist reservoir every two weeks in cold weather (if so equipped).

The reservoir is located directly beneath the brake master cylinder and is plainly marked.

## Ball Joint Lubrication

The ball joints should be lubricated: every 32,000 miles or 24 months on 1971–73 cars; on 1974–75 cars, the interval is 24,000 miles/24 months on 1976–77 cars (except GLC), the interval is 24,000 miles/24 months; on 1978 cars and all GLC, 1986 and later 323, and 626 Models, no lubrication is required. To grease the ball joints, proceed in the following manner:

1. Take the set ring out of the groove on the dust boot. Turn the boot inside out.
2. Remove the plug and install a grease fitting in its place.

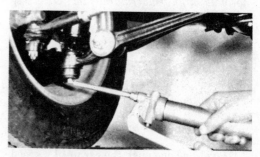

**Ball joint lubrication**

3. Use molybdenum disulphide lithium grease, NGLI No. 2, to grease the ball joint. Apply the grease with a grease gun. Drive out the old grease in the dust boot and socket by slowly pumping in new grease.
4. Once the old grease has been completely removed, secure the dust boot back in its original position with the set ring.
5. Add grease until the dust boot begins to balloon. Squeeze the boot gently with your fingers until about half of the grease remains on it.
6. Wipe off any excess grease from around the ball joint.
7. Remove the grease fitting and install the plug.

NOTE: *Replace the dust boot if it is worn or damaged. See Chapter Eight.*

## Body Lubrication

The door and hood hinges and the door holders should be lubricated with light oil each time the engine oil is changed. It is also a good idea, in very cold weather, to squirt a small amount of lock antifreeze into the door locks at this time.

## Wheel Bearings

The wheel bearings should be repacked with lithium grease, NGLI No. 1, every 32,000 miles or 24 months on 1971–73 cars; 30,000 miles or 24 months on 1974–75 cars; 24,000 miles or 24 months on 1976–78 cars; and 30,000 miles or 30 months on 1979 and later cars. For the correct repacking procedure, see Chapter Nine.

## PUSHING AND TOWING

CAUTION: *Do not attempt to push start a vehicle equipped with a catalytic converter unless absolutely necessary. Damage to the converter will occur caused by raw gas flowing into the converter and then burning at an abnormally high temperature which adversely affects the catalyst.*

Mazda models equipped with manual transmissions are started in the same manner as any other car:

1. Place the car in High gear and turn the ignition switch to ON. If the car is a diesel, make sure the glow plugs have had time to operate (the WAIT) light has gone out.)

CAUTION: *Be sure that the steering column is unlocked.*

2. Have someone push the car until a speed of 10 mph is reached.

CAUTION: *Never attempt to start the automobile by towing it. Once the automobile starts, it could crash into the rear of the tow vehicle.*

3. Slowly let the clutch pedal out until the engine catches. As soon as it has caught, depress the clutch pedal and select First gear.

Mazda models equipped with automatic transmission cannot be push-started. Not only will pushing the car with the automatic transmission in gear fail to start the car, but it could also cause serious damage to the transmission.

The following precautions should be observed when towing the vehicle:

1. Always place the transmission in Neutral and release the parking brake.

2. 1971–72 and 1979–82 models equipped with automatic transmissions may be towed with the transmission in Neutral, but only for short distances at speeds below 20 mph. If the car must be towed beyond this distance or if the transmission is inoperative, tow the car with its drive wheels off the ground or the driveshaft disconnected at the differential end. 1973–78 models with automatic transmissions cannot be towed unless the driveshaft is disconnected or the wheels are off the ground.

3. If the rear axle is defective, the car must be towed with the rear wheels off the ground.

4. Always be sure that the steering column is unlocked before towing the car with its front wheels on the ground.

CAUTION: *The steering column lock is not designed to hold the wheels straight while the automobile is being towed. Therefore, if the car is being towed with its front end down, and the wheel cannot be unlocked, place a dolly under the front wheels.*

## JACKING

Specific instructions for the use of the jack and the proper jacking points are found on stickers which are attached to the jack and located in the luggage compartment.

There are, however, some general precautions to observe when jacking the automobile:

1. Never climb underneath the car when it is supported only by the jack. Always use jackstands as an additional means of support.

2. Always keep the car on level ground when jacking it. Otherwise, the car may roll or fall off the jack.

3. When raising the FRONT of the car, set the parking brake and block the rear wheels.

4. When raising the REAR of the car, securely block the front wheels.

## TUNE-UP PROCEDURES

### Spark Plugs

A typical spark plug consists of a metal shell surrounding a ceramic insulator. A metal electrode extends downward through the center of the insulator and protrudes a small distance. Located at the end of the plug and attached to the side of the outer metal shell is the side electrode. The side electrode bends in at a 90° angle so that its tip is even with, and parallel to, the tip of the center electrode. The distance between these two electrodes (measured in thousandths of an inch) is called the spark plug gap. The spark plug in no way produces a spark but merely provides a gap across which the current can arc. The coil produces anywhere from 20,000 to 40,000 volts which travels to the distributor where it is distributed through the spark plug wires to the spark plugs. The current passes along the center electrode and jumps the gap to the side electrode, and, in so doing, ignites the air/fuel mixture in the combustion chamber.

#### SPARK PLUG HEAT RANGE

Spark plug heat range is the ability of the plug to dissipate heat. The longer the insulator (or the farther it extends into the engine), the hotter the plug will operate; the shorter the insulator the cooler it will operate. A plug that absorbs little heat and remains too cold will quickly accumulate deposits of oil and carbon since it is not hot enough to burn them off. This leads to plug fouling and consequently to misfiring. A plug that absorbs too much heat will have no deposits, but, due to the excessive heat, the electrodes will burn away quickly and in some instances, preignition may result. Preignition takes place when plug tips get so hot that they glow sufficiently to ignite the fuel/air mixture before the actual spark occurs.

This early ignition will usually cause a pinging during low speeds and heavy loads.

The general rule of thumb for choosing the correct heat range when picking a spark plug is: if most of your driving is long distance, high speed travel, use a colder plug; if most of your driving is stop and go, use a hotter plug. Original equipment plugs are compromise plugs, but most people never have occasion to change their plugs from the factory recommended heat range.

NOTE: *Some of the spark plugs listed in this chapter are especially designed and built for use in the Mazda rotary engine. They are available from the manufacturers listed. The spark plugs listed for the rotary engine are specified for use by Toyo Kogyo Co., Ltd. Use only these plugs, do not substitute a different type of plug.*

#### REMOVAL AND INSTALLATION

A set of spark plugs usually requires replacement after about 10,000 miles on cars with conventional ignition systems and after about 20,000 to 30,000 miles on cars with electronic ignition, depending on your style of driving. In normal operation, plug gap increases about 0.001" (0.0254mm) for every 1,000–2,500 miles. As the gap increases, the plug's voltage requirement also increases. It requires a greater voltage to jump the wider gap and about two to three times as much voltage to fire a plug at high speeds than at idle.

When your're removing spark plugs, you should work on one at a time. Don't start by removing the plug wires all at once, because unless you number them, they may become mixed up. Take a minute before you begin and number the wires with tape. The best location for numbering is near where the wires come out of the cap.

NOTE: *On rotary engines both the distribu-*

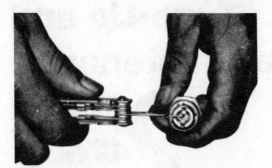

**Checking the electrode gap—note dual electrodes**

*tor and the engine housing are marked to aid in identification of the spark plug and distributor connections. However, to avoid confusion, it is easier to remove one plug at a time.*

1. Twist the spark plug boot and remove the boot and wire from the plug. Do not pull on the wire itself as this will ruin the wire.

2. If possible, use a brush or rag to clean the area around the spark plug. Make sure that all the dirt is removed so that none will enter the cylinder after the plug is removed.

3. Remove the spark plug using the proper size deep-well socket. Turn the socket counterclockwise to remove the plug. Be sure the socket goes all the way onto the plug to avoid breaking the plug, or rounding off the hex on the plug.

4. Once the plug is out, check it against the plug shown in this section to determine engine condition. This is crucial since plug readings are vital signs of engine condition.

5. Inspect the plug for unusual wear problems. See the color insert on spark plug analysis. Note any problems and, if necessary, replace an individual plug that shows excessive wear or damage.

6. Use a round wire feeler gauge to check the plug gap. The correct size gauge should pass through the electrode gap with a slight drag. If you're in doubt, try one size smaller and one larger. The smaller gauge should go through easily while the larger one shouldn't go through at all. If the gap is incorrect, use the electrode bending tool on the end of the gauge to adjust the gap. When adjusting the gap, always bend the side electrode. The center electrode is non-adjustable.

7. Squirt a drop of penetrating oil on the threads of the new plug and install it. Don't oil the threads too heavily. Turn the plug in clockwise by hand until it is snug.

8. When the plug is finger tight, tighten it with a wrench. If you don't have a torque wrench, tighten the plug as shown.

9. Install the plug boot firmly over the plug. Proceed to the next plug.

## Firing Orders

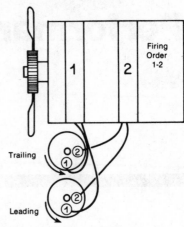

**1971–73**

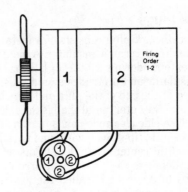

**1974**

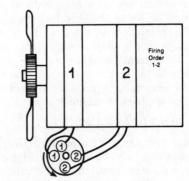

**1975–78**

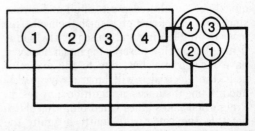

**GLC front wheel drive models, firing order; 1-3-4-2**

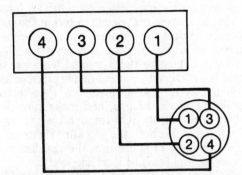

All models except the GLC front wheel drive, firing order 1-3-4-2. Number one distributor tower location may vary, depending on model

## Spark Plug Wires
### CHECKING AND REPLACING

Visually inspect the spark plug cables for burns, cuts, or breaks in the insulation. Check the spark plug boots and the nipples on the distributor cap and coil. Replace any damaged wiring. If no physical damage is obvious, the wires can be checked with an ohmmeter for excessive resistance. (See the tune-up and troubleshooting section).

When installing a new set of spark plug cables, replace the cables one at a time so there will be no mixup. Start by replacing the longest cable first. Install the boot firmly over the spark plug. Route the wire exactly as the original was routed. Insert the nipple firmly into the tower on the distributor cap. Repeat the process for each cable.

## Breaker Points

Mazda rotary engines, through 1973, are equipped with two distributors. One distributor operates the leading set of plugs and the other the trailing set. When checking or re-placing the points, remember to serve both distributors. 1974 and later rotary engines have a single distributor with either dual or triple point sets.

Most piston engines are equipped with breaker point distributors through 1979, GLC models from 1977 use a breakerless distributor except those built for California and Canada 1977–78 and the 1979 Canadian models. The 1979 and later 626 are equipped with breakerless ignition. On the breakerless distributors there are no points or condenser to replace.

### REMOVAL AND INSTALLATION

New points should be installed on 1971–75 cars at 12,000 miles or 12 months. On 1976 and later models, no set interval for replacement is recommended. Clean, gap, and inspect the points every 12,000 miles and replace them if they're excessively pitted or worn.

1. Perform steps 1 and 2 of the adjustment.
2. Unplug the blade type electrical connector from the contact set.
3. Remove the two mounting screws, noting the location of any condenser lead wires, and remove the contact set.
4. Install the new set of points, any condenser lead wires, and the screws, tightening the screws just enough to hold the contact set in place.

**Point gap adjustment**

## Spark Plug Usage—Rotary Engine

| Year | Manu. | Part Number | | |
| | | Hot | Standard | Cold |
|---|---|---|---|---|
| 1974–75 | NGK | — | B7-EM or B-7EJ | B8-EM or B-8EJ |
| | Nippondenso | — | W-22EA | W-25EA |
| | Champion | — | N-80B | N-78B |
| 1976 | NGK | — | B-7ET | B-8ET |
| | Nippondenso | — | W-22EB | W-25EB |
| | Champion | — | N-278B | N-280B |
| 1977–78 | NGK | BJET | B-7ET | B-8ET |
| | Nippondenso | W-20EB | W-22EB | W-25EB |
| | Champion | N-278B | N-280B | N-282B |

5. Reconnect the blade connector. Then, adjust point gap as described in the procedure above.

6. Repeat the procedure for additional contact sets or the other distributor as required.

7. Check and adjust dwell as described in the appropriate procedure below.

## Condenser

The condenser should be replaced every time the points are replaced. If the condenser is suspect, the easiest way to check it is by replacing it with a new one. The condenser capacity is 0.27 mfd. To replace the condenser, perform the following steps:

1. Remove the distributor cap. Leave the wires connected. Withdraw the rotor.

2. Loosen the condenser lead retaining screw from inside the distributor and withdraw the clip.

3. Unfasten the condenser retaining screw which is located on the outside of the distributor housing.

NOTE: *The smaller condenser, mounted next to the ignition condenser, is for radio noise suppression. It need only be replaced if a clicking sound is heard over the radio.*

4. Remove the condenser. Install the new condenser in the reverse order of removal.

### CONTACT ADJUSTMENT

NOTE: *The procedure given here covers adjustment of the ignition points after replacement or cleaning. See the DWELL ANGLE ADJUSTMENT procedure below for what is required to check and fine tune the adjustment with an electronic dwell meter.*

On 1971–75 cars, the ignition points should be checked and gapped every 4,000 miles or four months and replaced every 12,000 miles or 12 months. On 1976 and later cars with ignition points, they should be checked and gapped every 12,500 miles or one year.

To check and adjust the point gap, proceed in the following manner:

1. Unfasten the clips and remove the cap from one of the distributors. Leave the leads attached to the cap.

2. Remove the rotor from the distributor.

3. Clean the points with a point file, if they are pitted. If they are badly pitted or burned, replace them as detailed in the section below.

4. Rotate the engine by using a remote starter switch, or have someone inside the car operate the ignition key until the rubbing block is at the top of the cam.

5. Check the point gap with a feeler gauge. The gap should be 0.018″ (0.457mm) on rotary engine cars, and 0.020″ (0.51mm) on piston engine cars.

6. Adjust the gap with a screwdriver. Loosen the lockscrew just enough to permit the stationary contact to be moved, using the screwdriver as a lever in the slot provided. The lockscrew must be tight enough, however, to hold the stationary contact in one place while you adjust it. Use a clean, flat type feeler gauge to check the gap, and make sure the blade is sliding straight through the gap, not at an angle. Recheck the gap after tightening the lockscrew to make sure the gap has not changed, and readjust it as necessary.

7. Make sure the cam follower is properly lubricated. If necessary, wipe dirty grease off the follower and cam and apply high melting point contact point lube to leading edge of the cam follower and cam.

8. If necessary, repeat these steps for the other set of points. Replace rotor and cap.

9. If there are two distributors, repeat the procedure for the other one. Check the swell angle as described in the appropriate procedures below.

NOTE: *On 1975–76 rotary engine distributors, the leading-retard points are located on a plate mounted in the top of the distributor. To gain access to the other two sets of points, holes are provided in the upper contact plate base or can be reached by disconnecting the wiring and removing the mounting screws for the plate and the connecting screw for the exterior adjusting lever, and removing the plate.*

## Electronic Ignition
### TROUBLESHOOTING

**1978 California and Canada GLC**
**1979 626**
**1979 GLC Except Canada**
**All 1980 and Later Models**

Electronic ignition replaces the contact points with an electromagnetic generator, consisting of a rotating pole piece, mounted on the distributor shaft, passes the pickup, current is generated, much as in the car's main electrical system generator. The spikes of current produced as each of the four corners on the pole piece pass the pickup operate transistors in the ignitor mounted on the coil. This provides the switching actions ordinarily handled by the contact points, but without the arcing and stress of opening and closing associated with their operation.

There are several checks unique to this system that can be made to locate or repair trouble. The gap between the pole piece and pickup can be checked and adjusted, and the electrical resistance of the pickup can be checked on vehicles built up until 1982. The resistance of the

**Adjusting pickup gap**

coil can be checked on all electronic ignition equipped vehicles.

## ADJUSTING PICKUP GAP

### 1978–82

1. Remove the distributor cap and rotor. Turn the engine over with the starter or by using a socket wrench on the crankshaft pulley bolt until one of the four high points on the pole piece lines up directly with the metallic portion of the pickup.

2. Using a non-magnetic (i.e. brass or paper) feeler gauge, check the gap. If it is not 0.010–0.018″ (0.254–0.457mm) for the GLC, or >0.008″ (>0.2mm) for the 626, wide loosen the two adjusting screws and slide the pickup in or out until the dimension is correct. Tighten screws and recheck the gap. Readjust if necessary.

## CHECKING PICKUP COIL RESISTANCE

### 1978–82

Unplug the primary ignition wire connector, and connect an ohmmeter between the two prongs of the connector on the distributor side. The resistance of the pickup coil should be 670–790Ω (GLC) or 720–1,050Ω (626) as measured at room temperature. If resistance is incorrect, replace the pickup.

## CHECKING IGNITION COIL RESISTANCE

### 1978–82

1. Run the engine until it reaches operating temperature (coil must be hot). Pull the high tension lead out of the coil tower.

2. Measure primary resistance with an ammeter, connecting between coil minus and plug primary terminals. Resistance should be 1.15–1.28Ω (GLC) or 0.9–1.15Ω (626).

3. Measure secondary resistance, connecting the ohmmeter between the coil tower and the plus primary terminal. Resistance should be 13,500Ω (GLC) or 7,000Ω (626).

4. Replace the coil if resistances are incorrect by plus or minus 10%.

## CHECKING ELECTRONIC IGNITION

### 1982–86

1. Pull the high tension lead from the coil out of the distributor cap and hold its electrical connector 0.020–0.040″ (0.51–1.01mm) from a good ground. Have someone crank the engine. The ignition system should produce a plainly visible, bluish/white spark. Reconnect the high tension lead.

2. If there is doubt about the adequacy of the spark, run the engine until it is hot and then make checks of the coil primary and secondary resistance.

First, connect an ohmmeter set to the X1 scale to the plug and minus primary connectors of the coil, as shown. The coil should have good continuity. That is, resistance should be approximately 1–1.3Ω.

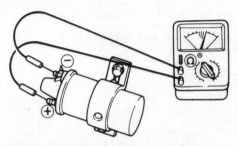

**Test the coil primary resistance as shown**

Second, disconnect the high tension wire and move the connector leading to the minus terminal over to the metallic connector inside the coil tower. Set the ohmmeter to the X1000 scale. Resistance must be 10,000–30,000Ω.

If either of these tests is failed, replace the coil.

You can also check for bad coil insulation by measuring the resistance between the coil (–)

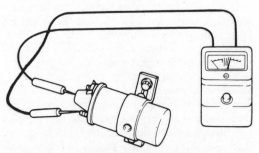

**Test the coil secondary circuit as shown**

## Tune-Up Specifications—Rotary Engine

When analyzing compression test results, look for uniformity among cylinders, rather than specific pressures.

| Year | Engine Displace. (cu in.) | Spark Plugs | | Distributors | | Ignition Timing (deg) | | | Idle Speed (rpm) | |
| | | | | Point Dwell (deg) | Point Gap (in.) | Leading | | Trailing Normal | | |
| | | Type | Gap (in.) | | | Normal | Retarded | | MT | AT |
|---|---|---|---|---|---|---|---|---|---|---|
| 1971–73 | 70 | N80B ① | .031–.035 | 58±3 | .018 | TDC | 10A | 10A | 900 | 750 ② |
| 1974 | 70 | N80B ① | .024–.028 | 58±3 | .018 | 5A | — | 15A | 900 | 750 ② |
| 1975 | 70, 80 | N80B ① | .024–.028 | 58±3 | .018 | TDC | 20A | 15A | 800–850 | 750–800 ② |
| 1976 | 70 | RN-278B ① | .039–.043 | 58±3 ③ | .018 | TDC | 15A | 20A | 700–750 | 700–750 ② |
| 1976 | 80 | RN-278B ① | .039–.043 | 58±3 ③ | .018 | 5A | 20A | 20A | 700–750 | 700–750 ② |
| 1977 | 70, 80 | RN-278B ① | .039–.043 | 58±3 | .018 | 5A | — | 25A | 725–775 | 725–775 ② |
| 1978 | 70 ④ | RN-278B ① | .039–.043 | 58±3 | .018 | 0 | — | 20A | 725–775 | 725–775 ② |
| 1978 | 80 | RN-278B ① | .039–.043 | 58±3 | .018 | 5A | — | 25A | 725–775 | 725–775 ② |

① See "Spark Plug Usage" chart above
② Transmission in Drive
③ Leading retarded dwell angle is 53±3
④ Used in RX-35P only
TDC—Top dead center
A—After top dead center
B—Before top dead center
MT—Manual transmission
AT—Automatic transmission
deg—degrees
NOTE: *The underhood specifications sticker often reflects tune-up specification changes made in production. Sticker figures must be used if they disagree with those in this chart.*

primary connection and the metal body of the coil. If resistance is less then 10,000Ω, replace the coil. This test may not be entirely satisfactory unless you have a megger tester that produces 500 Volts. If the tests below do not reveal the problem and, especially, if operating the engine at night may produce some bluish sparks around the coil, you may want to remove the coil and have it tested at a diagnostic center.

If the coil tests out ok, replace the igniter and pickup coil. However, you should make sure before doing this work that there are no basic maintenance problems in the secondary circuit of the system, since it is often impossible to return electrical parts. We suggest that before you replace the igniter and pickup coil, you carefully inspect the cap and rotor for carbon tracks or cracks and disconnect the wires and measure their resistance with an ohmmeter. Resistance should be 16,000Ω per length of 3.28 feet. Also, check for cracks in the insulation. Replace secondary parts as

inspection/testing deems necessary before replacing the igniter and pickup coil. See the procedure below for general information on replacing these units.

### DWELL ANGLE ADJUSTMENT

**Rotary Engines**

*1971–74*

Make separate checks of dwell angle for each distributor, in the following manner:

1. Disconnect the vacuum line from the distributor and plug it with a pencil or a golf tee.
2. Connect the dwell meter in accordance with the manufacturer's instructions. The dwell meter must be connected to the coil which fires the leading plugs to test the leading distributor, and to the coil which fires the trailing plugs to test the trailing distributor. Then, to test the leading retard ignition points (used on 1972–73 RX-2 and RX-3), do the following:

## Tune-Up Specifications—Piston Engine

When analyzing compression test results, look for uniformity among cylinders, rather than specific pressures.

| Year | Engine Displace (cu in.) | Spark Plugs Type | Gap (in.) | Distributor Point Dwell (deg) | Point Gap (in.) | Ignition Timing (deg) MT | AT | Intake Valve Opens (deg) | Fuel Pump Pressure (psi) | Idle Speed (rpm) | Valve Clear (in.) In. | Ex |
|---|---|---|---|---|---|---|---|---|---|---|---|---|
| 1974 | 96.8 | BP-6ES | .031 | 49–55 | .020 | 5B | 4B ① | 13 | 2.8–3.6 | 800–850 ② | .012 | .012 |
| 1975 | 96.8 | BP-6ES | .031 | 49–55 | .020 | 5B | 5B | 13 | 2.8–3.6 | 800–850 ② | .012 | .012 |
| 1976–78 | 96.8 | BP-6ES | .031 | 49–55 | .020 | 5B ③ | 5B ③ | 13 | 2.8–3.6 | 800–850 ④ | .012 | .012 |
| | 77.6 | BP-6ES | .031 | 49–55 | .020 | 7B ⑤ | 11B | 13 | 2.84–3.84 | 700–750 ⑥ | .010 | .012 |
| 1979 | 86.4 | BP-5ES BPR-5ES | .031 | 49–55 | .020 | 7B ⑦ | 7B ⑧ | 15 | 2.8–3.8 | 700–750 ⑩ ⑪ | .010 | .012 |
| | 120.2 | BP-5ES BPR-5ES | .031 | — | — | 8B | 8B | 10 | 2.8–3.6 | 650–700 | .012 | .012 |
| 1980 | 86.4 | BP-5ES BPR-5ES | .031 | — | — | 5B | 5B | 15 | 2.8–3.8 | 700–750 ⑩ | .010 | .012 |
| | 120.2 | BP-5ES BPR-5ES | .031 | — | — | 5B ⑨ | 5B ⑨ | 10 | 2.8–3.6 | 650–700 | .012 | .012 |
| 1981–82 | 90.9 | BP-5ES BPR-5ES | .031 | — | — | 8B | 8B | 15 | 2.8–3.8 | ⑫ | .010 | .012 |
| | 120.2 | BP-5ES BPR-5ES | .031 | — | — | ⑬ | ⑬ | 10 | 2.8–3.6 | ⑭ | .012 | .012 |
| 1983–84 | 90.9 | BPR-5ES BPR-6ES | .031 | — | — | 6B | 6B | 15 | 4.3–5.9 ⑮ | ⑰ | .007 | .009 |
| | 121.9 | BPR-5ES BPR-6ES | .031 | — | — | 6B | 6B | 17 | 2.9–4.2 | ⑯ | .012 | .012 |
| 1985 | 90.9 | BPR-5ES BPR-6ES | .031 | — | — | 6B | 6B | 15 | 4.3–6 | ⑰ | .010 | .012 |
| | 121.9 | BPR-5ES BPR-6ES | .031 | — | — | 6B | 6B | 17 | 2.8–4.3 | ⑯ | .012 | .012 |
| 1986 | 97.4 | BPR-5ES11 BPR-6ES11 | .041 | — | — | 7B | 7B | 14 | 4.5–6.0 | ⑱ | .012 | .012 |
| | 121.9 | BPR-5ES ⑲ BPR-6ES | .031 | — | — | 6B | 6B | 16 | 35.6–40.5 | ⑳ | .012 | .012 |

① Refers to distributor in retard position—8B in advance position
② In Neutral
③ California—8B
④ Automatic—650–700 in Drive
⑤ California—11B
⑥ Automatic—600–650 in Drive
⑦ California—5B
  Canada—8A
⑧ California—5B
  Canada—8B
⑨ Canada—8B
⑩ Federal:
  Automatic—600–650
⑪ Canada:
  Manual—800–850
  Automatic—700–750

⑫ Manual transmission 800–850 rpm
  Automatic transmission 750 rpm in "Drive"
⑬ 1981; USA-5B
     Canada-8B
  1982; All-8B
⑭ Manual transmission 650–700 rpm
  Auto transmission 650 rpm in "Drive"
⑮ Applies to '84–'83—2.84–3.84
⑯ Set automatic to 700 in "D"; Manual—750
⑰ Set automatic to 750 in "D"; Manual—850
⑱ Set automatic 1000 in N; Manual 850
⑲ Non turbo engine only
⑳ Set automatic 900–950 in N; Manual 750–800

## Diesel Engine Tune-Up Specifications

| Year | Engine Displace (cu in.) | Valve Clearance (cold) ① | | Intake Valve Opens (deg) | Injection Pump Setting (deg) | Injection Nozzle Pressure (psi) | | Idle Speed (rpm) | Cranking Compression Pressure (psi) |
|------|------|------|------|------|------|------|------|------|------|
| | | Intake (in.) | Exhaust (in.) | | | New | Used | | |
| 1985 | 121.9 | .008–.012 | .012–.016 | 13 | 0TDC | 1,920 | — | 800–850 | 427 ① |

① Minimum—384. Maximum difference between cylinders—43

a. Disconnect both the Thermosensor connections (see Chapter 4).

b. Unfasten the idle and/or vacuum switch connections.

c. Detach the choke switch connector. The leading retard points can be identified by the fact that their position on the mounting plate can be rotated to adjust ignition timing. The dwell meter must be connected to the leading coil to test them.

3. Run the engine at idle, after it has warmed up.

4. Observe the dwell meter reading. It should be within the range specified in the tune-up chart.

5. If it is not within specifications, adjust the contact point gap as outlined above.

NOTE: *If dwell angle is above the specified amount, the point gap is too small; if it is below, the gap is too large.*

6. If both the dwell angle and the contact point gap cannot be brought to within specifications, check for one or more of the following:

a. Worn distributor cam

b. Worn rubbing block

c. Bent movable contact arm

7. Replace any of the parts, as necessary.

8. When the dwell angle check is complete, disconnect the meter and reconnect the vacuum line.

### 1975–76

1. Run the engine until it is warm.

2. Connect the dwell meter in accordance with the manufacturer's instructions. The dwell meter must be connected to the coil which fires the leading plugs to test the leading contact points, and to the coil which fires the trailing plugs to test the trailing contact points.

3. Run the engine at idle speed and observe the meter reading. It should be within the range specified in the tune-up chart.

4. If dwell is not within the specified range, adjust the contact gap as described above. If dwell angle is too high, the point gap is too small; if dwell angle is too low, the point gap is too wide.

5. After setting dwell of leading and trailing contact points, stop the engine and disconnect the connector in the wiring harness which leads to the distributor. Then, run two jumper wires exactly as shown in the illustration. This will cause the leading ignition coil to be operated through the leading-retard contact points, and enable you to read the dwell for those contacts. Dwell for this set of contacts is 58° on 1975 models, and 53° on 1976 models.

6. Be sure to recheck dwell after tightening the adjusting screw, because the point gap (and dwell) sometimes change when this is done. If dwell cannot be brought to specification, check for a bent contact arm, worn rubbing block, or worn distributor cam or shaft.

### 1977–78

The method of dwell angle adjustment described here requires that some of the high tension wiring be re-routed to permit the engine to run with the distributor cap and rotor off. While this re-routing process requires some extra time, the dwell adjustment may be made with the engine running, which will save considerable time and make it possible for the dwell to be brought to specification on the first adjustment.

1. Run the engine until it is hot and stop it.

2. Note their locations, and then disconnect high tension leads at leading and trailing ignition coils.

3. Note its location in the distributor cap, and then disconnect the leading spark plug wire for the front rotor at the cap. Connect it to the tower of the leading ignition coil.

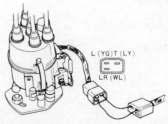

**Run jumper wires as shown to set dwell on leading-retard contacts**

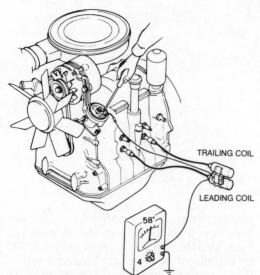

**Re-route high tension wiring as shown to set dwell with engine running on 1977–78 rotary cars**

4. Note its location in the distributor cap, and then disconnect the leading spark plug wire for the rear rotor at the cap. Connect it to the tower of the trailing ignition coil.

5. Remove the distributor cap and rotor.

6. Check the high tension wiring with the illustration. The plug wires for the top two plugs will still be connected to the rotor, but the bottom two plugs must be wired as shown.

7. Connect the dwell angle tester to the trailing ignition coil. Then, start the engine and read the dwell. If the dwell is incorrect, loosen the set screw for the trailing contact set only slightly (or the engine will stop). Then, very gradually move the stationary contact back and forth until dwell is within the specified range (55–61°).

8. When dwell is correct, tighten the set screw and recheck dwell. Readjust it as necessary.

9. Connect the dwell meter to the leading ignition coil and repeat steps 7 and 8 for the leading contacts.

10. Reconnect all wiring and reinstall the cap and rotor.

## Piston Engine Cars

1. Start the engine and run until it is hot and running at normal idle speed.

2. Connect a dwell meter to the ignition coil as described in the manufacturer's instructions. Read the dwell and compare the reading to the specification shown in the Tune-Up Chart.

3. If dwell is incorrect, stop engine, remove distributor cap and rotor and adjust point gap as described above. If dwell is very far from the

specified range, simply set contacts to the specified gap. If dwell is just a little too high, open the contact gap just slightly; if dwell reading is too low, close the point gap just slightly.

4. After contact adjustment, replace cap and rotor, start engine, and read dwell again. Readjust if necessary.

## ELECTRONIC IGNITION

### Ignition Timing
#### ROTARY ENGINES
#### 1971–73

As in other tune-up procedures involving the ignition system, both distributors must be adjusted separately. Begin with the leading distributor when checking the timing:

1. Connect a timing light to the leading distributor spark plug cable which runs to the number one (front) rotor. Check the manufacturer's instructions for specific hook-up details.

2. Start the engine and run it at idle speed.

3. Loosen the distributor locknuts so that the distributor can be rotated.

4. Aim the timing light at the timing indicator pin in the front housing.

5. The yellow mark (0 TDC) should align with the pin on the housing.

6. If it does not, rotate the distributor until it aligns.

7. Tighten the locknuts and recheck the timing.

The ignition timing for the trailing distributor is checked and adjusted in the same manner, except that the timing light lead should be connected to the trailing distributor spark plug cable which runs to the number one rotor.

When the timing light is pointed at the eccentric shaft pulley, the orange mark (10° ATDC) should align with the timing pointer.

When the adjustment of normal timing has been completed for both distributors on 1972–73 models, proceed with the next section. On

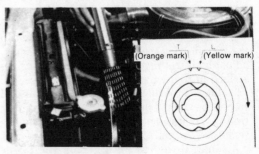

**Ignition timing marks**

1972–73 Mazda RX-2 and RX-3 models, the leading distributor is equipped with dual points. One set of points is for normal ignition system operation and the other is used for retarded operation during engine warm-up. To test and adjust retarded timing, proceed in the following manner:

1. Disconnect both of the thermosensor connections (see Emission Controls, in Chapter Four).

NOTE: *Only manual transmission models have two thermosensors; automatics only have one.*

2. Unfasten the idle and/or vacuum switch connections.

3. Detach the choke switch connector.

4. Connect the timing light to the leading spark plug cable of the number one (front) rotor.

5. Check the timing at idle with the strobe, as above. The pointer should align with the orange mark on the timing pulley (10 ATDA 2 ).

If the retarded timing setting is incorrect, adjust in the following manner:

1. Turn the engine off.

2. Unfasten the slips and remove the distributor cap. Withdraw the rotor.

3. Loosen the adjusting screws and move the point set base to correct the retarded timing setting.

NOTE: *Do not rotate the distributor housing.*

4. Assemble the distributor and check the retarded timing again with the strobe.

5. When the timing is satisfactory, disconnect the timing light and connect all of the leads which were disconnected for this test.

NOTE: *If the timing cannot be brought to specifications, check the components of the air flow control system, as detailed in Chapter Four.*

### 1974

1. Disconnect the vacuum line leading to the distributor and plug it. Connect the timing light to the upper (trailing) plug of the front housing. Warm the engine up and operate it at normal idle speed. This should be checked with a tachometer, which may be read as for a conventional four cylinder engine.

2. Check the trailing timing. If it is not to the specification specified in the tune-up chart, adjust both trailing and leading timing as described in the remaining steps.

3. Loosen the distributor mounting bolt and rotate the distributor to adjust the trailing timing. Tighten bolt and make sure timing has remained correct.

4. Install the timing light on the lower (leading) plug and start the engine. Check the

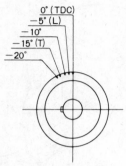

**Timing marks—1974 rotary engine**

leading timing and estimate how far off specification it is and determine which direction. Then, stop the engine and remove the distributor cap and rotor. Loosen the breaker base setscrews (directly opposite each other near the outside of the distributor body) and turn the base plate the right number of degrees as indicated on the scale inside the distributor. To advance timing, turn the points against the rotation of the rotor. Then, tighten the setscrews.

5. Replace the cap and rotor, recheck timing, and readjust if necessary.

### 1975

1. Run the engine until it reaches operating temperature. Install a tachometer, and, reading it as for a conventional four cylinder engine, make sure engine is idling at the proper speed. Stop engine and connect a timing light to the leading (lower) spark plug in the front rotor housing. Then, restart the engine.

2. The timing should be 0°. The indicator pin on the front cover should line up with the first notch in the pulley. If timing is not correct, loosen the distributor locknut just lightly and rotate the distributor until the correct reading is obtained. Then, tighten the locknut and recheck.

3. Then, stop the engine and disconnect the distributor wiring connector. Jumper four connectors together as was done to check the dwell for the leading-retard contacts in the appropri-

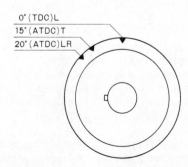

**Timing marks—1975 rotary engine**

ate procedure above. Then, start the engine and run it at idle speed and check timing again. The timing should now be 20° After Top Center. The pin should line up with the last notch in the pulley. If not, loosen the screw (see illustration) located on the external adjusting lever for leading-retard timing, and gradually move the lever back and forth until the correct timing is obtained. Then, retighten the screw and recheck timing.

4. Finally, stop the engine and move the timing light over to the trailing (upper) spark plug for the front rotor.

5. Start the engine and check timing again. It should be 15° After Top Center, lined up with the middle mark on the pulley. If necessary, adjust the timing by loosening the lockscrew and moving the trailing contacts adjusting lever. When the timing is correct, tighten the lockscrew and recheck the timing.

6. Stop the engine and remove the timing light.

### 1976

1. Connect a tachometer to the engine, and run the engine until it is warmed up. Reading the tach as for a conventional four cylinder engine, verify that the engine is operating at its normal idle speed. Then, stop the engine and hook up the timing light to the leading (lower) spark plug for the front rotor.

2. Aim the timing light at the indicator pin on the front cover and check to see if spark occurs when the pin is lined up with the first notch. If not, loosen the distributor locknut, and slowly turn the distributor back and forth until the timing is correct. Then, tighten the distributor locknut and recheck.

3. Stop the engine and move the timing light to the trailing (upper) plug for the front rotor. Start the engine and check to see if the spark occurs at the last notch on the pulley. If not, note the direction timing is off and stop the engine. Remove the cap and rotor. Disconnect the primary wire from the leading retard points located in the top of the distributor, remove the attaching screws for the upper breaker base plate and external adjusting lever, and remove the upper base plate. Then, loosen the lower base plate attaching screws and rotate the plate and trailing contacts. If timing is too far advanced, turn the plate in the direction of distributor shaft rotation; otherwise, turn it the opposite way. Then, completely reassemble the distributor an recheck trailing timing. Repeat this adjustment until trailing timing is correct.

4. Stop the engine and disconnect the distributor wiring connector. Jumper four of the connectors together as was done to check the

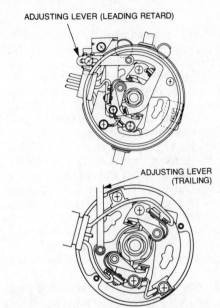

Adjusting points for leading retard and trailing ignition timing—1975–76 rotary engines

dwell for the leading-retard contacts in the appropriate procedure above. Then, start the engine and recheck timing. Timing should be 20° After Top Center again, as in the preceding step on RX-4 engines, or 15° After Top Center (middle notch), on RX-3 engines. If not, loosen the setscrew on the external adjusting lever, and move the lever until the timing is correct. Tighten the setscrew and verify that timing is still correct or readjust as necessary.

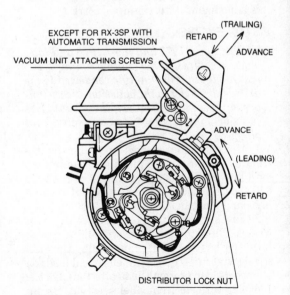

Method of adjusting 1978 distributors with external trailing timing adjustment

## 1977–78

1. Warm the engine up until it reaches operating temperature. Connect a tachometer. On automatic transmission cars, securely apply the handbrake, block the wheels, and put the car in Drive. Reading the tach as for a conventional four cylinder engine, verify that the engine is running at its normal idle speed. If not, adjust idle speed to specification.

2. Stop the engine and connect a timing light to the leading (lower) spark plug on the front rotor. Then, restart the engine. Aim the timing light at the pin on the front housing cover, and observe timing. If spark does not occur when the pin is lined up with the first mark to pass it, loosen the distributor locknut and rotate the distributor back and forth until timing is correct. Tighten the locknut and check that timing is still correct.

3. Stop the engine and switch the timing light to the trailing (upper) spark plug on the front rotor. Start the engine (putting automatic transmission cars in Drive), and check trailing timing. On 1978 cars except RX-3SP with automatic, if timing does not occur at the second notch on the pulley, loosen the vacuum advance attaching screws and pull the unit in or out to correct timing. Then, tighten screws and recheck timing. In 1977 cars, and 1978 RX-3SP with automatic, stop the engine and remove distributor cap and rotor. Then, slightly loosen the set screws which fasten the slotted breaker plate in place and turn the plate in the direction of distributor shaft rotation to retard timing, or against shaft rotation to advance. Tighten screws, replace cap and rotor, and restart engine and check timing. Repeat this adjustment until timing is correct.

### PISTON ENGINE

NOTE: *Some 1977 and most 1978 and later models require that the ignition timing be adjusted with the vacuum line connected to the distributor. Refer to the emission sticker (under the hood) to determine if the vacuum line is to be connected or disconnected and plugged.*

1. If required, disconnect and plug the distributor vacuum line. This is not required on most late model cars. It is required on the 1986 626. On that model, disconnect BOTH vacuum lines and plug them.

2. Set the parking brake and block the front wheels. Put automatic transmission cars in N. If the car has an electric fan, unplug the electrical connector. Turn off all electrical loads on all models (don't forget the heater fan). On the 1986 323 with electronic fuel injection, disconnect the black connector at the distributor. Start and run the engine until it reaches the

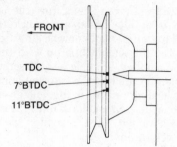

**Timing mark—1978–79 GLC**

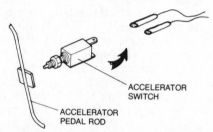

**Disconnect connectors shown to check advance timing (1978 GLC)**

normal operating temperature. Shut off the engine and connect a tachometer. On cars with an electrically driven fan, disconnect the fan's electrical connector. Restart and check engine idle speed. Adjust if necessary. Shut off engine.

NOTE: *Prior to starting the engine, clean off any grease or oil that will prevent seeing the timing marks on the crankshaft pulley. Mark the pulley notches with chalk or paint.*

3. Connect a timing light to the engine following the manufacturer's instructions. Start the engine and observe the timing by pointing the light at the timing marks on the crankshaft pulley.

NOTE: *If the car is equipped with an automatic transmission put the lever in* **D**; *check emission sticker of tune-up specs for requirement.*

4. If the timing is not correct, loosen the distributor mounting bolt and rotate the distribu-

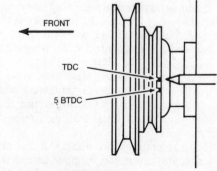

**Timing mark—1980 GLC**

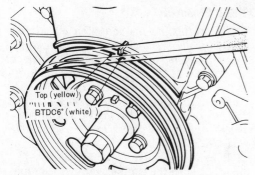

**Timing marks on 1983–84 626**

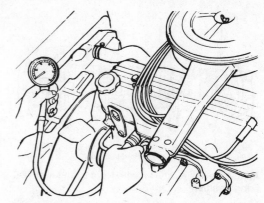

**Checking engine compression**

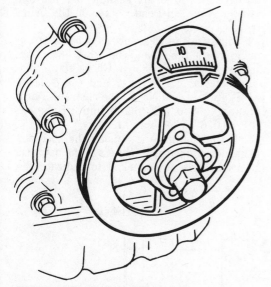

**GLC front wheel drive, timing marks**

tor as necessary to produce the correct timing mark alignment. Recheck the timing after tightening the lock bolt. Readjust if necessary. Check idle speed.

5. On 1978 non-California cars with manual transmissions, the advance timing may be checked by disconnecting the leads to the switch which is operated by the accelerator pedal. If the advance setting is not at 11° BTC, check the dwell angles of both sets of points. If the advance setting is not correct, it indicates unequal dwell angles, or more rarely, faulty parts in one or both contact sets or a worn distributor shaft or cam.

NOTE: *Some Canadian models require the bullet connectors at the water temperature connector disconnected before timing the ignition; check the emission sticker for requirements.*

6. Reconnect the vacuum line, accelerator switch or bullet connectors if disconnected. Recheck idle speed, readjust if necessary.

## Compression

Because of the unusual shape of the combustion chamber, the lack of valves, and because there are three chambers for each rotor, a normal gauge is useless for the measurement of rotary engine compression.

Mazda makes a special recording compression tester which produces a separate graph for each of the three chambers.

This is a fairly expensive piece of equipment and not one that back yard mechanics are likely to have around. If low compression is suspected, your best bet is to take the car to your local Mazda dealer, who does have this instrument.

Compression may be checked on piston engines in the conventional manner; that is, with engine hot, all spark plugs removed, and cranking the engine with the starter until the compression gauge reading ceases to rise. Follow this procedure for each cylinder.

## Valve Lash Adjustment

### GASOLINE ENGINES

Valve lash adjustment is performed on gasoline piston engines in 1978 and earlier models at 2,000 miles and then at 12,500, 25,000, etc. On 1979 and later models, no 2,000 mile adjustment is required, and adjustment is needed only at 15,000 mile intervals. This adjustment is performed to correct for wear in the valve train and changes in dimensions of various engine parts that occur during normal engine operation, and, at a faster rate, during the break-in process. Failure to keep valves properly adjusted can result in excessive wear or burning of valves or valve train parts, poor performance, and/or noisy operation of the valve train. To perform gas engine valve adjustment, proceed as follows:

1. Operate the engine until several miles after temperature gauge indicates operating

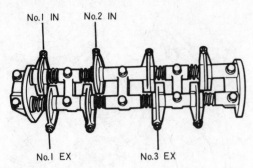

No.1 IN          No.2 IN

No.1 EX                    No.3 EX

**Adjust the valves shown with No. 1 cylinder at TDC firing position**

temperature has been reached. Then, stop engine and remove the valve cover.

2. Rotate the engine forward only with a wrench on the crankshaft pulley bolt or with the starter until the mark on the crankshaft pulley indicates it has reached Top Dead Center, and the valves for Number 1 cylinder (at front) are both fully closed (are not moving as the crankshaft is turned). If engine is at TDC and these valves are still open, rotate the crankshaft one full turn until it is again at Top Dead Center.

3. Insert a flat feeler gauge of proper dimension (see tune-up chart) between the exhaust valve and the exhaust valve rocker lever for No.1 cylinder. The exhaust valve is in line with the front exhaust manifold passage. The gauge should slide between these two parts with a slight pull. If the gauge will not slide readily, or there is not resistance in pulling it through, loosen the locknut and use a screwdriver to rotate the adjusting screw clockwise to tighten the adjustment or counterclockwise to loosen it. When a slight pull is obtained, hold the adjusting screw in place with a screwdriver and use a box wrench or open end wrench to tighten the locknut. If the adjustment has tightened up, readjust the position of the adjusting screw. If a great deal of effort is required to pull the gauge (adjustment too tight) burned valves may result.

4. Select the gauge for the adjusting dimension of the intake valves (see the Tune-up chart). Repeat Step 2 for the front intake valve (lined up with the front intake manifold passage.

5. Adjust the remaining valves shown in the illustration (No. 2 Intake and No. 3 Exhaust). Then, rotate the engine forward only exactly one full revolution, so that the timing marks for Top Dead Center are again lined up. Finally, adjust the remaining valves (No. 3 and No. 4 intake and No. 2 and No. 4 exhaust). Make sure you use the gauge of proper thickness on each side.

## DIESEL ENGINES

NOTE: *Adjusting the valves on the Mazda diesel involves replacing discs that rest in a recess in the top of each tappet. To do this, a special tool MAZDA tappet holder 49 S120 220 or equivalent is required, along with a selection of discs of different dimensions. The tool depresses the valve tappet, opening the valve slightly, for access to the replaceable disc.*

1. Remove the valve cover as described in Chapter 3. Turn the engine over by the crankshaft pulley bolt until the valve cams of the No. 1 cylinder are both pointing generally upward and the timing marks indicate that No. 1 cylinder is at Top Dead Center on the firing stroke.

2. Measure the clearance between the top surface of the tappet and the cam's lower surface, in the manner shown. Check the intake valves of No. 1 and No. 2 and the exhaust valves of No. 1 and No. 3. The clearances are, Intake: 0.008–0.012″ (0.2–0.3mm); Exhaust: 0.012–0.016″ (0.3–0.4mm).

3. If the clearance is outside the specified range, determine the thickness of the new disc required. Discs are marked to indicate the

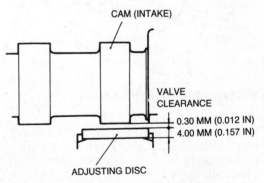

CAM (INTAKE)

VALVE CLEARANCE

0.30 MM (0.012 IN)
4.00 MM (0.157 IN)

ADJUSTING DISC

**Measuring valve clearance—diesel engines**

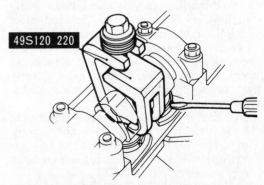

49S120 220

**A tappet holder 49 S120 220 or equivalent must be used to depress the valve tappets on the diesel engine during adjustment**

thickness in mm. Thicknesses range from 3.70mm (0.146″) to 4.30mm (0.169″) in intervals of 0.050mm or 0.002″. For example: 3825 means 3.825mm or 0.156″. Figure the required thickness of the new disc with the following, simple formula: Thickness of the original disc + (the clearance you measured minus the standard clearance specification) = the required thickness for the new disc. For example, if you measured the intake valve clearance at 0.012″ (0.3mm) and the disc was 4.00mm or 0.157″ thick, you would figure it this way: 0.157″ + (0.012–0.010″) = 0.159″.

NOTE: *The engine must be positioned so that the cam above each valve is positioned upward before installing the special tool. Attempting to depress the valve without properly positioning the engine can damage the valve by bending it.*

4. If the valves you have checked require adjustment, turn each of the tappets around so one of the notches is facing toward the left side of the car for access to the discs. Before working on each valve, turn the engine over so that the intake cam for that cylinder is pointing straight upward. Then, install the tool in the position shown (right between the cams). Tighten the bolt to force the tool halves together and depress the tappets. Then, pry the disc out with a screwdriver and replace it with one of the proper thickness.

5. Turn the engine 360°. Repeat the checking procedure for the intake valves of cylinders No. 2 and 4 and the exhaust valves of Nos. 3 and 4. Then, adjust those valves, as necessary. Install the valve cover as described in Chapter 3.

## Idle Speed and Mixture Adjustment

### 1971–73 ROTARY ENGINES

1. Start the engine and allow it to warm up. Remove the air cleaner assembly.

2. Operate the secondary throttle valve. Be sure that it returns fully.

3. Connect a tachometer to the engine in accordance with its manufacturer's instructions, or if none is available, have someone sit in the car and watch the tachometer on the instrument panel.

4. Adjust the mixture by seating the mixture control screw lightly and then unscrewing it four or five turns.

5. Turn the idle screw until the specified idle is obtained; it may also be necessary to turn the mixture control screw slightly.

NOTE: *The carburetor is equipped with an idle limiter screw, as an aid in controlling emissions; do not attempt to defeat its purpose by adjusting it.*

6. Remove the tachometer (if used) and install the air cleaner once idle adjustments are completed.

### 1974–78 ROTARY AND 1974 AND LATER PISTON ENGINES

Idle speed adjustments are easily performed, but you must be careful to perform them under the proper conditions. The engine must be fully warmed up--the best procedure is to drive the vehicle for several miles after the temperature gauge indicates that the cooling water has reached operating temperature. The gas tank cap should be removed on 1975 and later rotary engine Mazdas, but all other normal operating conditions should be maintained. For example, the air cleaner and all vacuum hoses should be installed or connected, the choke should be wide open, and all accessories should be off. This includes the engine cooling fan if it's electrical. If necessary, unplug it. Also, avoid extremes of outside temperature, and replace a thermostat that makes the engine operate too hot or too cold before proceeding. On the 1978–79 GLC and the 1979 626 models disconnect the canister purge hose between the canister and the air cleaner. On the 1986 626, run the engine at 2,500–3,000 rpm in neutral for three minutes before proceeding.

Identify the idle speed screw on the carburetor. This screw acts directly on a flange which is integral with the throttle shaft; it does not act through any cams or levers. On models with electronic fuel injection, the air throttling screw is located on top of the throttle body (see the illustration). Connect a reliable tachometer according to manufacturer's instructions (usually between the coil (–) terminal and ground). Turn off all accessories. Read the tach as for a 4 cylinder engine on all engines--both rotary and piston. If the tach has a six cylinder

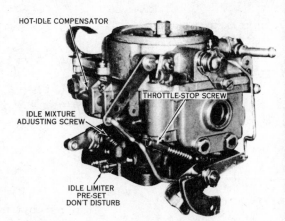

**Carburetor idle adjustment screws—typical 1971–73**

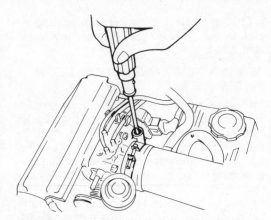

**Adjusting the idle speed on 323 models with electronic fuel injection. 626 models with injection use a similar adjusting screw.**

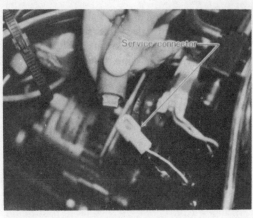

**Location of the service connector for the A/F solenoid on 1983–84 GLC and 626**

scale and an eight cylinder scale, read the right cylinder scale and be sure to multiply all readings by two to get the correct rpm. For example, if the specified rpm is 700, set the idle speed at 350 rpm on the right cylinder scale.

Idle mixture adjustment for all Mazda cars built from 1979–82 and on the 1986 323 requires the use of an HC/CO analyzer. Since this is an extremely expensive piece of equipment, the adjustment procedure is complex, and this adjustment is not required as a part of ordinary maintenance, no procedures are in-

cluded here. This adjustment can, however, be checked at reasonable cost at many diagnostic centers or may be checked as a matter of routine during required vehicle inspection procedures. If the engine exhibits rough idle and/or smoke combined, in some cases, with hesitation or poor running at low speeds, idle mixture might be at fault. You should first check all the basic tune-up adjustments such as dwell, ignition timing, and spark plug condition and verify that there are no vacuum leaks due to disconnected or leaking hoses. Then, if

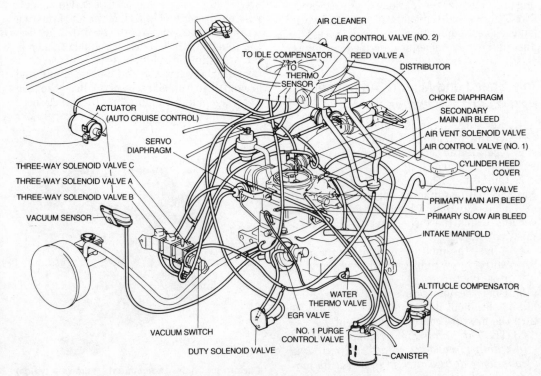

**Layout of vacuum hoses for '83–'84 626. California models are similar.**

these symptoms persist, the next step would be to have the idle mixture checked with an HC/CO meter at a dealer or diagnostic center. If incorrect readings are uncovered, we suggest your take the vehicle to a shop or dealer familiar with Mazdas and have the mixture adjusted according to the procedure specified by the factory. On the 1986 323 with electronic injection, and all 1986 626 cars (which also have injection), idle mixture is constantly adjusted electronically and cannot be adjusted.

On 1983–1985 models, the air/fuel mixture can readily be checked with a tachometer. It normally needs adjustment only when the carburetor is overhauled, and the unit must be disassembled off the car to gain access to the mixture screw. An incorrect reading can indicate either improper mixture adjustment or an bad oxygen sensor. Make sure the engine is in proper tune generally and that all vacuum hoses are properly connected before suspecting improper mixture.

To check the mixture on these models, first warm the engine fully and make sure idle speed on 1983–84 models is: 850 rpm in neutral for GLCs with manual transmissions and 1,050 rpm in neutral for GLCs with automatics; 750 rpm in neutral and 700 rpm in Drive for 626s. On 1985 models, all figures are the same except that the GLC automatic is set at 750 in Drive. Disconnect the check connector for the Air/Fuel solenoid. On 1984 626s only, disconnect and plug the idle compensator, thermosensor, and reed valve hoses. Connect a dwell meter for four cylinder engines between the check connector (hook the red lead of the meter to this) and the engine itself. The meter should read 32–40° on 1983–84 models and 20–70° on 1985 models. Disconnect the dwell meter and reconnect the connector.

## DIESEL

NOTE: *Adjusting the idle speed on the diesel requires you to have a special tachometer which measures idle speed off a special sensor on the injection pump.*

1. Place a ruler near the accelerator pedal and then depress the pedal to determine the play in the cable. It should be 0.04–0.12″ (1–3mm). If necessary, lengthen the cable (to increase play) by loosening the nut on the

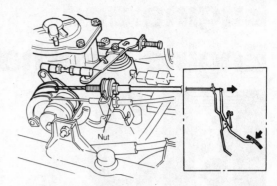

**Checking and adjusting accelerator cable deflection on the 626 diesel**

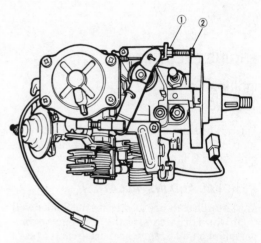

**To adjust the idle speed on the 626 diesel, loosen the locknut (1) and then turn the adjusting bolt (2). See text.**

firewall side of the cable bracket and then tightening the nut on the other side. Do the opposite to decrease play, if necessary.

2. Drive the car until several miles after the temperature gauge indicates normal operating temperature to warm up the engine. Measure the engine rpm with the tachometer.

3. If the rpm is outside the range of 800–850 rpm, loosen the locknut on the idle adjusting bolt on the injection pump. Then, turn the bolt clockwise to increase the idle speed and counterclockwise to decrease it. Lock the adjusting bolt with the locknut.

# Engine and Engine Overhaul

## 3

## ENGINE ELECTRICAL

### Ignition Coil

#### TESTING

For coil testing procedures, see the Electronic Ignition Troubleshooting section near the beginning of Chapter 2.

#### REMOVAL AND INSTALLATION

Most Mazda coils are located on the fender well (rear wheel drive cars) or the front engine compartment panel (front wheel drive cars) to keep them away from engine heat. Replacement is very simple, but you should be sure to disconnect the battery before starting, be careful about reconnecting the primary wiring to the + and terminals correctly, and make sure the terminal connections are clean.

1. Disconnect the negative battery cable and make sure the ignition switch is off. Remove any protective boots from the top of the coil, if necessary by sliding them back the coil-to-distributor wire.

2. Carefully pull the high tension wire out of the coil, twisting it gently as near as possible to the tower to get it started.

3. Note the routing and colors of the primary wires, and then remove nuts and lockwashers, retaining all parts for installation. Clean the primary terminals with sandpaper, if necessary, to ensure a clean connection. Then, loosen the through bolt which clamps the coil in place and slide the coil out of its mount.

4. Install the new coil in exact reverse order, making sure the primary connections are tight. Ensure also that the coil-to-distributor wire is fully seated in the tower and that the protective boot is fully installed on the outside of the tower.

### Ignitor

#### REMOVAL AND INSTALLATION

#### 626 without Turbocharging

1. Remove the distributor cap. Unscrew the two attaching screws and remove the rotor.

2. Remove the snap ring and then pull the governor weights assembly off the shaft. Slide the reluctor off the shaft.

3. Disconnect the two electrical connectors for the pick-up coil. Then, remove the two attaching screws and remove the coil from the mounting plate.

4. Remove the attaching screws and remove the igniter.

5. Installation is the reverse of removal. Make sure all wires are properly routed so no contact with rotating parts will occur.

#### 626 with Turbocharging

1. Unscrew the attaching screws and remove the distributor cap. Remove the rotor by sliding it up and off the distributor shaft. Do the same with the No. 1 cylinder sensor's rotating element, located right underneath.

2. Remove the dust cover and then unscrew and remove the No. 1 cylinder sensor stator. Remove the baseplate on which the No. 1 cylinder sensor components are mounted.

3. Remove the snap ring with snap ring pliers. Then, pull off the reluctor. Note the locations of the wires and then disconnect the primary wiring at the pick-up coil. Then, remove the two attaching screws and remove the pick-up coil, the pick-up coil mounting plate, and the ignitor.

4. Install a new ignitor in reverse order. Make sure all wiring connectors are plugged in securely and check that the snap ring seats securely in the groove in the distributor shaft.

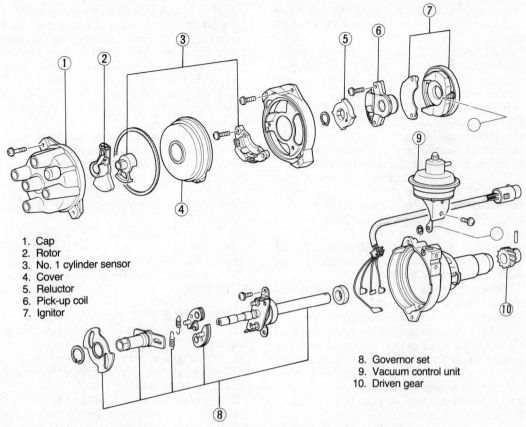

1. Cap
2. Rotor
3. No. 1 cylinder sensor
4. Cover
5. Reluctor
6. Pick-up coil
7. Ignitor

8. Governor set
9. Vacuum control unit
10. Driven gear

**Exploded view of the distributor used on the turbocharged 626**

## GLC and 323

1. Unscrew the attaching screws and remove the distributor cap. Remove the rotor by sliding it up and off the distributor shaft.

2. Remove its two mounting screws and remove the pole piece (it has two vertical prongs) and the insulator underneath it. Then, remove the grease cap and mounting screw and remove the reluctor with its locating key. Note the locations of the wires and then disconnect the three primary wiring connectors from the ignitor.

3. Remove the two mounting screws and remove the ignitor. On the 323, be careful to retain and remove the two mounting insulators from underneath; on the GLC, retain and remove the insulator block from underneath.

4. Install a new ignitor in reverse order. Make sure the wiring connectors are securely connected. When installing the reluctor, make sure to turn it to the correct angle for installation of the key and install the key with the reluctor to retain proper timing.

## Distributors

### REMOVAL AND INSTALLATION

#### 1971–73 Rotary Engines

The removal procedure for both the leading and trailing distributor is the same. To remove either or both of them, proceed in the following manner:

NOTE: *It is a good idea to remove and install the distributors separately, to avoid confusion.*

1. Disconnect the vacuum advance line at the distributor.

2. Unfasten the vacuum advance switch connector (trailing distributor).

3. Disconnect the primary wire at the coil.

4. Note the letters and numbers identifying them, and remove the spark plug cables.

5. Matchmark the distributor housing and sockets. Matchmark the position of the rotor, in relation to the distributor housing. These marks are to be used as an aid when installing the distributor in a properly timed engine.

6. Remove the distributor clamping screw and carefully lift the distributor out of its socket.

NOTE: *Try to avoid rotating the engine while the distributors are removed. Unnecessary rotation of the engine under these conditions only means more work.*

If the engine has not been rotated with either of the distributors removed, their installation is performed in the reverse order of removal. Use the matchmarks made during removal to correctly position the distributors in their sockets. If both distributors were removed at the same time, use care to see that they are returned to their proper sockets. Both the distributors and the front cover are marked to aid in correct installation.

Once the distributors are installed, adjust the point gap, the dwell angle, and the timing, as detailed in Chapter Two.

If the engine was rotated, or otherwise disturbed, such as for engine rebuilding, install the distributors in the following manner:

1. Turn the engine until the white mark on the eccentric shaft pulley is aligned with the pointer on the front cover. This will always be top dead center (TDC) of the number one rotor's compression cycle, because each rotor only make ⅓ of a turn for each full rotation of the eccentric shaft.

NOTE: *TDC cannot be found by feeling for compression at the number one spark plug hole, as in a conventional piston engine.*

2. Align the marks stamped on each distributor housing and driven gear.

3. Install either distributor, so that the key on the end of its drive engages with the slot in the socket.

**Align the distributor identification marks prior to installation**

NOTE: *If both distributors were removed at the same time, be careful not to mix their parts or confuse them upon installation. Both distributor and the front housing are marked insert the distributor having the same letter as the housing into its proper socket.*

4. Rotate each distributor slightly, until its points just start to open and then tighten its locknut.

5. Check the point gap and install the cap.

6. Connect all of the vacuum lines and the wires carefully, to ensure their connection to the proper distributor.

NOTE: *Spark plug position and leads are marked, as is each distributor cap, to aid in installation.*

7. Check and adjust the dwell angle and ignition timing, using the procedures outlined above in Chapter Two.

8. Connect the vacuum advance lines to the distributors.

### 1974–78 Rotary Engines

1. Rotate the engine in normal direction of rotation until the first (TDC or Leading) timing mark aligns with the pin on the front cover. Matchmark the body of the distributor and the engine rotor housing.

2. The easiest way to clear the high tension wires out of the way is to simply remove the cap and set it aside with the wires still attached. However, if you wish to deep the cap with the distributor, pull the wires out of the cap, observing markings.

3. Disconnect vacuum advance and, if so equipped, retard hoses. Disconnect the primary electrical connector.

4. Remove the distributor adjusting bolt. Pull the distributor vertically out of the engine.

5. To install the distributor, first make sure the engine has not been disturbed. If it has been moved, again turn the crankshaft until

**Distributor alignment marks—1974–76 rotary engines**

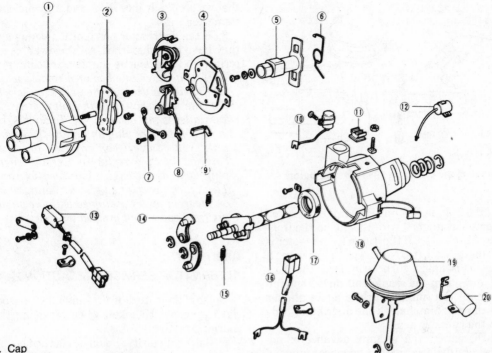

1. Cap
2. Rotor
3. Point set
4. Breaker plate
5. Cam
6. Spring
7. Ground wire
8. Point set
9. Felt
10. Ignition condenser
11. Terminal
12. Radio suppression condenser
13. Vacuum switch— trailing distributor only
14. Governor
15. Governor spring
16. Shaft
17. Oil seal
18. Distributor housing
19. Vacuum advance unit
20. Ignition condenser

**Distributor components**

the first timing mark lines up with the pin on the front cover. Then align the dimple in the distributor gear with the notch or line cast into the body of the distributor (see illustrations).

6. Insert the distributor carefully and slowly into the engine with distributor body and rotor housing matchmarks aligned. Avoid allowing the shaft to turn and be careful not to damage the housing when inserting the gear into it.

7. Install the adjusting bolt, but do not tighten. Turn the distributor until the leading points just start to open, and then tighten the locking bolt.

8. Install vacuum hoses, electrical connectors, and high tension wires in reverse of the removal procedure.

9. If ignition points have been disturbed or replaced, set the dwell as described in the previous chapter. Set ignition timing.

### Piston Engines

1. Unfasten the clips or remove the screws which hold the distributor cap to the top of the distributor, and remove the cap. Note the location of the wire going to No. 1 (the front cylinder on rear drive cars and the cylinder on the left side of the car on front drive cars) cylinder where it enters the cap.

2. Rotate the engine with the starter or by using a socket wrench on the bolt which re-

**Distributor alignment marks—1977-78 rotary engines**

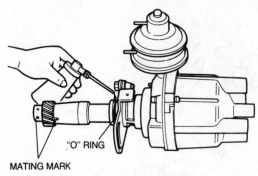

"O" RING

MATING MARK

**Lubricating the O-ring on 1983–84 distributors**

tains the front pulley until the timing mark on the pulley is aligned with the pin on the front cover. Check to see if the contact on the rotor is pointing toward the No.1 spark plug wire. If the rotor is half a turn away from the No.1 plug wire, turn the crankshaft ahead one full turn until the timing mark is again aligned with the pin. Matchmark the distributor body with the cylinder head.

3. Disconnect the vacuum advance or advance/retard line(s) at the advance unit and disconnect the primary wire or wires at the connector near the distributor.

4. Remove the adjusting bolt, and pull the distributor out of the engine.

5. On 1982–86 models, lightly oil the O-ring located near the top of the distributor shaft. To install the distributor, first align the dimple on the distributor drive gear with the mark cast into the base of the distributor body by rotating the shaft. Then, being careful not to rotate the shaft, insert the distributor back into the cylinder head with distributor body and cylinder head match marks aligned and seat it.

6. Install the mounting bolt, but do not tighten it.

7. Install the distributor cap, and reconnect

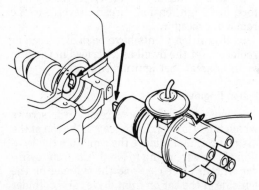

**On GLC front wheel drive models, the distributor engages a notch in the rear of the camshaft. Do not remove the seal block (not shown) at the rear of the valve cover**

the vacuum advance line and the primary connector.

8. If the distributor has ignition points and they have been disturbed, set the dwell as described in the previous chapter. Set timing.

NOTE: *If the engine has been rotated while the distributor was out, it will be necessary to turn the crankshaft until the point where No. 1 cylinder is just about to fire. To do this, remove No. 1 spark plug and rotate the engine until you can feel compression pressure building (with your finger over the spark plug hole) as the engine is turned forward. Then, turn the engine until the timing mark on the front pulley is aligned with the pin on the front cover, and proceed with step 5.*

## Alternator

### ALTERNATOR SERVICE PRECAUTIONS

Because of the nature of alternator design, special care must be taken when servicing the charging system.

1. Battery polarity should be checked before any connections, such as jumper cables or battery charger leads, are made. Reversed battery connections will damage the diode rectifiers.

2. The battery must never be disconnected while the alternator is running, because the regulator will be ruined.

3. Always disconnect the battery ground cable before replacing the alternator.

4. Do not attempt to polarize an alternator.

5. Do not short across or ground any alternator terminals.

6. Always disconnect the battery ground cable before removing the alternator output cable whether the engine is running or not.

7. If electric arc welding equipment is to be used on the car, first disconnect the battery and alternator cables. Never start the engine with the electric arc welding equipment attached.

8. If the battery is to be quick charged, disconnect the positive cable from the battery.

Do not use any kind of high voltage resistance tester, such as a megger tester, in the electrical circuits of the car while the alternator is connected.

### REMOVAL AND INSTALLATION

1. Disconnect the battery ground cable at the negative (–) terminal.

2. Remove the air cleaner. Remove the nut, and disconnect the alternator **B** terminal. Unplug the connector from the rear of the alternator.

3. Remove the alternator adjusting link bolt. Do not remove the adjusting link. Remove

the alternator drive belt. On the 626 diesel, this requires first loosening the air conditioner idler pulley; then remove the two alternator belts and the single A/C drive belt.

4. Remove the alternator securing nuts and bolts. Pull the drive belt off the pulley and remove the alternator.

Installation is performed in the reverse order of removal. Adjust the drive belt tension as detailed below:

1. Check the drive belt tension by applying about 22 lbs. of thumb pressure to the belt, midway between the eccentric shaft and alternator pulleys. The belt should deflect to the following specifications:

Old belt: approximately 0.6″ (15mm)
New belt: approximately 0.5″ (13mm)

2. If belt deflection is not within specifications, loosen, but do not remove, the bolt on the adjusting link.

3. Push the alternator in the direction required to obtain proper belt deflection.

CAUTION: *Do not pry or pound on the alternator housing as you adjust the belt.*

4. Tighten the adjusting link bolt to 20 ft. lbs.

## Regulator

NOTE: *Some later models have the voltage regulator mounted within the alternator as part of the unit. No adjustments can be make to the regulator and the alternator must be removed and disassembled to replace the regulator.*

### REMOVAL AND INSTALLATION

**1971–79 except 626**

1. Disconnect the battery ground cable at the negative (−) battery terminal.
2. Disconnect the wiring from the regulator.
3. Remove the regulator mounting screws.
4. Remove the regulator.
5. Installation is performed in the reverse order of removal.

### VOLTAGE ADJUSTMENTS

**1971–79 except 626**

1. Remove the cover from the regulator.
2. Check the air gap, the point gap, and the back gap with a feeler gauge (see illustration).
3. If they do not fall within the specifications given in the Alternator and Regulator chart, adjust the gaps by bending the stationary contact bracket.
4. Connect a voltmeter between the **A** and the **E** terminals of the regulator, except on GLC. On GLC, connect a voltmeter between the top terminal of the alternator and the coil mounting bolt.

## Alternator and Regulator Specifications

| | | Alternator | | Regulator | | | | | | | |
|---|---|---|---|---|---|---|---|---|---|---|---|
| | | | | | Regulator | | | Field Relay | | | |
| Year | Model | Field Current @ 14V | Output (amps) | Air Gap (in.) | Point Gap (in.) | Back Gap (in.) | Air Gap (in.) | Point Gap (in.) | Back Gap (in.) | Volts @ 75° |
| 1971–73 | RX-2, RX-3 | 32 | 40. | — | — | — | .028–.043 | .012–.016 | .028–.043 | 14 |
| 1974 | All Rotary | — | 56 | .035–.047 | .028–.043 | .028–.043 | .028–.043 | .012–.016 | .028–.043 | 14 |
| 1975–76 | RX-3, RX-4 | — | 56 | .035–.055 | .028–.043 | .028–.059 | .028–.051 | .012–.018 | .028–.059 | 14–15 |
| 1974–78 | 808 | — | 40 ① | .035–.055 | .028–.043 | .028–.059 | .028–.051 | .012–.018 | .028–.059 | 14–15 |
| 1977–78 | All Rotary | — | 63 | .035–.055 | .028–.043 | .028–.049 | .028–.051 | .012–.018 | .028–.059 | 14 |
| 1977–80 | GLC | — | 30 | .039–.059 | .020–.035 | .028–.059 | .028–.051 | .012–.018 | .028–.059 | 14–15 |
| 1981–85 | GLC | — | 50 | ←————————— Not Adjustable —————————→ | | | | | | |
| 1981–85 | 626 | — | 60 | ←————————— Not Adjustable —————————→ | | | | | | |
| 1986 | 323 | — | 53 ② | ←————————— Not Adjustable —————————→ | | | | | | |
| 1986 | 626 | — | 65 | ←————————— Not Adjustable —————————→ | | | | | | |

① —1974 808—50
② 60 amps with Electronic Fuel Injection

## Regulated Voltage Test Chart

| Model/Year | Alternator rpm | Engine rpm | Regulated Voltage |
|---|---|---|---|
| 1971–73 RX-2, RX-3 | 4000 | 2000 | 13.5–14.5 |
| 1974–75 All Rotary | 4000 | 1800 | 14–15 |
| 1974–78 808 | 4000 | 2000 | 14–15 |
| 1976–78 All Rotary | 4000 | 2000 | 14–15 |
| 1977–82 GLC ① | — | 2000 | 14–15 |
| 1981–83 GLC ② 1982 626 | 5000 | 2000 | 14.1–14.7 |
| 1983–86 626 1984–85 GLC 1986 626 | 5000 | 2500 | 14.4–15.0 |

① without internal regulator
② with internal regulator

NOTE: *Be sure that the car's battery is fully charged before proceeding with this test. The ammeter must read 5 amps or less.*

5. Start the engine and run it at the rpm specified in the chart below. The voltage reading should be to the specification shown in the same chart.

6. Stop the engine.

7. Bend the upper plate down to decrease the voltage setting, or up to increase the setting, as required.

8. If the regulator cannot be brought within specifications, replace it.

9. When the test is completed, disconnect the voltmeter and replace the regulator cover.

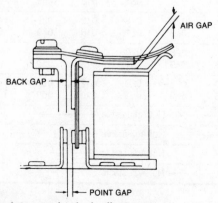

**Regulator mechanical adjustments**

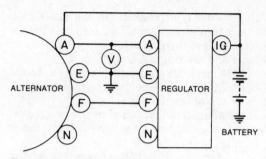

**Testing the voltage regulator**

## REGULATED VOLTAGE TEST

NOTE: *For these tests, you will need a voltmeter and an ohmmeter.*

### 1980 GLC

1. Disconnect the wire from the **B** terminal of the alternator, and connect an ammeter between the **B** terminal and the wire's connector. Then, disconnect the alternator's wiring connector and make wiring connections with jumper wires, as shown.

2. Start the engine and run it at 2,000 rpm (you can use a dwell/tach to measure rpm). Read the ammeter, and note the reading. Then, pull the wire off the female **F** terminal and connect it to the female **A** terminal just long enough to get a reading on the amperage. Shut off the engine.

3. If the amperage reading increases significantly, the trouble is in the regulator, and if it remains exactly the same, the trouble is in the alternator.

This test assumes that you know the battery is undercharged, and that the alternator drive belt and basic wiring are in working condition. If the specific gravity of the battery cells indicate inadequate charging (is less than 1.260) and the vehicle has been driven in a normal manner (without too many extremely short trips), the alternator is not charging properly.

### 1980–82 626

1. With the ignition switch off, connect the voltmeter between the **R** terminal and ground and read the voltage. Do the same for the **L** terminal. If there is voltage at either terminal, the alternator is defective.

2. With the voltmeter still connected to the **L** terminal, turn the ignition switch on and read the voltmeter. Note the reading and then check the voltage across the battery terminals. **L** terminal voltage should be within 1–3 Volts

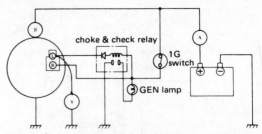

Connect the voltmeter between the "L" terminal and ground, as shown. Connect the ammeter as shown, also.

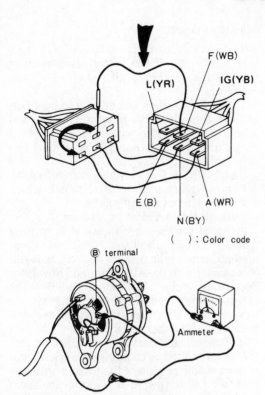

Regulated Voltage Test—1980 GLC

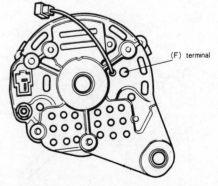

The "F" terminal on 1980–82 626 is located by the arrow

of battery voltage. If there is no voltage, the alternator or associated wiring is bad, If the voltage is ok, connect a jumper wire between the **F** terminal, located about 0.079″ (2mm) from the hole near the **B** terminal, and ground. If the voltage at the **L** terminal now drops significantly lower than the battery voltage, this indicates that the IC regulator may be faulty.

On 1982 models, only, you can go a step further and check no-load voltage.

3. With the battery fully charged, connect a voltmeter between the battery positive terminal and ground. Connect a voltmeter between the **L** terminal on the rear of the alternator and ground. Jumper the ammeter with a heavy wire to get the engine started. Then, remove the jumper. Run the engine at 2,000–2,500 rpm (check rpm with a dwell/tach). This will turn the alternator 5,000 rpm. The ammeter should read less than 5 amps, and the voltmeter 14.1–14.7. Now, turn on the lights. If the unit responds by putting out increased amperage, and the voltage is higher than the battery voltage, it is ok.

### 1981–85 GLC
### 1983–85 626

Perform all the tests for 1982 626, as described above, but use these specifications:

- 1981–83 GLC: 14.1–14.7 volts
- 1984–85 GLC: 14.4–15 volts
- 1983–85 626: 14.4–15 volts

#### 1985 626 Diesel

1. With the ignition switch off, connect the voltmeter between the **L** terminal and ground and read the voltage. If there is voltage at the terminal, the alternator is defective.

2. Turn the ignition switch on and read the voltmeter. If the reading is 0 volts, there is a malfunction, most probably in the alternator,

The location of the "F" terminal on the 626 diesel alternator

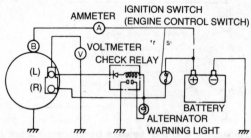

Make the connections shown to test the output of the 626 diesel alternator

but you should check the wiring before condemning it.

3. Disconnect the negative battery cable. Connect an ammeter and a voltmeter as shown. Then, reconnect the negative battery connector.

4. Start the engine and turn on the headlights. Gradually increase the engine speed as you read the output voltage and current. If the voltage is higher than battery voltage and there is output current, the alternator is operating satisfactorily.

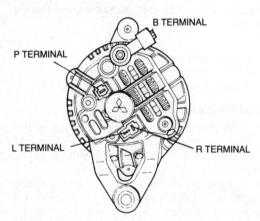

Alternator terminal locations for the '86 323

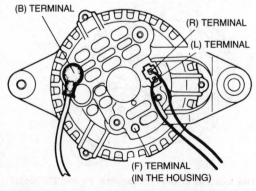

Alternator terminal locations for the '86 626

### 1986 323 and 626

The following tests should be used if the battery discharges. If the battery is constantly overcharged, proceed to the next series of tests, below.

1. Start the engine and allow it to idle. Disconnect the alternator **B** terminal wire and connect an ammeter with a capacity of 60 amps or more between the wire and the terminal.

CAUTION: *Make connections carefully so as to avoid grounding the* **B** *terminal, which would burn out the alternator.*

Turn all lights and accessories on.

2. Speed the engine up until it is turning 2,500–3,000 rpm. Read the output on the ammeter. Compare the reading with the nominal output shown on the Alternator and Regulator Specifications chart. If the output is 90% of the rated output given there, the alternator is okay (on the 626, use 51 amps). Otherwise, proceed with further tests.

3. Turn off all electrical accessories. Charge the battery until the charging rate is less than 5 amps at idle or replace the battery with one that is fully charged, if it is available. Then, read the ammeter at 2,500 rpm. If the reading is now more than 5 amps, there is a short (ground) somewhere in the vehicle wiring. If the indication is still less than 5 amps, proceed with the test of the rotor coil (Step 6).

4. This test should be done with the car at normal, room temperature (about 68°F [20°C]). Disconnect the ammeter and reconnect the alternator **B** terminal. Connect a voltmeter to the **L** terminal of the alternator. Accelerate the engine to 2,500 rpm and read the voltage. If the reading is 14.4–15 volts, the problem is in the alternator stator coil and/or diodes. If it is less than 14.4–15 volts, the problem is in the regulator and you should proceed with the next test.

5. Disconnect the **R** connector from the alternator terminal. Connect a voltmeter between the connector female side (that is, coming from the wiring harness) and a good ground. Then, turn the ignition switch on and measure the voltage. If it is equal to battery voltage, proceed to the next step. Otherwise, correct problems in the wiring harness.

6. Turn the ignition switch off. Disconnect the **B** terminal from the alternator. Measure the resistance between the **L** and **F** terminals with an ohmmeter. The resistance should be 3–6Ω. If resistance is within the proper range, proceed with the tests following. If it is outside the range, proceed with electrical checks of the rotor coil and slip rings. If not, the problem is in the field rotor or slip rings and the alternator must be disassembled and repaired.

7. Reconnect the **B** terminal connector to the alternator. Turn the ignition switch back on. Pull the connector which includes the **L** terminal out just slightly, so contact is maintained but you can get the probe of a voltmeter in to read the voltage. Measure the voltage at the **L** terminal prong. If it is over 3 volts, the problem is in the regulator. If it is 1–3 volts, the problem is in the stator coil or diodes.

**Perform the following tests if the battery is overcharged:**

1. Turn off all electrical loads. Run the test with the vehicle as close to room temperature (68°F [20°C]) as possible. Disconnect the wiring connector for the **B** terminal. Connect an ammeter of more than 60 amps capacity between the wiring harness connector and the connector on the alternator. Start the engine and run it to charge the battery until the charging rate is less than 5 amps. If you have a fully charged battery available, it will save time to install it in place of the present one. Pull the connector which includes the **L** terminal out just slightly, so contact is maintained but you can get the probe of a voltmeter in to read the voltage. Run the engine at 2,500 rpm and measure the voltage at the **L** terminal prong. If the voltage is 14.4–15 volts, the alternator is ok. If it is over 15 volts, proceed with the next test. Turn the engine off.

2. Disconnect the **R** connector at the alternator. Connect a voltmeter between the **R** connector and a good ground. Turn the ignition switch on and measure the voltage at the connector. If the voltage is less than battery voltage, repair the wiring harness. If the voltage is equal to battery voltage, proceed with the next test.

3. Turn the ignition switch off and then disconnect the **B** terminal at the alternator. Connect an ohmmeter and measure the resistance between the **L** and **F** terminals. If resistance is 3–6Ω, the problem lies in the voltage regulator. If it is outside that range, it is in the field coil or the slip rings and brushes.

## Starter

### REMOVAL AND INSTALLATION

There are two possible locations for the starter motor; one is the lower right hand side of the engine and the other is on the upper right hand side.

1. Remove the ground cable from the negative (–) battery terminal.

2. If the car is equipped with the lower mounted starter, remove the gravel shield from underneath the engine. On 1976 and later vehicles equipped with automatic transmission, remove the two bolts attaching the starter bracket to the transmission.

CAUTION: *Be extremely careful not to contact the hot exhaust pipe, while working underneath the car.*

3. Remove the battery cable from the starter terminal.

4. Disconnect the solenoid leads from the solenoid terminals.

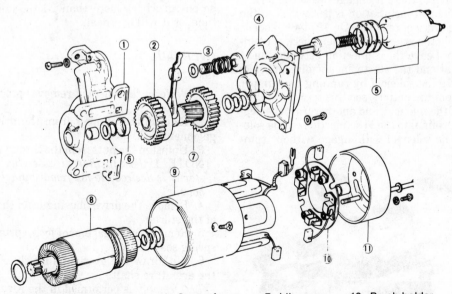

| 1. Front housing | 4. Center frame | 7. Idler gear | 10. Brush holder |
| 2. Overrunning clutch | 5. Solenoid | 8. Armature | 11. End frame |
| 3. Engagement fork | 6. Stop | 9. Field coil | |

**Starter components—typical of models from 1974–82**

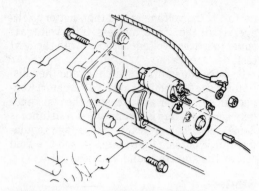

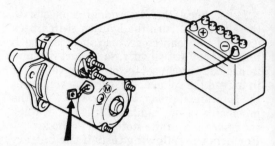

To check pinion gap, energize the solenoid with jumper wires, as shown

**Starter removal and installation—typical of 1983–84 models**

5. Remove the starter securing bolts and withdraw the starter assembly.

6. Installation is the reverse of the above steps.

### SOLENOID REPLACEMENT

Perform solenoid replacement with the starter motor removed from the car.

CAUTION: *Disconnect the negative battery cable. This is necessary as the wiring coming from the battery could ground and cause a fire or other damage!*

1. Detach the field strap, hot wire from the battery, and ignition wiring connector from the solenoid terminals.

2. Remove the solenoid securing bolts.

3. Withdraw the solenoid, washers, spring, and plunger, lifting the assembly to disconnect the plunger where it engages with the fork.

4. Solenoid installation is performed in the reverse order of removal. On 1974–86 models, assemble the solenoid and then check the pinion gap. Leave the connection between the M terminal and the starter motor disconnected. Energize the solenoid by running one jumper wire from the battery positive terminal to the body of the solenoid, and another from the negative terminal to the M connection on the solenoid. The solenoid will engage without spin-

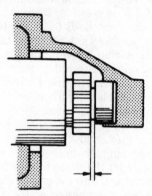

Insert the feeler gauge between the front of the pinion gear and the starter body to check pinion gap

ning starter. Measure the pinion gap with a feeler gauge, as shown, If it is not 0.020–0.079" (0.5–2.0mm), change it by changing the number of washers (increase the number of washers to reduce the gap). The solenoid should not be energized for more than 20 seconds at a time, or it will overheat.

### OVERHAUL

**1971–73**

1. Perform the solenoid removal procedure, above.

2. Remove the plunger from the drive engagement fork.

3. Unfasten the nuts from the through bolts. NOTE: *Unless further disassembly of the starter is desired, do not remove the through bolts.*

4. Remove the drive housing from the front of the starter.

5. Remove the engagement fork, spring, and spring seat.

6. Withdraw the over-running clutch from the armature shaft.

7. Assembly is performed in the reverse order of disassembly. Check the clearance between the pinion and the stop collar with the solenoid closed. It should be 0.0012–0.0060" (0.03–0.15mm).

**Starter solenoid removal**

**1974 and Later**

1. On 1976 and later cars with automatic transmissions, remove the bracket from the rear of the starter.

2. Disconnect the field strap from the terminal on the solenoid, remove the solenoid attaching screws, and remove the solenoid, spring, and washers.

3. Detach the plunger at the drive lever, and remove it.

4. Remove the starter through bolts and the brush holder attaching screws. Remove the rear cover.

5. Remove the insulator and washers from the rear end of the armature shaft. Remove the brush holder.

6. Pull the yoke off the drive housing. Remove the rubber packing, spring, and spring seat.

7. Pull the armature, drive lever, and overrunning clutch assembly from the drive housing.

8. Position the armature with the front end upward in a soft jawed vise. Drive the pinion stop collar rearward until the stop ring can be removed. Then, remove the stop ring, stop collar, and overrunning clutch.

9. Assemble in exact reverse order. Then, energize the solenoid by connecting the **M** terminal on the solenoid to the battery + terminal, and grounding the solenoid housing to the battery − terminal. Check the clearance between pinion and stop collar with a feeler gauge. It should be 0.020–0.079″ (0.5–2.0mm). If the clearance is incorrect, install adjusting washers, which are available for insertion between the solenoid and drive housing.

### STARTER BRUSH REPLACEMENT

Inspect the brushes for excessive wear (limit is 0.45″ [1.14mm]). If worn beyond the limit, they must be replaced.

1. Remove the brush from the holder. Smash the brush in order to free the lead from it. Clean old solder and corrosion from the lead.

2. Insert the lead into the new brush, going into the end with the smaller chamfer.

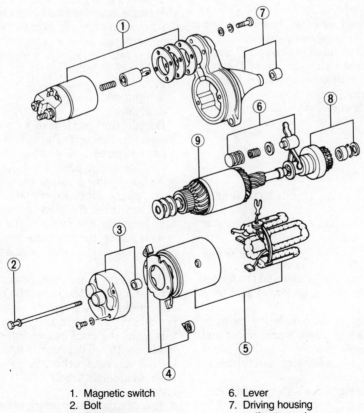

1. Magnetic switch
2. Bolt
3. Rear over
4. Brush-holder assembly
5. Yoke
6. Lever
7. Driving housing (front cover)
8. Drive pinion
9. Armature

**Disassemble 1983–84 starters in the numbered order**

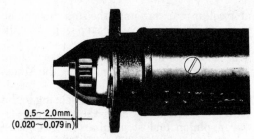

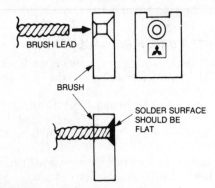

**Checking pinion-to-stop collar clearance**

BRUSH LEAD

BRUSH

SOLDER SURFACE
SHOULD BE
FLAT

**Soldering brush leads to brushes**

3. Solder the lead into the brush by filling the large chamfer with rosin core solder. A small soldering iron rated at about 150 watts is best. Smooth the outer surface of the soldered connection with sandpaper after the soldering is complete.

4. Install the brush in the brush holder under the spring.

## Battery

### REMOVAL AND INSTALLATION

1. Protect the paint finish with fender covers.

2. Disconnect the battery cables from the battery terminal posts.

3. Remove the battery holddown clamp and remove the battery from the vehicle.

4. Inspect the battery carrier and the fender panels for damage caused by loss of acid from the battery.

5. If the battery is to be reinstalled, clean its top with a solution of clean, warm water and baking soda. Scrub heavily deposited areas with a stiff bristly brush, being careful not to scatter corrosion residue.

6. Rinse off the top of the battery with clean, warm water.

NOTE: *Keep the cleaning solution and water out of the battery cells.*

7. Examine the battery case and cover for cracks.

8. Clean the battery posts and cable connectors with a wire brush. Replace damaged or worn cables.

9. Install the battery in the car. Tighten the holddown clamp nuts.

10. Connect the cables to their correct battery terminals and, after tightening the connections, coat all connections with petroleum jelly to prevent corrosion.

11. If the electrolyte level is low, fill the battery to the recommended level with distilled water.

## ENGINE MECHANICAL

### Design

#### ROTARY ENGINE

The Mazda rotary engine replaces conventional pistons with three-cornered rotors which have rounded sides. The rotors are mounted on a shaft which has eccentrics rather than crank throws.

The chamber in which the rotor travels is roughly oval shaped, but with the sides of the oval bowed in slightly. The technical name for this shape is a two lobe epitrochoid.

As the rotor travels its path in the chamber, it perform the same four functions as the piston in a regular four-cycle engine:

1. Intake
2. Compression
3. Ignition
4. Exhaust

But all four functions in a rotary engine are happening concurrently, rather than in four separate stages.

Ignition of the compressed fuel/air mixture occurs each time a side of the rotor passes the spark plugs. Since the rotor has three sides there are three complete power impulses for each complete revolution of the rotor.

As it moves, the rotor exerts pressure on the cam of the eccentric shaft, causing the shaft to turn.

Because there are three power pulses for every revolution of the rotor, the eccentric shaft must make three complete revolutions for every one revolution of the rotor. To maintain this ratio, the rotor has an internal gear that meshes with a fixed gear in a three-to-one ratio. If it was not for this gear arrangement, the rotor would spin freely and timing would be lost.

The Mazda rotary engine has two rotors mounted 60° out of phase. This produces six power impulses for each complete revolution of both rotors and two power impulses for each revolution of the eccentric shaft.

## Battery and Starter Specifications
All cars use 12 volt, negative ground electric systems

| Year | Model | Battery Amp Hour Capacity | Lock Test Amps | Lock Test Volts | Torque (ft./lbs.) | No Load Test Amps | No Load Test Volts | No Load Test RPM | Brush Spring Tension (oz) | Min. Brush Length (in.) |
|---|---|---|---|---|---|---|---|---|---|---|
| 1971 | RX-2 | 60 | 600 | 6 | 19.5 | 70 | 12 | 3,600 | 40.0 | .45 |
| 1972–75 | RX-2 and RX-3 w/MT | 70 | 600 | 6 | 19.5 | 70 | 12 | 3,600 | 56.3 | .45 |
| | RX-2 and RX-3 w/AT | 70 | 1,200 | 4 | 19.5 | 100 | 12 | 5,400 | 56.3 | .45 |
| 1974–78 | RX-4 w/MT | 70 | 780 | 5 | 7.96 | 75 | 11.5 | 4,900 | 56 | .45 |
| | RX-4 w/AT | 70 ① | 1,100 | 5 | 17.36 | 100 | 11.5 | 7,800 | 56 | .45 |
| 1975–77 | 808 | 60 | 400 | 6 | 6.7 | 53 | 10.5 | 5,000 | 56 | .45 |
| 1976 | RX-3 w/MT | 60 | 780 | 5 | 8.0 | 75 | 11.5 | 4,900 | 56 | .45 |
| | RX-3 w/AT | 60 | 1,100 | 5 | 17.4 | 100 | 11.5 | 7,800 | 56 | .45 |
| 1977–78 | Cosmo w/MT | 45 | 600 | 5 | 6.9 | 50 | 11.5 | 5,600 | 56 | .45 |
| | Cosmo w/AT | 70 | 1,050 | 5 | 15.9 | 100 | 11.5 | 6,600 | 56 | .45 |
| 1977–82 | GLC | 45 ② | 310 | 5 | 5.4 | 53 | 11.5 | 6,800 | 56 | .45 |
| | 626 | 45 | 310 | 5 | 5.4 ③ | 53 ④ | 11.5 | 6,800 | 56 | .45 |
| 1983–85 | GLC | ⑤ | — | — | — | 53 | 11.5 | 6,800 | — | .453 |
| | 626 | ⑥ | — | — | — | 60 | 11.5 | 6,500 ⑦ | — | .453 |
| | 626 (Diesel) | 80 | — | — | — | 130 | 11.0 | 4,500 | — | .452 |
| 1986 | 323 | ⑧ | — | — | — | 60 | 11.5 | 6,500 | 31.75 | .453 |
| | 626 | ⑨ | — | — | — | 60 | 11.5 | 6,500 ⑦ | 31.75 | .453 |

MT—Manual transmission
AT—Automatic transmission
①—60 amp w/MT
②—1977    Canada 45 amp
             Exc Calif. 60 amp
             Calif. 35 amp
     1978    Calif. 35 amp
     1979–80 Calif. 33 amp
③ 1982; 8.3
④ 1982; 60 amp or less
⑤ 50D23L: 60A

50D20L: 50A
  N540ZAL: 33A (Calif.)
⑥ 50D20N: 50A
  55D23L: 60A
⑦ Automatic Trans: 6,600
⑧ N540ZAL(S) 33A
  50D20L: 50A
  55D23L: 60A
⑨ 50D20L: 50A
  55D23L: 60A

Because of the number of power impulses for each revolution of the rotor and because all four functions are concurrent, the rotary engine is able to produce a much greater amount of power for its size and weight than a comparable reciprocating piston engine.

Instead of using valves to control the intake and exhaust operations, the rotor uncovers and covers ports on the wall of the chamber, as is turns. Thus, a complex valve train is unnecessary. The resulting elimination of parts further reduces the size and weight of the engine, as well as eliminating a major source of mechanical problems.

Spring loaded carbon seals are used to prevent loss of compression around the rotor apexes and cast iron seals are used to prevent loss of compression around the side faces of the rotor. These seals are equivalent to compression rings on the conventional piston, but must be more durable because of the high rotor rpm to which they are exposed.

Oil is controlled by means of circular seals mounted in two grooves on the side face of the rotor. These oil seals function to seep oil out of the combustion chamber and gasoline out of the crankcase, in a similar manner to the oil control ring on a piston.

The rotor housing is made of aluminum and the surfaces of the chamber are chrome plated.

## PISTON ENGINE

The Mazda piston engines incorporate many of the design features used to make small and efficient engines both clean and willing performers. They incorporate a slightly undersquare (stroke slightly longer than bore) design in combination with hemispherical combustion chambers for minimal hydrocarbon emissions. The hemi-head also provides room for large valves, and these, in combination with the crossflow cylinder head design, permit free breathing and high output for the engine's size. Because the exhaust manifold is on the opposite side from the intake, engine coolant is used to warm the intake passages instead of exhaust gas.

Free breathing is aided further through the use of a progressive, 2 venturi carburetor. An overhead camshaft design minimizes valve train mass so that the engine's breathing ability can be translated into higher rpm and the higher maximum output this creates. The use of rocker levers not only allows a single camshaft to operate both intake and exhaust valves, but ensures easy adjustment of valve clearances without the use of special tools or shims or spacers. The camshaft is operated via a chain for maximum durability.

The 90.9 cu. in. engine has been retained for use in the GLC in the 1983–85 model years, but the 626 uses a very different engine, the FE. The long stroke design of its predecessor has been supplanted by a square design, one in which bore and stroke are equal. The shorter stroke (3.39″ [86mm] vs 3.86″[98mm]) is more appropriate where emissions are largely controlled by the catalytic converter. This type of engine revs more freely and runs with reduced friction. The timing chain of the former design has been replaced by a timing belt for reduced weight and noise. The 1986 626 FE engine uses fuel injection and is available with or without a turbocharger.

There is also a diesel version of the FE, known as the RF, used only in 1985. It uses the same basic cylinder dimensions, although there are minor changes in the dimensions or various crankshaft and connecting rod parts. Its cylinder head is a completely different design from that on the gas engine, except that it is also of aluminum alloy. It employs radically changed head bolts because of the increased compression and combustion pressures of a diesel. Prechamber inserts form the lower halves of the precombustion chambers required to ensure smooth diesel running. An overhead camshaft operates bucket type valve lifters directly. Valve clearance is adjusted by replacing the adjusting discs, provided in various thicknesses, located in the tops of the lifters. The camshaft is operated by a timing belt which also operates the rotary type injection pump.

The 1986 323 uses a new engine, the B6. This uses a slightly undersquare bore/stroke relationship (3.07″ x 3.29″ [77.9mm x 83.5mm]) and a substantially higher compression ratio (9.3:1 rather than 8.6:1). The distributor, on this engine, is driven directly off the rear of the camshaft through a coupling. An exhaust manifold mounted catalytic converter, used on the FE engine, has been eliminated, partly because of the use of fuel injection and the longer stroke, both of which tend to reduce hydrocarbon emissions.

## Engine Overhaul Tips

Most engine overhaul procedures are fairly standard. In addition to specific parts replacement procedures and complete specifications for your individual engine, this chapter also is a guide to accepted rebuilding procedures. Examples of standard rebuilding practice are shown and should be used along with specific details concerning your particular engine.

Competent and accurate machine shop services will ensure maximum performance, reliability and engine life. Procedures marked with the symbol shown above should be performed by a competent machine shop, and are provided so that you will be familiar with the procedures necessary to a successful overhaul.

In most instances it is more profitable for the do-it-yourself mechanic to remove, clean and inspect the component, buy the necessary parts and deliver these to a shop for actual machine work.

On the other hand, much of the rebuilding work (crankshaft, block, bearings, piston rods, and other components) is well within the scope of the do-it-yourself mechanic.

## TOOLS

The tools required for an engine overhaul or parts replacement will depend on the depth of your involvement. With a few exceptions, they will be the tools found in a mechanic's tool kit

(see Chapter 1). More in-depth work will require any or all of the following:
- a dial indicator (reading in thousandths) mounted on a universal base
  - micrometers and telescope gauges
  - jaw and screw type pullers
  - scraper
  - valve spring compressor
  - ring groove cleaner
  - piston ring expander and compressor
  - ridge reamer
  - cylinder hone or glaze breaker
  - Plastigage®
  - engine stand

Use of most of these tools is illustrated in this chapter. Many can be rented for a one time use from a local parts jobber or tool supply house specializing in automotive work.

Occasionally, the use of special tools is called for. See the information on Special Tools and Safety Notice in the front of this book before substituting another tool.

### INSPECTION TECHNIQUES

Procedures and specifications are given in this chapter for inspecting, cleaning and assessing the wear limits of most major components. Other procedures such as Magnaflux® and Zyglo® can be used to locate material flaws and stress cracks. Magnaflux® is a magnetic process applicable only to ferrous materials. The Zyglo® process coats the material with a fluorescent dye penetrant and can be used on any material. Checks for suspected surface cracks can be more readily made using spot check dye. The dye is sprayed onto the suspected area, wiped off and the area sprayed with a developer. Cracks will show up brightly.

### OVERHAUL TIPS

Aluminum has become extremely popular for use in engines, due to its low weight. Observe the following precautions when handling aluminum parts:
- Never hot tank aluminum parts (the caustic hot tank solution will eat the aluminum.
- Remove all aluminum parts (identification tag, etc.) from engine parts prior to the tanking.
- Always coat threads lightly with engine oil or anti-seize compounds before installation, to prevent seizure.
- Never over torque bolts or spark plugs, especially in aluminum threads.

Stripped threads in any component can be repaired using any of several commercial repair kits (Heli-Coil®, Microdot®, Keenserts®, etc.).

When assembling the engine, any parts that will be in frictional contact must be prelubed

to provide lubrication at initial start-up. Any product specifically formulated for this purpose can be used, but engine oil is not recommended as a prelube.

When semi-permanent (locked, but removable) installation of bolts or nuts is desired, threads should be cleaned and coated with Loctite® or other similar, commercial non-hardening sealant.

### REPAIRING DAMAGED THREADS

Several methods of repairing damaged threads are available. Heli-Coil® (shown here), Keenserts® and Microdot® are among the most widely used. All involve basically the same principle – drilling out stripped threads, tapping the hole and installing a prewound insert – –making welding, plugging and oversize fasteners unnecessary.

Two types of thread repair inserts are usually supplied– –a standard type for most Inch Coarse, Inch Fine, Metric Course and Metric Fine thread sizes and a spark plug type to fit most spark plug port sizes. Consult the individual manufacturer's catalog to determine exact applications. Typical thread repair kits will contain a selection of prewound threaded inserts, a tap (corresponding to the outside diameter threads of the insert) and an installation tool. Spark plug inserts usually differ because they require a tap equipped with pilot

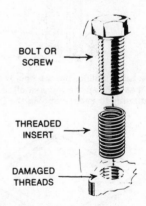

BOLT OR SCREW

THREADED INSERT

DAMAGED THREADS

**Damaged bolt holes can be repaired with thread repair inserts**

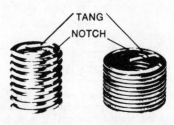

TANG

NOTCH

**Standard thread repair insert (left) and spark plug thread insert (right)**

threads and a combined reamer/tap section. Most manufacturers also supply blister packed thread repair inserts separately in addition to a master kit containing a variety of taps and inserts plus installation tools.

Before effecting a repair to a threaded hole, remove any snapped, broken or damaged bolts or studs. Penetrating oil can be used to free frozen threads; the offending item can be removed with locking pliers or with a screw or stud extractor. After the hole is clear, the thread can be repaired, as follows:

Drill out the damaged threads with specified drill. Drill completely through the hole or to the bottom of a blind hole

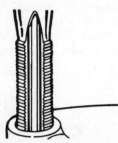

With the tap supplied, tap the hole to receive the thread insert. Keep the tap well oiled and back it out frequently to avoid clogging the threads

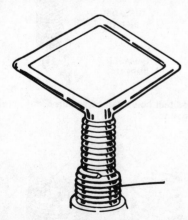

Screw the threaded insert onto the installation tool until the tang engages the slot. Screw the insert into the tapped hole until it is ¼–½ turn below the top surface. After installation break off the tang with a hammer and punch

## Checking Engine Compression

A noticeable lack of engine power, excessive oil consumption and/or poor fuel mileage measured over an extended period are all indicators of internal engine war. Worn piston rings, scored or worn cylinder bores, blown head gaskets, sticking or burnt valves and worn valve seats are all possible culprits here. A check of each cylinder's compression will help you locate the problems.

As mentioned in the Tools and Equipment section of Chapter 1, a screw-in type compression gauge is more accurate that the type you simply hold against the spark plug hole, although it takes slightly longer to use. It's worth it to obtain a more accurate reading. Follow the procedures below for gasoline and diesel engined cars.

### GASOLINE ENGINES

1. Warm up the engine to normal operating temperature.
2. Remove all spark plugs.

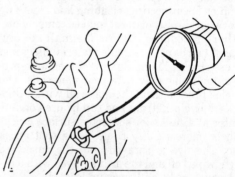

The screw-in type compression gauge is more accurate

3. Disconnect the high tension lead from the ignition coil.
4. On fully open the throttle either by operating the carburetor throttle linkage by hand or by having an assistant floor the accelerator pedal.
5. Screw the compression gauge into the no.1 spark plug hole until the fitting is snug.
NOTE: *Be careful not to crossthread the plug hole. On aluminum cylinder heads use extra care, as the threads in these heads are easily ruined.*
6. Ask an assistant to depress the accelerator pedal fully on both carbureted and fuel injected cars. Then, while you read the compression gauge, ask the assistant to crank the engine two or three times in short bursts using the ignition switch.
7. Read the compression gauge at the end of

## Standard Torque Specifications and Fastener Markings

In the absence of specific torques, the following chart can be used as a guide to the maximum safe torque of a particular size/grade of fastener.

- There is no torque difference for fine or coarse threads.
- Torque values are based on clean, dry threads. Reduce the value by 10% if threads are oiled prior to assembly.
- The torque required for aluminum components or fasteners is considerably less.

### U.S. Bolts

| SAE Grade Number | 1 or 2 | | | 5 | | | 6 or 7 | | |
|---|---|---|---|---|---|---|---|---|---|
| Number of lines always 2 less than the grade number. |  | | |  | | |  | | |
| Bolt Size (Inches)—(Thread) | Maximum Torque | | | Maximum Torque | | | Maximum Torque | | |
| | Ft./Lbs. | Kgm | Nm | Ft./Lbs. | Kgm | Nm | Ft./Lbs. | Kgm | Nm |
| ¼—20 | 5 | 0.7 | 6.8 | 8 | 1.1 | 10.8 | 10 | 1.4 | 13.5 |
| —28 | 6 | 0.8 | 8.1 | 10 | 1.4 | 13.6 | | | |
| ⁵⁄₁₆—18 | 11 | 1.5 | 14.9 | 17 | 2.3 | 23.0 | 19 | 2.6 | 25.8 |
| —24 | 13 | 1.8 | 17.6 | 19 | 2.6 | 25.7 | | | |
| ³⁄₈—16 | 18 | 2.5 | 24.4 | 31 | 4.3 | 42.0 | 34 | 4.7 | 46.0 |
| —24 | 20 | 2.75 | 27.1 | 35 | 4.8 | 47.5 | | | |
| ⁷⁄₁₆—14 | 28 | 3.8 | 37.0 | 49 | 6.8 | 66.4 | 55 | 7.6 | 74.5 |
| —20 | 30 | 4.2 | 40.7 | 55 | 7.6 | 74.5 | | | |
| ½—13 | 39 | 5.4 | 52.8 | 75 | 10.4 | 101.7 | 85 | 11.75 | 115.2 |
| —20 | 41 | 5.7 | 55.6 | 85 | 11.7 | 115.2 | | | |
| ⁹⁄₁₆—12 | 51 | 7.0 | 69.2 | 110 | 15.2 | 149.1 | 120 | 16.6 | 162.7 |
| —18 | 55 | 7.6 | 74.5 | 120 | 16.6 | 162.7 | | | |
| ⅝—11 | 83 | 11.5 | 112.5 | 150 | 20.7 | 203.3 | 167 | 23.0 | 226.5 |
| —18 | 95 | 13.1 | 128.8 | 170 | 23.5 | 230.5 | | | |
| ¾—10 | 105 | 14.5 | 142.3 | 270 | 37.3 | 366.0 | 280 | 38.7 | 379.6 |
| —16 | 115 | 15.9 | 155.9 | 295 | 40.8 | 400.0 | | | |
| ⅞— 9 | 160 | 22.1 | 216.9 | 395 | 54.6 | 535.5 | 440 | 60.9 | 596.5 |
| —14 | 175 | 24.2 | 237.2 | 435 | 60.1 | 589.7 | | | |
| 1— 8 | 236 | 32.5 | 318.6 | 590 | 81.6 | 799.9 | 660 | 91.3 | 894.8 |
| —14 | 250 | 34.6 | 338.9 | 660 | 91.3 | 849.8 | | | |

### Metric Bolts

| Relative Strength Marking | 4.6, 4.8 | | | 8.8 | | |
|---|---|---|---|---|---|---|
| Bolt Markings |  | | |  | | |
| Bolt Size Thread Size x Pitch (mm) | Maximum Torque | | | Maximum Torque | | |
| | Ft./Lbs. | Kgm | Nm | Ft./Lbs. | Kgm | Nm |
| 6 x 1.0 | 2–3 | .2–.4 | 3–4 | 3–6 | .4–.8 | 5–8 |
| 8 x 1.25 | 6–8 | .8–1 | 8–12 | 9–14 | 1.2–1.9 | 13–19 |
| 10 x 1.25 | 12–17 | 1.5–2.3 | 16–23 | 20–29 | 2.7–4.0 | 27–39 |
| 12 x 1.25 | 21–32 | 2.9–4.4 | 29–43 | 35–53 | 4.8–7.3 | 47–72 |
| 14 x 1.5 | 35–52 | 4.8–7.1 | 48–70 | 57–85 | 7.8–11.7 | 77–110 |
| 16 x 1.5 | 51–77 | 7.0–10.6 | 67–100 | 90–120 | 12.4–16.5 | 130–160 |
| 18 x 1.5 | 74–110 | 10.2–15.1 | 100–150 | 130–170 | 17.9–23.4 | 180–230 |
| 20 x 1.5 | 110–140 | 15.1–19.3 | 150–190 | 190–240 | 26.2–46.9 | 160–320 |
| 22 x 1.5 | 150–190 | 22.0–26.2 | 200–260 | 250–320 | 34.5–44.1 | 340–430 |
| 24 x 1.5 | 190–240 | 26.2–46.9 | 260–320 | 310–410 | 42.7–56.5 | 420–550 |

each series of cranks, and record the highest of these readings. Repeat this procedure for each of the engine's cylinders. Compare the highest reading of each cylinder to the compression pressure specification in the Tune-Up Specifications chart in Chapter 2. The specs in this chart are maximum values.

A cylinder's compression pressure is usually acceptable if it is not less than 80% of maximum. The difference between each cylinder should be no more than 12–14 pounds.

8. If a cylinder is unusually low, pour a tablespoon of clean engine oil into the cylinder through the spark plug hole and repeat the compression test. If the compression comes up after adding the oil, it appears that the cylinder's piston rings or bore are damaged or worn. If the pressure remains low, the valves may not be seating properly (a valve job is needed), or the head gasket may be blown near that cylinder. If compression in any two adjacent cylinders is low, and if the addition of oil doesn't help the compression, there is leakage past the head gasket. Oil and coolant water in the combustion chamber can result from this problem. There may be evidence of water droplets on the engine dipstick when a head gasket has blown.

### DIESEL ENGINES

Checking cylinder compression on diesel engines is basically the same procedure as on gasoline engines except for the following:

1. A special compression gauge adaptor suitable for diesel engines (because these engines have much greater compression pressures) must be used.

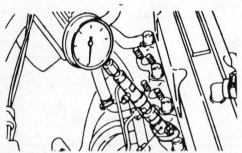

**Diesel engines require a special compression gauge adaptor**

2. Remove the fuel lines and gaskets and then remove the injectors from each cylinder. See Chapter 4.

NOTE: *Don't forget to remove the washer and gasket underneath each injector; otherwise, it may get lost when the engine is cranked.*

3. When fitting the compression gauge adaptor to the cylinder head, make sure the bleeder of the gauge (if equipped) is closed.

4. When reinstalling the injector assemblies, install new washers underneath each injector. See Chapter 4.

## Engine Removal and Installation
### ROTARY ENGINES

Be sure that the engine has completely cooled before attempting to remove it.

1. Scribe matchmarks on the hood and hinges. Remove the hood from the hinges.

2. Working from underneath the car, remove the gravel shield then drain the cooling system and the engine oil.

3. Disconnect the cable from the negative (−) battery terminal.

4. Remove the air cleaner, its bracket, and its attendant hoses.

5. Detach the accelerator cable, choke cable, and fuel lines from the carburetor.

6. Remove the nuts which secure the thermostat housing. Disconnect the ground cable from the housing and install the housing again after the cable is removed.

7. Disconnect the power brake vacuum line from the intake manifold.

8. Remove the fan shroud securing bolts and then remove the shroud itself.

9. Remove the bolts which secure the fan clutch to the eccentric shaft pulley. Withdraw the fan and clutch as a single unit.

CAUTION: *Keep the fan clutch in an upright position so that its fluid does not leak out.*

10. Unfasten the clamps and remove both radiator hoses.

11. Note their respective positions and remove the spark plug cables. Disconnect the primary leads from the distributors and remove both distributor caps.

12. Detach all of the leads from the alternator, the water temperature sender, the oil pressure sender, and the starter motor.

13. Disconnect all the wiring from the emission control system components. See Chapter 4.

14. Detach the heater hoses at the engine.

15. Detach the oil lines from the front and the rear of the engine.

16. Disconnect the battery cable from the positive (+) battery terminal and from the engine.

17. Unfasten the clutch slave cylinder retaining nuts from the clutch housing and tie the cylinder up and out of the way.

NOTE: *Do not remove the hydraulic line from the slave cylinder.*

18. Remove the exhaust pipe and the thermal reactor.

CAUTION: *Be sure that the thermal reactor*

## How the Rotary Engine Works

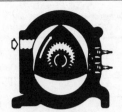   

**1. INTAKE.**
Fuel/air mixture is drawn into combustion chamber by revolving rotor through intake port (upper left). No valves or valve-operating mechanism needed.

**2. COMPRESSION.**
As rotor continues revolving, it reduces space in chamber containing fuel and air. This compresses mixture.

**3. IGNITION.**
Fuel/air mixture now fully compressed. Leading sparkplug fires. A split-second later, following plug fires to assure complete combustion.

**4. EXHAUST.**
Exploding mixture drives rotor, providing power. Rotor then expels gases through exhaust port.

## How Your Piston Engine Works

 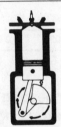  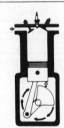

**1. INTAKE.**           **2. COMPRESSION.**           **3. IGNITION.**           **4. EXHAUST.**

## General Engine Specifications—Rotary Engine

| Model | Engine Displacement Cu In. (cc) | Carburetor Type | Net Horsepower @ rpm | Net Torque @ rpm | Rotor Displacement (cu in.) | Compression Ratio | Oil Pressure @ rpm (psi) |
|---|---|---|---|---|---|---|---|
| RX-3 | 70/1,146 | 4-bbl | 90 @ 6,000 | 96 @ 4,000 | 35 | 9.4:1 | 71.1 @ 3,000 |
| RX-2, RX-3SP | 70/1,146 | 4-bbl | 97 @ 6,500 | 98 @ 4,000 | 35 | 9.4:1 | 71.1 @ 3,000 |
| RX-4, Cosmo | 80/1,308 | 4-bbl | 110 @ 6,000 | 120 @ 4,000 | 40 | 9.2:1 | 71.1 @ 3,000 |

## General Engine Specifications—Piston Engine

| Year | Engine Displacement Cu In. (cc) | Fuel System Type | Horsepower (@ rpm) | Torque @ rpm (ft. lbs.) | Bore x Stroke (in.) | Compression Ratio | Oil Pressure @ rpm (psi) |
|---|---|---|---|---|---|---|---|
| 1975–78 | 96.8 (1,586) | 2-bbl | 64 @ 5,000 | 78 @ 3,000 | 3.07 x 3.27 | 8.6:1 | 57 @ 3,000 |
| 1976–78 | 77.6 (1,272) | 2-bbl | — | — | 2.87 x 2.99 | 9.2:1 | 57 @ 3,000 |
| 1979–82 | 86.4 (1.415) | 2-bbl | — | — | 3.03 x 2.99 | 9.0:1 | 57 @ 3,000 |
| | 90.9 (1,490) ① | 2-bbl | — | — | 3.03 x 3.15 | 9.0:1 | 57 @ 3,000 |
| | 120.2 (1,970) | 2-bbl | — | — | 3.15 x 3.86 | 8.6:1 | 57 @ 3,000 |
| 1983–84 | 90.9 (1,490) | 2-bbl | — | — | 3.03 x 3.15 | 9.0:1 | 57 @ 3,000 |
| | 121.9 (1,998) | 2-bbl | — | — | 3.39 x 3.39 | 8.6:1 | 57 @ 4,000 |

## General Engine Specifications—Piston Engine (cont.)

| Year | Engine Displacement Cu In. (cc) | Fuel System Type | Horsepower (@ rpm) | Torque @ rpm (ft. lbs.) | Bore x Stroke (in.) | Compression Ratio | Oil Pressure @ rpm (psi) |
|---|---|---|---|---|---|---|---|
| 1985 | 90.9 (1,490) | 2 bbl | 85 @ 5,500 | 90 @ 3,500 | 3.03 x 3.15 | 9.0:1 | 50–60 @ 3,000 |
| | 121.9 (1,998) | 2 bbl | 83 @ 4,800 | 110 @ 2,500 | 3.39 x 3.39 | 8.6 | 43–57 @ 3,000 |
| | 121.9 (1,998) | ② | 72 @ 4,650 | 100 @ 2,750 | 3.39 x 3.39 | 22.7 | 58–70 @ 3,000 |
| 1986 | 97.4 (1,597) | 2 bbl | 82 @ 5,000 | 92 @ 2,500 | 3.07 x 3.29 | 9.3 | 43–57 @ 3,000 |
| | 121.9 (1,998) | EFI | 93 @ 5,000 | 115 @ 2,500 | 3.39 x 3.39 | 8.6 | 43–57 @ 3,000 |
| | 121.9 (1,998) | EFI Turbo | 120 @ 5,000 | 150 @ 3,000 | 3.39 x 3.39 | 7.8 | 43–57 @ 3,000 |

① 1981 and later
② Diesel injection

## Eccentric Shaft Specifications—Rotary
All measurements are given in inches.

| Model | Journal Diameter Main Bearing | Journal Diameter Rotor Bearing | Oil Clearance Main Bearing | Oil Clearance Rotor Bearing | Eccentric Shaft End-Play Normal | Eccentric Shaft End-Play Limit | Min. Shaft Runout |
|---|---|---|---|---|---|---|---|
| All | 1.6929 | 2.9134 | 0.0016–0.0028 | 0.0016–0.0031 ① | 0.0016–0.0028 | 0.0035 | 0.0008 |

① 1971—0.0020–0.0035

## Crankshaft and Connecting Rod Specifications—Piston Engine
All measurements given in inches.

| Year | Engine Displacement Cu In. (cc) | Crankshaft Main Brg Journal Dia | Crankshaft Main Brg Oil Clearance | Crankshaft Shaft End-Play | Crankshaft Thrust on No. | Connecting Rod Journal Dia | Connecting Rod Oil Clearance | Connecting Rod Side Clearance |
|---|---|---|---|---|---|---|---|---|
| 1972–78 | 96.8 (1,586) | 2.4804 | 0.001–0.002 | 0.003–0.009 | 5 | 2.0866 | 0.001–0.003 | 0.004–0.008 |
| 1976–78 | 77.6 (1,272) | 2.4804 | 0.0012–0.0024 | 0.003–0.009 | 5 | 1.7717 | 0.0011–0.0029 | 0.004–0.008 |
| 1979–82 | 86.4 (1,415) | 1.9685 | 0.0009–0.0017 | 0.004–0.006 | 5 | 1.5748 | 0.0009–0.0019 | 0.004–0.008 |
| | 90.9 (1,490) ① | 1.9668 | 0.0009–0.0017 | 0.004–0.006 | 5 | 1.5734 | 0.0009–0.0019 | 0.004–0.010 |
| | 120.2 (1,970) | 2.4804 | 0.0012–0.0020 | 0.003–0.009 | 5 | 2.0866 | 0.001–0.003 | 0.004–0.008 |
| 1983–85 | 90.9 (1,490) | 1.9668 ② | 0.0009–0.0017 | 0.0039–0.0059 | 5 | 1.5734 | 0.0009–0.0019 | 0.004–0.010 |
| 1985 | 121.9 (1,998) Diesel | 2.361 | 0.0012–0.0019 | 0.0016–0.0110 | 3 | 2.0063 | 0.0012–0.0024 | 0.0043–0.0102 |
| 1983–86 | 121.9 (1,998) | 2.360 | 0.0012–0.0019 | 0.0031–0.0071 | 3 | 2.006 | 0.0010–0.0026 | 0.004–0.010 |
| 1986 | 97.4 (1,597) | 1.9668 | 0.0011–0.0027 | 0.0031–0.0071 | 3 | 1.7699 | 0.0011–0.0027 | 0.0043–0.0103 |

① 1981 and later
② Taper/out-of-round not to exceed 0.002 in. In ground undersize for oversize bearings, dimension of finished size is:
   0.25 mm undersize—1.9563–1.9569
   0.50 mm undersize—1.9465–1.9471
   0.75 mm undersize—1.9366–1.9372

## Rotor and Housing Specfications—Rotary Engine

All measurements are given in inches.

| Model | Rotor | | | Housings | | | | | | |
|---|---|---|---|---|---|---|---|---|---|---|
| | Side Clearance | Stardard Protrusion of Land | Limit of Protrusion of Land | Front and Rear | | Rotor | | Intermediate | | |
| | | | | Distortion Limit | Wear Limit | Width | Distortion Limit | Distortion Limit | Wear Limit |
| RX-3, RX-3SP, and RX-2 | 0.0051–0.0067 | 0.004–0.006 | 0.003 | 0.002 | 0.004 | 2.7539 | 0.002 | 0.002 | 0.004 |
| 1974 RX-4 | 0.0047–0.0083 | — | — | 0.002 | 0.004 | 3.1438 | 0.002 | 0.002 | 0.004 |
| 1975–78 RX-4, Cosmo | 0.0039–0.0083 | — | — | 0.0016 | 0.0039 | 3.150 | 0.0024 | 0.0016 | 0.0039 |

## Seal Clearances—Rotary Engine

All measurements are given in inches.

| Model | Apex Seals | | | | Corner Seal to Rotor Groove | | Side Seal | | | |
|---|---|---|---|---|---|---|---|---|---|---|
| | To Side Housing | | To Rotor Groove | | | | To Rotor Groove | | To Corner Seal | |
| | Normal | Limit | Normal | Limit | Normal | Limit | Normal | Limit | Normal | Limit |
| RX-2, RX-3, RX-3SP | 0.0020–0.0028 ① | 0.0039 | 0.0014–0.0029 | 0.0039 | 0.0008–0.0019 | 0.0031 | 0.0016–0.0028 | 0.0039 | 0.002–0.006 | 0.016 |
| RX-4, Cosmo | 0.0051–0.0067 | 0.0118 | 0.0020–0.0035 | 0.006 | 0.0008–0.0019 ② | 0.0031 ② | 0.0016–0.0028 | 0.0040 | 0.0020–0.0059 | 0.016 ③ |

① Arctic Specifications—0.0004–0.0020
② Applies only to 1974 models
③ 1975–78 models—0.0157

## Seal Specifications—Rotary Engine

All measurements are given in inches.

| Model | Apex Seal | | Corner Seal Width (OD) | Side Seal | | Oil Seal Contact Width of Lip | |
|---|---|---|---|---|---|---|---|
| | Normal Height | Height Limit | | Thickness | Width | Normal | Limit |
| RX-2, RX-3, RX-3SP | 0.03927 | 0.03150 | 0.2756 | 0.0394 | 0.1378 | 0.008 | 0.031 |
| RX-4, Cosmo | 0.33500 | 0.27600 | 0.4331 | 0.0394 | 0.1378 | 0.008 | 0.031 |

## Torque Specifications—Rotary Engine

(All figures in ft. lbs.)

| Engine Displacement Cu In. (cc) | Front Cover | Bearing Housing | Rear Stationary Gear | Eccentric Shaft Pulley Bolt | Flywheel to Eccentric Shaft Nut | Manifolds | | Oil Pan | Tension Bolts |
|---|---|---|---|---|---|---|---|---|---|
| | | | | | | Intake | Exhaust | | |
| 70 (1,156) | 15 | 15 | 15 | 45 | 350 | 15 | 30 | 7 | 20 |
| 80 (1,308) | — | — | — | 54–69 ① | 289–362 | 15 | 32–43 ② | 5–7 | 23–27 |

① 1977–78—72–87
② 1975–78—22–40

## Torque Specifications—Piston Engine
(All figures in ft. lbs.)

| Year | Engine Displacement Cu In. (cc) | Cylinder Head Bolts (cold) | Rod Bearing Bolts | Main Bearing Bolts | Crankshaft Pulley Bolt | Flywheel-to-Crankshaft Bolts | Manifolds | |
|------|------|------|------|------|------|------|------|------|
| | | | | | | | Intake | Exhaust |
| 1974–78 | 1600 | 56–60 | 36–40 | 61–65 | 101–108 | 112–118 | 14–19 | 16–21 |
| 1976 | 1300 | 56–60 | 36–40 | 61–65 | 101–108 | 112–118 | 14–19 | 16–21 |
| 1977–78 | 1300 | 47–51 | 29–33 | 43–47 | 80–87 | 60–65 | 14–19 | 12–17 |
| 1979–82 | 1415 | 47–51 | 22–25 | 43–47 | 80–87 | 60–65 | 14–19 | 12–17 |
| | 1970 | 59–64 | 29–33 | 61–65 | 101–108 | 112–118 | 14–19 | 16–21 |
| 1979–85 | 1490 | 56–59 | 22–25 | 48–51 | 80–87 | 60–65 ① | 14–19 | 14–17 |
| 1985 | 1998 Diesel | ② | 51–54 | 61–65 | 116–123 | 130–137 | 14–19 | 16–20 |
| 1983–86 | 1998 | 59–64 | 37–41 | 61–65 | 80–87 | 71–76 | 14–19 | 16–21 |
| 1986 | 1600 | 56–60 | 37–41 | 40–43 | 36–45 | 71–76 | 14–19 | 12–17 |

① Autotransaxle 51–61. All '85 engines 80–87
② See text

## Piston and Ring Specifications
All measurements are given in inches.

| Year | Engine Displacement Cu In. (cc) | Piston Clearance | Ring Gap | | | Ring Side Clearance | | |
|------|------|------|------|------|------|------|------|------|
| | | | Top Compression | Bottom Compression | Oil Control | Top Compression | Bottom Compression | Oil Control |
| 1972–78 | 96.8 (1586) | 0.0022–0.0028 | 0.008–0.016 | 0.018–0.016 | 0.008–0.016 | 0.0014–0.0028 | 0.0012–0.0025 | 0.008–0.016 |
| 1976–78 | 77.6 (1272) | 0.0021–0.0026 | 0.008–0.016 | 0.008–0.016 | 0.008–0.016 | 0.0014–0.0028 | 0.0012–0.0025 | 0.008–0.016 |
| 1979–80 | 86.4 (1415) | 0.0021–0.0026 | 0.008–0.016 | 0.008–0.016 | 0.012–0.035 | 0.0012–0.0025 | 0.0012–0.0025 | 0.008–0.016 |
| 1979–82 | 120.2 (1970) | 0.0014–0.0030 | 0.008–0.016 | 0.008–0.016 | 0.012–0.035 | 0.0012–0.0028 | 0.0012–0.0028 | 0.008–0.016 |
| 1981–85 | 90.9 (1490) | 0.0010–0.0026 | 0.008–0.016 | 0.008–0.016 | 0.012–0.035 | 0.0012–0.0028 | 0.0012–0.0028 | 0.008–① 0.016 |
| 1985 | 121.9 (1998) Diesel | 0.0012–0.0020 | 0.0079–0.0157 | 0.0079–0.0157 | 0.0079–0.0157 | 0.0020–0.0035 | 0.0016–0.0031 | ① |
| 1983–86 | 121.9 (1998) | 0.0014–0.0030 | 0.008–0.014 | 0.006–0.012 | 0.012–0.035 | 0.0012–0.0028 | 0.0012–0.0028 | ① |
| 1986 | 97.4 (1597) | 0.0015–0.0020 | 0.008–0.016 | 0.006–0.012 | 0.012–0.035 | 0.001–0.003 | 0.001–0.003 | ① |

① Only ring groove width is given for 1983–85: 0.1583–0.1591

has completely cooled; severe burns could result if it has not.

19. Remove the nuts and bolts, evenly and in two or three stages, which secure the clutch housing to the engine.

20. Support the transmission by a jack placed underneath it.

21. Remove the nuts from each of the engine mounts.

22. Attach a lifting sling to the lifting bracket on the rear of the engine housing.

23. Use a hoist to take up the slack on the sling.

CAUTION: *Be sure that the hoist is secure to prevent personal injury or damage to the engine.*

24. Pull the engine forward until it clears the transmission input shaft. Lift the engine straight up and out of the car.

CAUTION: *Be careful not to damage any of the components remaining in the car.*

25. Remove the heat stove from the exhaust manifold.

26. Remove the thermal reactor as outlined below.

27. Mount the engine on a workstand.

## Valve Specifications—Piston Engine

| Year | Engine Displacement Cu In. (cc) | Seat Angle (deg) | Face Angle (deg) | Spring Test Pressure (lbs. @ in.) | Spring Installed Height (in.) | Stem-to-Guide Clearance (in.) | | Stem Diameter (in.) | |
|---|---|---|---|---|---|---|---|---|---|
| | | | | | | Intake | Exhaust | Intake | Exhaust |
| 1972–78 | 96.8 (1586) | 45 | 45 | ① | ② | 0.0007–0.0021 | 0.0007–0.0023 | 0.3150 | 0.3150 |
| 1976–78 | 77.6 (1272) | 45 | 45 | ③ | ④ | 0.0007–0.0021 | 0.0007–0.0023 | 0.3150 | 0.3150 |
| 1979–80 | 86.4 (1415) | 45 | 45 | ③ | ④ | 0.0007–0.0021 | 0.0007–0.0023 | 0.3150 | 0.3150 |
| 1981–82 | 90.9 (1490) | 45 | 45 | ⑤ | 1.319 | 0.0007–0.0021 | 0.0007–0.0021 | 0.3150 | 0.3150 |
| 1983 | 90.9 (1490) | 45 | 45 | ⑤ | — | 0.0007–0.0021 | 0.0007–0.0023 | 0.3161–0.3167 | 0.3159–0.3167 |
| 1984–85 | 90.9 (1490) | 45 | 45 | 164 @ 1.00 | 1.555 | 0.0007–0.0021 | 0.0007–0.0021 | 0.3161–0.3167 | 0.3159–0.3167 |
| 1979–82 | 120.2 (1970) | 45 | 45 | ① | ② | 0.0007–0.0021 | 0.0007–0.0023 | 0.3150 | 0.3150 |
| 1983–84 | 121.9 (1998) | 45 | 45 | ⑥ | — | 0.0010–0.0024 | 0.0010–0.0024 | 0.3161–0.3167 | 0.3159–0.3165 |
| 1985 | 121.9 (1998) Diesel | 45 | 45 | 211 @ 1.00 | ⑦ | 0.0016–0.0031 | 0.0020–0.0031 | 0.3138–0.3144 | 0.3136–0.3142 |
| 1985–86 | 121.9 (1998) | 45 | 45 | 101 @ 1.00 | ⑧ | 0.0010–0.0024 | 0.0010–0.0024 | 0.3161–0.3167 | 0.3159–0.3165 |
| 1986 | 97.4 (1597) | 45 | 45 | 157 @ 1.565 | 1.555–1.575 | 0.0018–0.0051 | 0.0019–0.0053 | 0.274–0.275 | 0.274–0.275 |

① Outer: 31.4 @ 1.339
　Inner: 20.9 @ 1.260
② Outer: 1.339
　Inner: 1.260
③ Outer: 43.7 @ 1.319
　Inner: 20.9 @ 1.260
④ Outer: 1.319
　Inner: 1.260
⑤ 63.3 @ 1.319
⑥ Outer: 50.5 @ 1.563
　Inner: 50.5 @ 1.3
⑦ Measure valve recession from the cylinder deck with a feeler gauge. The standard valve is 0.030–0.041 with a maximum valve of 0.100 in.
⑧ Applies only to 1985. 1986: outer—90 @ 1.00; inner—95 @ 1.00

NOTE: *A special three part workstand, designed for the rotary engine, is available from Mazda.*

28. Engine installation is performed in the reverse order of removal. Remember to refill all fluids according to specifications and to adjust the ignition timing after installation.

### PISTON ENGINES

**808**

1. Remove the hood.
2. Remove the oil pan cover.
3. Drain coolant from radiator and cylinder block drain cocks (located on right rear). Drain engine oil.

4. Disconnect battery cables, remove clamp bolts and nuts, and remove battery.
5. Disconnect air control valve air hose and vacuum sensing tubes.
6. Disconnect primary and high tension wires at distributor and alternator wiring at the connector and **B** terminal.
7. Disconnect oil pressure switch wire and engine ground wire. Disconnect the wiring connector located near the rear of the cylinder head.
8. Remove the radiator water hoses. Remove the radiator cowling bolts and radiator attaching bolts, and remove both cowling and radiator from the car.

9. Remove the hot air hose. Remove air cleaner mounting bolts, and remove the air cleaner.

10. Disconnect the choke wire and throttle linkage at the carburetor.

11. Disconnect fuel supply and return lines at the carburetor, noting which is which.

12. Disconnect heater hoses from the manifold.

13. Disconnect the wires at the water temperature sending unit and carburetor solenoid.

14. Disconnect the power brake unit vacuum sensing tube at the intake manifold.

15. On California cars, disconnect the vacuum sensing tubes from the three way solenoid.

16. Disconnect the accelerator switch wiring.

17. Disconnect all starter motor wiring, and remove the starter.

18. Disconnect the exhaust pipe at the manifold.

19. Remove the clutch cover and brackets.

20. Support the transmission with a suitable jack. Then, install a suitable lifting sling to the engine hanger brackets, and connect the sling to a suitable hoist, and take up all slack.

21. Remove the nuts and bolts which connect the transmission to the engine, and the engine mount through bolts on both sides.

22. Pull the engine forward until it clears the clutch shaft. Then, lift the engine from the vehicle.

23. Installation is the reverse of the removal procedure.

### Rear Wheel Drive GLC

1. Remove the hood.

2. Disconnect the negative battery cable.

3. Drain the cooling system by opening radiator drain cock.

4. Disconnect upper and lower water hoses.

5. Remove radiator.

6. Remove air cleaner.

7. Disconnect: ECS hoses, heater hose, accelerator and choke cables, fuel lines, vacuum hoses, and distributor, starter, temperature sending unit, thermostatic switch, and alternator wiring.

8. Disconnect the exhaust pipe at the exhaust manifold.

9. Remove the starter.

10. Support the car on axle stands. Support the transmission with a jack. Connect a suitable lifting sling to the engine hanger brackets and to a hoist, and remove slack. Then, remove engine mount bolts.

11. Remove transmission mounting bracket from left side, and transmission-to-engine bolts from right side.

12. Pull the engine forward until it clears the clutch shaft, and then remove it from the vehicle.

13. Installation is the reverse of the removal procedure.

### Front Wheel Drive GLC

NOTE: *The factory recommends that the engine and transaxle be removed from the car as a unit.*

1. Mark the outline of the hood hinges for reinstallation alignment. Remove the hood.

2. Disconnect the battery cables from the battery; negative cable first. Remove the battery.

3. Loosen the front wheel lugs. Jack up the car and safely support it on jackstands. (Refer to Chapter 1 for jacking instructions).

4. Remove the two front wheels. Remove the bottom and side splash shields. Drain the coolant, engine oil and transaxle fluid.

5. Remove the air cleaner assembly. Remove the radiator hoses and the radiator shroud and electric fan assembly.

6. Connect an engine lifting sling to the engine. Connect a chain hoist or portable engine crane to the lifting sling and apply slight upward pressure to the engine and transaxle assembly.

7. Remove the mounting bolts from the engine crossmember. Remove the crossmember.

8. Disconnect the lower ball joints. Dismount the steering knuckles and drive axles. (See Chapters 6 and 7).

9. Cars equipped with manual transaxles: Disconnect the shifting rod and extension bar. Cars equipped with an automatic transaxle: Disconnect the selector rod and counter rod.

10. Remove the front and rear transaxle mounting bushings. Disconnect the exhaust pipe from the converter. Remove the transaxle crossmember.

**Engine mount through bolt—front wheel drive GLC to 1982**

**Engine mount through bolt—front wheel drive GLC 1983 and later**

11. Disconnect all wires and hoses from under the engine and transaxle. Label them for identification.

12. Disconnect all wires, heater hoses and vacuum hoses from the upper side of the engine and transaxle. Label them for correct installation.

13. Disconnect the accelerator cable, speedometer cable, clutch cable, power brake booster line and fuel lines.

14. Check to be sure all remaining hoses and wiring are disconnected. Remove the evaporative canister. Remove the right side upper engine mount through bolt.

15. Lift the engine and transaxle assembly from the car. Take care not to allow the assembly to swing forward into the radiator.

16. If the car must be moved from underneath the engine: Remount the steering knuckles, secure the drive axles so that they can still turn, mount the front wheels and lower the car from the jackstands.

17. Installation is in the reverse order of removal.

**GLC Wagon**

1. Mark its location on the hinges and remove the hood. Disconnect the negative battery cable. Allow the engine to cool and drain coolant.

2. Disconnect the upper and lower radiator hoses. On vehicles with automatic transmissions, disconnect the transmission cooler lines at the radiator. Collect the transmission fluid that drains out.

3. Remove the radiator and cooling fan. Remove the air cleaner (first disconnect air hoses). Disconnect the accelerator cable. Cover the carburetor inlet to keep dirt out.

4. Disconnect the following wiring:
   a. distributor primary leads
   b. coil-to-distributor high tension wire

c. oil pressure gauge line
   d. water temperature gauge line
   e. accelerator switch wire
   f. slow fuel cut solenoid wire
   g. automatic choke wire
   h. engine ground strap
   i. starter motor wiring

5. Remove the right side engine mount through bolt.

6. Disconnect the wire from the alternator **B** terminal and the alternator wiring connector.

7. Disconnect the air control valve and air vent hoses, all vacuum hoses, and the fuel lines.

8. Disconnect the accelerator cable, power brake vacuum hose, and heater hoses. Remove the hot air hose leading to the air cleaner.

9. Remove the left side engine mount through bolt.

10. Raise the vehicle and support it on axle stands or a lift. Working underneath, disconnect the exhaust pipe and clutch cable. Remove the clutch cable bracket, and the lower clutch cover.

11. Support the transmission securely from underneath. Then, on automatic transmission equipped vehicles, remove the bolts fastening the torque converter to the drive plate. Then, remove transmission support bolts and nuts (automatic or manual tansmission).

12. Remove the starter motor. Remove the forward catalytic converter.

13. Install a lifting sling on the engine hooks, and support the engine with a sling and a lift. Slide the engine forward until it clears the clutch shaft (manual transmission) or torque converter (automatics), and lift it out of the vehicle.

14. Install the engine in reverse order, torquing the clutch cover to 13–20 ft. lbs. or the drive plate-to-torque converter bolts to 25–36 ft.lb. and converter housing-to-engine bolts to 23–34 ft.lb.

**626 through 1984**

1. Remove the hood.

2. Disconnect the negative battery cable.

3. Drain the cooling system.

4. Remove the upper and lower radiator hoses.

5. On cars equipped with an automatic transmission disconnect the cooler lines.

6. Remove the radiator cowling and fan.

7. Remove the radiator.

8. Remove the air hoses from the air cleaner and remove the air cleaner.

9. Disconnect the wiring from the distributor primary, coil wire, oil pressure gauge unit, alternator **B** terminal, alternator wiring cou-

pler, and the right side engine mounting nut.

10. Disconnect the wiring from the water temperature gauge unit, fuel cut solenoid, automatic choke, starter motor.

11. Disconnect the air hoses (reed valve), vacuum hoses (three way solenoid valve), fuel hoses, acceleration wire, master vacuum hose, and the left side engine mounting nut.

12. Raise the front of the vehicle and support with jackstands.

13. Remove the under cover.

14. Disconnect the exhaust pipe.

15. Remove the clutch under cover plate.

16. On cars equipped with automatic transmission, remove the torque converter and driving plate support bolts.

17. Support the transmission with a suitable jack and remove the transmission support bolts and nuts.

18. Remove the starter motor and the clutch release cylinder.

19. Connect a suitable lifting sling to the engine hanger brackets and to a hoist, and remove the slack.

20. Pull the engine forward until it clears the clutch shaft, then lift the engine from the vehicle.

21. To install reverse the removal procedure.

### 1985–86 626 (Gas Engine Only)

NOTE: *To perform this procedure, you will need a special tool, a differential side gear holder, Mazda part number 49 G030 455 or equivalent. For details, see the Driveshaft Removal and Installation procedure in Chapter 6. You will also have to support the vehicle with front wheels off as you remove the engine from above.*

1. Scribe matchmarks on the hood where the hinges fit up against it and remove it. Disconnect both battery cables.

2. Remove the air cleaner. Disconnect the fuel supply hose and, on '85 models, the return hose. Disconnect the accelerator cable at the carburetor or injection system throttle body.

3. Disconnect the clutch cable ('85 models) or remove the clutch slave (or release) cylinder ('86 models) at/from the transaxle. On automatic transmission equipped models, disconnect the control cable.

4. Disconnect the engine ground wire. On '86 models, disconnect the related connector at the same time. Disconnect the power brake unit vacuum hose. Remove the three-way valve vacuum switch and its mounting bracket from the firewall.

5. Drain the cooling system through both the radiator drain cock and the block drain plug. Then, disconnect and remove both heater hoses.

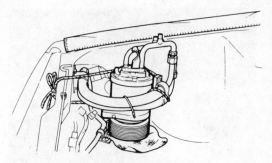

**Tie the air conditioner compressor as shown while removing the engine on the '85–'86 626**

6. On 1985 models, disconnect the duty solenoid valve and vacuum sensor.

7. On all models, label and then disconnect all wiring going to the engine and transaxle.

8. Disconnect both the air vent and vacuum hoses from the storage canister.

9. Remove the electric fan and radiator (see the Piston Engine Cooling section later in this chapter).

10. On air conditioned models only (for other models, go to Step 12), remove the windshield washer tanks, and the alternator (refer to the appropriate procedure earlier in this chapter for alternator removal).

11. Remove the air conditioner compressor from its mounts without attempting to disconnect any refrigeration lines. Tie the compressor in a secure manner to the front cowl in such a way that the refrigerant lines are not under stress.

12. Raise the car and support it securely. Remove the front wheels and splash shields.

13. On cars with manual steering, go on to Step 14. On cars with power steering, loosen the power steering pump pulley bolt. Then, remove the pump drive belt. Remove the power steering pump pulley and pump installation bolts, holding the pump so hoses will not be stressed. Support the pump above the crossmember so that the hoses can remain connected without any stress.

14. Remove the driveshafts as described in Chapter 6. Make sure to use a holder to prevent misalignment of the differential side gear splines and to keep the gears in position.

15. On cars with manual transmissions, remove the shift rod and torque rod and related joints and nuts. Then, install a lifting sling and support the engine securely by the lifting hooks.

16. Remove the cap and then the bolts shown in the illustration. Remove the arrowed bolts and then remove the torque rods.

17. Remove the exhaust pipe.

18. Remove the mounting bolts (arrowed in

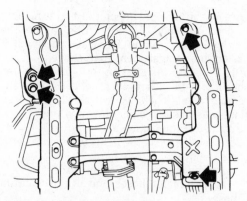

Remove the engine mount bolts from the locations shown (1985–86 626)

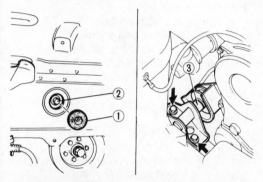

Remove the cap (1) and then the bolts (2). Remove the arrowed bolts and then remove the torque rods (3) (1985–86 626).

the illustration) for the engine mounts. Then, lift the engine and transaxle assembly cautiously out of the engine compartment, being especially careful not to damage air conditioner or power steering parts.

19. To begin installation first carefully line the engine up with its eventual position in the compartment. Then, work it slowly into position so as to avoid damaging anything.

20. Install the exhaust pipe. Install the torque rods and bolts, and then the cap. Install the engine mount bolts.

21. Install each of the items below in reverse of its removal:

a. Shift rod and torque rod and related parts

b. Driveshafts (refer to Chapter 6)

c. Power steering pump

d. Splash shields and front wheels

22. Lower the car. Then, continue replacing parts as listed:

e. Air conditioner compressor

f. Alternator (if necessary)

g. Electric fan and radiator

h. Air vent and vacuum hoses

i. Wiring

j. Heater hoses

k. Three-way valve vacuum switch and bracket and the power brake unit vacuum hoses (make sure connections are secure!)

l. Engine ground wire and connector

m. Clutch release cylinder or cable or automatic transmission control cable

n. Speedometer and accelerator cables

o. Fuel hose(s) and the air cleaner

p. Replace the hood, making sure it is lined up. Reconnect the battery.

23. Check all fluid levels and replenish as necessary, using approved anti-freeze/water mixture, power steering fluid, and engine oil.

## 626 Diesel

NOTE: *To perform this procedure, you will need a special tool, a differential side gear holder, Mazda part number 49 G030 455 or equivalent. For details, see the Driveshaft Removal and Installation procedure in Chapter 6. You will also have to support the vehicle with front wheels off as you remove the engine from above.*

1. Scribe matchmarks on the hood where the hinges fit up against it and remove it. Disconnect both battery cables.

2. Remove the oil filler and radiator caps. Then raise the vehicle and support it in a secure manner.

3. Drain the engine oil and coolant. Drain the transaxle fluid. Remove both front wheels.

4. Disconnect the starter motor cable and ignition switch wire at the starter. Disconnect the oil pressure switch connection nearby.

5. Disconnect the lower radiator hose from the water inlet pipe on the block.

6. Disconnect the two rubber hoops which support the exhaust pipe via the crossbar. Then, unbolt the exhaust pipe both at its support bracket and at the flange adjacent to the exhaust manifold.

7. Disconnect the shift control rod and torque rod at the transaxle.

8. Remove the tie rod clinch bolts and nuts, and then pry the lower control arms on both sides downward to separate the knuckle and lower ball joint.

9. Pry the right driveshaft out of the transaxle. See Chapter 6.

10. Remove the engine mount attaching nuts. Then, lower the vehicle to the ground.

11. Remove the Quick Start and Afterglow relays from the air cleaner bracket. Then, unbolt and remove the air cleaner assembly and bracket.

12. Unbolt and remove the clutch release (slave) cylinder from the transaxle housing. Disconnect the speedometer cable from the transaxle housing, as well.

13. Remove the engine wiring harness

bracket. Disconnect the ground cable from the transaxle case. Disconnect the speedometer cable at the case, as well.

14. Disconnect the left side driveshaft from the transaxle (see Chapter 6). Make sure to install the required holder to prevent misalignment of the differential side gear splines and to keep the gears in position.

15. Disconnect the electric fan motor and back-up lamp switch connectors.

16. Disconnect:
    a. The fuel supply and return hoses at the injection pump, draining the fuel into a metal container. Cap the open ends to keep the connections clean.
    b. The glow plug connector
    c. The tachometer sensor connector
    d. The engine stop valve connector
    e. The water temperature sensor connector (at the thermostat housing)

17. Disconnect the upper radiator hose at the thermostat housing. Disconnect the water lever sensor connector, water temperature switch connector and ground wire. Disconnect the lower hose and then remove the radiator and its rubber mounts.

18. Disconnect the accelerator cable at the injection pump. Disconnect the cold start device cable at the injection pump. Then, disconnect the plug and terminal type connector from the alternator.

19. Disconnect the power brake vacuum hose at the pipe leading from the vacuum pump. Disconnect the two coolant hoses and two oil hoses from the oil cooler, draining them into a convenient container to avoid spillage.

20. Disconnect the engine ground at the body. Unbolt and remove the torque damper at the body. Then, refer to the previous procedure, covering the gas engine removal procedure for the 626, and unbolt the engine mounts as described there. Hook a lifting sling to the two hooks on top of the engine and pull it out of the engine compartment from above.

21. To begin installation first carefully line the engine up with its eventual position in the compartment. Then, work it slowly into position so as to avoid damaging anything.

22. Install the engine mount bolts.

23. Install each of the items below in reverse of its removal:
    a. The engine torque damper.
    b. Oil cooler hoses and brake vacuum hose.
    c. The alternator wiring.
    d. Cold start and accelerator cables to the injection pump.
    e. Radiator and mounts.
    f. Radiator hoses and wiring.
    g. Water temperature sensor connector, fuel cut valve connector, tachometer connector, glow plug wiring connector, and fuel injection pump supply and return hoses.
    h. Back-up light and electric fan connectors.
    i. The left side driveshaft as decribed in Chapter 6.
    j. The speedometer cable and engine ground (at the transaxle housing).
    k. The engine electrical harness bracket.
    l. Clutch release hydraulic cylinder.
    m. Install the quick start and afterglow relays onto the air cleaner bracket.
    n. Install the air cleaner and air cleaner bracket.
    o. The right side driveshaft as described in Chapter 6. Then, reconnect the tie rod ends.
    p. Reconnect the exhaust pipe and reinstall the rubber supports.
    q. Reconnect the oil pressure sending unit, radiator lower hose (at the inlet pipe on the block), and the starter wiring.
    r. Replenish all fluids, reinstall the wheels and lower the vehicle to the ground.
    s. Install filler caps, and the hood, and then reconnect the battery.

323

1. Scribe matchmarks on the hood where the hinges fit up against it and remove it. Disconnect both battery cables.

2. Drain the engine oil, transaxle, and coolant.

3. Remove the battery and the battery carrier. Remove the air cleaner assembly.

4. Remove the oil level dipstick and tube. Remove the cooling fan and the radiator assembly.

5. Remove the accelerator cable and, if the

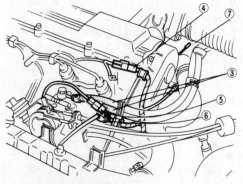

3. Fuel supply and return hoses
4. Glow plug connector
5. Tachometer electrical connector
6. Engine stop valve connector
7. Water temperature sensor connector

**Disconnecting diesel engine electrical connectors**

car has cruise control, the cruise control cable. Disconnect the speedometer cable.

6. Disconnect the fuel hoses, draining them into a metal container.

7. Disconnect and remove the heater hoses and the brake vacuum hose.

8. Disconnect and remove the three-way solenoid valve hoses and canister hoses.

9. Disconnect and remove the engine harness connectors. Disconnect the engine ground wire.

10. Disconnect and remove the upper and lower radiator hoses. On vehicles with automatic transmissions, remove the secondary air pipe from the exhaust manifold.

11. Disconnect and lower the exhaust pipe, supporting it in a safe manner.

12. Unbolt and dismount the air conditioner compressor without attempting to disconnect the lines. Tie the compressor in a convenient spot so that the refrigerant lines will not be under tension.

13. Unbolt and dismount the power steering pump without attempting to disconnect the lines. Tie the pump in a convenient spot so that the lines will not be under tension.

14. Disconnect the driveshafts at the transaxle on either side, as described in Chapter 6.

15. Disconnect and remove the clutch control cable and shift control rod on manual transmission cars and the shift control cable on automatic transmission cars.

16. Remove the splash shields from under the engine and on both sides.

17. Unbolt the engine mounts at the body and remove them. Place a lifting sling on the engine and remove it from above.

18. To begin installation first carefully line the engine up with its eventual position in the compartment. Then, work it slowly into position so as to avoid damaging anything. Install each item below in the reverse of the removal procedure.

a. Engine mount-to-body bolts.

b. Splash shields.

c. Shift control rod and clutch cable (manual transmission) or automatic transmission shift control cable.

d. Driveshafts (see Chapter 6).

e. Power steering pump, avoiding putting stress on the lines.

f. Air Conditioner compressor, avoiding putting stress on the lines.

g. Exhaust pipe and, on cars with automatic transmissions, the secondary air lines.

h. Upper and lower radiator hoses.

i. Engine ground strap.

j. Engine electrical connectors.

k. Emission canister hoses.

l. Three-way solenoid valve hoses.

m. Brake vacuum hose.

o. Heater hoses.

p. Fuel hoses.

q. Speedometer cable.

r. Accelerator and cruise control cable (if necessary).

s. Cooling fan and radiator. Connect the hoses and electrical connectors.

t. Oil dipstick tube and dipstick.

u. Air cleaner assembly.

v. Battery tray and battery.

w. Hood, aligning the hinges as they were, using the matchmarks.

19. Check all fluid levels and replenish as necessary, using approved antifreeze/water mixture, power steering fluid, and engine oil.

## Rocker Arm Cover
### REMOVAL AND INSTALLATION

1. If so equipped, disconnect the choke cable and the air bypass valve cable.

2. On carbureted models, remove the air cleaner. On fuel injected models, loosen the clamps and remove the air intake crossover. On the turbocharged 1,998 engine, loosen the clamps at either end and remove the turbocharger outlet line.

3. Disconnect the PCV valve at the cover or PCV line (diesels).

4. Remove the retaining bolts and remove the cam cover.

5. To install the cover, first supply new gaskets and, on the 1,998 engine, seal washers for the bolts. On the 1,597 engine, apply a suitable sealant to the groove in the cam cover prior to installing the new gasket.

6. Tighten the bolts in several stages, going back and forth across the cover. You can use the torque figures given for late model engines if you want, but the important point is to tighten the bolts evenly and just until they are slightly snug. The torques are: 1,998 gas engine, 2.2–2.9 ft.lb.; 1,597, 3.6–6.5 ft.lb.

7. Complete installation of the valve cover in reverse order of the removal procedure.

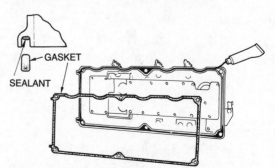

**Apply sealant to the valve cover prior to installing the gasket on the 1,597 engine**

## Rocker Shafts

### REMOVAL AND INSTALLATION

This operation should only be performed when the engine is cold; the bolts which hold the rocker shafts in place also hold the cylinder head to the block, and releasing the head when hot can cause it to warp. This does not apply to the 1998 and 1597 engines, which have a rocker shaft assembly incorporating separate bolts. Note that the diesel engine uses no rocker shaft assembly.

1. Remove the rocker cover as described above.

2. Loosen the rocker shaft bolts, going in reverse of the torquing sequence in several stages.

3. Remove the rocker shaft assembly and bolts as an assembly.

4. Installation is generally in reverse of removal. Make sure all the spherical valve operators at the outer ends of the rocker levers are

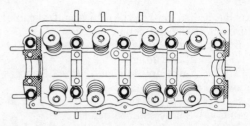

On the '83 and later 626, coat the block surfaces at either end with sealer as shown before installing the rocker assembly

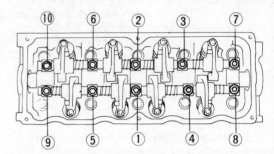

Torque pattern for rocker arm/shaft assembly on the 1597 engine

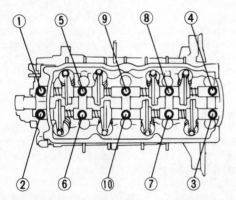

Rocker shaft assembly loosening sequence for 1983 and later 626

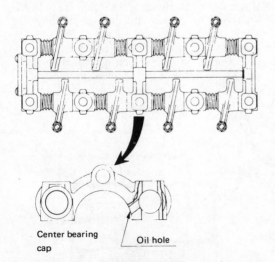

Center bearing cap        Oil hole

Locate the rocker assembly on '82 and earlier 626 engines so the oil passage lines up as shown

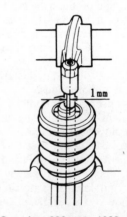

On the GLC, and on 626 up to 1982, shift the rocker assembly until the adjusting studs are offset 0.04 in. from the centers of the valve stems.

positioned so the flat surface is against the top of the valve stem. Then, except on the 1998 and 1597 engines, position the rocker assembly toward the exhaust side of the engine so that the exhaust valve rocker arms are offset 0.04″ (1mm) from the centers of the valve stems (see illustration). Then, torque the head bolts in several stages using the torquing pattern shown under, Cylinder Head Installation. On the 1998 engine, torque the bolts in the order shown to 13–19 ft.lb. On the 1597 engine, torque the bolts to 14–17 ft.lb. in the order shown for that engine.

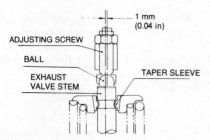

**Position of valve actuating ball and offset of rocker arms—1600 and 1970 engines**

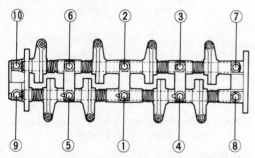

**Torque sequence for rocker assembly bolts on the 1998 engine**

## Thermostat

### REMOVAL AND INSTALLATION

#### Piston Engines

1. Drain several quarts of coolant from the radiator so that the coolant level is below the thermostat.

2. Disconnect the radiator hose from the thermostat housing. On the 1597 engine, disconnect the electrical connector going to the coolant temperature sensor in the housing.

3. Remove the thermostat housing mounting bolts, housing, gasket and thermostat.

4. Clean all gasket surfaces. Install the new thermostat with the temperature sensing pellet downwards or inside the block. On the 1998 gas and diesel engines, install the thermostat gasket with the printed side of the gasket facing the thermostat. Also, on all models, make sure the thermostat goes into the head or manifold before the gasket goes on. Use a new mounting gasket and install the housing.

5. The rest of the installation is in the reverse order of removal.

#### Rotary Engines

1. Drain the engine coolant.

2. Remove the thermostat housing and the thermostat.

3. Installation is the reverse of removal.

CAUTION: *The thermostat is equipped with a plunger which covers and uncovers a by-pass hole at its bottom. Because of this unusual construction, only the specified Mazda thermostat, or one specifically and accurately designed for this particular application, should be used for replacement. A standard thermostat will cause the engine to overheat. You should examine any replacement unit you use and assure yourself that it will work properly.*

## Intake Manifold

### REMOVAL AND INSTALLATION

#### Rotary Engine

To remove the intake manifold and carburetor assembly, with the engine remaining in the automobile, proceed in the following manner:

1. Perform Steps 2, 3, 4, 5, 7, and 13 of Engine Removal and Installation, above. Do not remove the engine.

2. Perform Steps 1, 2, 3, and 4 of Engine Disassembly, above.

3. Install the intake manifold and carburetor assembly in the reverse order of removal. Tighten the manifold securing nuts working from the inside out, and in two or three stages, to specification.

#### Piston Engine

1. Drain the cooling system and remove the air cleaner. On fuel injected engines, remove the crossover pipe. On turbocharged engines, remove the turbo compressor discharge line leading to the throttle body.

2. Disconnect: throttle and choke linkage; fuel line(s); PCV valve hose; heater hoses; distributor vacuum line; ventilation valve hose (at the manifold); air pump hose at the anti-afterburn valve.

3. Remove bolts attaching the manifold and remove it and the gasket from the head (on the

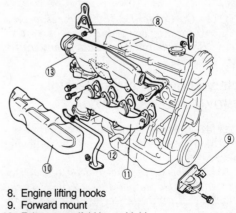

8. Engine lifting hooks
9. Forward mount
10. Exhaust manifold heat shield
11. Exhaust manifold
12. Air pump discharge line
13. Intake manifold

**Diesel intake and exhaust manifolds—exploded view**

diesel, an engine lifting hook will come off with the manifold).

4. Replace gaskets, make sure all surfaces are clean and smooth, and check manifold for warpage as described in the cylinder head overhaul procedures. Repair if necessary.

5. Install the manifold and tighten bolts gradually and in several stages, going from the center outward, to specifications.

6. Install auxiliaries in reverse of the above procedure. Refill the cooling system with engine idling.

## Piston Engine Exhaust Manifold

### REMOVAL AND INSTALLATION

NOTE: *On turbocharged engines, the turbo and exhaust manifold are removed as a unit. For exhaust manifold removal, see the Turbocharger Removal and Installation procedure below.*

1. Make sure engine is cold. Disconnect the inlet hose going to the anti-afterburn valve on the air injection manifold.

2. Disconnect the heat stove air pipe and remove the heat stove.

3. Disconnect the exhaust pipe or converter attaching nuts, and disconnect the exhaust pipe or converter.

4. Remove exhaust manifold attaching bolts, and remove the manifold and port liners.

5. Check the manifold for distortion as described under, Cylinder Head Overhaul and repair it as necessary.

6. Install manifold with new gaskets, and torque bolts in several stages, going from the center outwards. Torque to 16–21 ft.lb. on the 1,998 engine (16–20 on the diesel), 14–17 ft.lb. on the 1,490 engine, and 12–17 on the 1597 engine. Install auxiliaries in reverse of the above.

NOTE: *On California 1600 engines, a thermal reactor may be used in place of a manifold. Removal and installation procedures are the same.*

## Rotary Engine Thermal Reactor

### REMOVAL AND INSTALLATION

To remove the thermal reactor, which replaces the exhaust manifold, proceed in the following manner:

CAUTION: *The thermal reactor operates at extremely high temperatures. Allow the engine to cool completely before attempting its removal.*

1. Remove the air cleaner assembly from the carburetor.

2. Unbolt and remove the air injection pump, as outlined in, Emission Control.

3. Remove the intake manifold assembly, complete with the carburetor. See the section above.

4. Remove the heat stove from the thermal reactor.

5. Unfasten the thermal reactor securing nuts.

NOTE: *The bottom nut is difficult to reach. Mazda makes a special wrench (part number 49 213 001) to remove it. If the wrench is unavailable, a flexible drive metric socket wrench may be substituted.*

6. Lift the thermal reactor away from the engine.

7. Installation of the thermal reactor is performed in the reverse order of removal.

## Diesel Injection Pump and Lines

### REMOVAL AND INSTALLATION

This procedure is covered in detail in Chapter 4, Emission Controls and Fuel System.

## Turbocharger

### REMOVAL AND INSTALLATION

CAUTION: *This work should be performed with the engine cold.*

1. Drain the cooling system. Turn the engine over until it is at TDC with the engine in No. 1 firing position. Use the front timing marks, and remove the distributor cap to check the position of the rotor to do this. Note or mark their locations and then remove the high tension wires. Remove the distributor mounting bolt and remove the distributor.

2. Loosen the clamps and remove the hose leading from the air cleaner to the turbo compressor intake. Do the same for the duct leading from the compressor discharge to the intake manifold.

3. Remove the thin secondary air injection pipe from the exhaust manifold. Remove the lower insulator cover from around the turbocharger turbine (the exhaust side of the unit).

4. Remove the thicker secondary air injection pipe from the exhaust manifold. Remove the oil supply line from the turbocharger. Disconnect the oil drain line.

5. Remove the insulator from the top of the exhaust manifold. Remove the EGR pipe.

6. Disconnect and remove the turbo cooling water hoses. Disconnect the oxygen sensor and then remove it.

7. Disconnect the front exhaust pipe at the catalytic converter and support it. Remove the bolts attaching the turbo mounting bracket to the turbo.

8. Support the manifold, remove the manifold mounting bolts, and then remove the manifold, turbocharger, and catalytic converter as

an assembly. Then, remove the attaching nuts and remove the converter from the turbo and the turbo from the manifold. Cover all openings in the turbo.

CAUTION: *Be careful to avoid dropping the turbocharger or handling it roughly. Be careful not to bend the wastegate actuator mounting and rod.*

9. Carefully clean all the gasket surfaces. Replace all the gaskets. Pour 25 cc of clean engine oil into the opening for the turbo oil line.

10. Install the turbo onto the exhaust manifold with a new gasket. Torque the attaching nuts to 23–32 ft.lb. Install the catalytic converter onto the manifold and tighten the attaching nuts. Install the exhaust manifold onto the block with new gaskets and torque the nuts to 16–21 ft.lb.

11. Install the remaining parts in reverse of the removal procedure. Before starting the engine, disconnect the negative wire at the coil. Then, crank the engine for 20 seconds to build up oil pressure. Reconnect the coil wire, but start the engine without applying throttle and idle it for 30 seconds to purge air from the turbo oil lines before power is applied. Check all parts for leaks and make repairs as necessary.

## Radiator

### REMOVAL AND INSTALLATION

#### Piston Engine

1. Drain the coolant from the radiator.
2. Remove the fan blades and shroud or disconnect the electric harness from the electric fan motor and remove the fan and cowling mount.
3. Remove the upper and lower hoses. Disconnect the transmission cooler lines, if equipped.
4. Remove the radiator mounting bolts and remove the radiator.
5. Install the radiator by reversing the removal procedure. Refer to Chapter 1 for coolant refill.

#### Rotary Engine

*1971–76*

1. Drain the engine coolant.
2. Remove the shroud.
3. Remove the upper, lower, and expansion tank hoses.
4. Remove the oil cooler.
5. Withdraw the radiator.
6. Install in the reverse order of removal.

*1977–78*

1. Drain the cooling system.
2. Remove the fan drive attaching bolts, and remove fan and fan drive as an assembly.

3. Loosen hose clamps, and disconnect inlet and outlet hoses and heater hose at radiator.
4. Disconnect oil cooler hoses at radiator, if the vehicle has an automatic transmission.
5. Remove oil cooler mounting brackets from the radiator. Remove radiator shroud from the radiator.
6. Remove mounting bolts, and remove the radiator.
7. To install, reverse the removal procedure.

## Water Pump

### REMOVAL AND INSTALLATION

#### Except Below

1. Drain the coolant from the radiator.
2. On GLC front wheel drive models, jack up the front of the car and safely support it on jackstands. Remove the splash shield. Remove the drive belt, lower hose and by-pass pipe with O-ring. Remove the water pump.
3. On other models, remove the air pump if interfering. Remove the fan from the fan pulley if not equipped with electric fan assembly. Loosen and remove the fan drive belt. Remove the radiator hose.
4. Loosen and remove the water pump mounting bolts, remove the water pump.
5. Clean all gasket surfaces. Mount the new water pump and gasket. Tighten the mounting bolts evenly in several stages. The rest of the installation is in the reverse order of removal.

#### 1,998 cc Engine

1. Set the crankshaft at TDC for No. 1 cylinder, and then remove the timing belt as described above.
2. Remove its mounting bolt and remove the timing chain tensioner spring and tensioner.
3. Drain the coolant and disconnect the water pump inlet pipe at the pump. Remove the gasket.
4. Remove the mounting bolts and remove the pump. Remove the gasket and seal.
5. To install use a new gasket and coat the seal with vegetable oil. Torque mounting bolts to 15 ft.lb. Reconnect the inlet pipe with a new gasket.
6. Install the timing belt tensioner with the bolt tightened only loosely and install the spring. Reinstall the timing belt as described above.
7. Fill the system with coolant, and operate the engine to check for leaks. Recheck the coolant level.

#### Rotary Engine 1971–75

1. Drain the engine coolant.
2. Remove the air cleaner.

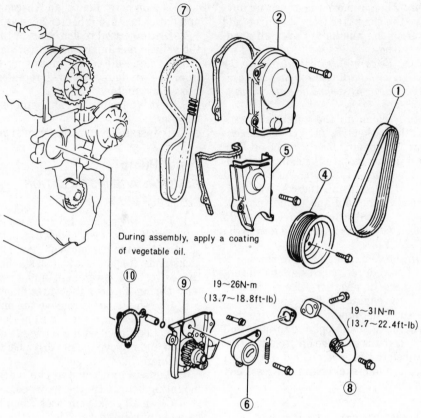

During assembly, apply a coating of vegetable oil.

19~26N-m
(13.7~18.8ft-lb)

19~31N-m
(13.7~22.4ft-lb)

1. V-ribbed belt (for alternator)
2. Timing belt cover (upper)
3. Splash shield
4. Crankshaft pulley
5. Timing belt cover (lower)
6. Tensioner
7. Timing belt
8. Inlet pipe
9. Water pump
10. Gasket

**1,998 cc engine water pump removal**

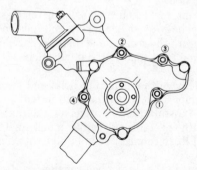

**Late model rotary engine water pump tightening sequence**

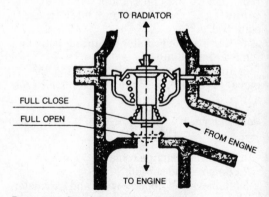

TO RADIATOR

FULL CLOSE

FULL OPEN

FROM ENGINE

TO ENGINE

**Rotary engine thermostat installation**

3. Loosen, but do not remove, the water pump pulley bolts.

4. Remove the alternator drivebelt.

5. Remove the water pump pulley.

6. Remove the pump.

7. Separate the pump body from the casing.

8. Installation is the reverse of removal.

**1976–78**

1. Drain the cooling system and remove the air cleaner.

2. Disconnect the water temperature sending unit.

3. Remove alternator and air pump and their belts.

4. Disconnect the upper radiator hose at the thermostat housing. Remove the upper fan shroud.

5. Remove the attaching bolts, and remove the fan and fan drive as an assembly.

6. Installation is in reverse order. Coat a new water pump gasket with sealer on both sides, and torque water pump attaching bolts, a little at a time, in the order shown to 13–20 ft.lb.

## Cylinder Head

### REMOVAL AND INSTALLATION

#### Gasoline Engines

Be sure that the cylinder head is cold before removal. This will prevent warpage. Do not remove the cam gear from the timing chain. The relationship between the chain and gear teeth should not be disturbed. Wire the chain and gear together.

1. Drain the cooling system.
2. Remove the air cleaner.
3. Disconnect all applicable electrical wires and leads.
4. Rotate the crankshaft to put the No. 1 cylinder at TDC on the compression stroke.
5. Remove the distributor.
6. Remove the rocker arm cover.
7. Raise and support the car. Disconnect the exhaust pipe from the manifold.
8. Remove the accelerator linkage.
9. Remove the nut, washer and the distributor gear from the camshaft, if equipped.
10. On the 1982 and later 626 with timing belt, remove the upper timing belt cover. Then, disconnect and remove the tensioning spring for the timing belt tensioner (use brake pliers, if necessary). Loosen the tensioner lock bolt until it is just finger tight. Front wheel drive (1490cc); remove the tensioner from the timing case cover. On all models remove the nut and washer and disconnect the camshaft gear from the camshaft. Support the timing chain so the tensioner will not come apart. On the front wheel drive 1490 cc GLC, even though the tensioner has been removed, you still must support the camshaft sprocket so the timing relationship between the chain links and upper and lower sprockets will not be lost. On the 626, be sure to support the camshaft sprocket so belt timing will not be lost.
11. On 1983 and later 626, first remove the rocker assembly bolts in sequence, in several stages. Remove the cylinder head bolts in several stages, reversing the torquing sequence or using the sequence shown. Remove the cylin-

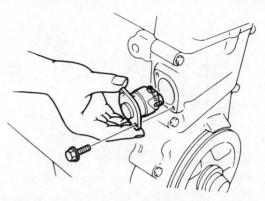

**Removing the tensioner. GLC front wheel drive models**

der head-to-front cover bolt, where so equipped.

12. Remove the rocker arm assembly.
13. Remove the camshaft.
14. Lift off the cylinder head.
15. Remove all tension from the timing chain, if necessary.
16. Check the cylinder head for warpage, as shown, by running a straightedge diagonally across the cylinder head and across either end, and attempting to insert a feeler gauge between the head surface and the straightedge. Permissible limit is 0.006″ (0.15mm). If distortion exceeds the limit, grind the head with a surface grinder.
17. Installation is the reverse of removal. Coat all the camshaft bearing surfaces with engine oil before installing it (that is, cylinder head and cap or bearing insert inner surfaces, and camshaft journal surfaces). Be sure to torque head bolts in proper sequence in several stages. On the 626 for 1982 and later, head bolts are torqued first, and then the rocker shaft assembly is installed and torqued in sequence and in several stages. Note the proper location of the oil hole on this model engine. It must be on the intake valve side. On 1983–84 626, coat the surfaces of the head at either end of the rocker assembly with sealer, as shown.

**Checking cylinder head for warpage**

Cylinder head torque sequence—all piston engines through 1980, 626—'81–'82

Cylinder head bolt loosening sequence—1981–84 GLC

Cylinder head bolt tightening sequence—1981–84 GLC

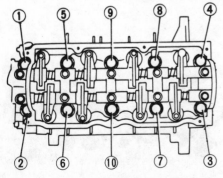

Cylinder head loosening sequence—1983 and later 626

On the GLC, and on the 626 engine up to 1982, the head bolts must not be tightened until the rocker assembly is positioned properly. Slide the rocker assembly to one side until the rocker adjusting studs are offset 0.04″ (1mm) from the centers of the valve stems. This is necessary for proper valve rotation. Then, torque the bolts.

**Diesel**

NOTE: *To perform this procedure, you will need two bolts size M8 x 1.25 x 45mm, a wheel puller with a selection of bolts with metric threads, and plastic caps or another appropriate means to seal off fuel injection line openings.*

1. Disconnect the negative battery cable. Disconnect the air cleaner hose at the intake manifold.

2. Drain the coolant by opening the radiator drain plug. Then, disconnect the following hoses/electrical connectors at the cylinder head:

   a. Heater outlet hose at the oil cooler.

   b. Upper radiator hose at both ends.

   c. Fuel supply and return hoses at the injection pump (and plug or cap the hoses and pump openings, once disconnected.)

   d. Temperature gauge sending unit electrical connector.

   e. Glow plug electrical connector.

   f. Engine ground strap.

3. Disconnect the exhaust pipe at the exhaust manifold. Then, remove the right side splash shield.

4. Remove the drive belts. Remove the attaching bolts and remove the cam cover and gasket.

5. Remove the rear timing belt mechanism as described below under Timing Belt Removal and Installation.

6. Put an open-end wrench on the flats of the camshaft to keep it from turning and loosen the camshaft rear pulley mounting bolt. Then, remove the pulley with a puller. Screw M8 x 1.25 x 45mm bolts into the rear seal plate so they pass through the two holes in the injection pump drive pulley. Remove the pulley lockbolt, and then remove the pulley and woodruff key.

7. Remove the tensioner, spring and lockbolt for the rear timing belt mechanism. Then, remove the rear seal plate.

8. Moving to the front timing belt mechanism, remove the right timing belt cover. Remove the top bolt from the left timing belt cover.

9. Turn the crankshaft to align the mark on the front camshaft pulley with the mark on the front seal plate. Then, turn the crankshaft 45° ahead, as shown.

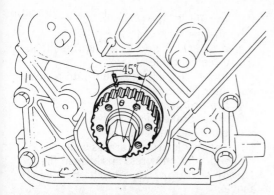

Turn the (diesel) crankshaft until the timing marks line up; then, turn it 45 degrees to the right, as shown. This is done at the injection pump end of the engine. In this position, the cylinder head can be removed or replaced without damaging the pistons or valves.

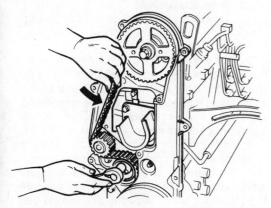

Loosen the timing belt tensioner lockbolt, depress the belt in the direction shown, and then retighten the lockbolt (diesel)

10. Loosen the tensioner lockbolt, and depress the timing belt toward the center of the engine. Hold the belt in the depressed position and then retighten the lockbolt.

11. Install a wrench onto the camshaft pulley and turn the pulley gently counterclockwise and hold it there in order to make it easier to remove the belt. Remove the belt.

12. Install a large, open-end wrench onto the camshaft flats and then loosen the camshaft pulley bolt and remove it. Discard the pulley lockbolt, as it must be replaced with a new one when the camshaft is reinstalled. Remove the pulley with a puller.

NOTE: *Do not attempt to hammer the pulley or camshaft to remove the pulley.*

13. Remove the front seal lockplate bolts and remove the lockplate and seals. Refer to Camshaft Removal and Installation below for proper seal removal procedures.

14. If you will probably be working on the valves or prechambers, remove the camshaft

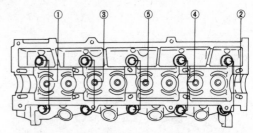

Loosen the diesel cylinder head bolts in the order shown

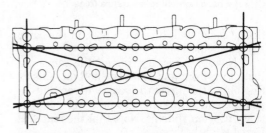

Check the flatness of the diesel cylinder head in the directions shown

cap bolts and the camshaft at this time (see the appropriate procedure below). Otherwise, remove the cylinder head mounting bolts, turning them a little at a time in the numbered order in several passes. Remove the cylinder head.

15. Thoroughly clean the block and head surfaces, being careful not to damage either surface.

16. Check the cylinder head for warpage, as shown, by running a straightedge diagonally across the cylinder head and across either end, and attempting to insert a feeler gauge between the head surface and the straightedge. Permissible limit is 0.004″ (0.1mm). If distortion exceeds the limit, replace the head.

NOTE: *Do not grind the head with a surface grinder!*

17. Supply a new head gasket, properly positioned, onto the block. Make sure the crankshaft is still positioned as described in Step 9. Then, put the cylinder head into position on the block.

18. Measure the length of every head bolt from the lower surface of the cap to the lower end of the bolt. If the length exceeds 4.5079″ (114.5mm) replace the bolt. Oil the threads on all the bolts you are going to use with engine oil.

19. Install the bolts just finger tight.

20. Torque the head bolts to 21.7 ft.lb. in the numbered sequence. Paint or punch a mark on the outer surface of the bolt head. Then, in the same sequence, turn each bolt 90°–105°. When

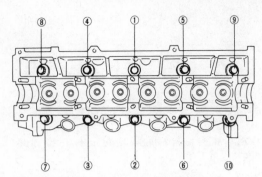

**Cylinder head tightening sequence (diesel)**

this is completed, turn each bolt, in the same sequence, another 90°–105°.

21. Now, if necessary, install the camshaft. Install the front and rear camshaft oil seals by first oiling the lips of the seals with engine oil, and then installing them by pressing on either side with your thumbs. Note that the rear seal is just slightly larger.

22. Install the front camshaft pulley with its woodruff key onto the camshaft. Hold the camshaft in position, using a wrench on the flats, and then install a new pulley lockbolt, torquing it to 41-48 ft.lb. Turn the camshaft to align the mark on the pulley with the mark on the front seal plate at about 2 o'clock).

23. Remove the cover for the inspection hole from the clutch housing. Then, turn the crankshaft back to Top Dead Center, as marked on the flywheel.

24. Install, time, and tension the timing belt as described below, under, Timing Belt Removal and Installation. Install the top bolt for the left side belt cover (removed in Step 8). Install the right side timing belt cover.

25. Install the rear seal plate. Install the fuel injection pump pulley with its woodruff key. Then, rotate the pulley until the mark on the pulley aligns with the mark on the rear seal plate. Install the two bolts used in removal, and then install the pulley bolt at torque it to 43-51 ft.lb. Leave the bolts in place.

26. Install the rear camshaft pulley and woodruff key onto the camshaft. Hold the camshaft in place, using a wrench on the flats, and install the lockbolt, torquing to 41-48 ft.lb. Install and tension the rear timing belt as described below under, Rear Timing Belt Removal and Installation. Check the valve clearance and adjust as necessary (see the appropriate procedure in Chapter Two).

27. Perform the remaining steps in reverse of the removal procedure.

323

1. Disconnnect the negative battery cable and drain the cooling system. Remove or disconnect the following parts:

a. the air cleaner.
b. oil dipstick.
c. accelerator and (if so equipped) the cruise control cable.
d. fuel hoses, draining fuel into a metal container. Then, plug them.
e. heater hoses.
f. power brake vacuum hose.
g. emissions canister hoses.
h. engine electrical harness connectors.
i. high tension wires (mark them first).
j. distributor (refer to the procedure above).
k. spark plugs.
l. secondary air piping (at the carburetor).
m. front engine hanger and the ground wire nearby.
n. upper radiator hose and the water by-pass hose and bracket.
o. intake and exhaust manifolds (see appropriate procedures elsewhere).
p. engine side cover.

2. Remove the timing belt covers as described below. Turn the crankshaft over until the matchmarks on the camshaft and crankshaft pulleys are aligned with the corresponding marks on the cylinder block. Then, remove the timing belt as described below.

3. If you will be removing the camshaft or doing other major work on the cylinder head itself, remove the camshaft sprocket. Use a screwdriver to hold it in position and unscrew the retaining bolt. Then, pull the sprocket off the camshaft.

4. Remove the rear engine hanger from the cylinder head.

5. If you will be removing the camshaft or doing other major work on the cylinder head itself, remove the rocker shaft assembly as described above.

6. Loosen the cylinder head bolts in the sequence shown, in several stages. Remove the head bolts. Then, lift off the head and head gasket.

7. Clean both sealing surfaces. Inspect the

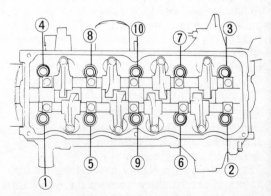

**Cylinder head loosening sequence (323 1597 engine)**

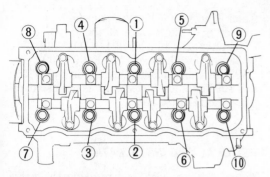

**Cylinder head tightening sequence (323 1597 engine)**

| Year | Engine | Intake | Exhaust |
|---|---|---|---|
| 1975–78 | 1600 | 1.7256 in. | 1.7592 in. |
| 1976 | 1300 | 1.7290 in. | 1.7290 in. |
| 1977 | 1300 | 1.7288 in. | 1.7288 in. |
| 1978 | 1300 | 1.7290 in. | 1.7290 in. |
| 1979–80 | 1415 | 1.7291 in. | 1.7291 in. |
| 1979–80 | 1970 | 1.7731 in. | 1.7784 in. |
| 1981–82 | 1970 | 1.7731 in. | 1.7718 in. |
| 1981–85 | 1490 | 1.7289 in. | 1.7289 in. |
| 1983–85 | 1998 | 1.4943 in. | 1.4945 in. |
| 1985 (Diesel) | 1998 | 1.728 | 1.768 |
| 1986 | 1998 | 1.4961 | 1.4961 |
| 1986 | 1597 | 1.4329 | 1.4329 |

cylinder head for warping or other damage as described immediately below.

8. Install the head gasket with all oil and water passages and bolt holes matching up.

9. Install the head into position. Install the head bolts finger tight. Then, torque the cylinder head bolts to 63–67 ft.lb. in three stages, using the numerical sequence shown.

10. Install the camshaft pulley onto the end of the camshaft with the dowel pin and key way in proper positions and the matchmark straight up. Install the retaining bolt and torque it to 36–45 ft.lb.

11. Perform the remaining installation steps in reverse of the removal procedure. Note the following points:

a. Install and adjust the timing belt as described below.

b. Install the rocker assembly according to the torque sequence and torque figures in the procedure for removing and installing it, above.

c. Torque intake and exhaust manifold bolts to specification.

d. Note that the distributor rotor should point near No. 1 cylinder and that the drive blade should then be aligned with the oil hole on the base of the distributor prior to attempting to engage the distributor drive gear with the corresponding gear on the camshaft.

e. Adjust the valves as described in Chapter 2.

f. Lay a coating of sealer along the groove in the camshaft cover before installing the gasket, and torque the bolts to 43–78 in.lb.

g. Make sure to replenish all fluids and check for leaks right after starting the engine.

## CLEANING AND INSPECTION

1. Check the cylinder head for distortion as described in the cylinder head removal and installation procedure above. Inspect water passages to make sure they are fully open and, if necessary, hot tank head in a solution that is compatible with aluminum to clean them. Repair or replace any damaged threads or broken studs.

2. Check the intake and exhaust manifolds for distortion with a straightedge, or by placing them against a surface plate. The limit is 0.006″ (0.15mm), (0.004″ [0.1mm] diesel). Regrind the surface of the manifold if excessive distortion is found.

3. Check clearance between rocker arms and shafts with rockers assembled to shafts. Limit is 0.004″ (0.1mm). Replace rocker or shaft, depending on characteristics of the wear (e.g., if all clearances are wide on the rocker shaft, replace the shaft; if clearance is wide under only one rocker, replace rocker, etc.).

4. Inspect the camshaft cam faces and bearing journals for roughness or obvious excessive wear. Measure the cam height with a micrometer. It should be:

Replace the camshaft if it is obviously worn

| Year | Engine | Front | Center | Rear |
|---|---|---|---|---|
| 1975–78 | 1600 | 1.7675 in. | 1.7671 in. | 1.7675 in. |
| 1976–78 | 1300 | 1.6516 in. | 1.6516 in. | 1.6516 in. |
| 1979–80 | 1415 | 1.6516 in. | 1.6516 in. | 1.6516 in. |
| 1979–82 | 1970 | 1.7695 in. | 1.7691 in. | 1.7695 in. |
| 1981–84 | 1490 | 1.6495 in. | 1.6431 in. | 1.6495 in. |
| 1985 | 1490 | 1.6515 | 1.6500 | 1.6515 |
| 1983 | 1998 | 1.255 in. | 1.254 in.① | 1.255 in. |
| 1984–86 | 1998 | 1.2575 | 1.2563 | 1.2575 |
| 1985 | Diesel | 1.254 | 1.254 | 1.254 |
| 1986 | 1597 | 1.7103 | 1.6870 | 1.7103 |

① Applies to three center journals

or damaged or if cam height is worn beyond limits.

5. Measure camshaft bearing journals with a micrometer. Wear limits are:

The cam journals should also be measured at 90° angles to determine elliptical wear. Subtract the smaller reading from the larger. The limit is 0.020″ (0.5mm). On 1300, 1490, 1998, and 1597 cc engines, camshaft must be replaced if worn beyond limits. On 1600 and 1970 cc engines, the journals may be ground and undersize bearings may be installed.

6. Check camshaft runout with a dial indicator, taking the measurement at the center bearing. Limit is 0.0012″ (0.03mm).

7. Check camshaft bearing clearance. This is done by installing Plastigage® inserts, which will then flatten out according to the bearing clearance when the camshaft bearing caps are torqued to specification. You can read the clearance by then removing the rocker assembly and inserts and reading them according to package directions.

• Torque rocker assembly bolts to 56–60 ft.lb. on all engines except the 1,998. On that engine torque them to 13–19 ft.lb.

• Torque the diesel engine camshaft bearing caps to 15–20 ft.lb.

• Clearance should be 0.0007–0.0027″ (0.01778–0.06858mm) for front and rear bearings and 0.0011–0.0031″ (0.028–0.079mm) for the center bearing on the 1600 and 1970 engines which use bearing inserts. On the 1490 engine, the clearance limit is 0.0059″ (0.15mm). On the 1,998 gasoline engine, clearance should be 0.0014–0.0033″ (0.035–0.084mm) on bearings 1 and 5 (at either end) and 0.0026–0.0045″ (0.066–0.114mm) on bearings 2 and 4. On the 1998 diesel, clearance should be 0.0014–0.0033″ (0.035–0.084mm) for the front and rear bearings and 0.0026–0.0045″ (0.066–0.114mm) for the three center bearings.

• On the 1597 engine, you must measure the outside diameter of the cam journals and use an inside diameter micrometer to measure the inside diameters of the bearing bores (these are integral with the cylinder head). Subtract the smaller figure from the larger to get the clearance. Normal limits are 0.0014–0.0033″ (0.035–0.084mm) for the front and rear bearings and 0.0026–0.0045″ (0.066–0.114mm) for the center bearings. Maximum dimension is 0.0059″ (0.15mm) for all bearings.

• Except on the 1600 and 1970 engines, which have replaceable bearings, if the cam is within limits and the clearance is still excessive, the cylinder head assembly and rocker assembly must be replaced.

8. Measure camshaft endplay by inserting a feeler gauge between the camshaft sprocket surface and the surface of the thrust plate. Clearance should be 0.001–0.007″ (0.0254–0.178mm) for all except the 1,490, 1,597, and 1,998cc engines; 0.008″ (0.2mm) on 1490, 1597 and 1998 engines. If clearance is excessive, replace the thrust plate.

## Valves

### REMOVAL AND INSTALLATION

Valves are removed by depressing the valve spring caps with a special tool. Mazda has a special tool set Valve Spring Lifter and Pivot No. 49 0636 100A and 49 G030 222, but this is a standard device that should be available at any well-equipped auto store.

The bottom of the tool rests against the valve head and the top rests against the valve spring cap. The tool is screwed down or

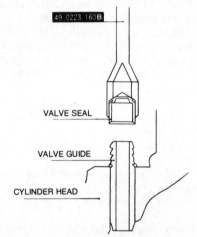

**Replacing the valve seal on the 1600 engine—The procedure is for all the other engines is the same, but the special tool is numbered 49 0223 160C**

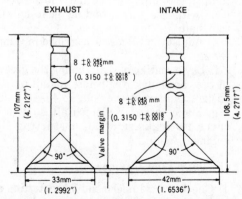

**Valve face angles and dimensions—1600 and 1970 cc engines**

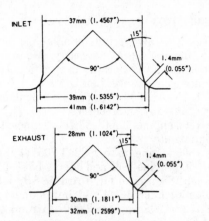

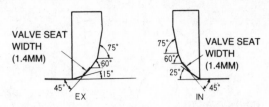

**Valve seat grinding angles and dimensions—1998 gas engine**

**Valve seat angles and dimensions—1600 and 1970 cc engines**

clamped with an actuating lever to depress the valve spring until two keepers, fitted into a groove in the valve head, can be removed. Remove the keepers and then slowly release spring tension. In installation, the valve is assembled into the head and the spring and cap are put into position. The tool depresses the spring via the cap until the keeper groove is fully exposed. The keepers are then positioned in the groove (make sure they are securely fitted all the way into the groove), and the tension is then released so the spring cap will lock the keepers in place.

## INSPECTION

Remove all carbon from the valves and inspect for warpage, cracks, or excessive burning. On the diesel, inspect the valves for stem wear, bending (of the stem in relation to the head), mechanical damage, or dents of any kind. Replace valves that cannot be cleaned up and refaced without removal of an excessive amount of metal. Measure stem diameter at three places, and check stem-to-guide clearance with the valve in the guide using a dial indicator. On the diesel, you must measure stem diameter and the inner diameter of the corresponding guide and subtract to determine the clearance. The limit is 0.004″ (0.1mm). Replace the guide and valve if stem-to-guide clearance is excessive, replace the valve if stem diameter is under specification, but a new valve will provide proper stem-to-guide clearance.

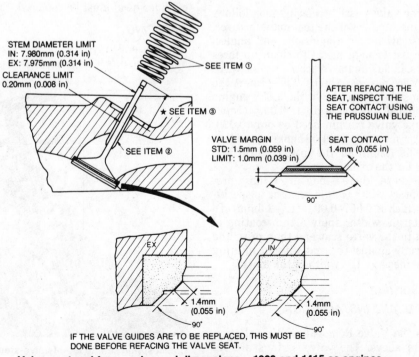

**Valve seat and face angles and dimensions—1300 and 1415 cc engines**

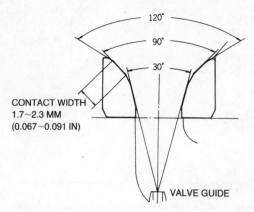

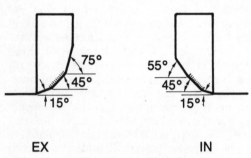

**Valve seat grinding angles and dimensions—1998 diesel**

EX            IN

**Valve seat grinding angles and dimensions—1597 engine**

### REFACING

Reface the valves with a refacing tool, following the instructions of the tool manufacturer. See illustrations for dimensions and angles. Remove just enough metal to clean up faces and seats. If, during the refacing process, valve margin becomes less then 0.039″ (1mm) the valve must be replaced. On the 1,998 engine only, exhaust valve margin is 0.039″ (1mm) but intake valve margin need be only 0.020″ (0.5mm) or more. On the 1,597 engine, the limit is 0.039″ (1mm) for the intake and 0.051″ (1.3mm) for the exhaust.

On the diesel, there is no margin limit, provided contact width can be brought to specification, which is 0.067–0.091″ (1.7–2.3mm). To check margin width, apply a thin coating of red lead to the valve seat and then press the valve firmly against the seat without rotating it. Then, measure the width of the mark.

## Valve Springs
### REMOVAL AND INSTALLATION

Refer to the Valve Removal and Installation procedure above. The valve springs are removed along with the valves.

### INSPECTION

Inspect the valve springs for breakage or corrosion and replace as necessary. Measure the free length for conformity to specification and replace as necessary. Limits are:
- 1970 and 1600 engine: 1.449″ (36.8mm) inner, 1.469″ (37.3mm) outer
- 1300 engine: 1.406″ (35.7mm) inner, 1.539″ (39mm) outer
- 1500 engine up to 1982: 1.705″ (43.3mm)
- 1500 engine 1983 and later: 1.654″ (42mm)
- 1998 engine through 1985: 1.984″ (50.4mm) outer, 1.744″ (44.3mm) inner
- 1986 1998 engine: 2.000″ (51mm) outer, 1.681″ (42.7mm) inner
- diesel: 1.764″ (44.8mm)
- 1597 engine: 1.673 in.″ (42.5mm)

On some engines, the spring should also be checked for straightness. Sit it flat next to a perpendicular surface and rotate the spring until there is a maximum gap between the top of the spring and the perpendicular. Then, measure that distance. The limit is:
- 1998 engine: 0.066″ (16.7mm)
- diesel: 0.062″ (15.7mm)
- 1597 engine: 0.055″ (14mm)

## Valve Seats
### REMOVAL AND INSTALLATION

While some Mazda engines use pressed-in seats, none are replaceable. If seats cannot be machined to restore proper dimensions, the cylinder head must be replaced.

### REFACING

If valve seats have cracks, burrs, or ridges, or angles and dimensions are not correct, remove

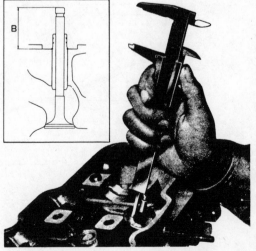

**Check spring seat to top-of-valve-stem dimension ("B") with vernier calipers as shown**

the minimum amount of metal that will correct them with a valve seat grinder. See the appropriate illustration for dimensions. Note that seat grinding must be done after valve guide replacement, where it is required. Contact of valve and seat must be checked by applying Prussian Blue dye to seat, seating valve, and then repeatedly reseating the valve while rotating it. If the dye marking on the valve is uneven, the valve must be lapped in.

When valve/seat machining has been performed, it is necessary to check the distance between the valve spring seat on the cylinder head and the top of the valve stem so that adequate spring tension is assured. Check dimension using vernier calipers as shown. Standard dimensions are:

- 1970 and 1600: intake 1.59″ (40.4mm), exhaust 1.48″ (37.6mm)
- 1300 and 1500: 1.555″ (39.5mm)
- 1,998: 1.831″ (46.5mm)

If this dimension is exceeded by more than 0.020″ (0.5mm), shims must be inserted on the spring seat so as to bring the dimension to within the dimension. If the dimension is greater than 0.069″ (1.8mm), replace the valve. On the 1,597 engine, the head can be used as-is if the dimension is 1.555–1.575″ (39.5–40mm). If the dimension is 1.575–1.614″ (40–41mm), shim the spring so that the total dimension is 1.555–1.575″ (39.5–40mm). If the dimension is beyond 1.614″ (41mm), replace the head.

On the diesel, valve recession below the height of the cylinder head deck is measured with the valve in its installed position. Place a straightedge across the center of the valve head diameter and then attempt to slide a flat feeler gauge of appropriate thickness under the straightedge. If the gauge fits without a great deal of pressure, valve recession is excessive. The limits are 0.030–0.041″ (0.762–1.041mm) for both intake and exhaust valves. If the recession dimension is 0.0610–0.100″ (1.55–2.54mm), you may re-use the cylinder head, but a washer of a thickness sufficient to compensate for the recession must be used under the valve spring. For example, if the recession were 0.090″ (2.3mm), you would use a washer of 0.090″ (2.3mm) minus 0.035″ (0.889mm) for a thickness of 0.055″ (1.4mm). If recession exceeds 0.100″ (2.54mm), the cylinder head must be replaced.

## Valve Guides

### REMOVAL AND INSTALLATION

Press out valve guides that require replacement with a valve guide removing tool and hammer. Press in a new guide in a similar manner, stopping when the rim on the guide

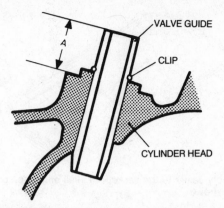

**Dimension "A" should be .752–.772 in. on the 1,998 engine**

touches the head. Be sure to hit the end of the tool as squarely as possible. Install a new seal onto replaced guides with a special tool. Note that on the 1,490 (GLC) engine, intake and exhaust valve guides are different. On the 1,998 (626 from '83) engine, guides originally used are different, but you should use exhaust type guides for replacement on both sides.

On the 1,998, both gas and diesel, install clips and then install the guide so the clip just touches the head. On the gas version only, dimension, A, from the valve spring seating surface to the top of the head should be 0.752–0.772″ (19–19.5mm). On the 1597, this dimension must be 0.520–0.543″ (13.2–13.8mm). Note that on the diesel, the longer type guide goes on the intake side, and the shorter on the exhaust side. Do not mix them up!

## Oil Pan

### REMOVAL AND INSTALLATION

#### Piston Engines

1. Jack up the front of the car and safely support on jackstands. Disconnect negative battery cable. Remove the engine splash shield or skid plate. On the diesel, remove the left front wheel and splash shield and then remove the crossmember.

2. Remove the clutch slave cylinder, if equipped. Do not disconnect the hydraulic line; let the cylinder hang.

3. Remove the engine rear brace attaching bolts and loosen the bolts on the left side, if equipped.

4. Disconnect the emission line from the oil pan, if equipped.

5. Loosen the front motor mounts, raise the front of the engine and block up to gain clearance if necessary. (Except GLC and other front wheel drive cars).

6. On front wheel drive cars, loosen the bolts

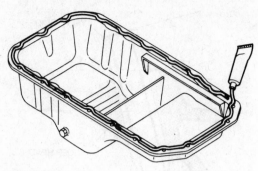

**Apply sealer to the gasketless 1998 engine oil pan, as shown**

attaching the exhaust pipe to the manifold and lower the pipe; also, disconnect the engine torque brace. On the 626, disconnect the No. 3 engine mount, located near the driver's side of the pan. On the diesel, also remove the lower clutch or torque converter cover and then remove the coolant return pipe, located under the pan.

7. On the 1597 engine, remove the stiffening strips that go under the oil pan bolts. Remove the oil pan and allow it to rest on the crossmember. Remove the oil pump pickup tube, if necessary, to remove the oil pan.

8. Install in the reverse order of removal. On late model 1998 engines, there is no gasket. Apply a gasket forming sealant as shown in the illustration before installing the pan, and make sure to install and toruqe the pan bolts within 30 minutes. On other cars, apply sealer to the joints between the front cover and the block and the rear main seal housing and the block.

### Rotary Engine

1. Drain engine oil. Remove attaching bolts, and remove the gravel shield.

2. Disconnect the oil level sensor and, if so equipped, the oil temperature sending unit.

3. Remove oil pan bolts and remove the pan.

4. Coat both sides of a new gasket with a sealer before installing the pan. Install bolts and torque to 5–7 ft.lb. Reverse the remaining removal procedures.

## Oil Pump

### REMOVAL AND INSTALLATION

#### 1490cc GLC w/Front Wheel Drive up to 1980 1600 and 1970 cc Engines

Remove the oil pan. Remove the oil pump gear attaching nut. Remove the bolts attaching the oil pump to the block. Loosen the gear on the pump. Remove the oil pump and gear.

#### 1981–84 1490 Engine

1. Unbolt and remove the oil pan. Then, remove the oil pump mounting bolts, disengage the drive chain, and remove the pump.

2. The drive gear will have to be pressed off the pump shaft using a suitable support for the gear and a press that will develop as much as 3,000 lbs. pressure.

3. Once the gear has been removed, remove the bolts and separate the pump cover from the body.

4. To assemble the pump, proceed in reverse order. The gear must be pressed back on until its outer edge is flush with the outer end of the shaft. A press that can measure the pressure must be used and pressure must be 1540–2860 lbs. or the gear and/or shaft must be replaced. Make sure the timing marks on inner and outer rotors are aligned.

#### 1300, 1415 and 1490 cc GLC Wagon

1. Remove the front cover as described below.

2. Remove oil pump drive sprocket retaining nut and lockwasher. Slide both oil pump drive sprockets and drive chain off crankshaft and oil pump shaft.

3. Remove oil pump cover, and pull out pump shaft and rotors.

4. Installation is the reverse of the removal procedure. Oil pump drive sprocket retaining nut is torqued to 22–25 ft.lb.

#### 1,998 cc Engine

1. Turn the engine so that No.1 cylinder is at TDC. Remove the timing belt cover as described below. Then, remove the timing belt as described above. Then, remove the retaining bolt and, with a puller, remove the lower timing belt sprocket.

2. Jack up and support the vehicle on safety stands. Remove the oil pan as described above.

3. Remove the pickup tube and tube brace mounting bolts and remove the pickup tube. Then, remove the pump mounting bolts and pump body from the front of the engine.

4. Gears may be inspected and removed after removing the screws and pump cover plate.

5. Install in reverse order, noting the following points.

   a. Coat the O-ring with grease and install it over the oil hole at the top right of the pump, viewed from the rear. Coat all sealing surfaces that touch the front of the block with sealer. Keep sealant out of the oil passages.

   b. Torque pump body mounting bolts to 15 ft.lb.

323

1. Remove the front cover and timing belt as described below. Remove the bolt at the center of the lower timing belt sprocket and remove the sprocket and key.

2. Remove the oil pan as described above. Unbolt and remove the oil strainer and its gasket. Remove the four bolts from the oil pump housing (lower front of the block) and remove it.

3. Install the assembly in reverse order, torquing the pump bolts to 14–19 ft.lb. and the pan bolts to 6–6.5 ft.lb.

## Rotary Engine Metering Oil Pump
### OPERATION

A metering oil pump, mounted on the top of the engine, is used to provide additional lubrication to the engine when it is operating under a load. The pump provides oil to the carburetor, where it is mixed in the float chamber with the fuel which is to be burned.

The metering pump is a plunger type and is controlled by throttle opening. A cam arrangement, connected to the carburetor throttle lever, operates a plunger. The plunger, in turn, acts on a differential plunger, the stroke of which determines the amount of oil flow.

When the throttle opening is small, the amount of the plunger stroke is small; as the throttle opening increases, so does the amount of the plunger stroke.

### TESTING

1. Disconnect the oil lines which run from the metering oil pump to the carburetor, at the carburetor end.

2. Use a container which has a scale calibrated in cubic centimeters (cc) to catch the pump discharge from the oil lines.
NOTE: *Such a container is available from a scientific equipment supply house.*

3. Run the engine at 2,000 rpm for six minutes.

4. At the end of this time, 2.4–2.9 cc of oil should be collected in the container on vehicles built up to 1976, and 2.0–2.5 cc on 1977 and later vehicles. If not, adjust the pump as explained below.

### ADJUSTMENTS

Rotate the adjusting screw on the metering oil pump to obtain the proper oil flow. Clockwise rotation of the screw increases the flow; counterclockwise rotation decreases the oil flow. After adjustment is completed, tighten the locknut.

If necessary, on 1971–76 vehicles, the oil dis-

Arrow indicates metering oil pump adjusting screw

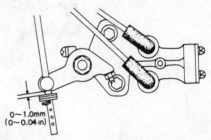
0~1.0mm
(0~0.04 in)

**Checking metering oil pump lever-to-washer clearance**

charge rate may further be adjusted by changing the position of the cam in the pump connecting rod. The shorter the rod throw the more oil will be pumped. Adjust the throw by means of the three holes provided.

On 1977 and later vehicles, after adjusting the adjusting screw, check the clearance between the pump lever and washer as shown, and if necessary, install washer(s) to create the proper clearance.

## Rotary Engine Oil Cooler
### REMOVAL AND INSTALLATION

1. Raise the car and support it with jackstands.
CAUTION: *Be sure that the car is securely supported.*

2. Drain the engine oil.

3. Unfasten the screw which retain the gravel shield and remove the shield.

4. Unfasten the oil lines from the oil cooler.

5. Unfasten the nuts which secure the oil cooler to the radiator.

6. Remove the oil cooler.

7. Examine the oil cooler for signs of leakage. Solder any leaks found. Blow the fins of the cooler clean with compressed air.

8. Installation is performed in the reverse order of removal

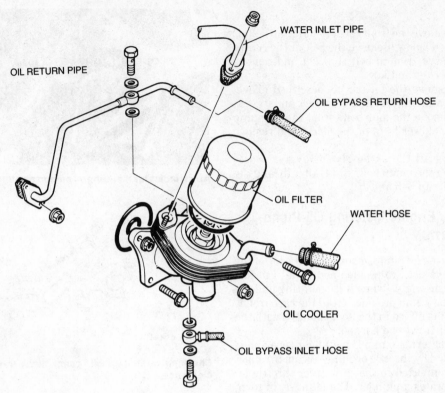

OIL RETURN PIPE

WATER INLET PIPE

OIL BYPASS RETURN HOSE

OIL FILTER

WATER HOSE

OIL COOLER

OIL BYPASS INLET HOSE

**Diesel oil filter and cooler—exploded view**

## Diesel Engine Oil Cooler
### REMOVAL AND INSTALLATION

1. Drain the engine coolant from the radiator and block. Use a clean container so it may be re-used.

2. Unclamp and then disconnect the heater hose located near the oil cooler.

3. Remove the oil filter.

4. Remove the bolts and then disconnect the water inlet pipe (retain the gasket). Unclamp and then disconnect the oil bypass return hose.

5. Remove the bolts mounting the oil return pipe to the block. Remove the through bolts and then disconnect the oil return pipe and the oil bypass inlet hose at the cooler.

6. Now, remove the two mounting bolts and two nuts and remove the cooler from the block. Make sure to remove the O-rings from the recesses where the cooler fits against the block.

7. To install the oil cooler, first apply clean engine oil to the area that is shaded in the illustration. Then, position the O-rings properly, put the cooler in position, install the bolts and nuts, and torque them to 23–34 ft.lb.

8. Perform the remaining steps in reverse of the removal procedure. Use a new oil filter. Make sure that all connections are tight, and

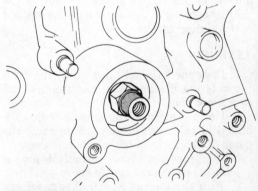

**Apply clean engine oil to the shaded area before installing the diesel oil cooler**

that you use a new gasket under the water inlet pipe. Inspect the water and oil hoses and replace any that are bulged or cracked. When all fittings are properly and snugly reconnected, close drain cocks, refill the cooling system, and start the engine. Run it to check for leaks, repairing any that occur. Stop the engine, allow the oil to drain into the pan, and then refill the oil pan with clean engine oil.

## Front Cover, Timing Chain, Tensioner, and Seal

### REMOVAL AND INSTALLATION

NOTE: *On front wheel drive GLC models, the engine must be removed from the car. Start procedure at Step 5.*

1. Bring number one piston to TDC (timing marks aligned). Drain the cooling system. Remove the radiator hoses, thermostat housing, thermostat, fan, water pump and radiator.

2. Remove all lower and side splash or skid shields. Remove the crankshaft pulley and any driven units (alternator, air pump etc.) that will interfere with front cover removal.

3. Remove the blind cover (small plate retained by two or three bolts that covers the chain adjuster). Install the special clamping tool or make a simple device to prevent the slipper head of the chain adjuster from popping out.

4. Remove the cylinder head, oil pan and timing chain front cover.

5. On GLC front wheel drive models: remove the chain tensioner (located on the left upper corner of the timing cover). Refer to the more complete procedure below for additional tips. Remove the crankshaft pulley and proceed as follows.

6. Remove the oil slinger from the crankshaft. Depending on engine, remove: the oil pump pulley and chain or the timing chain with sprockets first, the remaining sprockets and chain second. Loosen the timing chain guide strip if necessary.

7. Installation is generally in the reverse order of removal. But, follow all the steps below to ensure that worn parts are replaced and that all parts are properly reassembled.

8. When installing the oil pump sprocket and check the chain for excessive slack. Replace the chain if necessary. On the 626 models (to 1982) slack should be 0.015" (0.38mm). Adjusting shims (between the oil pump and mounting) are available in thicknesses of 0.006" (0.15mm).

9. Inspect the slipper head of the chain adjuster, the chain guide strip and the vibration damper for wear or damage. Check the adjuster spring for loss of tension. Replace parts as necessary.

10. Place the camshaft sprocket into the timing chain as shown on the appropriate illustration. Wire the sprocket and chain in position.

11. Install the timing chain onto the crankshaft sprocket as illustrated. Tighten the chain guide. Install the timing chain tensioner (except front wheel drive GLC). Make sure the snubber spring is fully compressed. Install clamping tool.

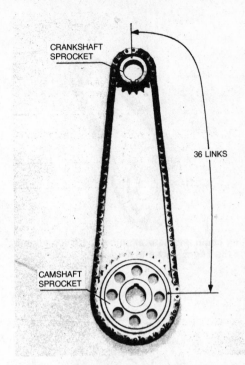

CRANKSHAFT SPROCKET

36 LINKS

CAMSHAFT SPROCKET

**Timing chain and gear alignment; 1978—1300cc engine, 1979–80—1415cc engine and 1981–82 GLC station wagon with the 1490cc engine**

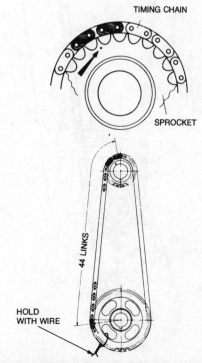

TIMING CHAIN

SPROCKET

44 LINKS

HOLD WITH WIRE

**Timing chain and gear alignment; 1970cc engine**

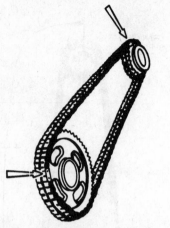

**Timing chain and gear alignment; 1586cc engine. Align the bright links and marks**

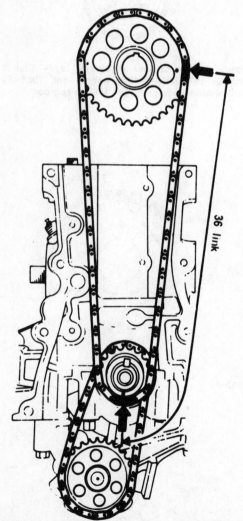

**Timing chain and gear alignment; 1490cc engine, GLC front wheel drive**

12. Install a new timing cover oil seal. Install the timing chain front cover, oil pan and cylinder head. When installing the front cover be sure tension is applied to the timing chain to prevent it from coming off of the crankshaft sprocket. If the chain comes off the sprocket, incorrect timing and engine damage will occur.

13. Install the sprocket and timing chain on the camshaft. Refer to illustrations. Adjust the timing chain tension.

14. Further installation is the reverse of removal.

## Front Cover and Timing Belt

### REMOVAL AND INSTALLATION

**1983 and later 626**

NOTE: *For access, first support the car and remove the right front wheel and splash shield.*

1. Loosen the alternator mounting bolts, release belt tension and remove the alternator belt.

2. Remove the attaching bolts and remove the upper front cover and gasket.

3. Remove the four attaching screws and remove the front pulley from the hub on the crankshaft. Then, remove the mounting bolts and remove the lower cover and gasket.

4. Now, rotate the engine in the normal direction of rotation until the camshaft pulley mark (A) aligns with the V-notch at the top of the front housing. At this point, the notch in the crankshaft pulley will align with the arrow on the front housing. Note that if the belt has jumped time, these marks will not align simultaneously, If that is true, your first step after belt removal should be to rotate the crankshaft until its marks align.

5. Loosen the tensioner lockbolt until it can be turned by hand. Then, remove the tensioner spring (brake pliers may be helpful).

6. Mark the direction of rotation of the belt if it may be reused and remove it. Inspect the belt and replace it if it is oil soaked, or shows excessive wear, peeling, cracking, or hardening. Inspect the tensioner for free and smooth rotation and replace it if it does not turn smoothly. Position the tensioner all the way toward the intake valve side.

7. Install a new bolt or reinstall the old one with the arrow indication the proper direction of rotation (that is, the arrow should point clockwise around the top pulley when viewed from the passenger side of the car). Make sure the bolt teeth engage the oil pump drive sprocket and upper and lower sprockets (pulleys) with the belt running straight from top to

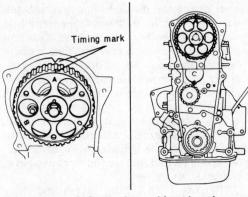

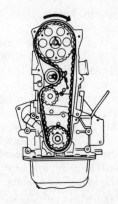

**Align the camshaft sprocket and front housing mark as shown**

**Install the belt around the sprockets and inside the tensioner pulley as shown. Make sure the arrow on the back of the belt, indicating direction of rotation, indicates rotation as shown**

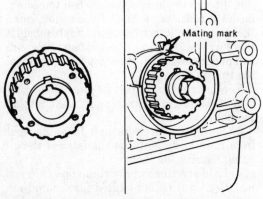

**Align the crankshaft sprocket and front housing as shown**

bottom on the right side. Then, route the bolt in around the tensioner pulley.

8. Install the tensioning spring to the tensioner. With a wrench on the crankshaft pulley, turn the engine in the normal direction of rotation (clockwise when viewed from the passenger's side) until the crankshaft has rotated two turns and the camshaft pulley returns to its former position. Now, torque the tensioner lockbolt to 28–38 ft.lb. If the belt is a used one, check deflection. Under 22 lbs. pressure, the belt should deflect 0.47–0.55" (12–14mm). You can repeat this step to reseat and retension the belt and then recheck deflection. If a used belt won't pass the test, replace it.

9. Install the lower timing belt cover with a new gasket. Torque the bolts to 5–7 ft.lb. Do the same with the upper cover. Replace the front pulley, and alternator belt in reverse of the above.

**323**

1. Disconnect the negative battery cable. Remove the engine side cover.

2. Remove the power steering and air conditioning belts, depending on how the car is equipped.

3. Remove the alternator drive belt and the alternator.

4. Remove the bolts and remove the water pump pulley. Remove the bolts and washer and remove the front portion of the crankshaft pulley together with its spacer.

5. Unbolt and remove the upper and lower timing belt covers and their gaskets.

6. Using a socket wrench on the front crankshaft bolt, turn the engine until the trailing (counterclockwise) timing mark on the camshaft sprocket aligns with the notch in the top of the plate behind the camshaft sprocket.

7. Remove the bolt mounting the timing belt tensioner to the front of the block. Remove the washer, the tensioner spring and the tensioner. Mark the direction of rotation of the timing belt if you may be re-using it.

8. Inspect all parts. Check the belt for peeling and cracks or for excessively worn or, of

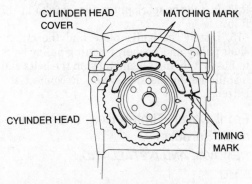

**Rotate the engine until it reaches the position shown before removing the timing belt (1597 engine)**

course, broken teeth. Check the tensioner for rough rotation.

9. Position the tensioner on the block and install the bolt and washer, just starting the threads. Connect the spring and then slide the tensioner as far as it will go to the left, or away from tensioning the belt and so as to maximize spring tension. Tighten the bolt enough to hold the tensioner in this position.

10. Check to make sure that the marks on the camshaft sprocket and backing plate are still aligned; and that the mark on the front of the block and the mark on the crankshaft pulley are still aligned, and realign the marks, if necessary.

11. Install the timing belt, making sure the direction arrow is facing in the direction of rotation if the belt is being re-used. The belt should be installed so that the right side is slightly tight, teeth are meshed, and the timing marks remain aligned. Remove all four spark plugs.

12. Now, loosen the tensioner lockbolt. Turn the crankshaft two full revolutions in the normal direction of engine rotation (clockwise), so that the timing marks again align. If the marks align, go to Step 13. If they do not align, reshift the tensioner away from tensioning the belt and lock it there with the bolt, and then re-mesh the teeth on the belt so the timing marks align and the right side of the belt is straight. Then, repeat this step.

13. Torque the tensioner lockbolt to 14–19 ft.lb. Place a ruler near the right side of the belt at the center of the span. Depress the belt with a thumb (to produce a little over 20 lbs. pressure) and measure deflection. It should move 0.35–0.39″ (8.9–9.9mm). If tension is correct, proceed to Step 14. If tension is incorrect, do not try to tension the belt by hand. Instead, fix any binding in the mechanism, if necessary; otherwise, replace the tensioning spring and then repeat Steps 11–13.

14. Install the timing covers in reverse of the removal procedure. Torque the bolts to 69–95 ft.lb. Install the spark plugs, torquing to 11–17 ft.lb.

15. Install the baffle plate and the crankshaft pulley and washer, torquing pulley bolts to 11–13 ft.lb. Install and tension the belts and install the engine side cover. Reconnect the battery.

## Front Cover, Timing Belt, and Camshaft Sprocket

### REMOVAL AND INSTALLATION

#### Diesel

NOTE: *To perform this procedure, you will need a 6 mm hex (Allen type) wrench. If you*
*need to remove the camshaft sprocket, you will need a puller with bolts that screw into the threaded holes in the sprocket. This procedure includes sprocket removal because belt and sprocket removal must be closely coordinated to prevent damaging the diesel engine. Simply skip those steps relating to the sprocket if you do not need to remove it.*

1. Disconnect the negative battery cable. Remove the drive belts and right side splash shield. Remove the cylinder head cover. Remove the bolts and remove the front portion of the crankshaft pulley.

2. Remove both timing covers and their gaskets.

3. Turn the crankshaft via the bolt at its center so the timing marks on the camshaft sprocket and front seal plate line up.

4. Loosen the lockbolt on the belt tensioner, push the tensioner to the left (so as to tighten the spring and loosen the belt) and then hold it there as you retighten the lockbolt. Now, unbolt and remove the torque stop from in front of the timing belt.

5. Mark the timing belt for direction of rotation, if you might be re-using it. Then, remove the belt.

6. Now, turn the crankshaft 45° to the right from the timing mark on the front of the oil pump housing, as shown.

7. Hold the camshaft with an open wrench installed on the flats located just behind the center bearing. Loosen the front sprocket lockbolt, but do not remove it. Then, install a puller onto the sprocket by screwing its two outer bolts into the threaded holes in the sprocket. When they are threaded in all the way, tighten the bolt at the center of the puller so its inner end rests against the lockbolt and then, as you turn it, forces the sprocket off the camshaft. Remove the puller and sprocket

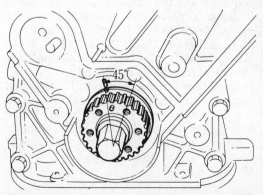

**On the diesel, rotate the crankshaft to the right, as shown, after removing the timing belt to remove the camshaft sprocket**

when the sprocket is free of the camshaft. Make sure to retain the key.

8. If the crankshaft sprocket must be removed, use a tire iron to hold the flywheel in place as you remove the lockbolt. The sprocket pulls right off the crankshaft. Make sure to retain both the washer and key.

9. Inspect all parts. Check the belt for peeling and cracks or for excessively worn or, of course, broken teeth. Check the tensioner for rough rotation.

10. Install the crankshaft sprocket with its key, the spacer, and the bolt. Restrain the flywheel and torque the bolt to 116–123 ft.lb.

11. Install the camshaft sprocket and lockbolt. Hold the camshaft by the flats with an open-end wrench as you torque the bolt to 41–48 ft.lb.

12. Realign the camshaft sprocket and front seal plate timing marks (Located at about 2 o'clock). Now, turn the crankshaft backward until the timing mark on the oil pump housing and the notch on the rear of the sprocket washer again line up.

13. Install the timing belt (in the same direction of rotation, if it is being re-used). The teeth should engage, the right side should be straight, i.e. without play, and the timing marks should align for both the camshaft and crankshaft sprockets. Make sure to route the belt over the tensioner and around the outside of the sprocket next to it (so the teeth engage that sprocket).

14. Loosen the tensioner lockbolt so that spring tension is fully free to tension the belt. Then, turn the engine via the crankshaft sprocket bolt two full revolutions in the direction of normal rotation. Torque the tensioner lockbolt to 23–34 ft.lb.

15. Recheck alignment of the timing marks (if they are not lined up, you will have to take the tension off the tensioner and reinstall the belt with timing marks properly aligned). Press the belt inward with thumb pressure on the (shorter) span on the left side. With a force of about 22 lb., it should deflect about 0.41–0.47" (10.4–12mm). If the tension is not correct and all procedures have been followed correctly, replace the tensioner spring and repeat Step 13. Do not try to tension the belt by adding tension to the tensioner mechanism manually!

16. Reinstall the torque stop. Reinstall the timing covers, using new gaskets if they are cracked or brittle. Torque bolts for the cover to 5–7 ft.lb. Install the crankshaft pulley and dowel pin, torquing the bolts to 17–24 ft.lb. Install the right side splash shield, cylinder head cover, and belts. Reconnect the battery.

## Rear Timing Belt and Sprockets
### REMOVAL AND INSTALLATION
#### Diesel

NOTE: *You'll need a puller suitable for removing the camshaft rear pulley and two bolts M8 x 1.25" x 1.77" to perform this procedure.*

1. Disconnect the negative battery cable. Remove the rear timing belt cover. Remove the cylinder head cover and gasket.

2. Turn the crankshaft until the rear camshaft sprocket and rear seal plate timing marks align.

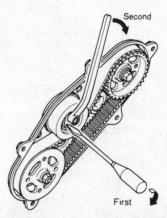

In removing tension from the diesel's rear timing belt, turn the tensioner with a screwdriver, in the direction shown

3. Loosen the lock bolt for the belt tensioner. Use a screwdriver as shown in the illustration to turn the tensioner so as to remove all tension from the belt. Hold the tensioner all the way in the released position and tighten the tensioner lock bolt to hold it in this position.

4. Mark the belt for reinstallation in the same position, if you may be re-using it. Then, remove the belt.

5. Hold the camshaft with an open-end wrench installed on the flats located just behind the center bearing. Loosen the rear sprocket lockbolt, but do not remove it. Then, install a puller onto the sprocket by screwing its two outer bolts into the threaded holes in the sprocket. When they are threaded in all the way, tighten the bolt at the center of the puller so its inner end rests against the lockbolt and then, as you turn it, forces the sprocket off the camshaft. Remove the puller and sprocket when the sprocket is free of the camshaft. Make sure to retain the key.

6. Install the two bolts described in the note above through the two holes in the injection

pump drive sprocket and into the rear seal plate. Then, unscrew the sprocket lockbolt. After the lockbolt is removed, use a puller to remove the pulley from the injection pump driveshaft.

7. Inspect all parts. Check the belt for peeling and cracks or for excessively worn or, of course, broken teeth. Check the tensioner for rough rotation.

8. Install the fuel injection pump sprocket to the pump shaft with the key. If necessary, rotate the sprocket slightly to align the timing marks. Install the bolts which prevent it from rotating. Leave these bolts in position as you complete the procedure. Then install the washer and lockbolt and torque it to 43–51 ft.lb.

9. Install the camshaft sprocket in reverse of the removal procedure, torquing it to 41–48 ft.lb. Then, make sure the mark on the camshaft pulley is still aligned with the mark on the rear seal plate.

10. Install the timing belt (in the proper direction of rotation, if it is being re-used). Engage it with the teeth of the injection pump sprocket first, and then with the teeth of the camshaft sprocket. The lower span should be tight with both sets of timing marks aligned. The upper span runs below the tensioner pulley.

11. Loosen the tensioner locknut so the tensioner spring is free to position the tensioner. Then turn the crankshaft two full turns in the normal direction of rotation. Make sure both sets of timing marks is still in alignment. If not, the belt has been installed a tooth or two off time and will have to be reinstalled properly, following which the first portion of this step should be repeated.

12. Torque the tensioner locknut to 15–20 ft.lb.

13. Check the deflection of the belt by pressing upward on the lower span with your thumb. With a force of about 22 lb. the belt should deflect about 0.37″ (9.4mm). If the tension is not correct and all procedures have been followed correctly, replace the tensioner spring and repeat Step 11. Do not try to tension the belt by adding tension to the tensioner mechanism manually!

14. Install the rear timing belt cover and the cylinder head cover and gasket. Reconnect the battery.

## Front Oil Seal

### REMOVAL AND INSTALLATION

#### Engines With Timing Belts

1. Remove the timing belt covers, timing belt, and crankshaft sprocket as described above and below.

2. With a flat bladed screwdriver, carefully pry the seal out of the front cover being careful not to damage the bore of the oil pump housing with the screwdriver blade.

3. Coat the lip of the new seal with engine oil. Using a piece of pipe that is just slightly smaller than the bore of the oil pump and about the diameter of the seal itself, tap a new seal in place. Position the seal so its front edge is aligned with the front edge of the oil pump body.

4. Perform the remaining installation steps in reverse of the removal procedure.

## Front Cover Oil Seal

### REMOVAL AND INSTALLATION

NOTE: *This procedure applies to engines with timing chains, in which the oil seals are located in the front cover, rather than the oil pump.*

#### Except Below

The front cover oil seal can be replaced, in most cases, without removing the front cover.

1. Drain the cooling system (except GLC front wheel drive).

2. Remove the radiator (except GLC front wheel drive).

3. Remove the drive belts and crankshaft pulley.

4. Pry the front oil seal carefully from the timing case cover.

5. Install the new oil seal. The rest of the installation is in the reverse order of removal.

#### 626 1,998 cc Engine

1. Align the engine timing marks and remove the timing belt as described above.

2. Remove the lower timing belt sprocket lockbolt and pull the sprocket off the crankshaft.

3. Pry out the seal with a flat tipped screwdriver. Pry against the inner surface of the seal, being careful not to touch the sealing surface of crankshaft.

4. Coat the lip of the new seal with engine oil. Start the seal by hand and then tap it in place with a 35mm socket wrench. Its front edge should align with the front edge of the pump body.

5. Reverse the above procedures to complete the installation.

## Camshaft Sprocket

### REMOVAL AND INSTALLATION

#### 1998 Gas Engine and 1597

1. Remove the timing belt as described above. On the 1597, remove the cam cover.

2. On the 1597, install an open-end wrench on the flats at the portion of the camshaft directly in front of the front bearing to hold the camshaft in place. On the 1998, install a socket wrench through one of the holes in the camshaft sprocket and onto the top bolt for the front seal plate. Then, remove the lockbolt for either type of camshaft.

3. Install in reverse order, torquing the lockbolt to 36–45 ft.lb. on the 1597 and 35–48 ft.lb. on the 1998.

## Timing Chain Tensioner

### REMOVAL, INSTALLATION AND ADJUSTMENT

#### Except GLC Front Wheel Drive

1. Remove the water pump.
2. Remove the tensioner cover.
3. Remove the attaching bolts from the tensioner. Remove the tensioner.

**To install the tensioner:**

4. Fully compress the snubber spring. Insert a screwdriver in the tensioner release mechanism on 1600 cc engines. On 1300, 1415, 1490 GLC wagon and 1970 cc engines, clamp the parts of the tensioner together with an appropriate tool (see illustration above).

5. Without removing the screwdriver, insert the tensioner and align the bolt holes. Install and torque the bolts.

6. Adjust the chain tension as follows:

   a. Remove the two blind plugs and aluminum washers from the front cover.

   b. Loosen the guide strip attaching screws.

   c. Press the top of the chain guide strip through the adjusting hole in the cylinder head.

   d. Tighten the guide strip attaching screws.

   e. Remove the screwdriver or clamping tool from the tensioner and let the snubber take up the slack in the chain.

   f. Install the blind plugs and aluminum washers.

   g. Install the tensioner cover and gasket.

   h. Install a new gasket and water pump.

7. Install the crankshaft pulley and drive belt and adjust the tension. Check the cooling system level.

#### Front Wheel Drive GLC

The chain tensioner is located on the left upper side of the timing case cover, it is operated by spring plus hydraulic pressure. The tensioner has a one-way locking system and an automatic release device. After assembly, it will automatically adjust when the engine is rotated

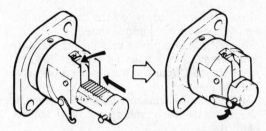

**Adjusting the tensioner before installation. GLC front wheel drive**

one or two times. No disassembly of the tensioner is required.

1. The tensioner is retained by two bolts. Remove the bolts and the tensioner.

2. Check the number of teeth showing on the sleeve of the tensioner. If thirteen or more notches are showing the timing chain is stretched and must be replaced.

3. To install the tensioner; push the sleeve back into the body and lock it with the swivel catch on the tensioner body. Install the tensioner into the timing cover. After installation the catch is released by the action of the timing chain when the engine is rotated one to two revolutions. The sleeve projects automatically providing the proper chain adjustment.

## Timing Belt Tensioner

### REMOVAL AND INSTALLATION

#### 1983 and Later 626

1. Loosen the alternator mounting bolts, release the belt tension and remove the alternator belt.

2. Remove the attaching bolts and remove the upper front cover and gasket. Rotate the engine in the normal direction of rotation until the camshaft pulley mark aligns with the V-notch at the top of the front housing. The notch in the crankshaft pulley will now be

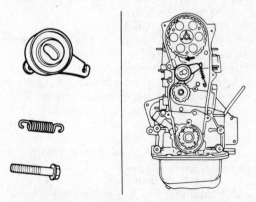

**The timing belt tensioner, tensioning spring, and bolt are shown at left. Installed position (minus the belt) is shown on the right**

aligned with the arrow on the front housing, unless the belt has jumped time.

3. With brake pliers or another suitable tool, remove the tensioning spring. Now, remove the bolt from the tensioner and remove the tensioner.

4. Inspect the tensioner for bearing wear. It should rotate freely and smoothly. If not, replace it.

5. Make sure the belt remains engaged at all three sprockets and that crankshaft and camshaft sprockets are properly in time. Locate the tensioner on its swivel pin with the slot through which the mounting bolt passes centered over the bolt hole. Install the bolt, but do not tighten it.

6. Install the tensioner spring. With a wrench on the crankshaft pulley, turn the engine in the normal direction of rotation (clockwise) exactly two full turns until the timing marks are again aligned. Torque the lockbolt to 28–38 ft.lb.

7. Install the upper cover and alternator belt in reverse of removal. Replace the cover gasket and torque the bolts to 57 ft.lb.

## Camshaft and Bearings

### REMOVAL AND INSTALLATION

**All Gasoline Engine Equipped Cars, Except 1983 and Later 626 and the 323**

Perform this operation on a cold engine only. Do not remove the camshaft gear from the timing chain. Be sure that the gear teeth and chain relationship is not disturbed. Wire the chain and cam gear to place so that they will not fall into the front cover. Maintain tension on the chain to avoid loss of timing at the crankshaft sprocket.

1. Remove the water pump (except GLC front wheel drive).

2. Rotate the crankshaft to place the No. 1 cylinder on TDC of the compression stroke.

3. Remove the distributor.

4. Remove the valve cover.

5. Release the tension on the timing chain by using a screwdriver or clamping tool (see Timing Chain Tensioner above).

6. Remove the cylinder head bolts in reverse of torquing sequence, in several stages.

7. Remove the rocker arm assembly.

8. Remove the nut, washer and distributor gear from the camshaft.

9. Remove the nut and washer holding the camshaft gear.

10. Remove the camshaft.

11. Installation is the reverse of removal. Torque in several stages using the torquing sequence shown under, Cylinder Head Overhaul. Camshaft endplay should be as specified in Cylinder Head Overhaul, above.

### 1983 and Later 626

1. Loosen the alternator mounting bolts, release belt tension, and remove the alternator belt.

2. Remove the cam cover and gasket and the upper front cover and gasket.

3. Rotate the engine in the normal direction of rotation until the camshaft sprocket mark aligns with the V-notch at the top of the front housing.

4. Loosen the tensioner lockbolt until it can be turned by hand.

5. Hold the camshaft sprocket to keep it from turning by passing a prybar of some sort through one of the holes, and remove the bolt from the center of the pulley. Remove the pulley from the camshaft, being careful to maintain tension on the timing belt so it won't jump out of time at the bottom. Support the sprocket in such a way as to maintain timing.

6. See the procedure for Cylinder Head Removal & Installation above and loosen the rocker assembly mounting bolts only in the specified sequence in several stages. Remove the rocker assembly and bolts as an assembly. Remove the camshaft.

7. Before replacing or reinstalling the camshaft and related parts, make checks for bearing clearance and end play and cam and journal dimensions as described above in the Cylinder Head overhaul section.

8. Lubricate all parts throughly with clean engine oil and position the camshaft on the head with the pin at front positioned at the top.

9. Lubricate the bearing surfaces and position the rocker assembly on the head. Torque bolts in the order shown in the Cylinder Head Removal & Installation procedure. Torque in several stages, in order, to 13–19 ft.lb.

10. Raise the camshaft sprocket into position at the front of the camshaft without losing timing. To do this, maintain upward tension on the sprocket while careful levering the tensioner upward against spring tension. When the sprocket is high enough, position it on the front of the camshaft with the lockpin on the camshaft in the hole on the sprocket. Install the lockbolt. Keep the sprocket from turning with a prybar inserted through on of its holes and torque the bolt to 35–48 ft.lb.

11. With a wrench on the crankshaft pulley bolt, turn the engine in the forward direction two full turns. You can check that belt timing is correct by positioning the pulley at the TDC (left) mark and checking that the marks on the cam sprocket and timing cover are still

aligned. Torque the tensioner bolt to 28–38 ft.lb.

12. Adjust the valves as described in Chapter 2.

13. Install the timing belt cover with a new gasket and torque the bolts to 5–7 ft.lb.

14. Reinstall the cam cover and alternator belt in reverse of removal.

### Diesel

NOTE: To perform this procedure, you will need a 6 mm hex (Allen type) wrench. You will need a puller with bolts that screw into the threaded holes in the camshaft sprocket. You'll also need a puller suitable for removing the camshaft rear pulley and two bolts M8 x 1.25" x 1.77" to perform this procedure.

1. Disconnect the negative battery cable. Remove the drive belts and right side splash shield. Remove the cylinder head cover and gasket. Remove the bolts and remove the front portion of the crankshaft pulley.

2. Remove the rear timing belt cover. Turn the crankshaft until the rear camshaft sprocket and rear seal plate timing marks align.

3. Loosen the lock bolt for the belt tensioner. Use a screwdriver to turn the tensioner so as to remove all tension from the belt. Hold the tensioner all the way in the released position and tighten the tensioner lock bolt to hold it in this position.

4. Mark the belt for reinstallation in the same position. Then, remove the belt.

5. Hold the camshaft with an open-end wrench installed on the flats located just behind the center bearing. Loosen the rear sprocket lockbolt, but do not remove it. Then, install a puller onto the sprocket by screwing its two outer bolts into the threaded holes in the sprocket. When they are threaded in all the way, tighten the bolt at the center of the puller so its inner end rests against the lockbolt and then, as you turn it, forces the sprocket off the camshaft. Remove the puller and sprocket when the sprocket is free of the camshaft. Make sure to retain the key.

6. Install the two bolts described in the note above through the two holes in the injection pump drive sprocket and into the rear seal plate. Then, unscrew the sprocket lockbolt. After the lockbolt is removed, use a puller to remove the pulley from the injection pump driveshaft.

7. Remove both front timing covers and their gaskets.

8. Turn the crankshaft via the bolt at its center so the timing marks on the camshaft sprocket and front seal plate line up.

9. Loosen the lockbolt on the belt tensioner,

push the tensioner to the left (so as to tighten the spring and loosen the belt) and then hold it there as you retighten the lockbolt. Now, unbolt and remove the torque stop from in front of the timing belt.

10. Mark the timing belt for direction of rotation. Then, remove the belt.

11. Now, turn the crankshaft 45° to the right from the timing mark on the front of the oil pump housing, as shown.

NOTE: *Do not attempt to hammer the pulley or camshaft to remove the pulley.*

12. Hold the camshaft with an open-end wrench installed on the flats located just behind the center bearing. Then, loosen the front sprocket lockbolt, but do not remove it. Then, install a puller onto the sprocket by screwing its two outer bolts into the threaded holes in the sprocket. When they are threaded in all the way, tighten the bolt at the center of the puller so its inner end rests against the lockbolt and then, as you turn it, forces the sprocket off the camshaft. Remove the puller and sprocket when the sprocket is free of the camshaft. Make sure to retain the key.

13. To remove the crankshaft sprocket, use a tire iron to hold the flywheel in place as you remove the lockbolt. The sprocket pulls right off the crankshaft. Make sure to retain both the washer and key.

14. Loosen the camshaft bearing cap nuts a little at a time, in several stages, in the numbered order. Then, remove the camshaft front and rear bearing caps. Now, remove both the front and rear camshaft oil seals.

15. Use a flat bladed screwdriver and carefully pry the oil pump (front crankshaft) oil seal out of the oil pump.

16. Remove the tensioner lockbolts, springs, and tensioners from both the front and rear of the engine. Remove the lockbolts and remove both the front and rear seal plates.

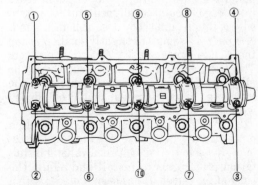

**Diesel engine camshaft caps must be loosened in the order shown**

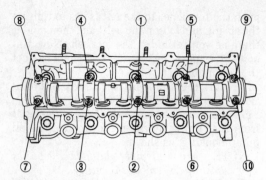

**Diesel engine camshaft caps must be tightened in the order shown**

17. Remove the attaching nuts and remaining camshaft bearing caps, and remove the camshaft.

18. Inspect the camshaft bearing surfaces and bearing clearances and check out cam dimensions as described earlier in this chapter. Thoroughly lubricate all bearing surfaces (saddles, caps, and cam journals), and carefully position the camshaft in the block.

CAUTION: *Install the camshaft so that the groove for the key of the front sprocket faces straight upward! Otherwise, the valve and pistons may be damaged when the caps are torqued!*

19. Install front and rear seal plates and their lockbolts. Coat the entire surfaces on which both the front and rear camshaft caps rest with a sealer. Then, install the camshaft caps and nuts. Tighten the nuts very slightly.

20. Install front and rear camshaft seals by hand. Note that the rear seal is slightly larger. Make sure you coat the seal lips with oil first.

21. Tighten the caps in the numbered order in three stages to 15–21 ft.lb. Now, install the front oil pump seal, oiling the lips first, around the crankshaft. Now use a hammer and a pipe 1.4″ (35.5mm) in diameter to gently tap the oil pump seal into position. The oil pump seal's front edge should be aligned with the front edge of the oil pump body. Use a slightly smaller pipe (1.3″ (33mm) or slightly smaller) to tap the front and rear camshaft seals into position. The front edge of the front seal should be aligned with the front edge of the head; the front edge of the rear seal should be aligned with the rear edge of the head.

22. The remaining steps of the installation procedure are the reverse of the removal procedure. Refer to timing belt removal and installation procedures to install and adjust the belts. If the camshaft has been replaced with a new one, adjust the valves before running the engine.

**323**

1. Remove the cylinder head as described above. Make sure to remove the camshaft sprocket and rocker assembly as specified there.

2. Remove the attaching bolt and remove the camshaft thrust plate from the front bearing. Carefully pry the camshaft oil seal out of the front cylinder head bore with a flat bladed screwdriver. Be careful not to damage the bore or camshaft! Slide the camshaft out of the bearing bores in the head.

3. Inspect the camshaft bearing surfaces and bearing clearances and check out cam dimensions as described earlier in this chapter. Thoroughly lubricate all bearing surfaces (bores and cam journals), and carefully slide the camshaft into position in the block.

4. Install the camshaft thrust plate and attaching bolt.

5. Coat the outer bore of a new camshaft oil seal and the inner bore of the cylinder head with a thin coat of engine oil. With a piece of pipe approximately the diameter of the oil seal (not larger!), gently tap the seal straight into position around the front of the camshaft.

6. Install the cylinder head and accessories in reverse of the removal procedure described above. Make sure to adjust the valve clearances before starting the engine.

### INSPECTION

See the Cylinder Head Cleaning and Inspection procedure above for camshaft cam, bearing, and endplay dimensional checks.

## Pistons and Piston Pins, Connecting Rods and Bearings
### REMOVAL AND INSTALLATION

NOTE: *This procedure requires the use of several special tools designed to permit the piston pins to be pressed out of the pistons and rods. This includes a hydraulic press that produces and measures total pressing pressures of 2,000–3,300 lbs. You may wish to remove the piston/rod assemblies yourself and have the pressing operations done at a competent automotive machine shop.*

Pistons and connecting rods are removed after the cylinder head and oil pan have been taken off the engine. It's best to have the engine out of the car and mounted on a stand that permits you to invert the engine for crankshaft removal. However, if you need to remove pistons and rods only, you can do so from underneath with the engine mounted in the car. On the 323 and 626, it is necessary to remove the engine from the car to remove the crankshaft.

Use a puller similar to that shown to remove the main bearing cap for the main which takes the end thrust. Late model 626 engine is shown—others are similar, although the center main may take the thrust

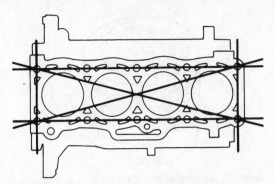

**Check the block deck for distortion by running a straightedge along both sides, both ends, and diagonally, as shown**

You must remove the engine, and then remove the transaxle from the engine. Remove the flywheel. Remove the oil pump from the front of the engine. Then, invert the engine and remove the main bearing caps, the bearings, and the crankshaft. Refer to appropriate procedures below.

All parts must be retained in order--both bearings and caps. Mark caps for installation in the same position in both directions if they are not already marked. Note that on all engines except those used in the 1983 and later 626 and the 323, thrust bearings are at the rear main. This main bearing cap must be removed with a puller. The 1983 and later 626 (1998) including the diesel has them on the center main and the 323 (1597) has them on the No. 4 main. Be careful not to lose or mix up thrust washers.

1. Inspect the upper area of the cylinder walls of each cylinder for a ridge above the top piston ring. If cylinder wall wear has created a noticeable ridge, it should be removed with a ridge reamer to prevent damage to the rings when the piston is removed. Ream the ridge out with the proper tools and with a rag covering the piston top to minimize the amount of metal getting into the cylinder. Remove all metal shavings before attempting to remove piston/rod assemblies.

2. Push piston/rod assemblies out from underneath after rod caps are removed.

3. On the 1983 and later 626 gas engines, test the oscillation torque of the rod by holding the piston in a horizontal position, raising the rod until it touches the piston skirt, and releasing it. The rod should descend freely, or the piston and pin must by replaced. Then, on all en-

gines, press the piston pin out of the piston with tools designed for this purpose.

*INSPECTION*

1. Check the top deck of the block for distortion by running a straightedge along both sides, both ends, and diagonally. Check for distortion exceeding 0.006″ (0.15mm), (0.004″ [0.1mm] on the diesel) by attempting to insert a flat feeler gauge of 0.006″ (0.15mm) between the block deck and the lower edge of the straightedge all along its length and in every direction shown. If the distortion exceeds the limit, have the block top deck ground by a competent machine shop or, if distortion is excessive, replace the block.

NOTE: *Do not attempt to save a diesel cylinder block through grinding! If the distortion exceeds the limit, the block must be replaced. Otherwise, the pistons will hit the valves!*

2. Also inspect the block for cracks or wetness indicating coolant has leaked through cracks. If you have any doubt about such problems, you should have the block inspected by the Zyglo® or a similar process to ensure it can be reused without risk of leakage.

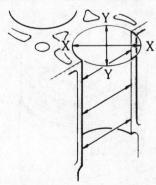

**Measure the diameter of each cylinder in the six directions/locations shown**

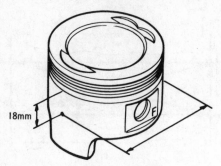

**Measure piston diameter as shown**

3. Measure the diameter of each cylinder at the six locations shown. Subtract the minimum dimension from the maximum dimension. If this difference exceeds 0.0059" (0.15mm), or the difference between cylinders exceeds 0.0007" (0.01778mm), cylinders must be bored and oversize pistons installed. On the diesel, maximum diameter must not exceed 3.39" (86mm) and the difference between cylinder bores must not exceed 0.009" (0.23mm). Wall scoring or signs of piston seizure also mean cylinders must be rebored. Even if only one cylinder is damaged, all must be bored and the same size oversize pistons installed (for balance). Pistons are offered in oversizes of 0.010" (0.254mm) and 0.020" (0.508mm) for most engines.

4. Measure piston diameter in the thrust direction 18mm (0.71") below the bottom of the oil ring groove. On the diesel, measure it 0.75" (19mm) above the bottom edge of the piston skirt. This dimension must compare with cylinder diameter so as to produce piston-to-cylinder clearance that is to specification. If clearance exceeds the maximum wear specification, cylinders must be bored oversize and oversize pistons of appropriate dimension must be installed.

5. Inspect the rings for damage or cracks and measure side clearance and end gap as

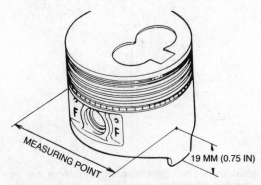

**Measure the diesel piston skirts for wear at the location shown**

shown. End gap must be measured with the rings near the bottom of the cylinder--below ring wear.

6. Install the connecting rods in a jig designed to test straightness and check that bend or twist is no more than 0.0016" (0.04mm), (0.006" [0.15mm] on the diesel) per 3.94" (100mm) of length.

7. Measure crankpin diameter and if it is under the limit specified, or if scoring is present, all the crankpins must be machined and undersize connecting rod bearings installed.

8. On the diesel, the upper ends of the connecting rods are bushed. (On all gas engines, proceed to the next step.) Measure the outside diameter of the piston pin with a micrometer; use an inside micrometer to measure the inside diameter of the bushing. Then, subtract the smaller figure from the larger. The standard inner diameter of the bushing is 0.9846–0.9854" (25.00–25.03mm). The limit on clearance between the two is 0.002" (0.05mm). If the clearance exceeds this figure, press the bushing out of the rod and replace it as follows:

a. Press the bushing out by supporting the upper rod end on a block with a suitable hole in it (for passage of the bushing downward). Place a pipe of 1.06–1.08" (27.0–27.4) diameter under the press and squarely aligned with the end of the pin (NOT touching the rod). Press the bushing out.

b. Thoroughly coat the outer bore of the new bushing and the inner bore of the rod with clean engine oil. Precisely align the oil holes of the bushing and rod bore. Then, press the new bushing in with the press and pipe until the edges of the bushing are aligned with the sides of the rod and the oil holes are precisely lined up.

c. Add the minimum piston pin-to-rod clearance to the actual pin diameter. Then, repeatedly measure the inside diameter of the bushing and ream it until the total clearance is to specification, using a spiral reamer.

9. Pistons and rods must be assembled (piston pins installed) with rods facing in the proper direction. With the **F** mark on the piston facing you, turn the connecting rod so the oil hole which lubricates the cylinder is on the left. This also applies to the diesel. On 1982 and earlier 626 engines, the rod is assembled with the connecting rod bolt heads pointing to the right, as shown.

The piston pin (and other related parts) must be thoroughly lubricated with clean engine oil and pressed in from the **F** mark side. On the diesel, heat the piston to 122°–168°F (50°C–76°C). Then, install the connecting rod

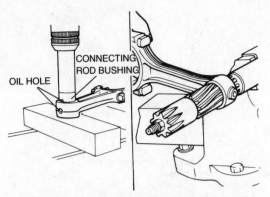

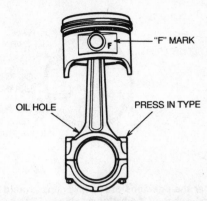

"F" MARK

OIL HOLE

CONNECTING ROD BUSHING

OIL HOLE

PRESS IN TYPE

Replacing the connecting rod bushing on the diesel. The left panel shows required alignment of the oil holes in the bushing and rod prior to pressing the bushing in; the right panel shows reaming the new bushing to create proper pin-to-bushing clearance.

Piston/connecting rod assembly—most engines

in the proper direction into the piston, slide the pin into position, and lock the pin with circlips. On the gas engines except the 1,272 cc engine, the job requires special tools and a press that can apply 1,100–3,300 lbs. while measuring

On the 1970 cc engine used in the 626 prior to 1983, the rod/piston assembly should look like this

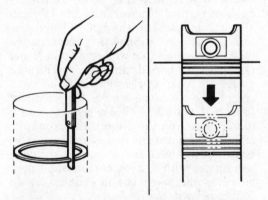

Measure ring end gap by placing the ring inside the cylinder below the area where rings have worn it, using an inverted piston to keep it square

the force. If the force is outside the limits, the pin or piston must be replaced. On the 1,998 cc engine used in late model 626, the completed assembly must pass the connecting rod oscillation torque test as described above. On the 1,272 cc engine, heat the piston slightly if the pin is a tight fit, press it into the piston, and install circlips.

10. Install all piston rings with rings and grooves thoroughly lubricated. Start with the oil control ring spacer. Then, install the upper oil control side rail by inserting one edge between the groove and spacer and holding it in place with your thumb. Then, run your other

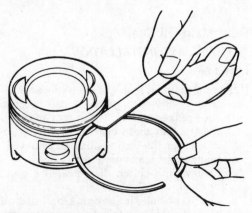

Check ring side clearance as shown

Installing the oil ring upper side rail

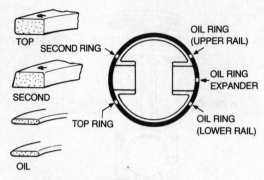

Stagger the positions of the ring gaps around the circumference of the piston as shown

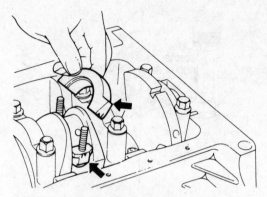

Install the connecting rod cap with matchmarks on the cap and rod aligned, as shown

thumb along the edge of the rail to work it into the ring groove. Install the lower side rail similarly.

Install the lower compression ring and then the upper ring, with **R** or **RN** markings facing upward. Use a ring expander and open rings up as little as possible. When the rings are installed, stagger their gaps as shown in the illustration, to prevent excessive oil consumption.

11. Install the connecting rod caps with the mark on one side of the cap aligned with that

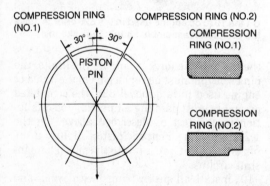

Install the rings for the 1597 engine as shown. Make sure the "R" mark faces upward

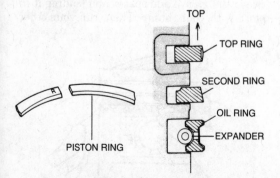

Install the rings for the 1998 diesel as shown. Make sure the "R" or "RN" mark faces upward

on one side of the rod itself. Install in original positions, using your marks or factory marks. Make sure on all engines that the **F** mark on the piston faces the front of the block. First, install and torque the cap with bearings dry and a Plastigage® insert installed. Make sure the connecting rod nuts are torqued to the proper value and that the Plastigage® insert is not seated on an oil hole. After proper bearing fit has been verified, remove the inserts, lubricate all parts thoroughly with engine oil, and reassemble and torque connecting rod caps and nuts. It is possible that while crankpin diameter may have passed minimum specification previously, bearing clearance may be excessive. If the clearance exceeds the maximum limit of 0.0039" (0.1mm), (0.0031" [0.07874mm] on the diesel), the crankpins must be machined and undersize bearings installed. If this work is necessary, it should be coordinated with a check of crankshaft main bearings and journals and endplay, as described below.

12. Measure the connecting rod end play between the side of the rod itself (not the cap) and the crankshaft. Replace rods that are worn excessively. Make sure the crankshaft rotates freely.

## Rear Main Oil Seal

### *REMOVAL AND INSTALLATION*

#### Except Below

If the rear main oil seal is being replaced independently of any other parts, it can be done with the engine in place. If the rear main oil seal and the rear main bearing are being replaced together the engine must be removed.

1. Remove the transmission.

2. Remove the clutch disc, pressure plate and flywheel.

3. Punch two holes in the crankshaft rear oil seal. They should be punched on opposite sides

of the crankshaft, just above the bearing cap-to-cylinder block split line.

4. Install a sheet metal screw in each hole. Pry against both screws at the same time to remove the oil seal.

5. Clean the oil recess in the cylinder block and bearing cap. Clean the oil seal surface on the crankshaft.

6. Coat the oil seal surfaces with oil. Coat the oil surface and the steel surface on the crankshaft with Lubriplate℗. Install the new oil seal and make sure that it is not cocked. Be sure that the seal surface was not damaged.

7. Install the flywheel. Coat the threads of the flywheel attaching bolts with oil resistant sealer.

8. Install the clutch, pressure plate and transmission.

### 626 1,998 cc Engine and 323 1597 Engine

NOTE: *You will need a seal installer designed for the seal you are replacing and an arbor press that you can use to press the seal into position. You might want to take the seal and rear cover (into which the seal fits) to an* automotive machine shop to have the seal pressed in.

1. Remove the transaxle. Remove the clutch pressure plate and disc or automatic transmission flex plate. Remove the flywheel mounting bolts and remove the flywheel.

2. Using a rag as a pivot point, pry the seal out with a flat tipped screwdriver.

3. Unbolt and remove the rear cover.

4. Apply a coating of oil to the lip of the new seal. Start the seal into the rear cover by hand and then press it in using a seal installer (which fits precisely into the inner seal bore) and an arbor press. It must be straight and the front edge of the seal must align with the front edge of the cover.

5. Install the rear cover onto the engine, torquing the bolts to 5.9–8.7 ft.lb. on the 1998 and 69–95 in.lb. on the 1597.

## Crankshaft and Main Bearings
### REMOVAL AND INSTALLATION AND BEARING REPLACEMENT

1. Remove the engine from the car. Remove the front pulley and the flywheel.

2. Invert the engine on a stand and remove the oil pan. Where so equipped, remove the rear main seal cover. Remove the front cover, timing chain, and oil pump. Mark all main and connecting rod bearing caps for location and remove them. On engines in which the rear bearing cap also retains oil seals, you'll have to use a puller. Remove the crankshaft with a secure hoist to prevent personal injury or damage to the crank. Keep all bearings and caps in position and order.

3. If the engine uses a manual transmission and has reached normal time for overhaul, remove the pilot bearing (which supports the transmission input shaft) from the rear of the crankshaft with an appropriate puller.

4. Inspect the crankshaft for any signs of scoring or cracks and for clogged oil passages. Clogged oil passages must be cleaned in a solvent tank or with solvent and brushes; scoring means that the crank should be machined and undersize bearings installed; and cracks may mean the crank must be replaced. Consult a competent machine shop in the case of the latter two problems.

5. Cradle the crankshaft in V-blocks, mount and a dial indicator as shown, and zero it. Now, rotate the crank to check for runout. The reading of the indicator should not exceed 0.0012″ (0.03mm), (0.0016″ [0.04mm] on the 1597). If it does, the crankshaft must be replaced.

6. Check the dimensions of all main journals and crankpins, as shown. If they are worn past the limit, they must be ground and under-

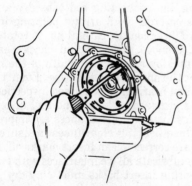

Removing the rear main seal from the 1,998 cc engine used in the 626

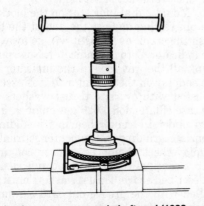

Pressing in a new rear crankshaft seal (1998 engine)

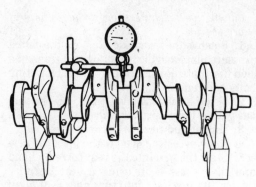

Checking crankshaft runout

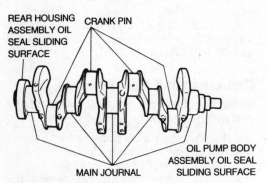

Measuring crankshaft wear surface dimensions

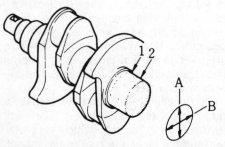

Measure as shown for elliptical wear of the crankshaft wear surfaces

size bearings installed. In addition, on 1981–86 engines, you must check all these dimensions in four places at 90° angles to each other and subtract the smaller from the larger to get the difference. This elliptical limit is 0.0020" (0.05mm). If the wear is elliptical beyond the limit, the crankshaft must be machined and undersize bearings installed regardless of the total wear.

In addition on the 1983–86 626 engines, you must measure the front and rear oil seal sliding surfaces. The rear seal surface must measure 3.5412–3.5434" (89.9–90.0mm). The front oil pump body assembly seal surface must measure 1.3371–1.3386" (33.96–34.00mm) Both must also be within the elliptical limit

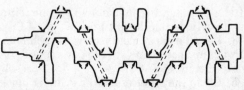

FILLET R DIMENSION

3MM (0.12 IN) R

**Make sure the "R" dimension is correct on 1983 and later 626, if the crankshaft is machined**

described above. If the crankshaft is machined, make sure the machinist is aware of the **R** dimension of 0.12" (3mm) on gas engine crankshafts and 0.102–0.118" (2.59–2.99mm) on diesels.

7. Inspect the bearings for scoring, flaking, grooving, blue color due to heat, partial elimination of the overlay (appearance of a different color in certain areas), or polished appearance and replace if any such indications appear.

8. Make sure all parts are clean and dry. Carefully position the bearings in the block and caps and then lower the crank into position carefully to avoid damaging it. Install Plastigage® inserts on the journals and crankpins, away from oil holes. Assemble and torque bearing and connecting rod caps dry and in numbered order with arrows pointing in the forward direction. Be careful not to rotate the crank. Remove the caps and check bearing clearances by reading the width of the mark left by the insert in each case. Even if the crank and bearings have passed inspections so far, the crank must be ground and undersize bearings installed if clearances are improper.

9. Once bearing clearances measured as above are correct, clean insert marks off, thoroughly lubricate all wear surfaces with engine oil (bearing insert backs must stay dry), and reassemble and retorque all caps and cap bolts. On late model GLC engines, insert the seals in the rear main cap with holes facing forward and backward, not side-to-side.

10. Mount a dial indicator on the block with the pin resting against the end of the crank. Push the crank as far as it will go away from the indicator. Zero the indicator. Now, pull the crank all the way toward the indicator. Read the endplay on the indicator. If it is excessive, adjust it with oversize thrust washers or, in the case of late model 626 gas engines, a standard undersize center bearing, including appropriate grinding of the center journal. The endplay check should be done in conjunction with a check of connecting rod side clearance as described above. Thrust washers must be installed with the groove outward (toward the crankshaft thrust surface).

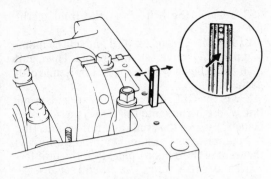

On the '81–84 GLC rear main cap, insert the side seals as shown

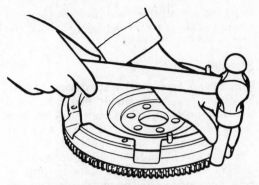

Removing the flywheel ring gear

11. On cars with manual transmissions, tap the pilot bearing into the rear of the crankshaft using a piece of pipe the diameter of the outer bearing race. Be careful to apply pressure to the outer race only.

12. Install the oil pan, rear main seal cover, oil pump and pump body, timing chain, front cover etc. by referring the appropriate procedures.

## Flywheel and Ring Gear

### REMOVAL AND INSTALLATION

1. Turn the engine over to TDC No. 1 firing position. Refer to the procedure for Transmission Removal and Installation in Chapter 6 and remove the transmission.

2. Install some sort of device to lock the flywheel. These typically bolt to the rear engine plate. Mazda supplies one numbered 49 E301 060 (on the 1998, use 49 V101 060); you should be able to find an equivalent part from many different sources in the automotive aftermarket. Turn the device in the direction which will hold the flywheel from turning as the flywheel mounting bolts are turned.

3. Remove the clutch as described in Chapter 6.

4. Support the flywheel in a secure manner, loosen and remove the bolts, and remove the flywheel.

5. On the 626 and 323, coat the bolt threads with a sealant such as Mazda part No. 8530 77 743. To install the flywheel, first put it into position and then install the bolts loosely.

6. Turn the flywheel locking device around so the bolts may be torqued without turning the flywheel. Torque the bolts to specification.

7. Install the transmission and clutch as described in Chapter 6.

### RING GEAR REPLACEMENT

NOTE: *To replace the ring gear, you will need a large oven capable of maintaining 500°F (260°C).*

1. Remove the flywheel as described above. Use a torch, confining the flame carefully to the ring gear itself, to heat the ring gear to expand it. Then, support the flywheel at its center and tap the ring gear all around to remove it.

2. Put the new ring gear in the oven and heat it to 480°–570°F (249–299°C). Give the ring gear plenty of time to come to the temperature of the oven (20 minutes plus).

CAUTION: *Handle the ring gear with insulated gloves only!*

3. Position the ring gear with the beveled side facing the engine side of the flywheel. Then, work it onto the flywheel. Install ring gear as described above.

## EXHAUST SYSTEM

For a number of different reasons, exhaust system work can be the most dangerous type of work you can do on your car. Always observe the following precautions:

1. Support the car extra securely. Not only will you often be working directly under it, but you'll frequently be using a lot of force--say, heavy hammer blows, to dislodge rusted parts. This can cause a car that's improperly supported to shift and possibly fall.

2. Wear goggles. Exhaust system parts are always rusty. Metal chips can be dislodged, even when you're only turning rusted bolts. Attempting to pry pipes apart with a chisel makes chips fly even more frequently.

3. If you're using a cutting torch, keep it at a great distance from either the fuel tank or lines. Stop what you're doing and feel the temperature of fuel bearing pipes or the tank frequently. Even slight heat can expand or vaporize the fuel, resulting in accumulated vapor or even a liquid leak near your torch.

4. Watch where your hammer blows fall. You could easily tap a brake or fuel line when you hit an exhaust system part with a glancing

blow. Inspect all lines and hoses in the area where you've been working before driving the car.

## Special Tools

A number of special exhaust system tools can be rented from auto supply houses or local stores that rent special equipment. A common one is a tail pipe expander, designed to enable you to join pipes of identical diameter.

It may also be quite helpful to use solvents designed to loosen rusted bolts or flanges. Soaking rusted parts the night before you do the job can speed the work of freeing rusted parts considerably. Remember that these solvents are often flammable. Apply them only after the parts are cool.

## Exhaust Manifold Mounted Catalytic Converter

### REMOVAL AND INSTALLATION

#### GLC

1. Remove the clamp supporting the pipe running from the exhaust mounted converter to the front of the rear converter. Remove the nuts and the springs which fasten the rear of this pipe to the front of the rear converter.

2. Remove the three nuts and washers fastening this pipe to the bottom of the exhaust manifold mounted converter. Disconnect the secondary air line where it passes into the top of this pipe. Then, pull the pipe down and off the exhaust mounted converter and forward and off the rear converter. Remove both gaskets.

3. Remove the nuts from the upper side of the flange on the exhaust manifold. Then, pull the converter downward and off the exhaust manifold. Remove the gasket.

4. Clean all flanges and supply new gaskets. Install a new exhaust manifold mounted converter in reverse order. Work the pipe connecting the two converters onto the studs of the rear converter before connecting it with the exhaust manifold mounted studs.

## Exhaust System Mounted Catalytic Converter

### REMOVAL AND INSTALLATION

#### 323 and GLC

1. Remove the attaching nuts and washers or springs from the exhaust manifold or exhaust manifold mounted converter studs. Disconnect the secondary air line from the pipe connecting the two converters on the GLC. Remove the nuts and washers from the studs or bolts on the front of the rear converter. On the

323, remove the bolts from the front of the front converter.

2. Pull the pipe downward and off the manifold mounted converter or manifold. Then, pull it off the exhaust system converter. Remove all gaskets.

3. On the GLC, disconnect the secondary air line where it runs into the converter. On both models, remove the studs and nuts connecting the main exhaust system mounted catalyst to the front of the exhaust pipe. Pull the unit forward and off the studs. Unbolt and remove the upper and lower heat shields on the GLC. Remove the gasket.

4. Clean all flanges and provide new gaskets. Install in reverse order.

### 626

1. The catalytic converter is integral with a pipe and the resonator, as well as the pipe linking the resonator to the exhaust pipe and muffler. First, support this assembly in front of the resonator.

2. Remove the nuts and springs holding the studs in the forward end of the catalytic converter to the front pipe flange. Then, remove the nuts from the forward ends of the bolts attaching the assembly to the center pipe and muffler. Pull the bolts out to the rear.

3. Remove the rubber support donuts at the forward hangers and at the resonator. Then, lower the assembly at the rear and when the rear is clear of the flange behind, slide the converter studs out of the flange in the front pipe. Remove the gaskets at both ends as well as the ring type seal located in the rear of the front pipe.

4. Install in reverse order, using new gaskets and seals.

## Muffler

### REMOVAL AND INSTALLATION

#### GLC

The GLC muffler assembly is attached at the front via a flange and at the rear via a clamped pipe connection. Unbolt the clamp at the rear and slide it forward and away from the connection. Remove the nuts from the rear side of the flange at the front. Then, support the assembly, and pull the bolts forward and out of the flange at the front. Remove the donut type hangers at the front and pull the rear hangers off the support prongs. Now, turn the assembly back and forth and pull the rear pipe out of the connector for the rear pipe and remove it. Unbolt the halves of the heat shield from the front pipe and install it onto the new assembly. Remove the gasket from the flange at the front

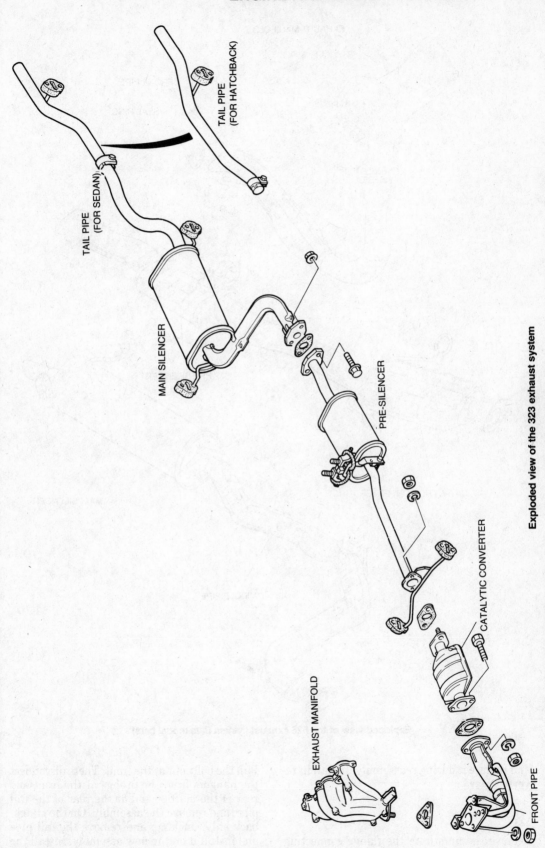

TAIL PIPE
(FOR HATCHBACK)

TAIL PIPE
(FOR SEDAN)

MAIN SILENCER

PRE-SILENCER

CATALYTIC CONVERTER

EXHAUST MANIFOLD

FRONT PIPE

Exploded view of the 323 exhaust system

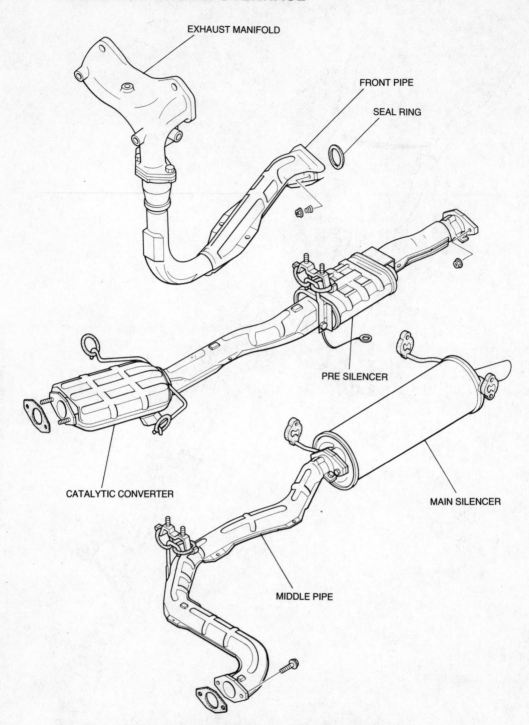

EXHAUST MANIFOLD

FRONT PIPE

SEAL RING

PRE SILENCER

CATALYTIC CONVERTER

MAIN SILENCER

MIDDLE PIPE

**Exploded view of the 626 exhaust system (late model cars)**

and replace it during reassembly. Install in reverse order.

**323**

Remove the nuts from the flange connecting the resonator rear pipe and muffler inlet pipe.

Pull the bolts out at the front. Then, disconnect the hangers from the prongs at the front and rear of the muffler and at the rear of the tail pipe, and remove the assembly. On the Hatchback only, unclamp and remove the tail pipe and install it on the new assembly. Install the assembly in reverse order with new gaskets.

**626 Gasoline and Diesel**

The 626 muffler assembly is flanged at the front. Remove the nuts and bolts connecting the muffler at the flange and then, on gas engines, unhook the hangers for the assembly at the prongs and remove it. On the diesel, unhook the donut type rubber connectors at the front and outboard on the rear support. Install in reverse order with a new gasket.

**Mark the front and rear rotor housings to prevent confusion during assembly**

# ROTARY ENGINE OVERHAUL

## 1971–73

### DISASSEMBLY

Engine disassembly should be performed in the following order, after it has been removed from the automobile and placed on a workstand:

1. Remove all of the components of the emission control system. See, Emission Controls in Chapter Four.
2. Detach the metering oil pump linkage, oil lines, and vacuum sensing lines from the carburetor.
3. Remove the intake manifold securing nuts, evenly and in several stages.
4. Remove the intake manifold assembly, complete with the carburetor.
5. Remove the alternator adjusting link bolt, but do not remove the adjusting link, itself.
6. Unfasten the alternator attaching bolts, then remove the alternator and its drive belt.
7. Remove the pulley from the water pump.
8. Unfasten the five nuts and two bolts which secure the water pump and remove the pump.
9. Remove the clamping nuts from both of the distributors and withdraw the distributors from their sockets.
10. Mark the distributor sockets for identification during assembly. Remove the nuts and withdraw the distributor sockets from the front housing.
11. Attach a brake to keep the ring gear from turning (Mazda tool, part number 49 0820 060A).
12. Unfasten the eccentric shaft pulley bolt. Remove the pulley and the key from the eccentric shaft.
13. Unfasten the clutch cover attachment bolts.
14. Remove the clutch assembly from the flywheel.
15. Straighten the tabs on the flywheel nut lockwasher.
16. Remove the flywheel nut with a wrench of a suitably large size.

CAUTION: *Do not use locking pliers or a hammer and chisel to remove the flywheel nut.*

17. Remove the flywheel with a puller.
18. Invert the engine on the workstand.
19. Remove the oil pan bolts and take the oil pan off the engine along with its gasket.
20. Remove the oil strainer bolts, the oil strainer, and its gasket.
21. Mark the front and rear rotor housings, which are identical in appearance, so that they will not be confused upon assembly.
22. With the front of the engine facing up in the stand, unfasten the front engine mount securing nuts and remove the mounts.
23. Remove the front engine cover securing bolts. Lift off the cover and its gasket.
24. Withdraw the O-ring from the passage on the front of the housing.
25. Remove the oil pump drive chain and related components from the engine on 1972–73 models, in the following manner:

    a. Slide the oil slinger, spacer, and distributor drive gear off the eccentric shaft.

    b. Remove the chain tensioner nuts and the chain tensioner.

    c. Remove the locknut and washer from the oil pump sprocket.

    d. Slide the sprockets off the eccentric shaft and oil pump drive shaft simultaneously, complete with the chain.

    e. Remove the key from the eccentric shaft.

26. Slide the oil pump drive gear (1971 models), balancing weight, thrust washer, and the first needle bearing off the eccentric shaft.
27. Unfasten the bearing housing securing bolts.
28. Remove the bearing housing, second needle bearing, spacer, and thrust washer.
29. Turn the engine on the workstand so that the top side of it is facing upward.
30. Loosen the engine housing tension bolts in the order illustrated.

CAUTION: *Do not loosen the tension bolts*

**Tension bolt removal sequence**

*one at a time. Loosen the bolts evenly and in two or three stages.*

31. With the front of the engine facing up, lift the front housing off the eccentric shaft.

32. Remove any side seals which are sticking to the surface of the front housing and place them in their original position on the rotor.

33. Remove the rotor seals and related components in the following order, after noting their original position so that they will not be confused during assembly.

    a. Three corner seals

    b. Three corner seal springs

    c. Six side seals

    d. Six side seal springs

NOTE: *Each seal has its own installation mark next to its groove on the rotor. Mazda has a special seal tray (part no. 49 0813 250) which uses the same marks so that the seals will not be confused during storage and assembly.*

34. Remove the oil seals and O-rings from the grooves in the rotor face.

35. Hold the front rotor housing down while threading a nut and bolt of the proper metric size into each of the hollow dowels on the engine housing.

36. Remove the dowels by holding the bolt with a wrench while tightening the nut. Once

the dowel contacts the nut, back off on the nut and insert a spacer between the nut and the housing. Continue tightening the nut and inserting spacers until each dowel is out of the housing.

37. Lift the front housing away from the rotor.

    CAUTION: *Use care when lifting the housing off the rotor, so that the apex seals do not fall off. If they strike a hard surface they will shatter.*

38. Remove the air injection nozzles, the O-rings, and the rubber seals from the front housing.

39. Remove the apex seals and their springs from the front rotor. When removing each seal, place an identification mark on the bottom, with a felt tipped pen, so that it can be installed in the proper location and direction. If any of the seals have come off, be sure to note their proper location.

    CAUTION: *When marking the seals, do not use a punch or scratch the surface of the seal.*

40. Remove the front rotor from the eccentric shaft and place it face down on a clean, soft cloth.

    NOTE: *The internal gear side of the front rotor is marked with an* **F** *to ensure installation in the proper rotor housing.*

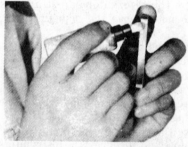

**Identify each apex seal by marking its bottom with a felt-tipped pen**

**Remove any side seals which adhere to the front housing**

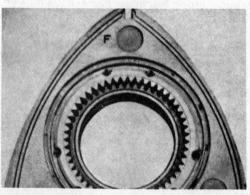

**The front rotor is marked with an "F" on its internal gear side and the rear with an "R" in the same manner**

41. Remove the seals and springs from the rear side of the rotor in the same manner as detailed for the front side in Step 38.

42. Hold the intermediate housing down and remove the hollow dowels, as outlined for the front rotor housing in Steps 35–36.

43. Lift the intermediate housing off the eccentric shaft by sliding it beyond the front rotor journal while pushing up on the shaft. Use care not to damage the eccentric shaft.

44. Withdraw the eccentric shaft.

45. Repeat Steps 35–41 to remove the rear rotor housing and rotor.

NOTE: *The internal gear side of the rear rotor is marked with a* **R** *to ensure installation in the proper rotor housing.*

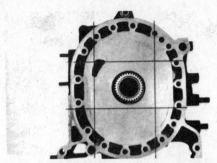

Measure the housing distortion along the axes indicated

## INSPECTION AND REPLACEMENT

### Front Housing

1. Check the housing for signs of gas or water leakage.

2. Remove the carbon deposits from the front housing with an extra fine emery cloth.

NOTE: *If a carbon scraper must be used, be careful not to damage the mating surfaces of the housing.*

3. Remove any old sealer which is adhering to the housing using a brush or a cloth soaked in ketone.

4. Check for distortion by placing a straightedge on the surface of the housing. Measure the clearance between the straightedge of the housing with a feeler gauge. If the clearance is greater than 0.002″ (0.05mm) at any point, replace the housing.

5. Use a dial indicator to check for wear on the rotor contact surfaces of the housing. If the wear is greater than 0.004″ (0.1mm), replace the housing.

NOTE: *The wear at either end of the minor axis is greater than at any other point on the housing. However, this is normal and should be no cause for concern.*

### Front Stationary Gear and Main Bearing

1. Examine the teeth of the stationary gear for wear or damage.

2. Be sure that the main bearing shows not signs of excessive wear, scoring, or flaking.

3. Check the main bearing-to-eccentric journal clearance by measuring the journal with a vernier caliper and the bearing with a pair of inside calipers. The clearance should be between 0.0018–0.0028″ (0.046–0.071mm), and the wear limit is 0.0039″ (0.01mm). Replace either the main bearing or the eccentric shaft if it is greater than this. If the main bearing is to be replaced, proceed as detailed in the following section.

Measure the housing wear with a dial indicator

### Main Bearing Replacement

1. Unfasten the securing bolts, if used. Drive the stationary gear and main bearing assembly out of the housing with a brass drift.

2. Press the main bearing out of stationary gear.

3. Press a new main bearing into the stationary gear so that it is in the same position as the old bearing before it was removed.

4. Align the slot in the stationary gear flange with the dowel pin in the housing and press the gear into place. Install the securing bolts, if required.

NOTE: *To aid in stationary gear and main bearing removal and installation. Mazda supplies a special tool, part number 49 0813 235.*

### Intermediate and Rear Housings

Inspection of the intermediate and rear housings is carried out in the same manner as detailed for the front housing above. Replacement of the rear main bearing and stationary gear (mounted on the rear housing) is given below.

### Rear Stationary Gear and Main Bearing

Inspect the rear stationary gear and main bearing in a similar manner to the front. In addition, examine the O-ring, which is located in

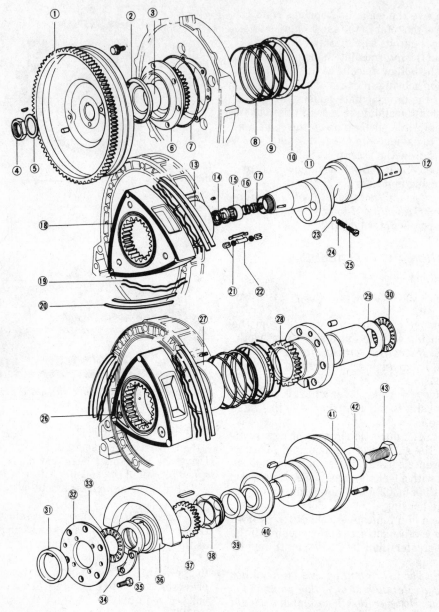

| | | |
|---|---|---|
| 1. Flywheel | 16. O-ring | 31. Spacer |
| 2. Oil seal | 17. Blind plug | 32. Bearing housing |
| 3. Main bearing | 18. Front rotor | 33. Needle bearing |
| 4. Locknut | 19. Side seal spring | 34. Washer |
| 5. Washer | 20. Side seal | 35. Thrust plate |
| 6. Rear stationary gear | 21. Corner seal and spring | 36. Balance weight |
| 7. O-ring | 22. Apex seal w/spring | 37. Oil pump drive sprocket |
| 8. Oil seal O-ring | 23. Steel ball | —1972–73 |
| 9. Oil seal | 24. Spring | 38. Distributor drive gear |
| 10. Oil seal | 25. Oil nozzle | 39. Spacer |
| 11. Oil seal spring | 26. Rear rotor | 40. Oil slinger |
| 12. Eccentric shaft | 27. Rotor bearing | 41. Eccentric shaft pulley |
| 13. Rotor bearing | 28. Front stationary gear | 42. Washer |
| 14. Grease seal | 29. Thrust washer | 43. Bolt |
| 15. Needle bearing | 30. Thrust bearing | |

**Rotor and eccentric shaft components**

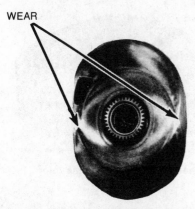

Most of the front and rear housing wear occurs at the ends of the minor axis, as indicated

Position the o-ring in the groove on the stationary gear (arrow)

Align the slot in the stationary gear flange with the pin on the housing (arrow)

the stationary gear, for signs of wear or damage. Replace the O-ring, if necessary. If required, replace the stationary gear in the following manner.

1. Remove the rear stationary gear securing bolts.

2. Drive the stationary gear out of the rear housing with a brass drift.

3. Apply a light coating of grease on a new O-ring and fit it into the groove on the stationary gear.

4. Apply sealer to the flange of the stationary gear.

5. Install the stationary gear on the housing so that the slot on its flange aligns with the pin on the rear housing.

CAUTION: *Use care not to damage the O-ring during installation.*

6. Tighten the stationary gear bolts evenly, and in several stages, to 15 ft.lb.

## Rotor Housings

1. Examine the inner margin of both housings for signs of gas or water leakage.

2. Wipe the inner surface of each housing with a clean cloth to remove the carbon deposits.

NOTE: *If the carbon deposits are stubborn, soak the cloth in a solution of ketone. Do not scrape or sand the chrome plated surfaces of the rotor chamber.*

3. Clean all of the rust deposits out of the cooling passages of each rotor housing.

4. Remove the old sealer with a cloth soaked in ketone.

5. Examine the chromium plated inner surfaces for scoring, flaking, or other signs of damage. If any are present, the housing must be replaced.

6. Check the rotor housings for distortion by placing a straightedge on the areas on the areas illustrated.

7. Measure the clearance between the straightedge and the housing with a feeler gauge. If the gap exceeds 0.002″ (0.05mm), replace the rotor housing.

8. Check the widths of both rotor housings, at a minimum of eight points near the trochoid surfaces of each housing, with a vernier caliper.

If the difference between the maximum and

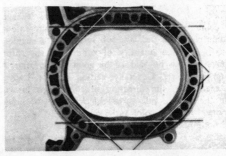

Measure the rotor housing distortion along the axes indicated

Check the rotor housing width at eight points along the trochoid surfaces

ROTOR ROTATING DIRECTION

**Normal shading of deposits on the rotor**

minimum values obtained is greater than 0.0031" (0.08mm), replace the housing. A housing in this condition will be prone to gas and coolant leakage.

NOTE: *Standard rotor housing width is 2.7559" (70mm).*

### Rotors

1. Check the rotor for signs of blow-by around the side and corner seal areas.

2. The color of the carbon deposits on the rotor should be brown, just as in a piston engine.

NOTE: *Usually the carbon on the leading side of the rotor is brown, while carbon on the trailing side tends toward black, as viewed from the direction of rotation.*

3. Remove the carbon on the rotor with a scraper or extra fine emery paper. Use the scraper carefully when doing the seal grooves, so that no damage is done to them.

4. Wash the rotor in solvent and blow it dry with compressed air after removing the carbon.

5. Examine the internal gear for cracks or damaged teeth.

NOTE: *If the internal gear is damaged, the rotor and gear must be replaced as a single assembly.*

6. With the oil seal removed, check the land protrusions by placing a straightedge over the lands. Measure the gap between the rotor surface and the straightedge with a feeler gauge. The standard specification is 0.004–0.006" (0.10–0.15mm); if it is less than this, the rotor must be replaced.

7. Check the gaps between the housings and the rotor on both sides.

    a. Measure the rotor width with a vernier caliper. The standard rotor width is 2.7500" (69.8mm).

    b. Compare the rotor width with the width of the rotor housing measured above. The standard rotor housing width is 2.7559" (70mm).

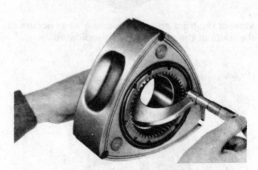

**Measure rotor width at the point indicated**

**Weight classification letter placement**

    c. Replace the rotor if the difference between the two measurements is not within 0.0051–0.0067" (0.13–0.17mm).

8. Check the rotor bearing for flaking, wearing, or scoring and proceed as indicated in the next section, if any of these are present.

The rotors are classified into five lettered grades, according to their weight. A letter between A and E is stamped on the internal gear side of the rotor. If it becomes necessary to replace a rotor, use one marked with a **C** because this is the standard replacement rotor.

### Rotor Bearing Replacement

Special service tools are required to replace a rotor bearing. Replacement is also a tricky procedure which, if done improperly, could result in serious damage to the rotor and could even make replacement of the entire rotor necessary. Therefore, this service procedure is best left to an authorized service facility or a qualified machine shop.

### Oil Seal Inspection

NOTE: *Inspect the oil seal while it is mounted in the rotor.*

1. Examine the oil seal for signs of wear or damage.

2. Measure the width of the oil seal lip. If it is greater than 0.031" (0.8mm), replace the oil seal.

3. Measure the protrusion of the oil seal, it should be greater than 0.020" (0.5mm). Replace the seal, as detailed below, if it is not.

### Oil Seal Replacement

NOTE: *Replace the rubber O-ring in the oil seal as a normal part of engine overhaul.*

1. Pry the seal out gently be inserting a screwdriver in the slots on the rotor. Do not remove the seal by prying it at only one point as seal deformation will result.

CAUTION: *Be careful not to deform the lip of the oil seal if it is to be reinstalled.*

2. Fit both of the oil deal springs into their respective grooves, so that their ends are facing upward and their gaps are opposite each other on the rotor.

3. Insert a new rubber O-ring into each of the oil seals.

NOTE: *Before installing the O-rings into the oil seals, fit each of the seals into its proper groove on the rotor. Check to see that all of the seals move smoothly and freely.*

4. Coat the oil seal groove and the oil seal with engine oil.

5. Gently press the oil seal into the groove with your fingers. Be careful not to distort the seal.

NOTE: *Be sure that the white mark is on the bottom side of each seal when it is installed.*

6. Repeat the installation procedure for the oil seals on both sides of each rotor.

### Apex Seals

CAUTION: *Although the apex seals are extremely durable when in service, they are easily broken when they are being handled. Be careful not to drop them.*

1. Remove the carbon deposits from the apex seals and their springs. Do not use emery cloth on the seals as it will damage their finish.

2. Wash the seals and the springs in cleaning solution.

3. Check the apex seals for cracks and other signs of wear or damage.

4. Test the seal springs for weakness.

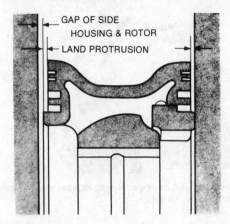

**Oil Seal protrusion**

**Position the oil seal spring gaps at arrows**

5. Use a micrometer to check the seal height. Replace any seal if its height is less than 0.3150" (8mm).

6. With a feeler gauge, check the side clearance between the apex seal and the groove in the rotor. Insert the gauge until its tip contacts the bottom of the groove. If the gap is greater than 0.004" (0.1mm), replace the seal.

7. Check the gap between the apex seals and the side housing, in the following manner:

   a. Use a vernier caliper to measure the length of each apex seal.

   b. Compare this measurement to the minimum figure obtained when rotor housing width was being measured.

   c. If the difference is more than 0.0059" (0.15mm), replace the seal.

   d. If, on the other hand, the seal is too long, stand the ends of the seal with emery cloth until the proper length is reached.

CAUTION: *Do not use the emery cloth on the faces of the seal.*

### Side Seals

1. Remove the carbon deposits from the side seals and their springs with a carbon scraper.

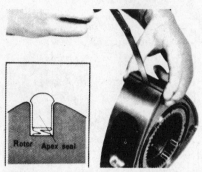

**Check the gap between the apex seal and groove with a feeler gauge**

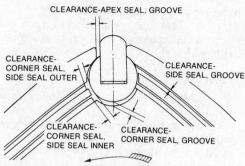

**Check the clearance of the seals at the points indicated**

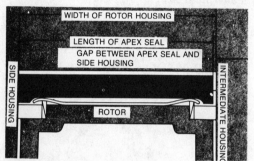

**Apex seal to side seal contact**

2. Check the side seals for cracks or wear. Replace any of the seals found to be defective.

3. Check the clearance between the side seals and their grooves with a feeler gauge. Replace any side seals if they have a clearance of more than 0.0039″ (0.01mm). The standard clearance is 0.002–0.003″ (0.05–0.07mm).

4. Check the clearance between the side seals and the corner seals with both of them installed in the rotor.

a. Insert a feeler gauge between the end of the side seal and the corner seal.

NOTE: *Insert the gauge against the direction of the rotor's rotation.*

b. Replace the side seal if the clearance is greater than 0.0016″ (0.04mm).

5. If the side seal is replaced, adjust the clearance between it and the corner seal as follows:

a. File the side seal on its reverse side, in the same rotational direction of the rotor, along the outline made by the corner seal.

b. The clearance obtained should be 0.002–0.006″ (0.05–0.15mm). If it exceeds this, the performance of the seals will deteriorate.

CAUTION: *There are four different types of side seals, depending upon their location. Do not mix the seals up and be sure to use the proper type of seal for replacement.*

**Corner seals**

1. Clean the carbon deposits from the corner seals.

2. Examine each of the seals for wear or damage.

3. Measure the clearance between the corner seal and its groove. The clearance should be 0.008–0.019″ (0.2–0.5mm). The wear limit of the gap is 0.0031″ (0.08mm).

4. If the wear between the corners seal and the groove is uneven, check the clearance with the special bar limit gauge (Madza part number 49 0839 165). The gauge has a "go" end and a "no go" end. Use the gauge in the following manner:

a. If neither end of the gauge goes into the groove, the clearance is within specifications.

b. If the "go" end of the gauge fits into the groove, but the "no go" end does not, replace the corner seal with one that is 0.0012″ (0.03mm) oversize.

c. If both ends of the gauge fit into the groove, then the groove must be reamed out as detailed below. Replace the corner seal with one which is 0.0072″ (0.18mm) oversize, after completing reaming.

NOTE: *Take the measurement of the groove in the direction of maximum wear, i.e., that of rotation.*

**Corner Seal Groove Reaming**

NOTE: *This procedure requires the use of special tools; if attempted without them, damage to the rotor could result.*

1. Carefully remove all of the deposits which remain in the groove.

2. Fit the jib (Mazda part number 2113 99 900) over the rotor. Tighten its adjusting bar, being careful not to damage the rotor bearing or the apex seal grooves.

3. Use the corner seal groove reamer (Mazda part number 49 0839 170) to ream the groove.

**Reaming the corner seal groove**

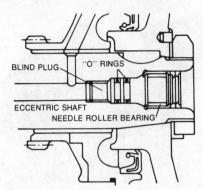

**Eccentric shaft blind plug assembly**

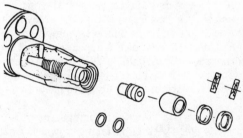

**Needle bearing components**

4. Rotate the reamer at least 20 times while applying engine oil as a coolant.
   NOTE: *If engine oil is not used, it will be impossible to obtain the proper groove surfacing.*
5. Remove the reamer and the jib.
6. Repeat Steps 1–5 for each of the corner seal grooves.
7. Clean the rotor completely and check it for any signs of damage.
8. Fit a 0.0079" (0.2mm) oversize corner seal into the groove and check its clearance. Clearance should be 0.0008–0.0019" (0.02–0.05mm).

### Seal Springs

Check the seal springs for damage or weakness. Be exceptionally careful when checking the spring areas which contact either the rotor or the seal.

### Eccentric Shaft

1. Wash the eccentric shaft in solvent and blow its oil passages dry with compressed air.
2. Check the shaft for wear, cracks, or other signs of damage. Make sure that none of the oil passages are clogged.
3. Measure the shaft journals with a vernier caliper. The standard specifications are:
   - Main journals: 1.6929" (43mm)
   - Rotor journals: 2.9134" (74mm)
   Replace the shaft if any of its journals shows excessive wear.
4. Check eccentric shaft runout by placing

**Position the dial indicator as shown, in order to measure shaft runout**

the shaft on V-blocks and using a dial indicator as shown. Rotate the shaft slowly and note the dial indicator reading. If runout is more than 0.0008" (0.02mm), replace the eccentric shaft.
5. Check the blind plug at the end of the shaft. If it is loose or leaking, remove it with an allen wrench and replace the O-ring.
6. Check the operation of the needle roller bearing for smoothness by inserting a mainshaft into the bearing for signs of wear or damage.
7. Replace the bearing, if necessary, with the special bearing replacer (Mazda part number 49 0823 073 and 49 0823 072).

### ASSEMBLY

1. Place the rear rotor on a rubber pad or a clean, thick cloth.
2. Install the oils seals on both sides of the rotor, if you have not already done so. Follow the procedure outlined in the appropriate section under Inspection and Replacement, below.
3. Place the rear rotor on the pad or cloth, so that its internal gear is facing upward.
   NOTE: *When installing the various seals, consult the marks made during engine disassembly in order to ensure installation of the seals in their proper location.*
4. Place each of the apex seals into their respective grooves without fitting the springs.

**Corner seal installation**

**The rear rotor must be positioned exactly as shown for installation**

5. Place each of the corner seal springs, followed by the corner seals, into the grooves on the rotor. Lubricate them with engine oil.

6. Check to see that the upper surface of the corner seal is 0.05–0.06″ (1.27–1.52mm) higher than the rotor. The corner seal should also move freely when finger pressure is applied to it.

7. Place the side seal springs into their grooves with both ends facing upward. Coat them with engine oil.

8. Install each of the side seals into the proper groove.

9. Be sure that each seal protrudes about 0.04″ (1mm) from the surface of the rotor. Test free movement of the seals by pressing them with your finger.

10. Lubricate all of the seals and the internal gear with engine oil.

11. Mount the rear housing in the workstand so that the top of it is facing upward.

12. Place the rotor on the rear housing so that both its rotor contact surface and the rotor are facing upward.

CAUTION: *Be sure that none of the seals fall off while the rotor is being moved.*

13. Mesh the rotor internal gear with the stationary gear on the housing so that the apexes of the rotor are positioned as illustrated.

NOTE: *When positioning the rotor, be sure that none of the corner seals drop into the parts.*

14. Remove the three apex seals from the rotor and place them so that they are near their proper installation positions.

15. Lubricate the eccentric shaft rear rotor and main bearing journals with engine oil.

16. Insert the eccentric shaft into the rotor and rear housing using care not to damage any of the bearings or journals.

17. Fit the air injection nozzles into place and apply sealer to the back of the rear rotor housing.

NOTE: *Use care not to get any sealer into the water or oil passages of the rear housing.*

18. Apply a small amount of rubber lubricant on new O-rings and rubber seals, then install them into the rear side of the rotor housing.

19. Invert the rear rotor housing, fit it over the rotor, and then onto the rear housing. Be sure that none of the O-rings or rubber seals fall out of the housing.

20. Coat the hollow dowels with engine oil. Fit the dowels through the holes in the rotor housing and into the holes on the rear housing.

21. Install the apex seals, complete with springs, in their proper positions and directions in the rotor.

22. Fit the corner and side seals, with their springs, into the proper grooves. Be sure that they are facing in the correct direction.

23. Lightly lubricate the rotor and the rotor contact surface of the rear housing, with engine oil.

24. Apply sealer to the O-rings and rubber seals. Install them on the intermediate housing in a similar manner to that outlined in Steps 17–18 above.

25. Hold the back end of the eccentric shaft up, so that the front end of the rear rotor journal does not extend beyond the front side of the rotor bearing.

26. Fit the intermediate housing on the rear rotor housing, while holding the eccentric shaft, as explained in the step above.

27. Install the front rotor and rotor housing in the same manner outlined for the rear rotor and housing in Steps 1–23.

NOTE: *The proper relationship between the timing of the front and rear rotors will be obtained when the front rotor is placed over the rotor journal on the eccentric shaft and positioned as the rear rotor is in Step 13.*

28. Apply engine oil to the front housing sta-

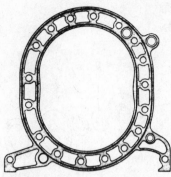

Apply sealer to the grey-shaded areas of the rotor housing

Intermediate housing installation

Installation of the apex seal and spring

Tension bolt tightening sequence

tionary gear and main bearing. Place the front housing over the front rotor housing. If necessary, turn the front rotor slightly to engage its internal gear with the front housing stationary gear.

29. Install the tension bolts in the following manner:

    a. Fit each bolt through the housings and turn it two or three times.

    b. Rotate the engine in the stand so that its top is facing upward.

    c. Tighten the bolts evenly and in two or three stages. Use the sequence illustrated below and the torque figure listed in the torque specifications chart.

CAUTION: *Do not tighten the bolts one at a time.*

    d. Rotate the eccentric shaft to see that it operates lightly and smoothly.

30. Coat the rear oil seal with engine oil. Apply Loctite[R] to the threads on the eccentric shaft through the key.

31. Install the flywheel on the rear of the eccentric shaft with its keyway over the key on the shaft.

32. Coat both sides of the flywheel lockwash-

er with sealer, then fit the washer on the eccentric shaft.

33. Finger tighten the flywheel locknut. Use a brake on the flywheel to deep it from rotating while tightening the nut on the flywheel to 350 ft.lb.

34. Turn the engine on the workstand so that its front end is facing up.

35. Slip the thrust plate, spacer, and the rear needle bearing over the front of the eccentric shaft. Lubricate the parts which were just installed, with engine oil.

36. Install the bearing housing, tighten its securing bolts, and bend up the lockwasher tabs on the bolts.

Flywheel installation

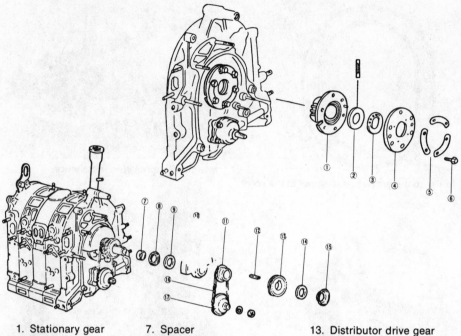

1. Stationary gear
2. Thrust-plate
3. Needle bearing
4. Bearing housing
5. Lockwasher
6. Bolt
7. Spacer
8. Needle bearing
9. Thrust washer
10. Balance weight
11. Oil pump drive sprocket
12. Key
13. Distributor drive gear
14. Spacer
15. Oil slinger
16. Drive chain
17. Oil pump drive sprocket

**Bearing housing assembly—1972–73 illustrated**

37. On 1972–73 models, fit the oil pump drive chain over both of the sprockets. Install the sprocket and chain assembly over the eccentric and oil pump shafts simultaneously. Place the key on the eccentric shaft.

NOTE: *Be sure that both of the sprockets are engaged by the chain before installing them over the shafts.*

38. Slip the oil pump drive gear (1971), distributor drive gear, the spacer, and the oil slinger over the eccentric shaft.

39. Align the keyway on the eccentric shaft pulley with the key on the shaft and install the pulley. Tighten the pulley securing bolt to 47 ft.lb. while holding the flywheel with the brake.

40. Check eccentric shaft endplay in the following manner:

a. Attach a dial indicator to the flywheel. Move the flywheel forward and backward.

b. Note the reading on the dial indicator; it should be 0.0016–0.0018″ (0.040–0.045mm).

c. If the endplay is not within specifications, adjust it by replacing the front spacer. Spacers come in four sizes, ranging from 0.3151–0.3181″ (8.0–8.1mm).

d. Check the endplay again and, if it is

**Use a dial indicator attached to the flywheel to measure eccentric shaft end-play**

now within specifications, proceed with the next step.

41. Remove the pulley from the front of the eccentric shaft. Tighten the oil pump drive sprocket nut and bend the locktabs on the lockwasher.

42. Fit a new O-ring over the front cover oil passage.

43. Install the chain tensioner and tighten its securing bolts, if so equipped.

**Cut off the excess front cover gasket**

**Position the distributor drive slot as shown**

44. Position the front cover gasket and the front cover on the front housing, then secure the front cover with its attachment bolts.

45. Install the eccentric shaft pulley again. Tighten its bolt to 47 ft.lb.

46. Use a spare mainshaft or an arbor to hold the clutch disc in place.

47. Install the clutch cover and pressure plate assembly over the flywheel.

NOTE: *Align the O-mark on the clutch cover with the hole in the flywheel.*

48. Tighten the clutch cover bolts to 15 ft.lb., while holding the ring gear with a brake. Install the self-tapping bolt into the reamed hole.

49. With the bottom of the engine pointing upward in the workstand, cut the excess front cover gasket at the oil pan mounting flange.

50. Install the oil strainer gasket and the strainer. Bolt them to the front housing.

51. Apply sealer to oil pan and housing mounting flanges. Install the oil pan and gasket. Tighten the bolts evenly and in several stages, to 7 ft.lb.

52. Align the white mark on the eccentric shaft pulley with the pointer on the front housing to obtain top dead center (TDC) of the number one rotor's compression cycle.

53. Place the distributor socket gaskets on the housing. Install the trailing distributor socket into the housing so that the driveshaft groove is inclined 34° to the right of the longitudinal axis of the engine.

54. Install the leading distributor socket in a similar manner, except that its driveshaft groove should be inclined 17° to the right of the longitudinal axis of the engine.

55. Install both distributors as outlined under Engine Electrical, above.

56. Install the water pump as detailed below.

57. Bolt the engine mounts on the front housing.

58. Perform alternator installation and drivebelt tension adjustment as detailed under Engine Electrical, above.

59. Position the intake manifold/carburetor

assembly and gaskets on the engine. Tighten the manifold securing nuts evenly, and working in two or three stages, to the specifications in the Torque Chart.

NOTE: *Start from the inside and work out when tightening the bolts.*

60. Attach the oil lines, the vacuum lines, and the metering oil pump linkage to the carburetor.

61. Remove the engine from the workstand.

62. Install the gaskets and then the thermal reactor on the engine. Tighten its securing nuts evenly, and working in two or three stages, to the specifications in the Torque Chart.

63. Place the heat stove over the thermal reactor and secure it with its mounting nuts.

64. Install the components of the emission control system as detailed in Emission Controls, below. See Chapter Four.

65. Install the engine in the car.

## 1974–78
### *DISASSEMBLY*

Because of the design of the rotary engine, it is not practical to attempt component removal and installation. It is best to disassemble and assemble the entire engine, or, go as far as necessary with the disassembly procedure.

1. Mount the engine on a stand.

2. Remove the oil hose support bracket from the front housing.

3. Disconnect the vacuum hoses, air hoses and remove the decel valve.

4. Remove the air pump and drive belt. Remove the air pump adjusting bar.

5. Remove the alternator and drive belt.

6. Disconnect the metering oil pump connecting rod, oil tubes and vacuum sensing tube from the carburetor.

7. Remove the carburetor and intake manifold as an assembly.

8. Remove the gasket and two rubber rings.

9. Remove the thermal reactor and gaskets.

10. Remove the distributor.

11. Remove the water pump.

12. Invert the engine.

13. Remove the oil pan.

14. Remove the oil pump.

15. Identify the front and rear rotor housing with a felt tip pen. These are common parts and must be identified to be reassembled in their respective location.

16. Turn the engine on the stand so that the top of the engine is up.

17. Remove the engine mounting bracket from the front cover.

18. Remove the eccentric shaft pulley.

19. Turn the engine on a stand so that the front end of the engine is up.

20. Remove the front cover.

21. Remove the O-ring from the oil passage on the front housing.

22. Remove the oil slinger and distributor drive gear from the shaft.

23. Unbolt and remove the chain adjuster.

24. Remove the locknut and washer from the oil pump drive sprocket.

25. Slide the oil pump drive sprocket and driven sprocket together with the drive chain off the eccentric shaft and oil pump simultaneously.

26. Remove the keys from the eccentric and oil pump shafts.

27. Slide the balance weight, thrust washer and needle bearing from the shaft.

28. Unbolt the bearing housing and slide the bearing housing, needle bearing, spacer and thrust plate off the shaft.

29. Turn the engine on the stand so that the top of the engine is up.

30. If equipped with a manual transmission, remove the clutch pressure plate and clutch disc. Remove the flywheel with a puller.

31. If equipped with an automatic transmission, remove the drive plate. Remove the counterweight.

32. Working at the rear of the engine, loosen the tension bolts.

NOTE: *Do not loosen the tension bolts one at a time. Loosen the bolts evenly in small stages to prevent distortion.*

33. Lift the rear housing off the shaft.

34. Remove any seals that are stuck to the rotor sliding surface of the rear housing and reinstall them in their original locations.

35. Remove all the corner seals, corner seal springs, side seal and side seal springs from the rear side of the rotor. Mazda has a special tray which holds all the seals and keeps them segregated to prevent mistakes during reassembly. Each seal groove is marked to prevent confusion.

36. Remove the two rubber seals and two O-rings from the rear rotor housing.

37. Remove the dowels from the rear rotor housing.

38. Lift the rear rotor housing away from the rear rotor, being very careful not to drop the apex seals on the rear rotor.

39. Remove each apex seal, side piece and spring from the rear rotor and segregate them.

40. Remove the rear rotor from the eccentric shaft and place it upside down on a clean rag.

41. Remove each seal and spring from the other side of the rotor and segregate these.

42. If some of the seals fall off the rotor, be careful not to change the original position of each seal.

43. Identify the rear rotor with a felt tip pen.

44. Remove the oil seals and the springs. Do not exert heavy pressure at only one place on the seal, since it could be deformed. Replace the O-rings in the oil seal when the engine is overhauled.

45. Hold the intermediate housing down and remove the dowels from it.

46. Lift off the intermediate housing being careful not to damage the eccentric shaft. It should be removed by sliding it beyond the rear rotor journal on the eccentric shaft while holding the intermediate housing up and, at the same time, pushing the eccentric shaft up.

47. Lift out the eccentric shaft.

48. Repeat the above procedures to remove the front rotor housing and front rotor.

## INSPECTION

The illustrations below detail and illustrate engine inspection procedures, and, in some cases, show usage and give the factory part numbers of special tools, or describe particular aspects of the assembly operation.

## ASSEMBLY

1. Place the rotor on a rubber pad or cloth.

2. Install the oil seal rings in their respective grooves in the rotors with the edge of the spring in the stopper hole. The oil seal springs are painted cream or blue in color. The cream colored springs must be installed on the front faces of both rotors. The blue colored springs must be installed on the rear faces of both rotors. When installing each oil seal spring, the painted side (square side) of the spring must face upward (toward the oil seal).

3. Install a new O-ring in each groove. Place each oil seal in the groove so that the square edge of the spring fits in the stopper hole of the oil seal. Push the head of the oil seal slowly with the fingers, being careful that the seal is not deformed. Be sure that the oil seal moves smoothly in the groove before installing the O-ring.

4. Lubricate each oil seal and groove with engine oil and check the movement of the seal. It should move freely when the head of the seal is pressed.

5. Check the oil seal protrusion and install the seals on the other side of each rotor.

6. Install the apex seals without springs and side pieces into their respective grooves so that each side piece positions on the side of each rotor.

7. Install the corner seal springs and corner seals into their respective grooves.

8. Install the side seal spring and side seals into their respective grooves.

9. Apply engine oil to each spring and check each spring for smooth movement.

10. Check each seal protrusion.

11. Invert the rotor being careful that the seals do not fall out, and install the oil seals on the other side in the same manner.

12. Mount the front housing on a workstand so that the top of the housing is up.

13. Lubricate the internal gear of the rotor with engine oil.

14. Hold the apex seals with used O-rings to keep the apex seals installed and place the rotor on the front housing. Be careful not to drop the seals. Turn the front housing so that the sliding surface faces upward.

15. Mesh the internal and stationary gears so that the one of the rotor apexes is at any one of the four places shown and remove the old O-ring which is holding the apex seals in position.

16. Lubricate the front rotor journal of the eccentric shaft with engine oil and lubricate the eccentric shaft main journal.

17. Insert the eccentric shaft. Be careful that you do not damage the rotor bearing and main bearing.

18. Apply sealing agent to the front side of the front rotor housing.

19. Apply a light coat of petroleum jelly onto new O-rings and rubber seals (to prevent them from coming off) and install the O-rings and rubber seals on the front side of the rotor housing.

NOTE: *The inner seal is of the square type. The wider white line of the rubber seal should face the combustion chamber and the seam of the rubber seal should be positioned as shown. Do not stretch the rubber seal.*

20. If the engine is being overhauled, install the seal protector to only the inner rubber seal to improve durability.

21. Invert the front rotor housing, being careful not to let the rubber seals and O-rings fall from their grooves, and mount it on the front housing.

22. Lubricate the dowels with engine oil and insert them through the front rotor housing holes and into the front rotor housing.

23. Apply sealer to the front side of the rotor housing.

24. Install new O-rings and rubber seals on the front rotor housing in the same manner as for the other side.

25. Insert each apex spring seal, making sure that the seal is installed in the proper direction.

26. Install each side piece in its original position and be sure that the springs seat on the side piece.

27. Lubricate the side pieces with engine oil. Make sure that the front rotor housing is free of foreign matter and lubricate the sliding surface of the front housing with engine oil.

28. Turn the front housing assembly with the rotor, so that the top of the housing is up. Pull the eccentric shaft about 1″ (25.4mm).

29. Position the eccentric portion of the eccentric shaft diagonally, to the upper right.

30. Install the intermediate housing over the eccentric shaft onto the front rotor housing. Turn the engine so that the rear of the engine is up.

31. Install the rear rotor and rear rotor housing following the same steps as for the front rotor and the front housing.

32. Turn the engine so that the rear of the engine is up.

33. Lubricate the stationary gear and main bearing.

34. Install the rear housing onto the rear rotor housing. If necessary, turn the rear rotor

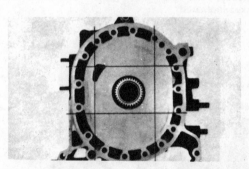

**Measure the housing distortion along the axes indicated**

**Measuring housing wear with a dial indicator**

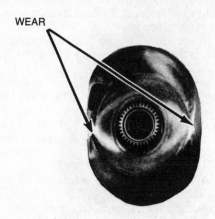

WEAR

Most of the front and rear housing wear occurs at the end of the minor axis as shown

Measure the rotor housing distortion along the axes indicated

Check the rotor housing width at eight points near the trochoid surface

ROTOR ROTATING DIRECTION

Normal shading of carbon deposits on rotor

Measure the rotor width at the point indicated

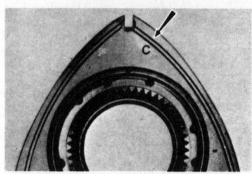

Weight classification letter placement (arrow)

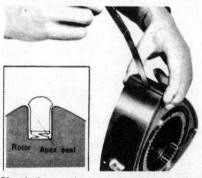

Rotor   Apex seal

Check the gap between the apex seal and groove with a feeler gauge

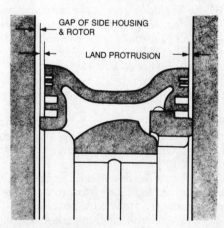

GAP OF SIDE HOUSING & ROTOR

LAND PROTRUSION

Oil seal protrusion

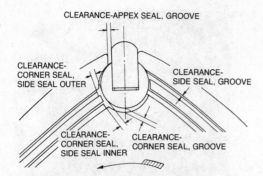

Check the clearance of the seals at the points indicated

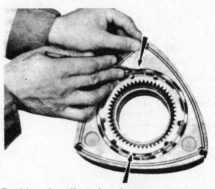

Position the oil seal spring gaps at arrows

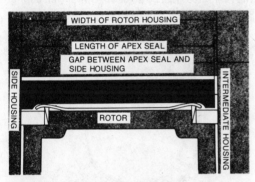

Apex seal-to-side seal housing gap

Insert the special bearing expander into the rotor

Reaming the corner seal groove

Installing a new rotor bearing

Corner seal installation

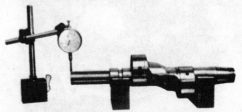

Position the dial indicator as shown in order to measure shaft runout

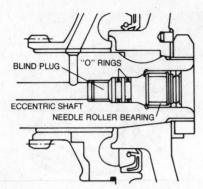

Eccentric shaft blind plug assembly

The rear rotor must be positioned as shown during engine assembly

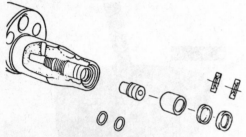

Needle bearing components

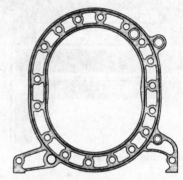

Apply sealer to the gray shadowed areas of the rotor housing

Align the slot in the stationary gear flange with the pin in the housing (arrow)

Intermediate housing installation

Position the o-ring in the groove on the stationary gear (arrow)

Installing oil pump

**Use a dial indicator attached to the flywheel to measure eccentric shaft end-play**

slightly to mesh the rear housing stationary gear with the rear rotor internal gear.

35. Install a new washer on each tension bolt, and lubricate each bolt with engine oil.

36. Install the tension bolts and tighten them evenly, in several stages following the sequence shown. The specified torque is 23–27 ft.lb.

37. After tightening the bolts, turn the eccentric shaft to be sure that the shaft and rotors turn smoothly and easily.

38. Lubricate the oil seal in the rear housing.

39. On vehicles with manual transmission, install the flywheel on the rear of the eccentric shaft so that the keyway of the flywheel fits the key on the shaft.

40. Apply sealer to both sides of the flywheel lockwasher and install the lockwasher.

41. Install the flywheel locknut. Hold the flywheel SECURELY and tighten the nut to THREE HUNDRED AND FIFTY FT.LB. (350 ft.lbs.) of torque.

NOTE: *350 ft.lbs. is a great deal of torque. In actual practice, it is practically impossible to accurately measure that much torque on the nut. At least a 3 ft. bar will be required to generate sufficient torque. Tighten it as tight as possible, with no longer than 3 ft. of leverage. Be sure the engine is held SECURELY.*

42. On vehicles with automatic transmission, install the key, counterweight, lockwasher and nut. Tighten the nut to 350 ft.lb. SEE STEP 41. Install the drive plate on the counterweight and tighten the attaching nuts.

43. Turn the engine so that the front faces up.

44. Install the thrust plate with the tapered face down, and install the needle bearing on the eccentric shaft. Lubricate with engine oil.

45. Install the bearing housing on the front

housing. Tighten the bolts and bend up the lockwasher tabs.

The spacer should be installed so that the center of the needle bearing comes to the center of the eccentric shaft and the spacer should be seated on the thrust plate.

46. Install the needle bearing on the shaft and lubricate it with engine oil.

47. Install the balancer and thrust washer on the eccentric shaft.

48. Install the oil pump drive chain over both of the sprockets. Install the sprocket and chain assembly over the eccentric shaft and oil pump shafts simultaneously. Install the sprocket and chain assembly over the eccentric shaft and oil pump shafts simultaneously. Install the key on the eccentric shaft.

NOTE: *Be sure that both of the sprockets are engaged with the chain before installing them over the shafts.*

49. Install the distributor drive gear onto the eccentric shaft with the **F** mark on the gear facing the front of the engine. Slide the spacer and oil slinger onto the eccentric shaft.

50. Align the keyway and install the eccentric shaft pulley. Tighten the pulley bolt to 60 ft.lb.

51. Turn the engine top of the engine faces up.

52. Check eccentric shaft endplay in the following manner:

a. Attach a dial indicator to the flywheel. Move the flywheel forward and backward.

b. Note the reading on the dial indicator: it should be 0.0016–0.0028″ (0.040–0.071mm).

c. If the endplay is not within specifications, adjust it by replacing the front spacer. Spacers come in four sizes, ranging from 0.3150–0.3181″ (8.0–8.1mm). If necessary, a spacer can be ground on a surface plate with emery paper.

d. Check the endplay again and, if it is now within specifications, proceed with the next step.

53. Remove the pulley from the front of the eccentric shaft. Tighten the oil pump drive

## Eccentric Shaft Spacer Thickness Chart

| Marking | Thickness |
|---|---|
| X | 8.08 ± 0.01 mm (0.3181 ± 0.0004 in.) |
| Y | 8.04 ± 0.01 mm (0.3165 ± 0.0004 in.) |
| V | 8.02 ± 0.01 mm (0.3158 ± 0.0004 in.) |
| Z | 8.00 ± 0.01 mm (0.3150 ± 0.0004 in.) |

sprocket nut and bend the locktabs on the lockwasher.

54. Fit a new O-ring over the front cover oil passage.

55. Install the chain tensioner and tighten its securing bolts.

56. Position the front cover gasket and the front cover on the front housing, then secure the front cover with its attachment bolts.

57. Install the eccentric shaft pulley again. Tighten its bolt to 60 ft.lb.

58. Turn the engine so that the bottom faces up.

59. Cut off the excess gasket on the front cover along the mounting surface of the oil pan.

60. Install the oil strainer gasket and strainer on the front housing and tighten the attaching bolts.

61. Apply sealer to the joint surfaces of each housing.

62. Install the gasket and oil pan. Tighten the bolts evenly in two stages to 3.5 ft.lb.

63. Turn the engine so that the top is up.

64. Install the water pump and gasket on the front housing. Tighten the attaching bolts.

65. Rotate the eccentric shaft until the yellow mark (leading side mark) aligns with the pointer on the front cover.

66. Align the marks on the distributor gear and housing and install the distributor so that the lockbolt is in the center of the slot.

67. Rotate the distributor until the leading points start to separate and tighten the distributor locknut.

68. Install the gaskets an thermal reactor and tighten the attaching nuts.

69. Install the hot air duct.

70. Install the carburetor and intake manifold assembly with a new gasket. Tighten the attaching nuts.

71. Connect the oil tubes vacuum tube and metering oil pump connecting rod to the carburetor.

72. Install the decel valve and connect the vacuum lines, air hoses and wires.

73. Install the alternator bracket, alternator and bolt and check the clearance. If the clearance is more than 0.006″ (0.15mm), adjust the clearance using a shim. Shims are available in three sizes: 0.0059″ (0.149mm), 0.0118″ (0.3mm), and 0.0197″ (0.5mm).

74. Install the alternator drive belt. Attach the alternator to the adjusting brace and adjust the belt tension to specification.

75. Install the air pump with the adjusting brace and install the air pump drive belt. Adjust the air pump drive belt to specifications.

76. Install the engine hanger bracket to the front cover.

77. Remove the engine from the stand.

78. Install the engine in the car.

79. Fill the engine with fresh engine oil and install a new filter. Fill the engine with coolant. Start the engine, check the oil pressure, and warm it to normal operating temperature. Adjust the idle speed, timing and dwell. Recheck all capacities and refill if necessary. Check for leaks.

# Emission Controls and Fuel System

## EMISSION CONTROLS

### Positive Crankcase Ventilation (PCV) System

*OPERATION*

The positive crankcase ventilation (PCV) valve is located on the intake manifold below the carburetor. In the case of the rotary engine the word crankcase is not quite correct, as the Mazda rotary engine has no crankcase in the normal sense of the term. Rather, the valve, which is operated by intake manifold vacuum, is used to meter the flow of fuel and air vapors through the rotor housing.

The diesel uses an extremely simple system designed to operate under the extremely low manifold vacuum conditions that exist in an engine which has no throttle valve. A simple breather hose connects the valve cover with a connector in the intake manifold. The system does not require routine periodic replacement of any part. You should inspect the breather hose occasionally and replace it if it deteriorates. And, at 30,000 mile intervals, or whenever removing the valve cover, you should clean the breather hose and the nipples in the valve cover and manifold in case of oil or carbon clogging.

### TESTING AND REPLACEMENT

The procedures for PCV valve testing and replacement may be found under Routine Maintenance, in Chapter One.

### Evaporative Emission Control System.

The evaporative emission control system is designed to control the emission of gasoline vapors into the atmosphere. On all models except the GLC and the 626 the vapors rising from the gasoline in the fuel tank are vented into a separate condensing tank which is located in the luggage compartment. There they condense and return to the fuel tank in liquid form when the engine is not running.

When the engine is running, the fuel vapors are sucked directly into the engine through the PCV valve and are burned along with the air/fuel mixture.

Any additional fuel vapors which are not handled by the condensing tank are stored in a charcoal canister or a filter which is incorporated into the air cleaner (1972–73). When the engine is running, the charcoal is purged of its stored fuel vapor. On some models, a check valve vents the fuel vapor into the atmosphere if pressure becomes too excessive in the fuel tank. The check valve is located in the luggage compartment, next to the condensing tank. On the GLC models the system consists of a charcoal canister, cut and check valve, liquid separator (wagon only), and purge control valves. The system on the model 626 consists of a charcoal canister, check and cut valve, purge control valves, Evaporator shutter valve in air cleaner.

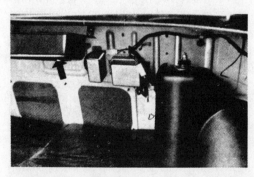

Arrow shows location of the condensing tank in the luggage compartment

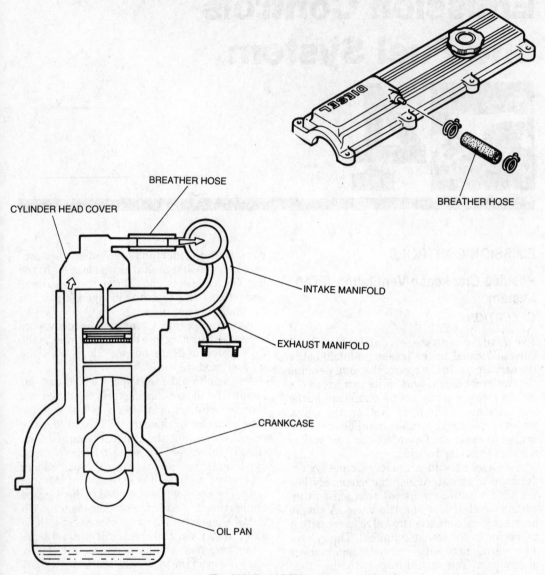

The 626 diesel PCV system

## SYSTEM TESTING

There are several things to check is a malfunction of the evaporative emission control system is suspected.

1. Leaks may be traced by using an infrared hydrocarbon tester. Run the test probe along the lines an connections. The meter will indicate the presence of a leak by a high hydrocarbon (HC) reading. This method is much more accurate than a visual inspection which would indicate only the presence of a leak large enough to pass liquid.

2. Leaks may be caused by any of the following, so always check these areas when looking for them:

a. Defective or worn lines.

b. Disconnected or pinched lines.

c. Improperly routed lines.

d. A defective check valve.

NOTE: *If it becomes necessary to replace any of the lines used in the evaporative emission control system, use only those hoses which are fuel resistant or are marked EVAP.*

3. If the fuel tank has collapsed, it may be the fault of clogged or pinched vent lines, a defective vapor separator, or a plugged or incorrect check valve.

### 1986 626

1. Warm up the engine and then allow it to idle. Disconnect the vacuum hose leading to the purge control valve on top of the canister.

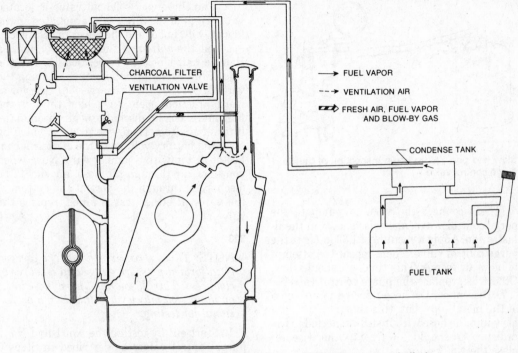

CHARCOAL FILTER
VENTILATION VALVE

→ FUEL VAPOR

--→ VENTILATION AIR

⟱ FRESH AIR, FUEL VAPOR
   AND BLOW-BY GAS

CONDENSE TANK

FUEL TANK

**Rotary engine emission control system—1972 (other years similar)**

Connect a vacuum gauge to the open end of the hose. Connect a tachometer to the ignition system.

2. Increase the engine rpm to 2,500 and read the vacuum gauge. Vacuum must be a minimum of 5.9 in.Hg. If vacuum is okay, go to Step 4. Otherwise, test the water temperature valve as described in Step 3.

3. Drain some coolant out of the system and then unscrew the water temperature valve from the intake manifold. Connect two short lengths of vacuum hose to the valve's connection points. Immerse the lower portion of the valve in a container of water with the vacuum hoses above the liquid level. With a thermometer capable of reading temperatures well past 100°F immersed in the water. Heat the water to more than 130°F and then attempt to blow air through it. If air passes, the valve is okay. Otherwise, replace it. Reconnect the disconnected vacuum hose.

4. Disconnect the vacuum hose labeled **B** from the No. 3 purge control valve and plug it. Then, with another length of hose, connect a vacuum gauge to the open port in the purge control valve, as is also shown. Run the engine up to more than 1,500 rpm and check for vacuum. If there is no vacuum, check out/inspect the three-way solenoid valve, No. 3 purge control valve and the EGR control unit 2P terminal. Disconnect the vacuum gauge and reconnect the disconnected hose.

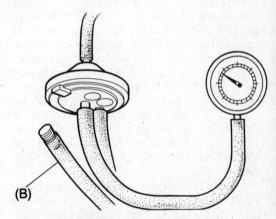

(B)

**Disconnect the vacuum hose "B" from the No. 3 purge control valve and plug it**

5. Disconnect the vacuum hose leading directly into the canister (not passing through the purge valve). Disconnect the hose right at the canister and connect a vacuum source to the open end of the rubber hose so air will be drawn out of the steel pipe mounted to the car body. Operate the vacuum pump. Air should be drawn into the pump freely. If the system holds vacuum, inspect the pipe or the three-way check valve (located near the fuel tank) for clogging.

6. Attempt to blow air into the port labeled **A**. No air should pass into it.

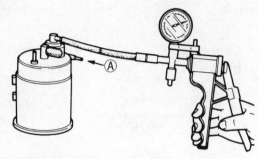

**Blow into port "A" to begin inspection of the No. 1 purge control valve**

Then, connect the vacuum pump to the purge control valve, as is also shown in the illustration. Apply a vacuum of 4.33 in.Hg to the purge control valve. Then, repeat the attempt to blow air into **A**. This time, air should flow. Otherwise, replace the purge control valve.

7. Disconnect the hose referred to in Step 5 at the metal pipe, but, this time, blow into the hose with it still connected to the canister. Air should flow freely. Otherwise, replace the No. 2 purge valve.

8. First label the connecting hoses, and then remove the No. 3 purge control valve. Blow into the center port on the flat side of the valve and check for airflow leaving the outboard port on the flat side. There should be no airflow without vacuum being applied to the valve. Apply vacuum of 2.95 in.Hg to the single port located on the convex side of the valve. Then, blow through the center port again, as you did at the beginning of this step. Air now should flow out of the outboard port. Install a new valve, if necessary, or reinstall the old one with all hoses properly connected according to your labeling.

9. Remove the three-way check valve located on the gas tank vent line near where the filler pipe connects with the fuel tank. Blow through Port **A**; and make sure air comes out Port **B**. Seal off Port **B** and blow again from Port **A**. Air should flow out of Port **C**. Now, block Port **B** and blow through port **C**. Air should come out of Port **A**. If the valve flunks any of these tests, replace it.

10. The three-way solenoid valve is located at the right of the three valves mounted on the fender well. Label and then disconnect the two hoses at the bottom of the valve. Connnect a short length of hose to the port leading into the side of the valve near the bottom, leaving the vertical port (which discharges out in a downward direction) open. First, blow through the hose and check for discharge of air through the filter at the top. Then, energize the valve by applying battery voltage to the electrical connector at top with a jumper wire. Now, when you blow air through the hose, air should be discharged through the port at the bottom of the valve. If either test is failed, replace the valve.

**323**

NOTE: *This test requires the use of a precisely calibrated pressure gauge and a source of compressed air. If you don't have these items on hand, you may wish to take it to a professional for testing.*

1. Start out by testing the No. 1 and No. 2 purge control valves as described in Steps 6 and 7 of the procedure for the 626 immediately above.

2. Remove the air cleaner. Place a finger on top of the air vent solenoid valve located on top of the carburetor. Have someone turn the ignition switch on and off as you feel for operation of the solenoid. If the solenoid does not click audibly or operate so that you can feel it, replace the valve.

3. Test the water temperature valve as described in Step 3 for the procedure for the 626 above. Replace the valve if it fails the test.

4. Remove the check and cut valve, noting that the horizontal connection goes to the fuel tank and the vertical connection is vented to the air. Tee a pressure gauge into the horizontal passage (normally connected to the tank).

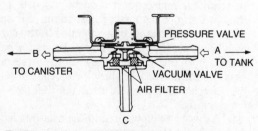

**Testing the three-way check valve**

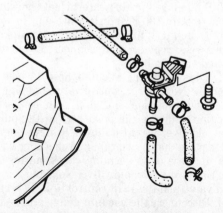

**Removing the check and cut valve (323)**

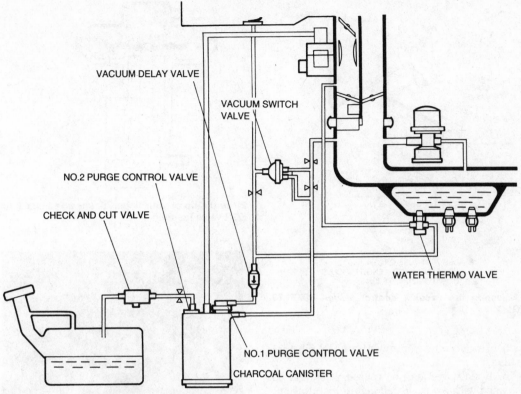

VACUUM DELAY VALVE

VACUUM SWITCH VALVE

NO.2 PURGE CONTROL VALVE

CHECK AND CUT VALVE

WATER THERMO VALVE

NO.1 PURGE CONTROL VALVE

CHARCOAL CANISTER

**Diagram of the 323 evaporative emission control system**

Hold the valve horizontally for proper internal airflow. Gradually valve air into the valve while watching the pressure. Air should start to flow through the valve at 0.14–0.71 psi. Connect the gauge over to the vertical (vented) connection. Again, gradually valve air into the valve while watching the pressure. It should open at 0.78–1.00 psi. Replace the valve if it fails either test.

5. Test the vacuum switching valve exactly as described in Step 8 in the procedure above for the 626.

6. Disconnect the vacuum delay valve. Connect the vacuum pump to the end of the valve away from the arrow with a length of hose 3'4" (1 meter) long. Draw a vacuum of 24 in.Hg. Then, watch as the vacuum decreases from 19.7 in.Hg to 3.9 in.Hg, timing how long it takes. It should take 0.2–1.2 seconds. If the valve fails the test, replace it.

## Exhaust Gas Recirculation System

### OPERATION

This system is used to meter a small amount of exhaust gas back into the intake manifold to slow the combustion process, slightly reduce the maximum temperatures in the combustion chambers, and thus reduce nitrogen oxides. A

water temperature switch or three way solenoid valve may stop exhaust gas recirculation when the engine is cold. On most models, the EGR Control Valve must be serviced periodically, and on some models, a maintenance warning system reset. Also, the EGR valve is by far the most sensitive part of the system, as it can become carbon clogged.

### EGR CONTROL VALVE TEST

1. Remove the air cleaner.
2. Run the engine at idle.
3. Disconnect the vacuum sensing tube from the EGR control valve, and make connections directly to an intake manifold (not carburetor) tap with a vacuum hose.
4. Connect this vacuum tube to the EGR control valve. The engine should stop. If not, clean or replace the EGR control valve.

### REPLACING EGR CONTROL VALVE

1. Remove air cleaner.
2. Disconnect the vacuum sensing tube from the EGR control valve.
3. Disconnect the EGR control valve-to-exhaust manifold pipe.
4. Disconnect the pipe between the EGR control valve and the intake manifold.

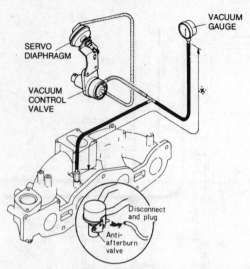

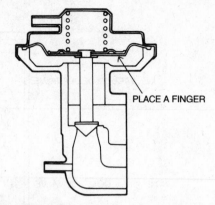

PLACE A FINGER

**Place the tip of your finger as shown to check for EGR valve function**

※ —USE TEST TUBE OF 3.0mm (0.12 in)
INNER DIAMETER. LENGTH SHOULD
BE WITHIN 2.0m (6.6 ft).

**Adjusting the vacuum control valve—1977–78 GLC**

5. Unbolt and remove the EGR control valve.

6. If old valve is to be reused, it should be cleaned with a wire brush before installation.

7. To install, reverse the above procedure.

### RESETTING EGR MAINTENANCE WARNING SYSTEM

This system is used on rotary engine cars. After the passages of the EGR valve have been cleaned with solvent and the outlet of the valve has been wire brushed, reset the maintenance warning system. On models to 1976, remove the cover from the switch and slide the knob in the opposite direction. On later models, disconnect the connector, which is located under the left of the dash, turn one side 180°, and reconnect it.

### TESTING THE EGR VALVE

If the EGR system gets clogged or the valve stem gets frozen due to carbon clogging, the engine may ping even when the proper fuel is used and ignition timing is correct.

One way to check the system is to run the engine at idle speed and place your finger on the EGR valve diaphragm by reaching in under the housing at the top of the valve. Have someone increase the opening of the throttle. The valve should open and its position should modulate as the throttle is open and closed, adjusting for each engine operating speed and throttle opening.

If you doubt that the system is performing properly, the best procedure is to test the EGR

**Route intake manifold vacuum directly to the EGR valve to test it**

valve with the engine at idle and full manifold vacuum applied to the valve diaphragm.

On the 626 1983–84 models, you should plug the hoses of the idle compensator, thermosenor, and reed valves. (Consult the underhood sticker showing vacuum hose routing to identify these).

Disconnect one of the vacuum lines going directly to an intake manifold tap below the carburetor. Most models have a purge line going to the charcoal canister that meets this requirement. Route a vacuum hose directly to the EGR valve from this tap. Disconnect the EGR valve diaphragm vacuum hose and plug it. With the engine idling and at normal operating temperature, plug the full-vacuum hose onto the EGR valve diaphragm. The valve should open all the way and make the engine suddenly run very rough or stall. Otherwise, clean or replace the EGR valve.

### TESTING THE EGR VALVE POSITION SENSOR

#### 1985 626

Disconnect the position sensor connector, which leads to the bottom of the EGR valve.

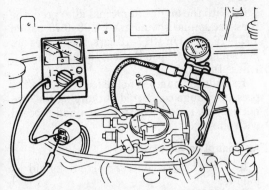

**Hook up the ohmmeter to test the EGR position sensor as shown ('85 626)**

Connect an ohmmeter as shown. If there is an open circuit, the position sensor is defective and the EGR valve should be replaced. If there is resistance, the sensor may be presumed to be okay.

## TESTING THE EGR MODULATOR VALVE

NOTE: *You will need a source of vacuum such as a vacuum pump and a vacuum gauge to make these tests. You may be able to plug off the hoses leading to this valve and then operate the engine and use engine vacuum to make them. In this case, you can tee a vacuum gauge into the line which will apply vacuum.*

### 1986 626

1. Note the routing of all hoses leading to the modulator valve, especially the hose which is connected to the exhaust side of the EGR valve. Remove the valve. Plug the ports numbered **2** and **3**. Attach a source of vacuum to the No. 1 port.

2. Attach a clean hose to the exhaust gas port. Blow into the end of the hose and maintain pressure. Apply vacuum to the No. 1 port and then seal off the source of vacuum. Vacuum should be maintained as long as air pressure is applied.

3. Stop applying air pressure. The vacuum should be released. If the valve fails to respond properly in either Step 2 or 3, replace it.

### 323

1. Note the routing of all hoses leading to the modulator valve, especially the hose which is connected to the exhaust side of the EGR valve. Remove the EGR Modulator valve. Plug the No. 1 port and then attach a source of vacuum to the No. 3 port.

2. Attach a clean hose to the exhaust gas port. Blow into the end of the hose and maintain pressure. Apply vacuum to the No. 3 port and then seal off the source of vacuum. Vacu-

um should be maintained as long as air pressure is applied.

3. Stop applying air pressure. The vacuum should be released. If the valve fails to respond properly in either Step 2 or 3, replace it.

## TESTING THE VACUUM DELAY VALVE

### 1985 626, 323

NOTE: *You will need a source of vacuum such as a vacuum pump and a vacuum gauge to make these tests. You may be able to plug off the hoses leading to this valve and then operate the engine and use engine vacuum to make them. In this case, you can tee a vacuum gauge into the line which will apply vacuum. You will also need about four feet of vacuum line the diameter of that used to connect this valve into the system.*

1. Remove the vacuum delay valve. Cut a vacuum hose of the size used to connect this valve into the system to 3'4″ (1 meter) in length. Then, connect the hose to the inlet end of this valve (the arrow on the valve should point away from the hose connection) and a source of vacuum and the vacuum gauge into the other end of the hose.

2. Hold your thumb tightly against the open end of the valve. Apply a vacuum of over 20 in.Hg. Then, seal off the source of vacuum. Release your thumb and watch the gauge as vacuum decreases to 4 in.Hg. This should take 1.3–2.3 seconds. If the time elapsed during the pressure drop is outside this range, replace the valve.

## Rotary Engine Air Injection System
### OPERATION

The air injection system used on the Mazda rotary engine differs from the type used on a conventional piston engine in two respects:

1. Air is not only supplied to burn the gases

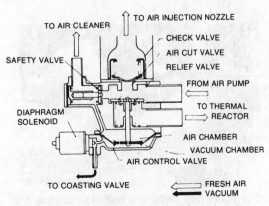

**Cross-section of the air control valve**

in the exhaust ports, but it is also used to cool the thermal reactor.

2. A three-way air control valve is used in place of the conventional anti-backfire and diverter valves. It contains an air cutout valve, a relief valve, and a safety valve.

Air is supplied to the system by a normal vane type air pump. The air flows from the pump to the air control valve, where it is routed to the air injection nozzles to cool the thermal reactor or, in the case of a system malfunction, to the air cleaner. A check valve, located beneath the air control valve seat, prevents the back-flow of hot exhaust gases into the air injection system in case of air pressure loss.

Air injection nozzles are used to feed air into the exhaust ports, just as in a conventional piston engine.

## COMPONENT TESTING

### Air Pump

1. Check the air pump drive belt tension by applying 22 lbs. of pressure halfway between the water pump and air pump pulleys. The belt should deflect 0.28–0.35" (7–9mm). Adjust the belt if necessary, or replace it if it is cracked or worn.

2. Remove belt and turn the pump by hand. If it has seized, the pump will be very difficult or impossible to turn.

NOTE: *Disregard any chirping, squealing, or rolling sounds coming from inside the pump these are normal when it is being turned by hand.*

3. Check the hoses and connections for leaks. Soapy water, applied around the area is question, is a good method of detecting leaks.

4. Connect a pressure gauge between the air pump and the air control valve with a T-fitting.

5. Plug the other hose connections (outlets) on the air control valve, as illustrated.

CAUTION: *Be careful not to touch the thermal reactor; severe burns will result.*

6. With the engine at normal idle speed, the pressure gauge should read 0.93–0.75 psi on 1971–76 cars. On 1977–78 cars, the figures are 800 rpm and 1.64 psi. Replace the air pump if it is less than this.

7. If the air pump is not defective, leave the pressure gauge connected but unplug the connections at the air control valve and proceed with the next test.

### Air Control Valve 1971–76

1. Test the air control valve solenoid as follows:

CAUTION: *When testing the air control valve, avoid touching the thermal reactor as severe burns will result.*

a. Turn the ignition switch off and on. A click should be heard coming from the solenoid. If no sound is audible, check the solenoid wiring.

b. If no defect is found in the solenoid wiring, connect the solenoid directly to the car's battery. If the solenoid still does not click, it is defective and must be replaced. If the solenoid works, then check the components of the air flow control system. See below.

2. Start the engine and run it at idle speed. The pressure gauge should still read 0.37–0.75

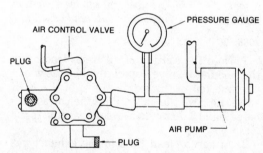

**Test connections for the air pump**

**Check the belt deflection halfway between the water pump and air injection pump pulleys**

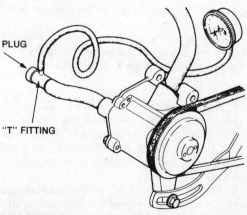

**Test connections for the air pump (1977 and later cars)**

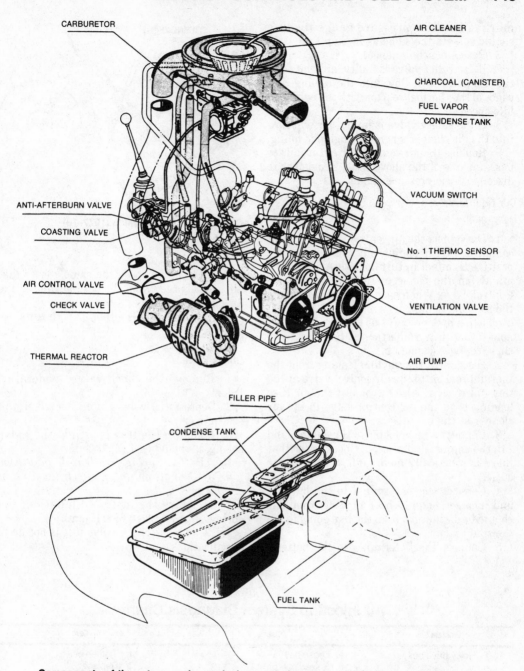

Components of the rotary engine emission control system—1972 (other years similar)

psi. No air should leak from the two outlets which were unplugged.

3. Increase the engine speed to 3,500 rpm w/MT, 3,000 rpm w/AT. The pressure gauge should now read 2.0–2.8 psi and the two outlets still should not be leaking air.

4. Return the engine to idle.

5. Disconnect the solenoid wiring. Air should now flow from the outlet marked (A) in the illustration, but not from the outlet

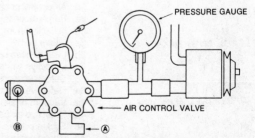

Test connections for the air control valve

marked (B). The pressure gauge reading should remain the same as in Step Two.

6. Reconnect the solenoid.

7. If the relief valve is faulty, air sent from the air pump will flow into the cooling passages of the thermal reactor with the engine at idle speed.

8. If the safety valve is faulty, air will flow into the air cleaner when the engine is idling.

9. Replace the air control valve if it fails to pass any one of the above tests. Remember to disconnect the pressure gauge.

### Air Control Valve

*1977–78*

1. Disconnect the air control valve electrical connector. With engine off, connect battery positive terminal in turn to both A and B terminals on the connector leading to the Air Control valve. When each connection is made, the solenoid being energized should click. If a connection at A produces no click, replace solenoid a, and if a connection at B produces no click, replace solenoid b.

2. Disconnect the air line leading from the thermal reactor to the air control valve at the thermal reactor. Also disconnect the air hose leading from the air control valve to the air cleaner at the air cleaner.

3. Connect a tachometer to the engine, and run the engine at idle speed. Check to see that there is practically no air inflow from either outlet.

4. Connect the A terminal to the battery, and increase engine speed to 2,000 rpm. Air should be discharged from the line going to the thermal reactor.

5. Connect the B terminal to the battery,

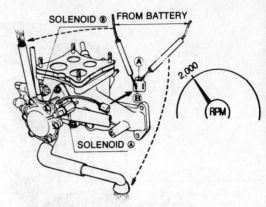

**Checking air control valve (1977–78)**

and, with engine speed the same, verify that air is discharged from the hose leading to the air cleaner.

6. If the valve fails either or both tests, replace it.

### Check Valve

1. Remove the check valve, as detailed below.

2. Depress the valve plate to see if it will seat properly.

3. Measure the free length of the valve spring; it should be 1.22″ (31mm). NOTE: *The spring free length should be 0.75″ (19mm) on automatic transmission equipped models.*

4. Measure the installed length of the spring: it should be 0.68″ (17mm).

5. Replace the check valve if it is not up to specifications.

## Air Injection System Diagnosis Chart

| Problem | Cause | Cure |
|---|---|---|
| 1. Noisy drive belt | 1a. Loose belt | 1a. Tighten belt |
| | 1b. Seized pump | 1b. Replace |
| 2. Noisy pump | 2a. Leaking hose | 2a. Trace and fix leak |
| | 2b. Loose hose | 2b. Tighten hose clamp |
| | 2c. Hose contacting other parts | 2c. Reposition hose |
| | 2d. Air control or check valve failure | 2d. Replace |
| | 2e. Pump mounting loose | 2e. Tighten securing bolts |
| | 2g. Defective pump | 2g. Replace |
| 3. No air supply | 3a. Loose belt | 3a. Tighten belt |
| | 3b. Leak in hose or at fitting | 3b. Trace and fix leak |
| | 3c. Defective air control valve | 3c. Replace |
| | 3d. Defective check valve | 3d. Replace |
| | 3e. Defective pump | 3e. Replace |
| 4. Exhaust backfire | 4a. Vacuum or air leaks | 4a. Trace and fix leak |
| | 4b. Defective air control valve | 4b. Replace |
| | 4c. Sticking choke | 4c. Service choke |
| | 4d. Choke setting rich | 4d. Adjust choke |

**Components of the check valve**

## COMPONENT REMOVAL AND INSTALLATION

### Air Pump

1. Remove the air cleaner assembly from the carburetor.

2. Loosen, but do not remove, the adjusting link bolt.

3. Push the pump toward the engine to slacken belt tension and remove the drive belt.

4. Disconnect the air supply hoses from the pump.

5. Unfasten the pump securing bolts and remove the pump.

CAUTION: *Do not pry on the air pump housing during removal and do not clamp the housing in a vise once the pump has been removed. Any type of heavy pressure applied to the housing will distort it.*

6. Installation is performed in the reverse order of removal. Adjust the belt tension by moving the air pump to the specification given in the Testing section, above.

### Air Control Valve

CAUTION: *Remove the air control valve only after the thermal reactor has cooled sufficiently to prevent the danger of a serious burn.*

1. Remove the air cleaner assembly.

2. Unfasten the leads from the air control valve solenoid or the electrical connector.

3. Disconnect the air hoses from the valve.

**Arrow indicates position of the air control valve**

4. Loosen the screws which secure the air control valve and remove the valve.

5. Valve installation is performed in the reverse order of removal.

### Check Valve

*1971–76*

1. Perform the air control valve removal procedure, detailed above. Be sure to pay attention to the CAUTION.

2. Remove the check valve seat.

3. Withdraw the valve plate and spring.

4. Install the check valve in the reverse order of removal.

### Check Valve

*1977–78*

1. Perform the air control valve removal procedure as described above.

2. Remove the check valve and gasket by unscrewing the valve from the manifold.

3. Install check valve in reverse order, and reinstall air control valve.

### Air Injection Nozzle

1. Remove the gravel shield from underneath the car.

2. Perform the oil pan removal procedure as detailed in Engine Lubrication, above.

3. Unbolt the air injection nozzles from both of the rotor housing.

4. Nozzle installation is performed in the reverse order of removal.

## Piston Engine Air Injection System

### OPERATION

Most Mazda piston engines use the conventional air injection system. This system uses a belt driven vane type pump to force air through air injection nozzles into the exhaust manifold or thermal reactor. The system employs a check valve near the exhaust manifold or thermal reactor to keep exhaust gases from traveling back into the air lines if the air pump fails. The system also uses an air control valve which regulates the amount of air sent to the exhaust manifold, increasing it when the vehicle is overruning (throttle closed at speeds beyond about 20 mph), at which time extra fuel is admitted to the manifold.

Various models replace the air pump with a pulse type system which utilizes pressure waves in the exhaust system and a reed valve to pump air into the exhaust manifold. Models not using pulse air employ a conventional air pump, a catalytic converter, and a system which protects the converter from overheating by interrupting airflow at high converter temperatures.

### CHECKING THE AIR PUMP

1. Disconnect the hose from the air pump outlet.
2. Connect a pressure gauge to the outlet.
3. Check the drive belt for proper tension and run engine at 1500 rpm. Gauge reading should be at least 1 psi. If not, replace the pump.

### CHECKING THE REED VALVE

1. Run the engine until it is hot. Disconnect the air hose at the reed valve.
2. Run the engine at idle speed, and place a finger over the inlet of the reed valve. Air should be sucked into the valve.
3. Increase speed to 1,500 rpm and make sure no exhaust gas is discharged from the reed valve inlet.

### CHECKING THE RELIEF VALVE

1. Run the engine at idle.
2. At idle, no air should be felt at the relief valve. If air flow is felt, replace the valve.
3. Increase the idle to 2000 rpm on 1600 engine, 4000 rpm on other engines. If air flow is felt, valve is working properly.

### CHECKING THE CHECK VALVE

1. Run the engine until it is hot. Disconnect the air hose at the check valve on the exhaust manifold.
2. Gradually increase the engine speed to 1,500 rpm while carefully checking for exhaust (hot) gas leakage from the check valve. Replace the valve if exhaust gases are present.

### AIR CONTROL VALVE TEST

1. Start the engine and run it at idle.
2. Hold a finger over the relief valve port of the air control valve. Discharge air should be felt.
3. Disconnect the vacuum sensing tube from the air control valve and plug the tube. No air should be felt at the relief port.

### AIR CONTROL VALVE CHECK VALVE TEST

1. Disconnect the vacuum sensing tube from the air control valve solenoid.
2. Blow through the vacuum tube. Air should pass through the valve. Suck on the tube. No air should pass through the valve.

### PUMP REPLACEMENT

1. Disconnect the inlet and outlet hoses at the pump.
2. Remove the adjusting bolt and lift off the drive belt.
3. Support the pump and remove the mounting bolts. Lift out the pump.
4. Installation is the reverse of removal. Ad-

just drive belt to specification. Correct belt adjustment will give a 5" flex at the midpoint with thumb pressure.

### REPLACING AIR CONTROL VALVE

1. Disconnect the vacuum lines from the valve.
2. Disconnect the wiring from the valve.
3. Disconnect the air hoses from the valve.
4. Unbolt and remove the valve.
5. Install in reverse of removal.

### CHECK VALVE OR REED VALVE REPLACEMENT

**Models to 1982**

1. Disconnect inlet air hose and unscrew valve from exhaust manifold.
2. To replace, screw in new valve and connect inlet air hose.

## Pulse Air Injection System

### INSPECTION/REPLACEMENT OF REED VALVE

This system is usually trouble free. One symptom of improper operation would be a high hydrocarbon emissions reading, assuming the basic engine functions, including idle mixture adjustment, are okay. To check the reed valves for proper function, proceed as follows:

**1983–85 Models**

1. Run the engine until it is fully warmed up. Stop it and remove the air cleaner cover and element. Get a small piece of ordinary paper.
2. Place the paper against the inlet port for the air injection system. Have someone start the engine and let it idle. Air flowing into the system should draw the paper against the air inlet.
3. Speed the engine up until rpm is 1,500 and check that the exhaust pressure does not force the paper away from the air inlet.

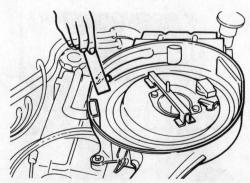

**Checking pulse air injection system—1983–84 626**

**Testing the pulse air system on 1983–84 GLC**

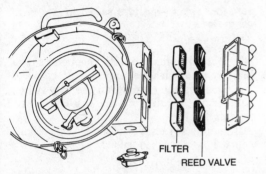

FILTER

REED VALVE

**Typical late model pulse air injection system reed valves**

4. If either test is flunked, replace the reed valves.

### 1986 Models

1. The Air Control Valve must be checked before checking the reed valves. It is located on the side of the air cleaner. Disconnect the vacuum hose, remove the screws and the mounting bracket, and remove the air control valve. Connect a vacuum source to the valve and tee in a vacuum gauge. You can use engine vacuum to do this if you have someone else start the engine, pinch off the vacuum line, and then release vacuum to the gauge and valve gradually.

2. Apply vacuum gradually while watching the stem of the Air Control Valve and the vacuum gauge. The valve stem must start to move at between 7.1–11.0 in.Hg. If the valve does not pass the test, replace it. If it does, install in back onto the air cleaner, leaving the gauge and vacuum source connected to it.

3. Apply a source of vacuum to the Air Control Valve. Vacuum must be 20 in.Hg. If necessary, start the engine. Now, lift the top of the air cleaner off. Check to make sure there is a flow of air into the intake of the ACV valve, accessible from the inside of the air cleaner. Now, have someone accelerate the engine to

2,55 rpm. Check the ACV valve intake again to make sure exhaust gas is not being expelled. If either test is failed, replace the reed valve.

## Thermal Reactor (Rotary Engine)

A thermal reactor is used in place of conventional exhaust manifold. It is used to oxidize unburned hydrocarbons and carbon monoxide before they can be released into the atmosphere.

If the engine speed exceed 4,000 rpm, or if the car is decelerating, the air control valve diverts air into passages in the thermal reactor housing in order to cool the reactor. In later models, air flow into the reaction chamber is cut off under these conditions.

A one-way valve prevents hot exhaust gases from flowing back into the air injection system. The valve is located at the reactor air intake.

### INSPECTION

CAUTION: *Perform thermal reactor inspection only after the reactor has cooled sufficiently to prevent the danger of being severely burned.*

1. Examine the reactor housing for crack or other signs of damage.

2. Remove the air supply hose from the one-way valve. Insert a screwdriver into the valve and test the butterfly for smooth operation. Replace the valve if necessary.

3. If the valve is functioning properly, connect the hose to it.

NOTE: *Remember to check the components of the air injection system which are related to the thermal reactor.*

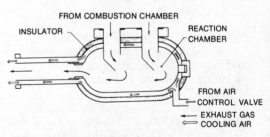

FROM COMBUSTION CHAMBER

INSULATOR

REACTION CHAMBER

FROM AIR CONTROL VALVE

← EXHAUST GAS
⇐ COOLING AIR

**Thermal reactor cooling circuit**

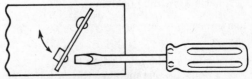

**Check one-way valve operation, as illustrated**

## REMOVAL AND INSTALLATION

Thermal reactor removal and installation are given in the Engine Mechanical section.

## Rotary Engine Deceleration Control System

### OPERATION

The deceleration control system uses an anti-afterburn valve, a coasting valve, and an air supply valve. In addition, either a throttle positioner (1971) or an idle sensing switch (1972–76) is fitted to the carburetor.

1971 models have a throttle positioner to seep idle speed at about 950 rpm during deceleration.

1972–76 models do not have a throttle positioner, but have an idle sensing switch attached to the carburetor in its place. When the throttle closes, its linkage contacts a plunger on the switch which completes the circuit from the No. 1 control box to the coasting valve, thus causing the coasting valve to operate. On automatic transmission equipped models, it also determines trailing distributor operation.

A solenoid operated air supply valve opens when the ignition is shut off to prevent the engine from dieseling (running on).

On 1977 models, these systems are replaced by a combination anti-afterburn and coasting valve, idle switch, and control unit. When the throttle is closed, a signal travels from the idle switch through the control box to a solenoid valve on the deceleration valve which supplies extra air to the intake manifold in order to reduce emissions.

These systems are highly complex and are covered by an extended warranty. Therefore, only simple adjustments are included here.

### COMPONENT TESTING

**Throttle Positioner**

*1971*

1. Remove the air supply hose from the coasting valve and plug up its intake.
2. Start the engine and increase its speed to 2,000 rpm.
3. Connect the solenoid on the coasting valve directly to the car's battery.
4. Release the throttle so that it snaps shut. The idle speed should go no lower than 950 rpm ( 50 rpm). If it does, adjust the throttle positioner, as outlined below.

**Idle Switch**

*1972–76*

1. Unfasten the idle switch leads.
2. Connect a test meter to the switch terminals (A and C - 1973).

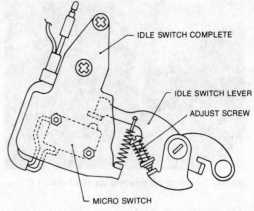

**1972 idle switch—the 1973 switch uses a multi-connector**

3. With the engine at idle, the meter should indicate a completed circuit.
4. Depress the plunger on the idle switch; the circuit should be broken (no meter reading).

If the idle switch is not functioning properly adjust it as described below.

### ADJUSTMENTS

**Throttle Positioner**

1. Disconnect the wiring from the coasting valve solenoid and connect the solenoid directly to the car battery.
2. Loosen the locknut on the solenoid adjuster.
3. Rotate the adjuster until an idle speed of 950 ± 50 rpm is obtained when the throttle is released from an engine speed of 2,000 rpm.
4. Tighten the locknut carefully once the proper idle speed has been obtained.
5. Disconnect the coasting valve solenoid from the battery and reconnect it as found.

NOTE: *As soon as the solenoid is disconnected from the battery; idle speed should drop to 800 rpm.*

**Idle Switch**

1. Warm up the engine until the water temperature is at least 159°F.
2. Make sure that the mixture and idle speed are adjusted properly.
3. Adjust the idle speed to 1,075–1,100 rpm w/MT; 1,200–1,300 rpm w/AT, by rotating the throttle adjusting screw.
4. Rotate the idle switch adjusting screw until the switch changes from off to on position.
5. Slowly turn the idle switch adjusting screw back to the point where the switch just changes from on to off.

6. Turn the throttle screw back so that the engine return to normal idle.

NOTE: *Be sure that the idle switch turns on when the idle speed is still above 1,000 rpm.*

## Piston Engine Deceleration Control System

### 1600 ENGINE ACCELERATOR SWITCH ADJUSTMENT

1. Remove the air cleaner. If the engine is not warm, open the throttle and choke and then release the throttle to ensure that throttle is at normal idle speed position (off the fast idle cam).

2. Fully loosen the adjusting screw of the switch (turning out until switch just clicks off), and then tighten very gradually until switch just clicks back on.

3. Turn the screw exactly an additional 1½ turns.

### 1977–78 GLC VACUUM THROTTLE OPENER ADJUSTMENT

1. Connect a tachometer to the engine. Run the engine until hot, and stop it and remove the air cleaner.

2. Disconnect the vacuum sensing tube **F** from the servo diaphragm, and connect a vacuum hose between the vacuum tap on the manifold and the diaphragm. Disconnect the vacuum line going from carburetor to distributor and plug the open end.

3. Start the engine and read the tachometer. Engine speed should be 1300–1500 rpm. If not to specification, adjust the throttle opener adjusting screw to bring engine speed to within the range.

4. Reconnect distributor and servo diaphragm vacuum lines, and then disconnect and plug the vacuum line going to the anti-afterburn valve. Disconnect the vacuum line going from the manifold to the vacuum control valve, and Tee in a vacuum gauge as shown.

5. Start the engine and accelerate to 3,000 rpm. Watch the vacuum gauge and release the throttle. After a rapid rise in vacuum, the gauge should stabilize at 22.0–22.8 in.Hg for a few seconds while the system gradually closes the throttle, and then fall off.

6. If vacuum does not stabilize in the right range, loosen the locknut and turn the adjusting screw in the end of the vacuum control valve until vacuum is in the specified range. Turn the screw clockwise to increase the vacuum reading, and counterclockwise to decrease it.

7. Tighten the locknut, and restore all vacu-

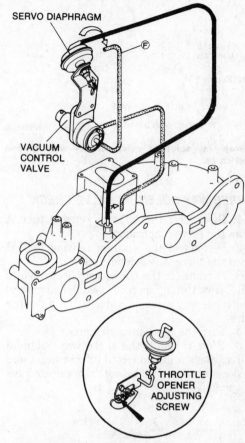

Adjusting the vacuum throttle opener system —1977–78 GLC

um connections. Replace the air cleaner and remove the tachometer.

### SERVO DIAPHRAGM ADJUSTMENT

1. Connect a tachometer to the engine.

2. Run the engine at idle to normal operating temperature.

3. Stop the engine and remove the air cleaner.

4. Disconnect the vacuum sensing tube **F** at the servo diaphragm.

5. Connect the inlet manifold and the servo diaphragm with a suitable tube so that the inlet manifold vacuum can be led directly to the servo diaphragm.

6. Disconnect the vacuum sensing tube from the carburetor to the distributor at the distributor and plug the tube.

7. Start the engine and check to see that the engine speed increases to 1100–1300 rpm (GLC), 1000–1200 rpm (626).

8. Turn the throttle positioner adjuster screw in or out to adjust to specifications.

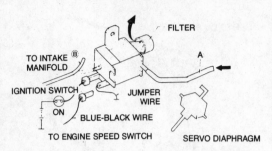

Three way solenoid valve check—with ignition switch on

Engine speed switch check

## THREE WAY SOLENOID VALVE CHECK

1. Disconnect the vacuum sensing tube **A** from the servo diaphragm.
2. Disconnect the vacuum sensing tube **B** from the three way solenoid valve.
3. Disconnect the connector (brown/white wire) from the engine speed switch and ground the three way solenoid valve using a jumper wire.
4. Turn the ignition switch on.
5. Blow through the three way solenoid valve from the disconnected tube in step 1 and make sure the air comes out from the air filter of the valve.

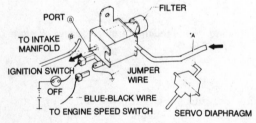

Three way solenoid valve check—with ignition switch off

6. Turn the ignition switch off.
7. Blow through the valve through the disconnected tube **A** in step 1, and make sure that the air comes through the port a.
8. Replace the three way solenoid valve if it does not operate properly.

## ENGINE SPEED SWITCH CHECK

1. Disconnect the engine speed switch connector.
2. Connect a voltmeter to the connector.
3. Increase the engine speed to 2,000 rpm then slowly decrease the engine speed.
4. Record the engine speed at which the current flows to the circuit. The engine speed should be 1,600–1,800 rpm (California AT) and 1,400–1,600 rpm (Canada MT).
5. Slowly increase the engine speed again

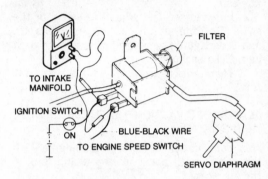

Engine speed switch check

and record the engine speed at which the current does not flow to the circuit. The difference between the engine speed recorded in step 3 and 5 should be 150–250 rpm.

6. The engine speed switch must be replaced if found defective.

## Catalytic Converter

### REMOVAL AND INSTALLATION

#### Rear Wheel Drive GLC

1. Raise the vehicle and support with jackstands.
2. Remove the four bolts and remove the heat insulator.
3. Disconnect the two hangers from the muffler and move the muffler assembly rearward.
4. Disconnect the exhaust pipes from the catalytic converter.
5. Remove the catalytic converter.
6. To install reverse the above.

#### Front Wheel Drive GLC

1. Raise the car and safely support it on jackstands.
2. Remove the heat shield from the front (at exhaust manifold) and rear (under car) converters.

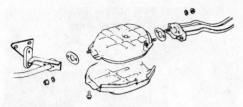

**Catalytic converter installation—GLC**

3. Unbolt the front converter from the exhaust manifold and exhaust pipe.

4. Remove the sensor tube from the rear converter. Disconnect the hangers, loosen and remove the front and rear mounting bolts. Remove the converter.

5. Installation is in the reverse order of removal. Always use new flange gaskets.

### 626 and 808 (1600)

1. Raise the vehicle and support with jackstands.

2. Remove the heat insulator from the catalytic converter.

3. Remove the nuts from the front and rear flanges of the converter and remove it from the vehicle.

4. To install reverse the above.

### 323

1. Raise the vehicle and support with jackstands.

2. Remove the two nuts and washers from behind the front flange of the pipe behind the converter.

3. Remove the nuts and washers from the forward side of the rear flange on the pipe leading into the converter. Pull the bolts outward to the rear through the holes in the forward converter flange. Then, pull the converter down at the front and pull the studs out of the flange to the rear.

4. Supply new gaskets and install in reverse order.

### 808 (1300)

1. Raise the vehicle and support with jackstands.

2. Disconnect the sensor wire connector at the converter.

3. Loosen and remove the sensor from the converter.

4. Remove the heat insulator from the converter.

5. Remove the nuts from the front and rear flanges of the converter.

6. Remove the nuts and rubber bushings between the converter and the body and remove the converter.

7. To install reverse the above procedure.

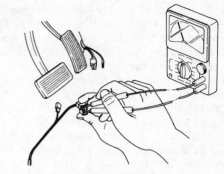

**Checking catalyst thermo sensor**

### CATALYST THERMOSENSOR CHECK

#### 808 (1300)

1. Remove the passenger's side trim plate and floor mat.

2. Disconnect the wire connector at the sensor.

3. Check the sensor with a circuit tester. If there is no current replace the sensor.

## CARBURETED FUEL SYSTEM

### Mechanical Fuel Pump

This pump is used on all GLC models and on the 323 with carburetor. The pump is located on the right side of the engine block on rear wheel drive models and on left side of the intake manifold on most front wheel drive models. An exception to the rule applying to the location on the manifold is the

### REMOVAL AND INSTALLATION

1. Slide the two fuel line clips back off the pump connectors. Then, pull fuel lines off the pump. Mark inlet and outlet lines. Note that the 323 has inlet and return lines on one side of the pump and an outlet on the other side.

2. Remove the two mounting bolts from the block, and remove the pump, gaskets, and spacer.

3. Reverse the removal procedure to install.

### TESTING

1. Disconnect the fuel inlet line going to the carburetor. Install a pressure gauge into the line coming from the pump. Be careful not to spill fuel or, if it does spill, to remove spillage before starting the engine.

2. Start the engine and run it at idle on the fuel in the carburetor float bowl until the pressure gauge reaches a maximum reading. Note the pressure reading. Specifications are 2.84–3.84 psi except on the 323. 323 spec's are 3.98–4.98 psi.

3. To test the volume of fuel discharged by the pump, the engine must be run at idle for one minute. Remove the pressure gauge, reinstall the fuel line into the carburetor, and run the engine until the carburetor float bowl is full of fuel. Procure a durable container (preferable metal) of well over 1 qt. capacity. Disconnect the fuel line at the carburetor, and put the open end into the container. Idle the engine until it stops (or for one minute) and time how long it has run. Then, reconnect the fuel line to the carburetor and run the starter or idle the engine until float bowl is full. Repeat the operation involving fuel discharge and timing until the engine has run for total of one full minute at idle speed and all the fuel discharged by the pump has been collected. The pump must discharge at least 1.1 qts. per minute.

4. If the pump fails either the pressure or volume test, replace it.

## Electric Fuel Pump

The electric fuel pump is located in the luggage compartment of the RX-2, RX-3, RX-4, Cosmo and 308 coupes and sedans, On RX-3 and RX-4 station wagon, it is located behind the left hand trim panel in the cargo compartment. The 626 and GLC wagon fuel pump is located under the floor of the car in front of the fuel tank. On the 323 with fuel injection, it is located in the top of the tank and is accessible by removing its cover on the floor of the trunk.

### REMOVAL AND INSTALLATION

#### 1971–75 Sedans and Coupes

1. Open the luggage compartment lid.
2. Remove the rear inside trim panel, after unfastening its two securing screws.
3. Disconnect the wiring and the fuel lines from the pump.
4. Unfasten the nuts and bolts which secure the pump assembly. Remove the pump.
5. Installation is performed in the reverse order of removal.

#### 1976–78 Sedans and Coupes

1. Open the trunk and remove the partition board or, on the Cosmo, the floor mat.
2. Disconnect the bullet type electrical connector.
3. Raise the Cosmo rear end upward and place on axle stands for access from underneath.
4. Remove the pump cover attaching bolts and remove the cover.
5. Disconnect inlet and outlet hoses from the pump.
6. Remove the nuts attaching the pump to the car body.

Fuel pump location—sedans and coupes

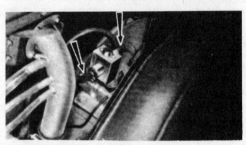

Fuel pump location—RX-3 wagon

7. Installation is the reverse of the removal procedure.

### Station Wagon – Except GLC

1. Remove the left hand cargo compartment trim panel.
2. Disconnect the wiring and fuel lines from the pump.
3. Unfasten the nuts which secure the pump and remove the pump.
4. Installation is performed in the reverse order of removal.

### 626 and GLC Wagons

1. Disconnect the negative battery cable at the battery.
2. Disconnect the fuel pump lead wire in the luggage compartment.
3. Raise the vehicle and support with jackstands.
4. Disconnect the fuel pump bracket.
5. Disconnect the fuel inlet and outlet hoses and remove the fuel pump.
6. Installation is the reverse of removal.

### TESTING

#### Electric Fuel Pump

1. Remove the air cleaner. Procure a durable container (preferably metal) of about 1½ qts. capacity.
2. Disconnect the carburetor fuel inlet hose. Turn the ignition switch on and allow air to be purged from the system with the hose pointed into the container.

3. Turn off ignition, install a pressure gauge into the line, and turn ignition back on. When pressure has stabilized, note the reading and turn ignition off. Pressure should be: 2.8–3.6 for cars built before 1974, 3.55–4.98 for 1974–75 cars; and 4.3–5.4 for 1976 and later cars.

4. Pull the pressure gauge out of the fuel line and position the line so fuel will be discharged into the container. Turn the ignition switch on for one minute. Volume should be 0.9 qts for 1971–73 cars; 1,22 qts for 1974–78 cars.

5. If the pump fails one or both tests, replace it.

## Carburetor

### REMOVAL AND INSTALLATION

#### Rotary, Except Below

1. Remove the air cleaner assembly, complete with its hoses and mounting bracket.

2. Detach the choke and accelerator cables from the carburetor.

3. Disconnect the fuel and vacuum lines from the carburetor.

4. Remove the oil line which runs to the metering oil pump, at the carburetor.

5. Unfasten the idle sensor switch wiring, if so equipped.

6. Remove the carburetor attaching nuts and/or bolts, gasket or heat insulator, and remove the carburetor.

7. Installation is performed in the reverse order of removal. Use a new gasket. Fill the float bowl with gasoline to aid in engine starting.

#### 1977–78 Cosmo

1. Disconnect battery (–) cable. Disconnect all hoses form the air cleaner and remove it.

2. Disconnect accelerator and choke cables at the carburetor.

3. Disconnect the two electrical connectors at the heater and the air vent solenoid and the vacuum lines.

4. Disconnect the sub-zero starting assist hose at the carburetor (except California cars).

5. Disconnect the metering oil pump hoses at the carburetor. Disconnect the metering oil pump rod at the connecting rod at the connecting lever.

6. Disconnect electrical connectors at the idle switch and the power valve solenoid (if so equipped).

7. If the car has a manual transmission, disconnect the connector at the richer solenoid.

8. Disconnect the duel inlet and return lines at the carburetor.

9. Remove carburetor attaching nuts, and remove the carburetor.

10. Install in reverse order, using new gaskets.

#### Piston Engines

1. Disconnect the negative battery cable.

2. Remove the air cleaner.

3. Disconnect the accelerator cable. Disconnect the cruise control cable, if so equipped.

4. Disconnect all wire connections, vacuum sensing tubes and fuel hoses, then remove the carburetor. Cover the opening to keep dirt out of the intake manifold.

5. Reverse the above to install.

### OVERHAUL

Carburetor rebuilding kits include specific procedures and exploded views for order of assembly and disassembly, and so only general applicable rebuilding suggestions are provided here. Efficient carburetion depends greatly on careful leaning and inspection during overhaul since dirt, gum, water, or varnish in or on the carburetor parts are often responsible for poor performance.

Overhaul your carburetor in a clean, dust-free area. Carefully dissemble the carburetor, referring often to the exploded views. Keep all similar and look-alike parts segregated during disassembly and cleaning to avoid accidental interchange during assembly. Make a note of all jet sizes.

When the carburetor is disassembled, wash all parts (except diaphragms, electric choke units, pump plunger, and any other plastic, leather, fiber, or rubber parts) in clean carburetor solvent. Do not leave parts in the solvent any longer than is necessary to sufficiently loosen the deposits. Excessive cleaning may remove the special finish from the float bowl and choke valve bodies, leaving these parts unfit for service. Rinse all parts in clean solvent and blow them dry with compressed air or allow them to air dry. Wipe clean all cork, plastic, leather, and fiber parts with a clean, lint-free cloth.

Blow out all passages and jets with compressed air and be sure that there are not restrictions or blockages. Never use wire or similar tools to clean jets and valves separately to avoid accidental interchange.

Check all parts for wear or damage. If wear or damage is found, replace the defective parts. Especially check the following:

1. Check the float needle and seat for wear. If wear is found, replace the complete assembly.

2. Check the float hinge pin for wear and the float(s) for dents or distortion. Replace the float if fuel has leaked into it.

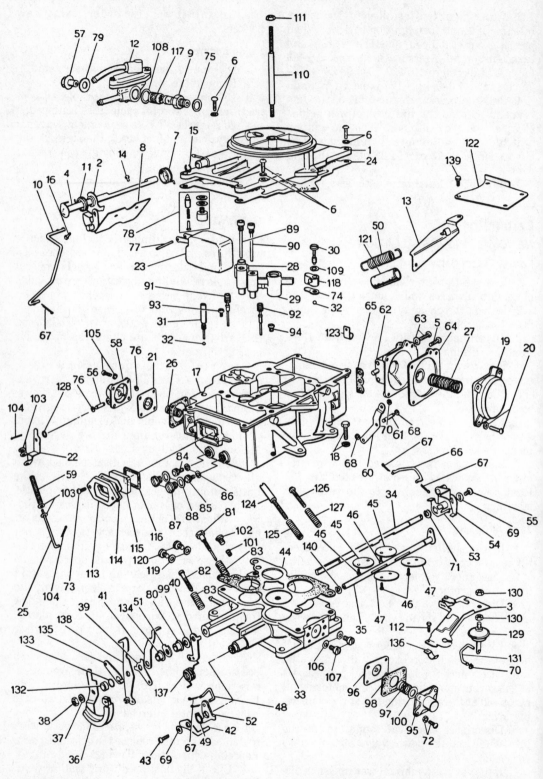

**Carburetor—exploded view**

| | | | |
|---|---|---|---|
| 1. Air horn | 5. Screw | 9. Connector | 13. Hanger |
| 2. Choke valve lever | 6. Setscrew | 10. Connecting rod | 14. Screw |
| 3. Clip | 7. Spring | 11. Spring | 15. Ring |
| 4. Choke lever shaft | 8. Choke valve | 12. Fuel return valve | 16. Bolt |

# CHILTON'S
# FUEL ECONOMY
# & TUNE-UP TIPS

**Tune-up • Spark Plug Diagnosis • Emission Controls**

**Fuel System • Cooling System • Tires and Wheels**

**General Maintenance**

**55 WAYS TO IMPROVE FUEL ECONOMY**

# CHILTON'S FUEL ECONOMY & TUNE-UP TIPS

Fuel economy is important to everyone, no matter what kind of vehicle you drive. The maintenance-minded motorist can save both money and fuel using these tips and the periodic maintenance and tune-up procedures in this Repair and Tune-Up Guide.

There are more than 130,000,000 cars and trucks registered for private use in the United States. Each travels an average of 10-12,000 miles per year, and, and in total they consume close to 70 billion gallons of fuel each year. This represents nearly ⅔ of the oil imported by the United States each year. The Federal government's goal is to reduce consumption 10% by 1985. A variety of methods are either already in use or under serious consideration, and they all affect you driving and the cars you will drive. In addition to "down-sizing", the auto industry is using or investigating the use of electronic fuel delivery, electronic engine controls and alternative engines for use in smaller and lighter vehicles, among other alternatives to meet the federally mandated Corporate Average Fuel Economy (CAFE) of 27.5 mpg by 1985. The government, for its part, is considering rationing, mandatory driving curtailments and tax increases on motor vehicle fuel in an effort to reduce consumption. The government's goal of a 10% reduction could be realized — and further government regulation avoided — if every private vehicle could use just 1 less gallon of fuel per week.

## How Much Can You Save?

Tests have proven that almost anyone can make at least a 10% reduction in fuel consumption through regular maintenance and tune-ups. When a major manufacturer of spark plugs sur-

## TUNE-UP

1. Check the cylinder compression to be sure the engine will really benefit from a tune-up and that it is capable of producing good fuel economy. A tune-up will be wasted on an engine in poor mechanical condition.

2. Replace spark plugs regularly. New spark plugs alone can increase fuel economy 3%.

3. Be sure the spark plugs are the correct type (heat range) for your vehicle. See the Tune-Up Specifications.

Heat range refers to the spark plug's ability to conduct heat away from the firing end. It must conduct the heat away in an even pattern to avoid becoming a source of pre-ignition, yet it must also operate hot enough to burn off conductive deposits that could cause misfiring.

The heat range is usually indicated by a number on the spark plug, part of the manufacturer's designation for each individual spark plug. The numbers in bold-face indicate the heat range in each manufacturer's identification system.

| Manufacturer | Typical Designation |
|---|---|
| AC | R **45** TS |
| Bosch (old) | WA **145** T30 |
| Bosch (new) | HR **8** Y |
| Champion | RBL **15** Y |
| Fram/Autolite | **415** |
| Mopar | P-**62** PR |
| Motorcraft | BRF-**42** |
| NGK | BP **5** ES-15 |
| Nippondenso | W **16** EP |
| Prestolite | 14GR **5** 2A |

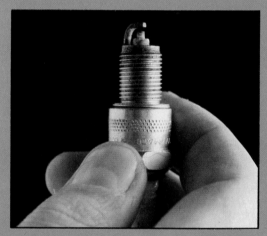

*Periodically, check the spark plugs to be sure they are firing efficiently. They are excellent indicators of the internal condition of your engine.*

On AC, Bosch (new), Champion, Fram/Autolite, Mopar, Motorcraft and Prestolite, a higher number indicates a hotter plug. On Bosch (old), NGK and Nippondenso, a higher number indicates a colder plug.

4. Make sure the spark plugs are properly gapped. See the Tune-Up Specifications in this book.

5. Be sure the spark plugs are firing efficiently. The illustrations on the next 2 pages show you how to "read" the firing end of the spark plug.

6. Check the ignition timing and set it to specifications. Tests show that almost all cars have incorrect ignition timing by more than 2°.

veyed over 6,000 cars nationwide, they found that a tune-up, on cars that needed one, increased fuel economy over 11%. Replacing worn plugs alone, accounted for a 3% increase. The same test also revealed that 8 out of every 10 vehicles will have some maintenance deficiency that will directly affect fuel economy, emissions or performance. Most of this mileage-robbing neglect could be prevented with regular maintenance.

Modern engines require that all of the functioning systems operate properly for maximum efficiency. A malfunction anywhere wastes fuel. You can keep your vehicle running as efficiently and economically as possible, by being aware of your vehicle's operating and performance characteristics. If your vehicle suddenly develops performance or fuel economy problems it could be due to one or more of the following:

| PROBLEM | POSSIBLE CAUSE |
|---|---|
| Engine Idles Rough | Ignition timing, idle mixture, vacuum leak or something amiss in the emission control system. |
| Hesitates on Acceleration | Dirty carburetor or fuel filter, improper accelerator pump setting, ignition timing or fouled spark plugs. |
| Starts Hard or Fails to Start | Worn spark plugs, improperly set automatic choke, ice (or water) in fuel system. |
| Stalls Frequently | Automatic choke improperly adjusted and possible dirty air filter or fuel filter. |
| Performs Sluggishly | Worn spark plugs, dirty fuel or air filter, ignition timing or automatic choke out of adjustment. |

Check spark plug wires on conventional point type ignition for cracks by bending them in a loop around your finger.

Be sure that spark plug wires leading to adjacent cylinders do not run too close together. (Photo courtesy Champion Spark Plug Co.)

7. If your vehicle does not have electronic ignition, check the points, rotor and cap as specified.

8. Check the spark plug wires (used with conventional point-type ignitions) for cracks and burned or broken insulation by bending them in a loop around your finger. Cracked wires decrease fuel efficiency by failing to deliver full voltage to the spark plugs. One misfiring spark plug can cost you as much as 2 mpg.

9. Check the routing of the plug wires. Misfiring can be the result of spark plug leads to adjacent cylinders running parallel to each other and too close together. One wire tends to pick up voltage from the other causing it to fire "out of time".

10. Check all electrical and ignition circuits for voltage drop and resistance.

11. Check the distributor mechanical and/or vacuum advance mechanisms for proper functioning. The vacuum advance can be checked by twisting the distributor plate in the opposite direction of rotation. It should spring back when released.

12. Check and adjust the valve clearance on engines with mechanical lifters. The clearance should be slightly loose rather than too tight.

# SPARK PLUG DIAGNOSIS

## Normal

APPEARANCE: This plug is typical of one operating normally. The insulator nose varies from a light tan to grayish color with slight electrode wear. The presence of slight deposits is normal on used plugs and will have no adverse effect on engine performance. The spark plug heat range is correct for the engine and the engine is running normally.

CAUSE: Properly running engine.

RECOMMENDATION: Before reinstalling this plug, the electrodes should be cleaned and filed square. Set the gap to specifications. If the plug has been in service for more than 10-12,000 miles, the entire set should probably be replaced with a fresh set of the same heat range.

## Oil Deposits

APPEARANCE: The firing end of the plug is covered with a wet, oily coating.

CAUSE: The problem is poor oil control. On high mileage engines, oil is leaking past the rings or valve guides into the combustion chamber. A common cause is also a plugged PCV valve, and a ruptured fuel pump diaphragm can also cause this condition. Oil fouled plugs such as these are often found in new or recently overhauled engines, before normal oil control is achieved, and can be cleaned and reinstalled.

RECOMMENDATION: A hotter spark plug may temporarily relieve the problem, but the engine is probably in need of work.

## Incorrect Heat Range

APPEARANCE: The effects of high temperature on a spark plug are indicated by clean white, often blistered insulator. This can also be accompanied by excessive wear of the electrode, and the absence of deposits.

CAUSE: Check for the correct spark plug heat range. A plug which is too hot for the engine can result in overheating. A car operated mostly at high speeds can require a colder plug. Also check ignition timing, cooling system level, fuel mixture and leaking intake manifold.

RECOMMENDATION: If all ignition and engine adjustments are known to be correct, and no other malfunction exists, install spark plugs one heat range colder.

Photos Courtesy Fram Corporation

## Carbon Deposits

APPEARANCE: Carbon fouling is easily identified by the presence of dry, soft, black, sooty deposits.

CAUSE: Changing the heat range can often lead to carbon fouling, as can prolonged slow, stop-and-start driving. If the heat range is correct, carbon fouling can be attributed to a rich fuel mixture, sticking choke, clogged air cleaner, worn breaker points, retarded timing or low compression. If only one or two plugs are carbon fouled, check for corroded or cracked wires on the affected plugs. Also look for cracks in the distributor cap between the towers of affected cylinders.

RECOMMENDATION: After the problem is corrected, these plugs can be cleaned and reinstalled if not worn severely.

## MMT Fouled

APPEARANCE: Spark plugs fouled by MMT (Methycyclopentadienyl Maganese Tricarbonyl) have reddish, rusty appearance on the insulator and side electrode.

CAUSE: MMT is an anti-knock additive in gasoline used to replace lead. During the combustion process, the MMT leaves a reddish deposit on the insulator and side electrode.

RECOMMENDATION: No engine malfunction is indicated and the deposits will not affect plug performance any more than lead deposits (see Ash Deposits). MMT fouled plugs can be cleaned, regapped and reinstalled.

## High Speed Glazing

APPEARANCE: Glazing appears as shiny coating on the plug, either yellow or tan in color.

CAUSE: During hard, fast acceleration, plug temperatures rise suddenly. Deposits from normal combustion have no chance to fluff-off; instead, they melt on the insulator forming an electrically conductive coating which causes misfiring.

RECOMMENDATION: Glazed plugs are not easily cleaned. They should be replaced with a fresh set of plugs of the correct heat range. If the condition recurs, using plugs with a heat range one step colder may cure the problem.

## Ash (Lead) Deposits

APPEARANCE: Ash deposits are characterized by light brown or white colored deposits crusted on the side or center electrodes. In some cases it may give the plug a rusty appearance.

CAUSE: Ash deposits are normally derived from oil or fuel additives burned during normal combustion. Normally they are harmless, though excessive amounts can cause misfiring. If deposits are excessive in short mileage, the valve guides may be worn.

RECOMMENDATION: Ash-fouled plugs can be cleaned, gapped and reinstalled.

## Detonation

APPEARANCE: Detonation is usually characterized by a broken plug insulator.

CAUSE: A portion of the fuel charge will begin to burn spontaneously, from the increased heat following ignition. The explosion that results applies extreme pressure to engine components, frequently damaging spark plugs and pistons.

Detonation can result by over-advanced ignition timing, inferior gasoline (low octane) lean air/fuel mixture, poor carburetion, engine lugging or an increase in compression ratio due to combustion chamber deposits or engine modification.

RECOMMENDATION: Replace the plugs after correcting the problem.

Photos Courtesy Champion Spark Plug Co.

# EMISSION CONTROLS

13. Be aware of the general condition of the emission control system. It contributes to reduced pollution and should be serviced regularly to maintain efficient engine operation.

14. Check all vacuum lines for dried, cracked or brittle conditions. Something as simple as a leaking vacuum hose can cause poor performance and loss of economy.

15. Avoid tampering with the emission control system. Attempting to improve fuel econ-

# FUEL SYSTEM

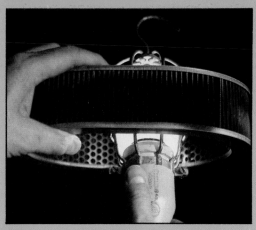

*Check the air filter with a light behind it. If you can see light through the filter it can be reused.*

*Extremely clogged filters should be discarded and replaced with a new one.*

18. Replace the air filter regularly. A dirty air filter richens the air/fuel mixture and can increase fuel consumption as much as 10%. Tests show that ⅓ of all vehicles have air filters in need of replacement.

19. Replace the fuel filter at least as often as recommended.

20. Set the idle speed and carburetor mixture to specifications.

21. Check the automatic choke. A sticking or malfunctioning choke wastes gas.

22. During the summer months, adjust the automatic choke for a leaner mixture which will produce faster engine warm-ups.

# COOLING SYSTEM

29. Be sure all accessory drive belts are in good condition. Check for cracks or wear.

30. Adjust all accessory drive belts to proper tension.

31. Check all hoses for swollen areas, worn spots, or loose clamps.

32. Check coolant level in the radiator or expansion tank.

33. Be sure the thermostat is operating properly. A stuck thermostat delays engine warm-up and a cold engine uses nearly twice as much fuel as a warm engine.

34. Drain and replace the engine coolant at least as often as recommended. Rust and scale

# TIRES & WHEELS

38. Check the tire pressure often with a pencil type gauge. Tests by a major tire manufacturer show that 90% of all vehicles have at least 1 tire improperly inflated. Better mileage can be achieved by over-inflating tires, but never exceed the maximum inflation pressure on the side of the tire.

39. If possible, install radial tires. Radial tires deliver as much as ½ mpg more than bias belted tires.

40. Avoid installing super-wide tires. They only create extra rolling resistance and decrease fuel mileage. Stick to the manufacturer's recommendations.

41. Have the wheels properly balanced.

omy by tampering with emission controls is more likely to worsen fuel economy than improve it. Emission control changes on modern engines are not readily reversible.

16. Clean (or replace) the EGR valve and lines as recommended.

17. Be sure that all vacuum lines and hoses are reconnected properly after working under the hood. An unconnected or misrouted vacuum line can wreak havoc with engine performance.

23. Check for fuel leaks at the carburetor, fuel pump, fuel lines and fuel tank. Be sure all lines and connections are tight.

24. Periodically check the tightness of the carburetor and intake manifold attaching nuts and bolts. These are a common place for vacuum leaks to occur.

25. Clean the carburetor periodically and lubricate the linkage.

26. The condition of the tailpipe can be an excellent indicator of proper engine combustion. After a long drive at highway speeds, the inside of the tailpipe should be a light grey in color. Black or soot on the insides indicates an overly rich mixture.

27. Check the fuel pump pressure. The fuel pump may be supplying more fuel than the engine needs.

28. Use the proper grade of gasoline for your engine. Don't try to compensate for knocking or "pinging" by advancing the ignition timing. This practice will only increase plug temperature and the chances of detonation or pre-ignition with relatively little performance gain.

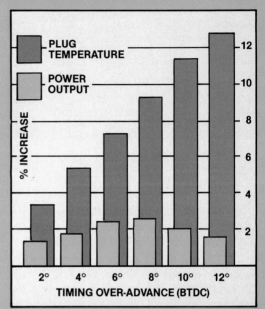

*Increasing ignition timing past the specified setting results in a drastic increase in spark plug temperature with increased chance of detonation or preignition. Performance increase is considerably less. (Photo courtesy Champion Spark Plug Co.)*

that form in the engine should be flushed out to allow the engine to operate at peak efficiency.

35. Clean the radiator of debris that can decrease cooling efficiency.

36. Install a flex-type or electric cooling fan, if you don't have a clutch type fan. Flex fans use curved plastic blades to push more air at low speeds when more cooling is needed; at high speeds the blades flatten out for less resistance. Electric fans only run when the engine temperature reaches a predetermined level.

37. Check the radiator cap for a worn or cracked gasket. If the cap does not seal properly, the cooling system will not function properly.

42. Be sure the front end is correctly aligned. A misaligned front end actually has wheels going in differed directions. The increased drag can reduce fuel economy by .3 mpg.

43. Correctly adjust the wheel bearings. Wheel bearings that are adjusted too tight increase rolling resistance.

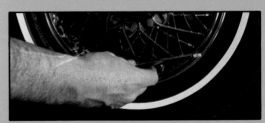

*Check tire pressures regularly with a reliable pocket type gauge. Be sure to check the pressure on a cold tire.*

# GENERAL MAINTENANCE

*Check the fluid levels (particularly engine oil) on a regular basis. Be sure to check the oil for grit, water or other contamination.*

*A vacuum gauge is another excellent indicator of internal engine condition and can also be installed in the dash as a mileage indicator.*

44. Periodically check the fluid levels in the engine, power steering pump, master cylinder, automatic transmission and drive axle.

45. Change the oil at the recommended interval and change the filter at every oil change. Dirty oil is thick and causes extra friction between moving parts, cutting efficiency and increasing wear. A worn engine requires more frequent tune-ups and gets progressively worse fuel economy. In general, use the lightest viscosity oil for the driving conditions you will encounter.

46. Use the recommended viscosity fluids in the transmission and axle.

47. Be sure the battery is fully charged for fast starts. A slow starting engine wastes fuel.

48. Be sure battery terminals are clean and tight.

49. Check the battery electrolyte level and add distilled water if necessary.

50. Check the exhaust system for crushed pipes, blockages and leaks.

51. Adjust the brakes. Dragging brakes or brakes that are not releasing create increased drag on the engine.

52. Install a vacuum gauge or miles-per-gallon gauge. These gauges visually indicate engine vacuum in the intake manifold. High vacuum = good mileage and low vacuum = poorer mileage. The gauge can also be an excellent indicator of internal engine conditions.

53. Be sure the clutch is properly adjusted. A slipping clutch wastes fuel.

54. Check and periodically lubricate the heat control valve in the exhaust manifold. A sticking or inoperative valve prevents engine warm-up and wastes gas.

55. Keep accurate records to check fuel economy over a period of time. A sudden drop in fuel economy may signal a need for tune-up or other maintenance.

3. Check the throttle and choke shaft bores for wear or an out-of-round condition. Damage or wear to the throttle arm, shaft, or shaft bore will often require replacement of the throttle body. These parts require a close tolerance of fit; wear may allow air leakage, which could affect starting and idling.

NOTE: *Throttle shafts and bushings are not included in overhaul kits. They can be purchased separately.*

4. Inspect the idle mixture adjusting needles for burrs or grooves. Any such condition requires replacement of the needle, since you will not be able to obtain a satisfactory idle.

5. Test the accelerator pump check valves. They should pass air one way but not the other. Test for proper seating by blowing and sucking on the valve. Replace the valve if necessary. If the valve is satisfactory, wash the valve again to remove breath moisture.

6. Check the bowl cover for warped surfaces with a straightedge.

7. Closely inspect the valves and seats for wear and damage, replacing as necessary.

8. After the carburetor is assembled, check the choke valve for freedom of operation.

Carburetor overhaul kits are recommended for each overhaul. These kits contain all gaskets and new parts to replace those that deteriorate most rapidly. Failure to replace all parts supplied with the kit (especially gaskets) can result in poor performance later.

Some carburetor manufacturers supply overhaul kits of three basic types: minor repair; major repair; and gasket kits. Basically, they contain the following:

**Minor Repair Kits:**
- All gaskets
- Float needle valve
- Volume control screw
- All diaphragms
- Spring for the pump diaphragm

**Major Repair Kits:**
- All jets and gaskets
- All diaphragms
- Float needle valve
- Volume control screw
- Pump ball valve
- Main jet carrier
- Float
- Complete intermediate rod
- Intermediate pump lever
- Complete injector tube
- Some cover holddown screws and washers

**Gasket Kits**
- All gaskets

After cleaning and checking all components, reassemble the carburetor, using new parts and referring to the exploded view. When reassembling, make sure that all screws and jets

| | | | |
|---|---|---|---|
| 17. Carburetor body | 48. Throttle lever link | 80. Collar | 111. Nut |
| 18. Bolt | 49. Ring | 81. Throttle adjusting | 112. Screw |
| 19. Diaphragm cover | 50. Throttle return spring | screw | 113. Cover |
| 20. Screw | 51. Arm | 82. Idle adjusting screw | 114. Gasket |
| 21. Diaphragm | 52. Retainer | 83. Spring | 115. Sight glass |
| 22. Accelerator pump | 53. Metering pump lever | 84. Main jet | 116. Gasket |
| arm | 54. Metering pump arm | 85. Main jet | 117. Filter |
| 23. Float | 55. Screw | 86. Gasket | 118. Accelerator nozzle |
| 24. Gasket | 56. Pin | 87. Plug | 119. Gasket |
| 25. Connecting rod | 57. Union bolt | 88. Gasket | 120. Plug |
| 26. Spring | 58. Cover | 89. Air bleed | 121. Cover |
| 27. Spring | 59. Diaphragm spring | 90. Air bleed | 122. Coasting valve |
| 28. Small venturi | 60. Diaphragm lever | 91. Slow jet | bracket |
| 29. Small venturi | 61. Diaphragm pin | 92. Step jet | 123. Clip |
| 30. Bolt | 62. Diaphragm chamber | 93. Air bleed screw | 124. Screw |
| 31. Check ball plug | 63. Screw | 94. Air bleed step | 125. Spring |
| 32. Steel ball | 64. Diaphragm | 95. Cover | 126. Screw |
| 33. Flange | 65. Gasket | 96. Diaphragm | 127. Spring |
| 34. Throttle shaft | 66. Connecting rod | 97. Spring | 128. Shim |
| 35. Throttle shaft | 67. Pin | 98. Gasket | 129. Throttle positioner |
| 36. Throttle lever | 68. Ring | 99. Washer | 130. Nut |
| 37. Spring washer | 69. Washer | 100. Shim | 131. Rod |
| 38. Nut | 70. Diaphragm stop ring | 101. Jet | 132. Collar |
| 39. Lock | 71. Diaphragm stop ring | 102. Bleed plug | 133. Shim |
| 40. Adjusting arm | 72. Screw | 103. Retainer | 134. Collar |
| 41. Starting lever | 73. Level gauge screw | 104. Pin | 135. Arm |
| 42. Arm | 74. Gasket | 105. Screw | 136. Plate |
| 43. Screw | 75. Gasket | 106. Gasket | 137. Retaining spring |
| 44. Gasket | 76. Stop ring | 107. Plug | 138. Lever |
| 45. Valve | 77. Float pin | 108. Gasket | 139. Setscrew |
| 46. Screw | 78. Needle valve seat | 109. Gasket | 140. Ring |
| 47. Throttle valve | 79. Gasket | 110. Bolt | |

**Carburetor—exploded view**

are tight in their seats, but do not overtighten, as the tips will be distorted. Tighten all screws gradually, in rotation. Do not tighten needle valves into their seat; uneven jetting will result. Always use new gaskets. Be sure to adjust the float level when reassembling.

### FLOAT AND FUEL LEVEL ADJUSTMENTS

#### 1971 Models

1. Adjust the amount of the fuel coming through the needle valve by bending the float stop so that the distance between the lowest part of the float and the lower air horn face is 2.1–2.2″ (53–56mm).

"1" is the float seal lip and "A" is the distance to be measured with the float in the raised position

2. Invert the air horn and lower the float so that the float seat lip is just contacting the needle valve.

3. Adjust the fuel level by adding or subtracting washers at the fuel intake so that the distance between the upper face of the float and the lower face of the air horn is 1.8–1.9″ (46–48mm).

#### 1972–73 Models

1. Perform Steps 1–2 of the 1971 procedure, above.

2. Measure the clearance between the float and the surface of the air horn gasket; it should be 0.22″ (5.6mm).

3. Bend the float seat lip in order to adjust the float setting.

On all models built after 1973, the float level can be checked without removing the carburetor from the car, utilizing a sight glass in a float bowl. In some cases, difficult access may require the use of a mirror.

With the engine operating at normal idle speed (choke off), observe the fuel level. The level of liquid should cross the glass within the diameter of the green dot or the thickness of the line which is printed onto the glass. If the level is incorrect, the carburetor must be removed from the engine and the air horn removed in order to correct the float level.

Float lowered—1972–73

#### 1974–76 Rotary Engines

1. Invert the air horn, raise the float, and lower it very gradually until the seat lip on the float just touches the needle valve. Then, measure the clearance between the bottom of the float and the face of the air horn gasket. The clearance should be:

- 1974: 0.43″ (11mm)
- 1975: 0.39″ (10mm)
- 1976: 0.30–0.38″ (7.6–9.7mm)

Bend the float seal lip to obtain the specified clearance.

2. Turn the air horn over into its normal position and allow the float to drop by its own weight. Measure the clearance between the bottom of the float and the air horn gasket. Clearance should be 2.03–2.07″ (51.5–52.5mm). If clearance is incorrect, bend the float stop to correct it.

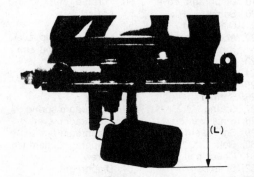

Measuring float drop—1974–76 rotary engines

#### 1977–78 Rotary Engines

1. Invert the air horn and allow the float to drop by its own weight.

2. Measure the clearance between the float and the air horn gasket. It should be 0.6–1.4″ (15–35mm). If necessary, bend the float seal lip until clearance is correct.

3. Turn the air horn over into its normal position, and measure the distance between the bottom of the float and the air horn gasket. The dimension should be 2.03–2.07″ (51.5–

52.5mm). If necessary, bend the float stop to correct the dimension.

### 1600cc Engine

To perform the float adjustment procedure on this carburetor, remove the carburetor assembly from the engine and remove the screws and glass cover from the float bowl.

Invert the carburetor and lower the float until the tang just touches the needle valve. Measure the distance between what is normally the top of the float and what is normally the top edge of the carburetor float bowl. The clearance should be 0.256″ (6.5mm). Bend the float tang to obtain the proper clearance.

### 1300, 1415, 1490cc Engine

1. Invert the air horn and lower the float slowly until the seat lip just touches the needle valve. Measure the clearance between the float and air horn gasket surface (remove the gasket). It should be 0.433″ (11mm). Bend the float seat lip as necessary to correct the dimension.

2. With air horn still inverted, lift the float upward until the float stop contacts the air horn. Measure the clearance between the top of the needle valve and the float seat lip. It should be 0.051–0.067″ (1.3–1.7mm). If not, bend the Float stop until the clearance is correct.

### 1970cc Engine

1. Invert the air horn and allow the float to lower by its own weight.

2. Measure the clearance between the float and the air horn bowl. The clearance should be 0.433″ (11mm). Bend the float seat lip to adjust.

3. Turn the air horn to the normal position and allow the float to lower by its own weight.

4. Measure the distance between the bottom of the float and the air horn bowl. The distance should be 1.811″ (46mm). Bend the float stopper to adjust.

### 1,998cc Engine

Follow the procedures for the 1970cc engine above, but use the following dimensions:

Float to air horn bowl: 0.53″ (13.5mm)

Bottom of float to air horn bowl: 1.929″ (49mm)

## *FAST IDLE ADJUSTMENT ROTARY*

### 1971–73

1. With the choke valve fully closed, measure the clearance between the primary throttle valve and bore with wire gauge.

2. Compare this measurement with the

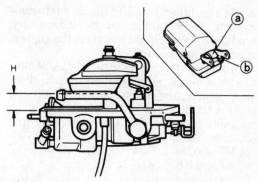

Adjusting float to air horn bowl adjustment on the 1,998 cc engine

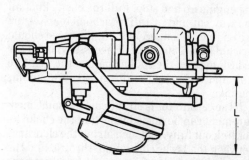

Adjusting float bottom to air horn bowl adjustment on the 1,998 cc engine

specifications given in the chart at the end of this section.

3. Bend the fast idle lever, if adjustment of the clearance is required.

4. Test the choke valve to make sure that it operates freely.

5. Open the choke all the way. The throttle valve should be opened less than 1°, when measured with a protractor.

6. Close the choke valve to an angle of 35. The throttle valve should just begin to open at this point.

7. Start the engine and run it at idle. The choke diaphragm rod should be pulled all the way out. If it is not, check for a clogged or an improperly connected vacuum line.

### 1974

If the carburetor is mounted on the car, center a protractor on the end of the throttle shaft and then have someone pull the choke knob all the way out. The angle through which the throttle

| Year | Throttle Valve Clearance |
|---|---|
| 1971 | 0.047 in. |
| 1972–73 (M/T) | 0.045 in. |
| 1973 (A/T) | 0.055 in. |

moves should be: 14–17° with manual transmission; 16–19° with automatic. If necessary, bend the connecting rod to correct the angle of movement and recheck.

If the carburetor is off the car, the same measurement can be taken by measuring the clearance between the lower edge of the throttle and the throttle bore with a wire gauge of appropriate diameter. Pull the choke lever link out fully. The dimensions are:

- MT: 0.0398–0.0524″ (1.0–1.3mm)
- AT: 0.0480–0.0618″ (1.2–1.6mm)

### 1975–78

If the carburetor is installed on the car, warm the engine up and stop. Pull the choke knot all the way out and install a tachometer. Restart the engine. In ten seconds, engine speed should reach 3,000–3,500 rpm. If necessary, bend the rod connecting the choke shaft to the fast idle cam and recheck fast idle speed in a similar manner.

If the carburetor is off the car, the same measurement can be made by pulling the choke lever link out fully, and measuring the clearance between the lower edge of the throttle and the throttle bore with a wire gauge. Specifications are:

- 1975: 0.069–0.085″ (1.7–2.2mm)
- 1976: 0.067–0.079″ (1.7–2.0mm)
- 1977–78: 0.037–0.045″ (0.93–1.1mm) 49 states; 0.050–0.058″ (1.3–1.5mm) in California

### PISTON ENGINE FAST IDLE ADJUSTMENT

#### 1,600cc Engine

NOTE: *This adjustment can be performed only with the carburetor off the car.*

1. Close the choke valve fully, and measure the clearance between the lower edge of the throttle and the throttle bore with a wire feeler gauge.
2. The clearance should be 0.07″ (1.8mm). If incorrect, bend the rod connecting the choke shaft to the fast idle cam to correct it.

#### 1976–78 1,300cc Engine

1. Follow the procedure above, if the carburetor if off the car. The dimension is: 0.048–0.060″ (1.2–1.5mm). The dimension can be checked with the carburetor on the car. Center a protractor on the throttle shaft and measure the angle that the throttle shaft moves from no choke to full choke. The angle should be 18.5°.
2. If necessary, bend the rod connecting choke shaft and fast idle cam to adjust.

#### 1,415, 1,490, 1,970cc Engines

1. On the 1415cc engine remove the bimetal cover.
2. Using your finger close the choke valve fully.

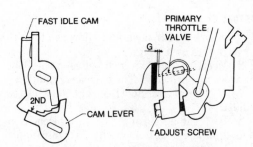

**Adjusting fast idle cam—1415 cc engine**

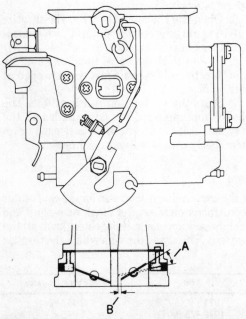

**Fast idle adjustments—measure the angle "A" and the clearance "B"**

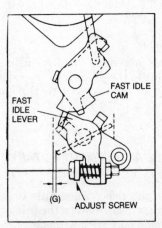

**Fast idle cam adjustment—1970 cc engine**

3. Make sure the fast idle cam is on the 1st position. 3rd position 1490cc engine.

4. The throttle valve opening (clearance G) should be:

• 1415cc engine: 0.054″ (1.4mm) in 1979; 0.041″ (1.04mm) in 1980

• 1490cc engine: 0.026″ (0.66mm)

• 1970cc engine: 0.041″ (1.04mm) in 1979; 0.024″ (0.61mm) for 1980 and later

5. Adjust by turning the adjustment screw. NOTE: *Turn the adjustment screw clockwise to increase the clearance.*

### SEMI-AUTOMATIC CHOKE ADJUSTMENT

#### Rotary Engines

*1974–78*

1. The engine must be overnight cold. Pull the choke knob all the way out and wire it in this position (or if carburetor is off the car, wire the link in position). Wire the choke vacuum break diaphragm in the fully withdrawn position, or, if a vacuum of over 15 in.Hg is available, apply vacuum to the diaphragm.

2. Measure the opening angle of the choke by gauging the clearance between the top of the choke and the air horn wall with a wire feeler gauge. Compare the reading to the appropriate chart and adjust the adjusting screw located on the end of the choke shaft, to correct the reading, if necessary.

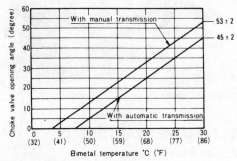

**Choke valve clearance—1974**

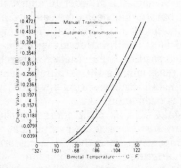

**Choke valve clearance—1975**

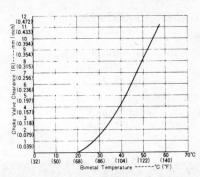

**Choke valve clearance—1976**

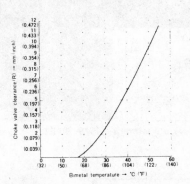

**Choke valve clearance—1977–78**

### AUTOMATIC CHOKE CHECK

#### 626 and GLC

1. Fully depress the accelerator pedal to make sure the choke valve closes properly.

2. Check for binding in the choke valve by pushing with your finger.

3. Make sure that the bimetal cover index mark is set at the center of the choke housing index mark.

4. Check the automatic choke heater source wiring for proper connection, then start the engine.

5. Make sure the choke valve is opened fully after the engine is warmed up.

6. If the automatic choke heater source wiring is normal and the choke valve does not operate after warm-up, replace the bimetal cover.

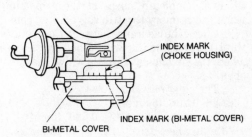

**Automatic choke check—models 626 and GLC 1979–80**

## UNLOADER ADJUSTMENT

### 626 and GLC

1. Close the choke valve fully, then open the primary throttle valve fully.

2. Measure the choke valve clearance. The clearance should be 0.09″ (2.3mm) for the GLC and 0.118″ (3.0mm) for the 626.

3. Bend the tab to adjust.

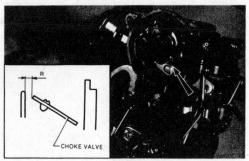

**Unloader adjustment—1979–80 GLC**

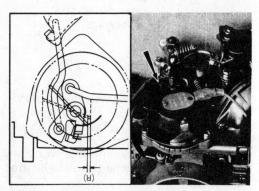

**Unloader adjustment—1979–80 626**

## SECONDARY THROTTLE VALVE ADJUSTMENT

### 626 and GLC

1. The secondary throttle valve starts to open when the primary throttle valve open 49–51° and completely opens at the same time when the primary throttle valve fully opens.

2. Check the clearance between the primary throttle valve and the wall of the throttle bore when the secondary throttle valve starts to open.

3. The clearance should be:
- 626: 0.266″ (6.8mm)
- Rear wheel drive GLC: 0.236″ (6mm)
- Front wheel drive GLC: 0.311″ (8mm)

4. To adjust the clearance, bend the connecting rod.

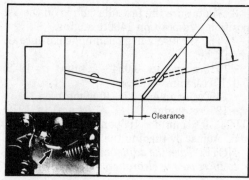

**Secondary throttle valve adjustment—1979–80 626 and GLC**

## ACCELERATOR PUMP ADJUSTMENT

### 1971–73

1. Remove the air cleaner assembly.

2. Move the primary throttle valve and check pump discharge.

3. If there is no discharge, check for a clogged pump nozzle or a binding pump lever.

4. If it is binding, dress the sliding surface of the lever with sandpaper and lubricate it with oil.

5. If pump discharge is still unsatisfactory, adjust the pump lever to one of the two other adjusting holes in the connecting rod.

**Arrow indicates pump adjustment**

## IDLE MIXTURE ADJUSTMENT CHECK

### 1983–84 Models

On these models, idle mixture can be checked with a tachometer in order to adjust it when the carburetor has been disassembled and initial adjustment lost. Note that the spring pin is tapped out of the throttle body with the body in inverted position before the screw is removed. When reassembling the carburetor remember not to install the new spring pin until the mixture has been adjusted.

1. Make sure all basic engine ignition settings are correct, that the engine is at operating temperature, and that all accessories are off. Unplug the electric cooling fan.

2. On the 626, adjust the idle speed to 750

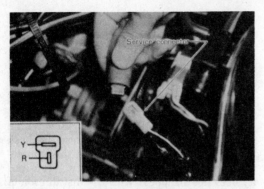

Connect a 4-cylinder tachometer between the "Y" terminal of the A/F solenoid and ground to read fuel/air mixture

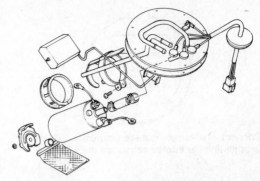

Exploded view of the fuel pump/gauge assembly showing removal of the fuel pump itself (323)

rpm in neutral with manual transmission and 700 in **D** (handbrake on tightly) with automatic. On the GLC, adjust idle speeds to 850 rpm in neutral with a manual transmission, and 1,050 rpm in neutral with automatic.

3. On the 626, plug the hoses of the idle compensator, thermosensor, and reed valves.

4. Connect a tach set up to read dwell for four cylinder engines to the **Y** terminal of the connector for the A/F solenoid. Ground the black lead.

5. Adjust the idle mixture screw until mixture is such that the dwell reads 32–40°. If the idle speed changes, reset it and recheck the mixture adjustment. Idle speed and mixture must meet the specified dwell reading and rpm at the same time. On the GLC with automatic, readjust the idle speed on the automatic to 750 rpm in **D** when the mixture is correct.

If mixture cannot be adjusted properly, the most likely cause is a faulty oxygen sensor.

## GASOLINE FUEL INJECTION SYSTEM

## Electric Fuel Pump

### REMOVAL AND INSTALLATION

#### 323, 626

1. Remove the rear seat cushion. Disconnect the electrical connector located near the pump cover. Remove the attaching screws and remove the cover.

2. Note the hookup locations of the fuel hoses. Disconnect fuel supply and return hoses and plug them. Remove the attaching screws and remove the pump/gauge unit assembly and gasket.

3. Unscrew and disconnect the electrical connectors for the pump from the assembly. Loosen the screw at the clamp which holds the pump in position. Loosen the clamps and remove the hose connecting the outlet of the pump to the assembly. Remove the pump.

4. Installation is the reverse of removal. Use a new connecting hose between the pump outlet and the top of the pump/gauge assembly.

### TESTING

1. Disconnect the negative battery cable. CAUTION: *Make sure the engine is cold. Otherwise, escaping fuel could start a fire!*

2. Cover the connection with a rag because the fuel is under pressure, and then disconnect the fuel line at the discharge side of the fuel filter. Connect a gauge directly into the discharge of the filter.

3. Reconnect the battery. On the 626, disconnect the fuel pump check connector, which is located on the firewall, and jumper the terminals. On the 323, turn the ignition on and then jumper the GW and B terminals of the fuel pump check connector. Observe the reading on the pressure gauge. It should be 64–85 psi. If the wiring to the pump and its relay are electrically sound, replace the fuel pump.

## Throttle Body

### REMOVAL AND INSTALLATION

The throttle body is calibrated at the factory. If there are problems with the adjustment of the throttle adjusting screw or with the action, air tightness, or operation of the throttle, replace the assembly.

#### 626

1. Drain engine coolant out of the bottom of the radiator. Unclamp and remove the air intake hose.

2. Disconnect the accelerator cable at the actuating cam on the throttle body. Disconnect the throttle sensor connector by pulling downward on the locking tab located underneath.

3. Label and then disconnect the vacuum hoses from the upper ports in the throttle body.

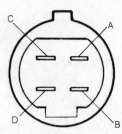

Connect an ohmmeter between terminals "B" and "D" in adjusting the throttle sensor on the 626

Note connections and then disconnect the water hoses and air bypass hose.

4. Remove the four attaching nuts from the studs and pull the throttle body off the air surge tank.

5. Install a new throttle body in reverse order using a new gasket. Then, install a 0.016" (0.4mm) between the throttle lever and adjusting screw. Connect an ohmmeter between the B and D terminals of the connector. There should be continuity.

6. Replace the 0.016" (0.4mm) gauge with a gauge of 0.022" (0.56mm) thickness. Recheck between the same terminals with the ohmmeter. There should not be continuity. If continuity does not disappear with the installation of the thicker gauge or is not there with the thinner gauge installed, adjust the throtttle adjusting screw so that the throttle sensor passes the test. Reconnect the throttle sensor electrical connector.

### 323

1. Disconnect the accelerator cable from the throttle linkage. Unclamp and disconnect the air intake tube.

2. Label and then disconnect the vacuum hoses at the throttle body. Disconnnect the PCV and evaporative control system hoses.

3. Disconnect the throttle position sensor connector. Then, remove the nuts from the mounting studs for the throttle body, and re-

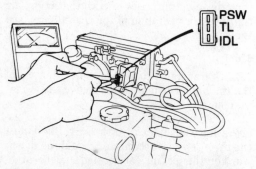

Connect an ohmmeter between terminals "TL" and "IDL" in adjusting the throttle sensor on the 323

move it from the air intake surge tank. Make sure to remove the two gaskets and spacer.

4. Install in reverse order, using new gaskets. Then, install a 0.020" (0.5mm) between the throttle lever and adjusting screw. Connect an ohmmeter between the **IDL** and **TL** terminals of the connector. There should be continuity.

5. Replace the 0.016" (0.4mm) gauge with a gauge of 0.027" (0.68mm) thickness. Recheck between the same terminals with the ohmmeter. There should not be continuity. If continuity does not disappear with the installation of the thicker gauge or is not there with the thinner gauge installed, adjust the throttle adjusting screw so that the throttle sensor passes the test. Reconnect the throttle sensor electrical connector.

## Injector
### *REMOVAL AND INSTALLATION*
#### 626

1. Allow the engine to cool. Disconnect the battery negative cable. Cover high pressure fuel connections with a rag and then disconnect the outlet connection from the end of the distribution pipe and the inlet connection from the bottom of the pressure regulator. Disconnect the vacuum line from the top of the pressure regulator.

2. Disconnect the injector electrical connectors.

3. Remove the two bolts that fasten the fuel distribution pipe to the intake manifold. Gently pull the assembly away from the intake manifold so the injectors and seals slide out of their recesses in the manifold. Then, pull the injectors and seals out of the distribution pipe.

4. Installation is the reverse of removal. Use new injector seals at both ends. Reconnect all connectors securely. Jumper the fuel pump connector as described above under the fuel pump removal and installation procedure and check for injector leaks, making repairs as necessary, before operating the engine.

#### 323

1. Allow the engine to cool. Disconnect the battery negative cable. Follow the first three steps of the procedure above for removal of the throttle body, but do not remove it. Then, remove the attaching nuts from the underside of the air intake surge tank (upper portion of the intake manifold) and remove it with its gasket, for clearance.

2. Disconnect the injector electrical connectors. Cover high pressure fuel connections with a rag and then disconnect the banjo connector from the top of the fuel distribution pipe and

the high pressure fuel line from the bottom of the fuel pressure regulator.

3. Remove the two mounting bolts from the underside of the fuel distribution pipe. Gently pull the assembly away from the intake manifold so the injectors and seals slide out of their recesses in the manifold. Then, pull the injectors and seals out of the distribution pipe.

4. Installation is the reverse of removal. Use new injector seals at both ends. Reconnect all connectors securely. Jumper the fuel pump connector as described above under the fuel pump removal and installation procedure and check for injector leaks, making repairs as necessary, before operating the engine.

### TESTING FUEL INJECTORS FOR CONTINUITY

You can test injectors electrically either on or off the car. Disconnect the electrical connector and connect an ohmmeter between the two prongs of the electrical connector. The injectors used in the 323 should have a resistance of $1.5–3\Omega$; those used in the 626 should have a resistance of $12–16\Omega$.

## DIESEL FUEL SYSTEM

### Injection Lines
#### REMOVAL AND INSTALLATION

CAUTION: *You should not remove the high pressure injection lines from the pump and nozzles unless you have a suitable means (plastic caps) to seal off the openings so dirt cannot enter the delicate diesel fuel system.*

The four injection pipes are clamped together as an assembly to dampen vibration. They are removed by simply unscrewing the four caps on the pump ends and the four on the nozzle ends, and removing the assembly. Make sure to plug all openings with suitable plastic caps if the assembly is to be removed for more than a few minutes.

When reinstalling the assembly, make sure all lines are positioned squarely in their openings at either ends to prevent crossthreading of the caps and nozzles or pump connections. The caps must be torqued to 23–34 ft.lb.

To remove the fuel return lines, first remove the high pressure injection lines as described. Then, disconnect the flexible drain line from the return line assembly and then plug the openings. Finally, remove the four nozzle nuts which retain the return line assembly to the injection nozzles and lift the assembly squarely off the nozzles. Remove the washers underneath and supply new ones. If the assembly will be removed for a significant length of time, cover the open ends of the nozzles with a clean rag. Installation is the reverse of removal.

### Injection Nozzles
#### REMOVAL AND INSTALLATION

NOTE: *It is not recommended that you attempt to work on the injection nozzles of your Mazda, as this service requires special tools and highly specialized training. However, if you keep all parts clean and seal off openings, you may want to remove the nozzles and take them to a qualified professional for service.*

1. Remove the injection lines, both high pressure and return, as described immediately above.

2. Unscrew the nozzles to be removed with a wrench located on the larger flats of the nozzle holder. Make sure to remove the ring type washer and the corrugated gasket underneath for each nozzle and provide new replacements.

3. To install, first install the new washer onto the bottom of the nozzle and then install a new, corrugated gasket to the underside of the nozzle with the red painted side facing upward.

4. Carefully screw the nozzle into the cylinder head. Torque it by the large flats of the nozzle holder to 43–51 ft. lbs. Install the injection lines in reverse of the above procedure.

### Fuel Injection Pump
#### REMOVAL AND INSTALLATION

NOTE: *You will need a suitable puller and two bolts M8 x 1.2 x 45mm to remove the injection pump drive pulley.*

1. Disconnect or remove the following items:

   a. Battery negative cable.

   b. Throttle cable.

   c. Cruise control cable (if the car has cruise control).

   d. Cold start device control cable.

   e. Fuel cut valve and pickup coil connectors.

   f. High pressure injection lines (remove and cap openings).

   g. Remaining fuel and vacuum hoses.

   h. The rear timing belt cover.

2. Rotate the crankshaft to align the matchmarks of the fuel injection pump pulley with the adjacent mark on the rear seal plate. The similar mark on the rear camshaft pulley should align with the nearby mark on the rear seal plate, also.

3. Mark the rear timing belt for direction of rotation. Loosen the rear tensioner lockbolt and then use a screwriver to turn the tensioner clockwise and loosen it; hold the tensioner in

this position. Tighten the lockbolt to retain the tensioner in the fully released position. Then, pull the timing belt off the pulleys.

4. Install the two bolts through the holes in the injection pump drive pulley and thread them into the seal plate behind it. Remove the locknut and washer from the center of the pulley. Remove the bolts. Then, use a puller to remove the pulley from the injection pump shaft, being careful not to lose the woodruff key.

5. Use a drift to precisely mark the relationship between the rear flange of the injection pump and the seal plate. This will avoid the need to re-time the injection pump if you are planning to service and re-use the present unit.

6. Have someone support the injection pump. Use a socket and long extension to remove the injection pump attaching bolt and nuts. Remove the pump.

7. To install the pump, first position it on the mounting flange and install the attaching bolt and nuts just until they touch the rear of the pump flange. Then, turn the pump carefully to precisely align the matchmarks made earlier. When these marks are precisely aligned, torque the nuts to 14–18 ft.lb. and the bolt to 24–34 ft.lb.

8. Install the woodruff key onto the pump driveshaft and lightly tap it with a lightweight hammer to make sure it is fully seated in the groove. Then slide the pulley on over it.

9. Align the matchmarks on the pulley and seal plate and then install the two bolts used to keep the pulley from turning during removal. Install the locknut and torque it to 44–50 ft.lb.

10. Install and adjust the timing belt as described in Chapter 3. Unless a new belt is being installed, make sure the belt will be turning in the same direction.

11. Install the rear timing belt cover. Then, install control cables and wiring, hoses, and injection lines in reverse of Step 1.

12. Operate the pump on top of the fuel filter by repeated depressing the large knob until it can no longer be readily moved. This will bleed the system.

13. If you installed a new injection pump, time it as described immediately below.

### SETTING INJECTION TIMING

NOTE: *To perform this procedure, you must have a special dial indicator and mounting jig designed for this particular job. The Mazda part number is 49 9140 074; you may want to shop around to get the equivalent tool from the least expensive source.*

1. Run the engine until it is hot so that timing will be as when the engine is running. Remove the high pressure injection lines as de-

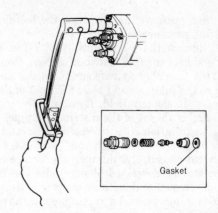

**Remove the delivery valve shown prior to installing the dial indicator on the diesel injection pump and timing the pump**

scribed above, leaving pump fittings uncapped.

2. Remove the service hole cover from the top of the flywheel housing and then rotate the engine to align the TDC (thicker) mark on the flywheel with the indicator pin inside the hole.

3. Remove the delivery valve from the top injection pump fitting, as shown in the illustration. The valve is removed by placing a socket wrench on the flats (the injection line cap screws onto the outer valve). Make sure you keep all valve parts together, in order, and in a clean environment. Supply a new gasket and discard the old one. Remove the hydraulic head plug from the front surface of the injection pump.

4. Mount the measuring jig and dial indicator onto the plug hole on the hydraulic head of the pump. The tip of the dial gauge should contact the plunger end of the pump.

5. Turn the flywheel clockwise (in reverse of normal rotation) to until the crankshaft pulley timing mark moves from TDC to about 30–50° BTDC and the dial indicator stops moving. Then, zero the indicator. Turn the crankshaft slightly to the right and left to make sure its motion does not effect the indicator. If it does, the timing must be advanced further before zeroing the indicator.

6. Now, turn the flywheel clockwise again to set the timing mark to TDC again. Read the dial indicator. The reading should be 0.04 plus or minus 0.0008" (0.02mm). If not, loosen the pump nuts and bolt and turn the pump until the figure is correct. Turn the pump clockwise if the figure is too high (timing is advanced) and clounterclockwise if it is too low (retarded). Retorque the nuts to 14–18 ft.lb. and the bolt to 24–34 ft.lb. Remove the timing device, and install the delivery valve with new gasket, torquing it to 36 ft.-lbs.

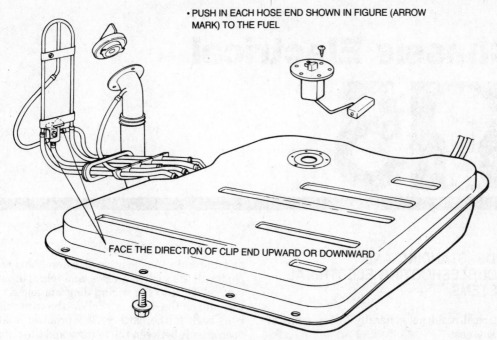

• PUSH IN EACH HOSE END SHOWN IN FIGURE (ARROW MARK) TO THE FUEL

FACE THE DIRECTION OF CLIP END UPWARD OR DOWNWARD

**Routing of hoses on the GLC Wagon fuel tank**

7. Install the injection lines and bleed the system as described above.

## FUEL TANK

### *REMOVAL AND INSTALLATION*

#### Except Front Wheel Drive GLC

On sedans and coupes, the fuel tank is located behind the partition board in the trunk. On wagons, it is under the rear of the car.

1. On sedans and coupes, open the trunk and remove the partition board. On the 626 diesel, remove the lower cushion for the rear seat. On Wagons, raise the vehicle and support securely on axle stands at this time.

2. On the 626, push the access hole cover inward toward the tank. Disconnect the inlet line from the fuel filter on carbureted vehicles built in years through 1985. Remove the tank filler hose clamp, and disconnect the hose at the tank. On fuel injected vehicles, there will be two hoses to disconnect at the top of the tank. Now, raise and support the vehicle securely on axle stands for the remaining models.

3. Disconnect the condensing tank hoses.

4. Remove mounting bolts and remove the tank.

5. Installation is in reverse order. Make sure that, where clamps are used, the clamp is well onto the hose, so that there is one clamp width of bare hose at the end. On the 626, install the large filler hose so that it is at least 1.4″ (36mm) onto the tank fitting or filler tube at either end.

#### Front Wheel Drive GLC

The fuel tank is located under the rear of the car.

1. Remove the rear seat.

2. Remove the fuel tank gauge unit and drain the gas tank. Siphon if necessary.

3. Raise the rear of the car and safely support it on jackstands.

4. Disconnect all hoses at the tank.

5. Remove the mountings, lower the fuel tank from the car.

6. Installation is the reverse of removal.

# Chassis Electrical

## UNDERSTANDING AND TROUBLESHOOTING ELECTRICAL SYSTEMS

Electrical problems generally fall into one of three areas:

1. The component that is not functioning is not receiving current.
2. The component itself is not functioning.
3. The component is not properly grounded.

Problems that fall into the first category are by far the most complicated. It is the current supply system to the component which contains all the switches, relays, fuses, etc.

The electrical system can be checked with a test light and a jumper wire. A test light is a device that looks like a pointed screwdriver with a wire attached to it. It has a light bulb in its handle. A jumper wire is a piece of insulated wire with an alligator clip attached to each end. To check the system you must follow the wiring diagram of the vehicle being worked on. A wiring diagram is a road map of the car's electrical system.

If a light bulb is not working, you must follow a systematic plan to determine which of the three causes is the villain.

1. Turn on the switch that controls the inoperable bulb.
2. Disconnect the power supply wire from the bulb.
3. Attach the ground wire on the test light to a good metal ground.
4. Touch the probe end of the test light to the end of the power supply wire that was disconnected from the bulb. If the bulb is receiving current, the test light will glow.

NOTE: *If the bulb is one which works only when the ignition key is turned on (turn signal), make sure the key is turned on.*

5. If the test light does not go on, then the problem is in the circuit between the battery and the bulb. As mentioned before, this includes all the switches, fuses, and relays in the system. Turn to the wiring diagram and find the bulb on the diagram. Follow the wire that runs back to the battery. The problem is an open circuit between the battery and the bulb. If the fuse is blown and, when replaced, immediately blows again, there is a short circuit in the system which must be located and repaired. If there is a switch in the system, bypass it with a jumper wire. This is done by connecting one end of the jumper wire to the power supply wire into the switch and the other end of the jumper wire to the wire coming out of the switch. Again, consult the wiring diagram. If the test light lights with the jumper wire installed, the switch or whatever was bypassed is defective.

NOTE: *Never substitute the jumper wire for the bulb, as the bulb is the component required to use the power from the source.*

6. If the bulb in the test light goes on, then the current is getting to the bulb that is not working in the car. This eliminates the first of the three possible causes. Connect the power supply wire and connect a jumper wire from the bulb to a good metal ground. Do this with the switch which controls the bulb turned on, and also the ignition switch turned on if it is required for the light to work. If the bulb works with the jumper wire installed, then it has a bad ground. This is usually caused by the metal area on which the bulb mounts to the car being coated with some type of foreign matter.

7. If neither test located the source of the trouble, then the light bulb itself is defective.

The above test procedure can be applied to any of the components of the chassis electrical system by substituting the component that is not working for the light bulb. Remember that for any electrical system to work, all connections must be clean and tight.

# HEATER

## Blower

### REMOVAL AND INSTALLATION

#### All Models

The heater blower is located underneath the dash panel, inside the passenger compartment. On most models, the blower is located next to the heater box and connected to it by a duct. On RX-2 models, it is attached directly to the heater box and therefore no connecting duct is used.

NOTE: *On models equipped with dealer installed air conditioning, blower access may be slightly more difficult.*

1. Disconnect the negative battery cable.
2. Remove the dash undercover if equipped. On the 323, remove the glovebox and the brace that locates the rear of the glovebox and remove the instrument panel bracket. Disconnect the multiconnector to the blower motor.
3. Remove the right side defroster hose for clearance if necessary. On the 323, remove the blower unit-to-heater unit duct.
4. If equipped with sliding heater controls, move the control to the HOT position and disconnect the control wire if it is in the way. On the 323, set the FRESH-REC air selector control to REC and then disconnect the FRESH-REC air selector control wire.
5. Remove the mounting screws and dismount the blower motor. On the late model 626 and the 323, you'll be removing the blower case assembly. Pull off the clips, split the case halves, and remove the blower motor and wheel.
6. Installation is the reverse of removal.

## Core

### REMOVAL AND INSTALLATION

#### Except RX-2 Models

NOTE: *On models equipped with air conditioning access to the heater core will be more difficult.*

1. Disconnect the negative battery cable. Drain the coolant from the radiator.
2. Disconnect the heater hoses at the engine firewall.
3. Disconnect the duct which runs between the heater box and the blower motor or, depending on the model, remove the crush pad and instrument panel pad from the dash. On the 323, disconnect the center duct, located in front of the heater box. See the following section for pad and panel removal.
4. Disconnect the defroster hose(s) if necessary, set the control to the DEF and HOT posi-

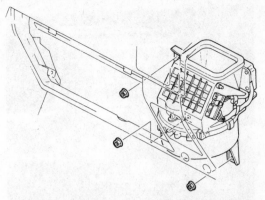

Remove the three nuts shown to remove the blower assembly (323)

tion and disconnect the control wires if they are in the way.
5. Unfasten the retaining screws or clips that secure the halves of the heater box together or remove the heater unit and separate the heater box for access to the heater core.
6. Detach the hoses if not already disconnected. Remove the mounting clips and the heater core. Reverse the removal procedure for installation.

### RX-2 Models

1. Perform Step 1 of the heater core removal above, then remove the blower motor.
2. Unfasten the screws securing the blower housing to the heater box.
3. Unfasten the screws that attach the bottom half of the heater box to the top.
4. Disconnect the heater box to the top.
5. Disconnect the heater hoses from the heater core.
6. Unfasten the clips securing the core to the heater box and remove the heater core.
7. Install in the reverse order of removal.

# RADIO

### REMOVAL AND INSTALLATION

CAUTION: *Never operate the radio with the speaker disconnected or with the speaker leads shorted together. Damage to the output transistors will result. Always replace the speaker with one of the same impedance (ohms) as was removed.*

### RX-3 Models

1. Unfasten the two upper and the two lower screws which secure the center panel to the dashboard.
2. Remove the ashtray.
3. Remove the knobs from both the radio and the heater controls.

Arrows show location of the four center panel securing screws used on RX-3 models

4. Tip the center panel forward.

5. Disconnect the power, speaker, and antenna leads from the radio.

6. Slip the radio out from behind the panel. NOTE: *With the panel tipped forward, access to the gauges, their pilot lights, and the heater controls may also be obtained.*

7. Installation is performed in the reverse order of removal. Remember to adjust the trimmer screw (condenser) on the radio if a new antenna or a new antenna lead has been used. Select a weak station around 1,400 kHz on the AM band and turn the trimmer until the strongest signal is obtained.

### RX-2 Models

1. Remove the knobs from the radio and heater controls.

2. Remove the knob from the hand throttle and its retaining collar.

3. Unfasten the two upper and the two lower screws which secure the center panel.

4. Working from underneath the panel, unfasten the rear brace from the radio.

5. Pivot the center panel sideways (to the left) and remove all the leads which are connected to the radio.

6. Withdraw the radio from the panel. NOTE: *With the center panel turned sideways, access to the heater controls, clock, switches, and the pilot light may also be obtained.*

7. Installation is performed in the reverse order of removal. If a new antenna or antenna head is installed, remember to adjust the trimmer (condenser) on the radio. Select a weak station around 1,400 kHz on the Am band and turn the trimmer screw until the strongest signal is obtained.

### RX-4

1. Remove mounting screws and remove right (passenger's) side console cover.

2. Disconnect power connector and unscrew aerial connector.

3. Remove rear mounting bolt.

4. Pull off radio knobs. Support radio assembly from the rear while removing mounting bezel nuts. Pull the unit back so shafts clear the front of the console, and slide the unit out the right side.

5. Installation is in reverse order.

### Cosmo

1. Pull off radio knobs. Remove radio bezel nuts.

2. Disconnect radio power connector and unscrew aerial connector.

3. Support radio while removing rear mounting bolt.

4. If necessary disconnect additional connectors that may be in the way, and then tilt the rear of the radio upward, pull it backward (to toward the front of the car) until the knob shafts clear the console, and remove out one side.

5. Installation is in reverse order.

### 808

1. Pull off radio knobs. Remove radio bezel nuts.

2. Disconnect radio power connector and unscrew aerial connector.

3. Remove rear radio bracket mounting nut while supporting radio.

4. Pull the back end of the radio slightly downward and to the rear until knob shafts clear the dash panel, and then pull the unit down and out from behind the panel.

5. Install in reverse order.

### GLC, to 1982

1. See the procedure for instrument cluster removal below, and remove the crash pad, meter hood, and wood grain center panel.

2. Disconnect the (−) cable from the battery. Then, remove attaching screws from either side of the dash panel, and pull the radio out. Disconnect aerial wiring, power connector, and speaker connector, and pull the radio out of the dash.

3. Install in reverse order.

### 1983–85 GLC

1. Disconnect the negative battery cable. Pull off the switch knobs.

2. Remove the mounting bolts and pull the radio backward and out of the dash.

3. Disconnect the antenna feeder and wiring connector and remove the radio.

4. Install in reverse order.

**626**

1. Disconnect the negative battery cable.

2. Remove the ashtray, radio knobs, heater control lever knob, and the fan control switch knob.

3. Remove the center panel attaching screws and pull the center panel rearward.

4. Remove the radio attaching screws and disconnect the antenna.

5. Installation is the reverse of removal.

**323**

1. Pull the ash tray out, depress the tang in back, and remove it from its slot in the dash.

2. Remove the two fastening screws from the area of the panel fascia behind the ash tray, and remove the panel, disconnecting the cigarette lighter when you can reach in behind it and unplug it.

3. Remove the two screws from the tops of the two mounting brackets, slide the radio out, disconnect the aerial and electrical connector plug, and remove it.

4. If the unit is actually being replaced, transfer the mounting brackets to the new radio. Install in reverse order.

## WINDSHIELD WIPERS

### Blade and Arm
*REMOVAL AND INSTALLATION*

The wiper arm is held in place with a screw which runs directly into the wiper arm drive shaft or a nut which screws onto the end of the shaft. Note the angle of the wiper arm so that it may be replaced in the same position on the splines on the drive shaft, and then remove the screw or nut and pull the arm off the drive shaft. To install, slide the arm into the splines in the same position, and install the screw or nut.

### Wiper Motor
*REMOVAL AND INSTALLATION*
#### Except Below

1. Remove the attaching screws or nuts and remove the wiper arms.

2. Raise the hood, and remove the screws from the front of the cowl plate or from the service hole panel on the firewall. Raise the front of the plate and disconnect the windshield washer hose at the nozzle. Then, remove the plate.

3. Disconnect the motor wiring. Remove motor and transmission attaching bolts and remove the motor and transmission.

4. Install the wiper motor in reverse order.

**1983 GLC Wagon**

1. Remove the attaching nuts and remove the two wiper arms. Disconnect the battery negative cable.

2. Remove the screws from the front of the cowl grille and remove it.

3. Mark the relationship between the linkage and motor shaft, and then disconnect linkage at the shaft.

4. Remove the three motor mounting bolts — two from the firewall and one from the bracket located directly in front of the windshield — and remove the motor.

5. Installation is the reverse of removal. Make sure the wiper arms are installed so they part in the proper position.

**1983 and Later GLC Sedan**

1. Disconnect the negative battery cable and remove the wiper arms.

2. Open the hood and remove the driver's side service hole cover from the cowl.

3. Disconnect the wiring connector and remove the motor and linkage, as an assembly. If it is necessary to disconnect the crank arm and linkage at the motor, mark the angle of installation first to ensure you can install the arm at the same angle for proper parking.

4. Install in reverse order.

**1983 and Later 626**

1. Disconnect the negative battery cable. Remove the attaching nuts and remove the wiper arms.

2. Pry out the attaching clips from the front of the cowl cover and then remove the cowl cover. Using a screwdriver to release the clips at the rear of the service hole covers, remove them.

3. Remove the two linkage mounting bolts from the cowl area.

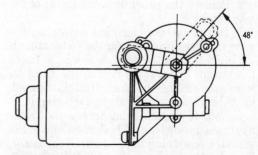

**Proper installation angle for wiper linkage on the 1983 and later 626**

4. Remove the mounting bolts and remove the motor and linkage.

5. If the motor and linkage must be separated to replace either, first mark the relationship between the crank arm and linkage, and then remove the nut. Use a large screwdriver to pry the linkage off the crank arm.

6. Install in reverse order.

### 323

1. Loosen the mounting screws and remove them. Remove the access cover adjacent to the wiper motor from the cowl.

2. Disconnect the motor electrical connector. Remove the three mounting bolts and pull the motor away from the cowl. Mark the angle of the linkage drive lever on the motor. Remove the nut and washer and pry the linkage lever off the motor shaft. Remove the motor.

3. Install a new motor in reverse order, installing the linkage lever at the same angle.

## Rear Wiper Motor
### REMOVAL AND INSTALLATION
#### 323

1. Note the installation angle of the wiper arm, and then remove the attaching nut from the end of the shaft and remove the arm.

2. The rear wiper motor on the 323 may be located either behind a panel in the rear hatch (hatchback) or behind the rear seat (sedan). Remove the door panel or rear seat back, depending on the model.

3. Disconnect the electrical connector. Remove the mounting bolts, and carefully pull the motor toward you, sliding the shaft straight through the rubber seal so as to avoid damaging it. Installation is the reverse of removal. Replace the rubber seal if it has been damaged.

#### 626

1. Note the installation angle of the wiper arm, and then remove the attaching nut from the end of the shaft and remove the arm.

2. Remove the panel from the inside of the rear hatch.

3. Disconnect the electrical connector. Remove the mounting bolts for the motor mounting bracket from the door. Remove the motor and bracket by carefully pulling the motor toward you, sliding the shaft straight through the rubber seal so as to avoid damaging it.

4. Remove the attaching screws and transfer the mounting bracket to the new motor. Reverse the remaining steps to install the motor. Replace the rubber shaft seal if it has been damaged.

## INSTRUMENT PANEL

### Crash Pad and Instrument Panel
#### REMOVAL AND INSTALLATION

1. Disconnect the negative battery cable.

2. Remove the steering wheel and the lower steering column cover.

3. Remove the glove box, switch panel and console.

4. Remove the meter (gauge) hood, heater control panel mounting screws and separate the heater controls from the instrument panel frame. Remove the combination meter.

5. Remove the air duct(s) and the steering shaft mounting bracket bolts. Allow the column to lower.

6. Disconnect and label the meter wiring. Remove the mounting bolts and unmount the crush pad and instrument panel.

7. Install in reverse order of removal.

### Instrument Cluster

Instrument cluster removal and installation procedures included here are those which can reasonably be performed utilizing the tools and skills possessed by the average do-it-yourself mechanic. Directions for performing this procedure on RX-4, 808, and Cosmo models are not included because of extreme complexity and the required use of certain special tools.

#### REMOVAL AND INSTALLATION
##### RX-3 Models

1. Disconnect the ground cable from the negative (–) battery terminal.

2. Pull the knob off the steering column-mounted headlight switch. Remove the screws which fasten the halves of the steering column shroud and separate the halves.

3. Open the left hand (driver's side) door to gain access to the screw which is located on the side of the instrument cluster. Remove the screw.

4. Unfasten the three retaining screws which are located underneath the instrument cluster.

5. Tip the top of the cluster toward the steering wheel.

6. Disconnect the wiring and the speedometer cable from the back of the instrument cluster.

7. Remove the cluster assembly completely.

8. Installation is performed in the reverse order of removal.

##### RX-2 Models

1. Disconnect the ground cable from the negative terminal (–) of the battery.

**Arrow indicates the screw which secures the instrument cluster to the side of the dashboard on RX-3 models**

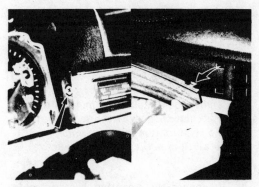

**Removing wood grain center panel—GLC**

2. Unfasten the screws which hold the halves of the steering column shroud together and pull off the headlight switch knob. Separate the halves of the shroud.

3. Working from underneath the instrument cluster, disconnect the speedometer cable.

4. Unfasten the two upper and the two lower screws which secure the instrument cluster.

5. Tip the top of the cluster toward the steering wheel.

6. Disconnect each component by unfastening its electrical connector.

7. Lift the cluster away from the dash panel.

8. Installation is performed in the reverse order of removal.

### GLC and GLC Wagon w/Standard Dash

1. Disconnect the (–) battery terminal. Place masking tape on the instrument panel pad directly below the instrument cluster to prevent damage to the pad during the procedure.

2. Remove the meter hood by removing the screw above either dial, and pulling the hood off the dash.

3. Remove the wood grain center panel cover by removing the screw from the left side and unclipping the panel on the right (see illustration).

4. Remove the three screws located under the front edge of the crash pad, and remove the pad.

5. Reach behind the speedometer and disconnect the cable by pressing on the flat surface of the connector.

6. Remove the three screws from the instrument cluster, and pull the cluster out of the dash.

7. Disconnect the multiple connectors.

8. Installation is the reverse of removal.

### GLC w/Sport Dash

1. Disconnect the (–) battery cable.

2. Put masking tape along the panel just below where the cluster will come out to protect it.

3. Remove the meter hood by removing the tripmeter knob (1), screws (2), clips (3), and the hood (4) (see illustration).

4. Remove the wood grain center panel cover as described in Step 3 of the procedure above.

5. Remove the instrument panel pad by removing the three screws located under the front edge of removing the pad.

6. Remove the three screws from the top of the combination instrument cluster, and pull the cluster outward.

7. Disconnect the speedometer cable by pressing on the flat surface of the plastic connector. Disconnect the wiring connectors. Remove the cluster.

8. Installation is the reverse of the removal procedure.

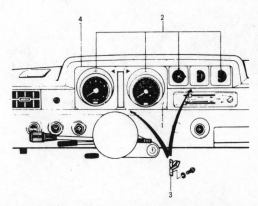

**Removing instrument hood, GLC sport dash**

### 626 up through 1984

1. Disconnect the negative battery cable.
2. Remove the steering wheel.
3. Remove the column cover.
4. Disconnect the speedometer cable.
5. Remove the meter hood.
6. Remove the combination meter attaching screws, disconnect the wire connections and remove the combination meter assembly.
7. Installation is the reverse of removal.

### 1985 626

1. Disconnect the negative battery cable. Tilt the steering wheel downward.
2. Remove the cover from the top of the meter hood. Remove the two screws from the top of the meter assembly.
3. Remove the two attaching screws from the underside of the meter hood. Then, remove the four screws from the underside of the assembly.
4. Remove the four screws attaching the meter assembly to the hood. Pull the assembly out slightly and disconnect the plugs and speedom-

eter cable, and remove the light (to disconnect the plugs, it is necessary to depress the retaining clip). Pull the assembly out.
5. Install the instrument cluster in reverse order.

### 1986 626

1. Disconnect the negative battery cable. Tilt the steering wheel downward.
2. Disconnect the speedometer cable from the rear of the cluster by reaching up behind the cluster and unscrewing the collar.
3. Remove the four screws from the underside of the instrument cluster assembly where it attaches to the underside of the dash and the three from the underside of the hood.
4. Remove the two screws attaching the cluster to the hood at the top. Then, pull the assembly slightly outward and disconnect the wiring connectors (to disconnect the plugs, it is necessary to depress the retaining clip). Then, the cluster assembly may be removed.
5. Install the instrument cluster in reverse order.

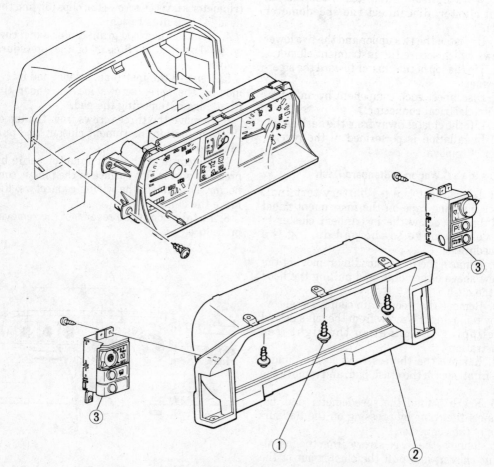

**Removing the instrument cluster (323)**

**323**

1. Disconnect the negative battery cable. Remove the three screws from under the top edge of the instrument hood.

2. Pull the hood out for access, unplug the electrical connectors to the cluster switches on either side, and remove it.

3. Remove the screw located near the bottom of the cluster on either side, and remove the cluster from the dash, unplugging connectors when you can reach them.

4. Installation is the reverse of removal.

## Instrument Cluster Mounted Switches
### REMOVAL AND INSTALLATION

On late model Mazdas, these switches are mounted in a cluster on either side of the instrument cluster. Remove the cluster as described above. Then, working from the rear, remove the attaching screws at top and bottom, and remove the cluster of switches involved.

Then, carefully pry the switch knob off the front of the cluster. Finally, release the lockpins at the rear and pull the switch out the back of the cluster. Install in revers order, making sure the plugs are securely connected.

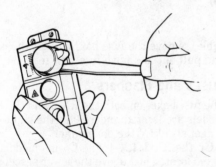

Prying a switch knob off a cluster of switches (typical of late model cars)

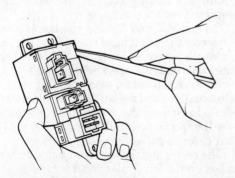

Release the lockpins and remove the switch from the rear of the cluster, as shown

## Speedometer Cable
### REPLACEMENT

Reach back behind the dash and disconnect the speedometer cable behind the instrument by depressing the flat portion of the connector, and then pulling the connector off. Then pull the cable core out of the cable housing.

If the entire cable core does not come out due to breakage, it will be necessary to raise and securely support the car, unscrew the speedometer cable housing at the transmission, and pull the lower end of the cable out. Then, reconnect the lower end of the cable housing.

Lubricate the new core with speedometer cable lubricant, and insert it into the top of the cable housing. Work the cable in until it bottoms against the drive gear in the transmission. Then, simultaneously press the core inward while rotating until the square end of the core engages the gear and seats. Reconnect the cable housing to the back of the speedometer.

## LIGHTING

### Headlights
#### REMOVAL AND INSTALLATION

On some models (for example the 626) you must remove the radiator grille to gain access to the headlights. If the grille blocks removal of the headlamp assembly or adjacent bezel, remove the attaching screws or disconnect the clips (usually 5 or 6 of them) and remove the grille. Then, remove the bezel, or half bezel that runs around the outside of the headlight by removing the attaching screws and removing it.

The next step is to clearly identify the two adjusting screws for the headlight. There are either two at the top or one on the side and one at top or bottom. These are always long screws which are tensioned by a spring. The spring is either working in opposition to the screw at the opposite side of the headlight or surrounds the screw. DO NOT TOUCH THESE SCREWS, AS THIS WILL CHANGE HEADLIGHT AIMING.

Remove the two to four short screws which actually fasten the headlight in place. On models with round headlights, these may retain a thin metal ring which actually holds the light in place. If the ring has elongated slots instead of round holes, just loosen the screws and rotate the ring until the rounded parts of the slots line up with the screw heads to remove it. Remove the ring, if necessary, and pull the headlight out until you can unplug it. Then, remove the assembly.

Be careful not to mix up the inner and outer lights if both must be replaced at the same time. The inner lights have only one filament, while the outer lights have two. To install the new headlight, first attach the plug securely. Then, position a square light so screw holes in the mounting plate will line up with screw slots in the headlamp assembly; turn a round light until the glass tab on the light locks into the notch in the mounting plate. Then, install the retaining screws or ring and retaining screws. Finally, install the bezel and, if necessary, the grille.

## Signal, Marker, and Turn Signal Lights
### REMOVAL AND INSTALLATION

To replace any of these lamps, simply remove the attaching screw or screw from the lens, remove the lens and gasket, and then depress and twist the lamp to the left (counterclockwise) to remove it. Install in reverse order.

## CIRCUIT PROTECTION

### Fusible Links

On the rotary engine cars and the 808, these are located in either one or two boxes next to the battery in the engine compartment. If these links blow, they may be replaced with the specified parts by disconnecting the battery, disconnect wiring to each link requiring replacement, removing the attaching screws an the link, and installing the new link or links in the reverse of the removal procedure.

On the GLC, there is a connector block located on the radiator panel on the right side of the radiator inside the engine compartment. On 1983 and later models, this has been moved the left inner fender panel, behind the battery. Two links connected there are color coded red and green and may simply be unplugged to remove them, and replace by plugging in replacement parts. Make sure to disconnect the battery before replacing them.

On the GLC wagon, the fusible link is located between connector plugs near the battery. On the 626 through 1985, three fusible links are visible in a box of links and relays mounted on the inner fender panel right behind the battery. In both cases, disconnect the negative battery cable before replacing the links.

On the 1986 626 and the 323, there are master fuses (30, 40 and 80 amps) located in a box mounted on the left side fender panel. To replace these, disconnect the battery negative

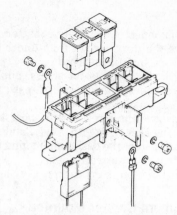

Replacing master fuses on the 323 and the 1986 626

Arrow shows location of RX-3 fusebox (RX-2 similar)

cable, remove the fuse box, pull off the cover, and pull out and push in a new fuse.

### Fuses and Flashers

The fuse boxes on both the RX-3 and the RX-2 models are located underneath the right (passenger's) side of the dash panel.

On the RX-3, RX-4, and Cosmo models, the box is located just above the lower parcel shelf and uses a back-hinged cover.

On RX-2 models, the box is located underneath the leading edge of the dash and is equipped with a sliding cover.

On the GLC and 626 the fuse box is located underneath the left hand side of the dash panel or on the left side kick panel. All covers have the location, amperage, and the circuit protected by each individual fuse, stamped on them. On the 323, the fuse box is located under the dash, in front of the driver. On 1986 models, use the special fuse puller provided in the fuse box cover to pull a fuse.

The relays and flashers are located either in a box on the left fender panel behind the battery or under the dash, near the fusebox (323).

Flasher units are replaced by simply unplugging them and plugging a new one in, but you should never work on them without first disconnecting the negative battery cable. In a few cases, the side of the flasher is also clipped to a mounting bracket. The clip passes through a slot, and all you have to do is lift the unit off the bracket.

## WIRING DIAGRAMS

Wiring diagrams have been left out of this book. As cars have become more complex, and available with longer and longer option lists, wiring diagrams have grown in size and complexity also. It has become virtually to reproduce them in a book this size.

# Drive Train

# ✛6

## MANUAL TRANSMISSION/TRANSAXLE

### Identification

Transmission codes are available from the vehicle information code plate on the cowl in the engine compartment. The first portion of the code is the transmission designation; following this, there is a blank box; at the right end of the line is the axle or final drive ratio.

### SHIFT LEVER ADJUSTMENT

The shift lever on most models may be adjusted during transmission installation by means of adjusting shims on the three bolts between the cover plate and the packing. The force required to move the shift knob should be 4.4-8.8 lbs.

### REMOVAL AND INSTALLATION

#### All Models Except GLC, 323 and 626

1. Remove the knob from the gearshift lever.

2. Unfasten the screws which secure the center console to the floor and remove the console over the shift lever.

3. Remove the floor mat.

4. Unfasten the screws which attach the shift lever boot and withdraw the boot over the shift lever.

5. Unbolt the cover and remove it from the gearshift lever retainer.

6. Pull the gearshift lever, complete with shims and bushings, straight up and out of its retainer.

7. Detach the ground lead from the negative (-) battery terminal.

8. Fasten the nuts which secure the clutch release cylinder and tie the cylinder up and out of the way. Do not disconnect the hydraulic line from the clutch release cylinder. On RX-4 and Cosmo, remove the upper starter bolt and loosen the three upper engine-to-transmission bolts.

9. Detach the back-up switch multiconnector which is located near the clutch release cylinder. On RX-4 and Cosmo, remove the brake booster line bracket from the clutch housing.

10. Raise the car and support it on jackstands.

CAUTION: *Be sure that the car is securely supported. Remember, you will be working underneath it.*

11. Unfasten the transmission drain plug and drain the oil. Wipe the drain plug clean and install it again.

12. Remove the driveshaft, as described below, and plug up the transmission extension housing.

NOTE: *An old U-joint yoke makes an excellent plug. Or, lacking this, secure a plastic bag over the opening with rubber bands.*

13. Detach the exhaust pipe from the thermal reactor flange. On RX-4 and Cosmo, remove the heat insulators first.

CAUTION: *Be sure that the reactor and exhaust pipe have cooled sufficiently to prevent severe burns.*

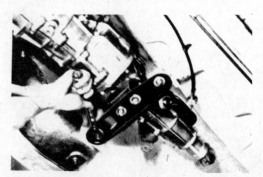

**Unfasten the bolts which secure the transmission support to the frame**

14. Unfasten the speedometer cable from the extension housing.

15. Detach the starter motor wiring. Remove its securing nuts and bolts and withdraw the starter motor.

16. Support the transmission with a block of wood mounted on a jack.

17. Remove the nuts which attach the transmission support to the frame members.

18. Evenly, and in several stages, remove the bolts which retain the bell housing to the engine.

19. Carefully slide the transmission assembly rearward until the input shaft has cleared the clutch disc.

20. Gently lower the transmission from the car.

21. Transmission installation is performed in the reverse order of removal. Align the clutch plate with an arbor or an old input shaft. Adjust the clutch and shift linkage as detailed elsewhere. Refill the transmission with gear oil:
   • Below 0°F: SAE EP80
   • Above 0°F: SAE EP90

**Rear Wheel Drive GLC and GLC Wagon**

1. Disconnect the (-) battery cable.

2. Put the transmission in neutral and remove the console and shift lever.

3. Remove the two upper bolts from the clutch housing.

4. Raise the vehicle and support it securely on axle stands or a lift.

5. Drain the transmission oil and replace the plug.

6. Remove the driveshaft, and plug or cover the hole in the extension housing.

7. Disconnect the speedometer cable and back-up light switch wires.

8. Disconnect the exhaust pipe hanger from the bracket on the clutch housing.

9. Remove the exhaust pipe support bracket from the clutch housing. Disconnect the clutch cable at the release lever.

10. Remove the lower clutch housing cover.

11. Remove the starter electrical connections, remove the bolts, and remove the starter.

12. Disconnect the exhaust pipe hanger at the extension housing.

13. Place a jack under the engine, using a block of wood to protect the oil pan. Make sure the jack can securely support the weight of the engine.

14. Disconnect the transmission support member at the transmission.

15. Remove transmission-to-engine attaching bolts.

16. Carefully slide the transmission rear-

ward until the input shaft has cleared the clutch disc, and lower it out of the car.

17. In installation, reverse above procedures, aligning the clutch plate with a arbor or old input shaft. Adjust clutch and shift linkage. Refill the transmission with the proper grade of gear oil.

**Front Wheel Drive GLC**

1. Raise the vehicle and support it safely. Disconnect the negative battery cable.

2. Disconnect all electrical wiring and connections. Mark these units to aid in reassembling. Drain the transaxle oil.

3. Remove the front wheels. Disconnect the lower ball joints from the steering knuckles. Pull the driveshafts from the differential gears.

NOTE: *A circlip is positioned on the driveshaft ends and engages in a groove, machined in the differential side gears. The driveshafts may have to be forced from the differential housing to release the clip from the groove. Do not apply a sharp impact. Do not allow the driveshaft's free end to drop. Damage may occur to the ball and socket joints and to the rubber boots. Wire the shafts to the vehicle body when released from the differential.*

4. Support the engine with a jack or lift, and raise it slightly. Now, separate the shift control rod from the shift rod.

5. Remove the extension bar from the transaxle. Remove the crossmember.

6. Remove the rubber mount from the transaxle case. Remove the starter.

7. Support the transaxle securely with a jack. Then remove the transaxle mounting bolts, and remove it from the car.

8. Installation is the reverse of removal. Observe the torque figures shown in the illustrations and below:
   • Lower arm-to-ball joint: 69-85 ft. lbs.

9. Fill the transaxle to proper level before moving the car. Adjust the shift linkage, if necessary.

**Rear Wheel Drive 626**

1. Remove the gearshift lever knob.

2. Remove the console box.

3. Remove the gearshift lever boot and the gearshift lever.

4. Disconnect the negative battery cable.

5. Raise the vehicle and support with jack stands.

6. Drain the transmission lubricant.

7. Disconnect the propeller shaft.

8. Disconnect the exhaust pipe hanger.

9. Remove the starter motor.

10. Disconnect the back-up switch wire.

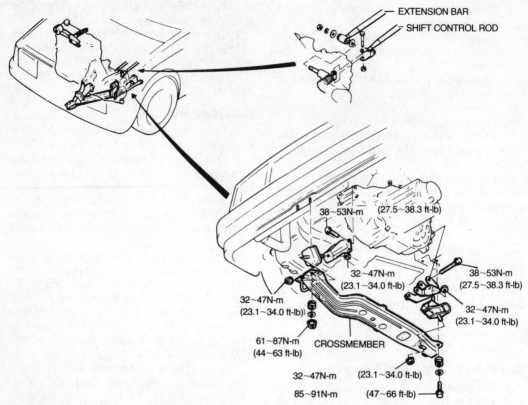

EXTENSION BAR

SHIFT CONTROL ROD

38~53N-m    (27.5~38.3 ft-lb)

32~47N-m
(23.1~34.0 ft-lb)

38~53N-m
(27.5~38.3 ft-lb)

32~47N-m
(23.1~34.0 ft-lb))

32~47N-m
(23.1~34.0 ft-lb)

61~87N-m      CROSSMEMBER
(44~63 ft-lb)

32~47N-m       (23.1~34.0 ft-lb)

85~91N-m       (47~66 ft-lb)

**Disconnecting shift linkage and removing the crossmember in GLC manual transaxle removal**

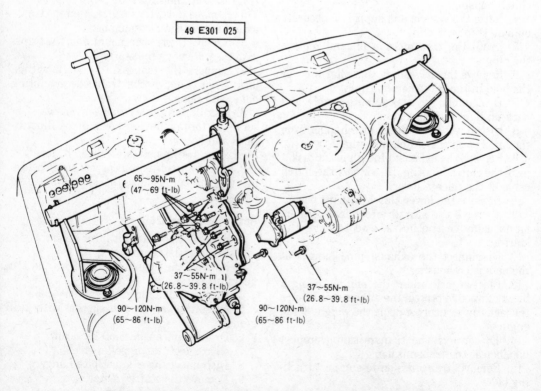

49 E301 025

65~95N-m
(47~69 ft-lb)

37~55N-m
(26.8~39.8 ft-lb)

37~55N-m
(26.8~39.8 ft-lb)

90~120N-m
(65~86 ft-lb)

90~120N-m
(65~86 ft-lb)

**Bolt torques to be observed in installing the GLC manual transaxle**

11. Disconnect the speedometer cable.

12. Place a jack under the engine, protecting the oil pan with a block of wood.

13. Remove the transmission attaching bolts and remove the transmission.

14. Transmission installation is performed in the reverse order of removal. Align the clutch plate with an old arbor or an old input shaft. Add lubricant until the level reaches the bottom of the filler plug hole.

### Front Wheel Drive 323 and 626

1. Disconnect the negative battery cable. Disconnect the speedometer cable at the transaxle. Remove the clutch cable bracket mounting bolts, disconnect the cable at the release lever, and remove the mounting bracket.

2. Remove the ground wire attaching bolt and the wiring harness clip from the transaxle. Remove the starter.

3. Support the engine via the hooks in a secure manner from above.

4. Now, remove the four bolts which couple the engine to the transaxle.

5. Jack up the vehicle and support it securely. Drain the transaxle oil.

6. Remove the front wheels and the splash shields. Remove the stabilizer bar control link.

7. Remove the protective cover, if so equipped. Remove its coupling bolt, and then pull the lower control arm ball joint out of the steering knuckle by pulling downward on the lower control arm. Be careful not to damage the ball joint dust cover.

8. Insert a lever between the left side driveshaft U-joint and the transaxle as shown, and gently tap the end of the lever to pull the driveshaft out of the differential side gear. Be careful not to damage the oil seal in the case. Pull outward on the brake rotor and caliper while holding the inner end of the shaft to guide it straight out of the transaxle case. This will prevent damage to the oil seal.

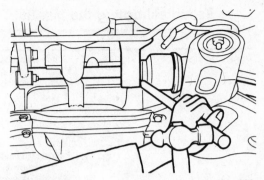

**Removing the right side driveshaft from the 626 transaxle**

9. Insert a lever between the right side driveshaft and cross-shaft, as shown, and gently tap the lever to uncouple the two. Pull forward on the brake caliper and rotor on this side and separate the two shafts. Now, remove the cross-shaft bracket mounting bolts and remove the shaft and bracket from the transaxle as an assembly.

10. Remove the nuts from the transaxle mounting bracket where it connects with the crossmember. Then, remove the crossmember and the left lower arm as an assembly.

11. Disconnect the shift control rod from the shift rod. Disconnect the locating rod at the transaxle. Remove the protective cover form under the transaxle.

12. Using a lift and chains or heavy rope, support the transaxle mounting bracket at two places and at the engine support. Support at three locations is necessary because the unit is not balanced. Now, remove the two bolts fastening the transaxle and engine together. Separate the transaxle from the engine. You can lower the unit out of the car now with a jack located underneath. But, make sure the chains or rope are kept under some tension to stop the unit from tipping. Remove the mount brackets from the unit.

13. To install, reverse the removal procedure, noting the following points:

    a. Coat the spline of the primary shaft gear with molybdenum disulphide grease prior to assembling the transmission to the engine.

    b. Make sure to steady the transaxle with chains or ropes while installing it.

14. Replace the clips at the inner ends of the driveshaft and cross-shaft back into the transaxle, first turn the differential side gear by inserting your finger into the shaft hole so the shaft splines and gear recesses will fit into one another. Force the shaft in so the spring clip will lock. After the shaft is installed, connect it to the driveshaft. Then, pull the front

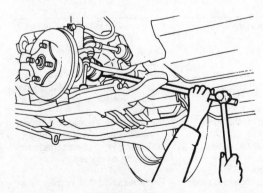

**Removing the left side driveshaft from the 626 transaxle**

## Troubleshooting the Manual Transmission and Transfer Case

| Problem | Cause | Solution |
|---|---|---|
| Transmission shifts hard | • Clutch adjustment incorrect<br>• Clutch linkage or cable binding<br>• Shift rail binding | • Adjust clutch<br>• Lubricate or repair as necessary<br>• Check for mispositioned selector arm roll pin, loose cover bolts, worn shift rail bores, worn shift rail, distorted oil seal, or extension housing not aligned with case. Repair as necessary. |
| | • Internal bind in transmission caused by shift forks, selector plates, or synchronizer assemblies | • Remove, dissemble and inspect transmission. Replace worn or damaged components as necessary. |
| | • Clutch housing misalignment | • Check runout at rear face of clutch housing |
| | • Incorrect lubricant<br>• Block rings and/or cone seats worn | • Drain and refill transmission<br>• Blocking ring to gear clutch tooth face clearance must be 0.030 inch or greater. If clearance is correct it may still be necessary to inspect blocking rings and cone seats for excessive wear. Repair as necessary. |
| Gear clash when shifting from one gear to another | • Clutch adjustment incorrect<br>• Clutch linkage or cable binding<br>• Clutch housing misalignment | • Adjust clutch<br>• Lubricate or repair as necessary<br>• Check runout at rear of clutch housing |
| | • Lubricant level low or incorrect lubricant | • Drain and refill transmission and check for lubricant leaks if level was low. Repair as necessary. |
| | • Gearshift components, or synchronizer assemblies worn or damaged | • Remove, disassemble and inspect transmission. Replace worn or damaged components as necessary. |
| Transmission noisy | • Lubricant level low or incorrect lubricant | • Drain and refill transmission. If lubricant level was low, check for leaks and repair as necessary. |
| | • Clutch housing-to-engine, or transmission-to-clutch housing bolts loose | • Check and correct bolt torque as necessary |
| | • Dirt, chips, foreign material in transmission | • Drain, flush, and refill transmission |
| | • Gearshift mechanism, transmission gears, or bearing components worn or damaged | • Remove, disassemble and inspect transmission. Replace worn or damaged components as necessary. |
| | • Clutch housing misalignment | • Check runout at rear face of clutch housing |
| Jumps out of gear | • Clutch housing misalignment | • Check runout at rear face of clutch housing |
| | • Gearshift lever loose | • Check lever for worn fork. Tighten loose attaching bolts. |
| | • Offset lever nylon insert worn or lever attaching nut loose | • Remove gearshift lever and check for loose offset lever nut or worn insert. Repair or replace as necessary. |
| | • Gearshift mechanism, shift forks, selector plates, interlock plate, selector arm, shift rail, detent plugs, springs or shift cover worn or damaged | • Remove, disassemble and inspect transmission cover assembly. Replace worn or damaged components as necessary. |
| | • Clutch shaft or roller bearings worn or damaged | • Replace clutch shaft or roller bearings as necessary |

# Troubleshooting the Manual Transmission and Transfer Case (cont.)

| Problem | Cause | Solution |
|---|---|---|
| Jumps out of gear (cont.) | • Gear teeth worn or tapered, synchronizer assemblies worn or damaged, excessive end play caused by worn thrust washers or output shaft gears<br>• Pilot bushing worn | • Remove, disassemble, and inspect transmission. Replace worn or damaged components as necessary.<br>• Replace pilot bushing |
| Will not shift into one gear | • Gearshift selector plates, interlock plate, or selector arm, worn, damaged, or incorrectly assembled<br>• Shift rail detent plunger worn, spring broken, or plug loose<br>• Gearshift lever worn or damaged<br>• Synchronizer sleeves or hubs, damaged or worn | • Remove, disassemble, and inspect transmission cover assembly. Repair or replace components as necessary.<br>• Tighten plug or replace worn or damaged components as necessary<br>• Replace gearshift lever<br>• Remove, disassemble and inspect transmission. Replace worn or damaged components. |
| Locked in one gear—cannot be shifted out | • Shift rail(s) worn or broken, shifter fork bent, setscrew loose, center detent plug missing or worn<br>• Broken gear teeth on countershaft gear, clutch shaft, or reverse idler gear<br>Gearshift lever broken or worn, shift mechanism in cover incorrectly assembled or broken, worn damaged gear train components | • Inspect and replace worn or damaged parts<br>• Inspect and replace damaged part<br>• Disassemble transmission. Replace damaged parts or assemble correctly. |
| Transfer case difficult to shift or will not shift into desired range | • Vehicle speed too great to permit shifting<br>• If vehicle was operated for extended period in 4H mode on dry paved surface, driveline torque load may cause difficult shifting<br>• Transfer case external shift linkage binding<br>• Insufficient or incorrect lubricant<br>• Internal components binding, worn, or damaged | • Stop vehicle and shift into desired range. Or reduce speed to 3–4 km/h (2–3 mph) before attempting to shift.<br>• Stop vehicle, shift transmission to neutral, shift transfer case to 2H mode and operate vehicle in 2H on dry paved surfaces<br>• Lubricate or repair or replace linkage, or tighten loose components as necessary<br>• Drain and refill to edge of fill hole with SAE 85W-90 gear lubricant only<br>• Disassemble unit and replace worn or damaged components as necessary |
| Transfer case noisy in all drive modes | • Insufficient or incorrect lubricant | • Drain and refill to edge of fill hole with SAE 85W-90 gear lubricant only. Check for leaks and repair if necessary.<br>Note: If unit is still noisy after drain and refill, disassembly and inspection may be required to locate source of noise. |
| Noisy in—or jumps out of four wheel drive low range | • Transfer case not completely engaged in 4L position<br>• Shift linkage loose or binding<br>• Shift fork cracked, inserts worn, or fork is binding on shift rail | • Stop vehicle, shift transfer case in Neutral, then shift back into 4L position<br>• Tighten, lubricate, or repair linkage as necessary<br>• Disassemble unit and repair as necessary |
| Lubricant leaking from output shaft seals or from vent | • Transfer case overfilled<br>• Vent closed or restricted | • Drain to correct level<br>• Clear or replace vent if necessary |

## Troubleshooting the Manual Transmission and Transfer Case (cont.)

| Problem | Cause | Solution |
|---|---|---|
| Lubricant leaking from output shaft seals or from vent (cont.) | • Output shaft seals damaged or installed incorrectly | • Replace seals. Be sure seal lip faces interior of case when installed. Also be sure yoke seal surfaces are not scored or nicked. Remove scores, nicks with fine sandpaper or replace yoke(s) if necessary. |
| Abnormal tire wear | • Extended operation on dry hard surface (paved) roads in 4H range | • Operate in 2H on hard surface (paved) roads |

disc-caliper assembly outward to make sure the drive-shaft will not come out of the transmission.

15. When installing the other driveshaft, use the dame general technique to first force the spring clip to lock and then check that it has locked in a similar manner.

Observe the following torque figures (ft. lbs.):
- Transaxle mount to transaxle: 28-38
- Transaxle to engine bolts: 66-85
- Cross-shaft bracket mounting bolts: 32-45
- Ball joint to steering knuckle: 32-40

When torquing the nuts fastening the stabilizer bar to the control link, make sure 1 in. of bare thread is visible.
- Engine to transaxle bolts: 66-68
- Engine mount installing nuts: 17-21

# CLUTCH

## Adjustments

### PEDAL HEIGHT ADJUSTMENT

1. Loosen the locknut on the adjusting bolt.
2. Turn the adjusting bolt until the clearance between the pedal pad and the floor mat is 7.28 in. (7.48-GLC rear wheel drive, 9.05 GLC-front wheel drive 7.60-626).
3. Carefully tighten the locknut.

### PEDAL FREE-PLAY ADJUSTMENT

#### RX-2, RX-3

1. Loosen the locknut on the master cylinder pushrod.
2. Rotate the pushrod until the clutch pedal has a travel of 0.8-1.2 in. before clutch disengagement.
3. Carefully tighten the locknut.

#### RX-4, Cosmo, 808, 626 Rear Drive

The free-play of the clutch pedal before the pushrod contacts the piston in the master cylinder should be 0.02-0.12 in.

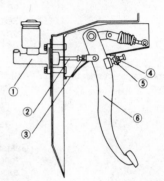

1. Master cylinder
2. Rod
3. Locknut
4. Adjusting bolt
5. Locknut
6. Clutch pedal

**Clutch pedal height adjustment**

To adjust the free-play, loosen the locknut and turn the pushrod until the proper adjustment is obtained. Tighten the locknut after the adjustment is complete.

#### 323 and 626 Front Wheel Drive

1. First, depress the clutch pedal and measure the distance between normal height and the point at which the clutch begins to disengage (effort increases). Play should be .45-.6 in.
2. If play is incorrect, loosen the locknut on the clutch cable. Pull the release fork backward so as to create a clearance between the adjusting nut roller and fork. The clearance should be about .1 in. Adjust the nut if necessary, and then recheck the adjustment at the pedal. When the adjustment is correct, tighten the locknut.
3. If the adjustment is correct, the distance from the bottom of the pedal and the floor when the clutch is fully disengaged should be 3.2 in. or more. If necessary, correct the adjustment to meet this specification.

### CLUTCH RELEASE CABLE ADJUSTMENT

#### GLC-Rear Wheel Drive

Loosen the locknut and put tension on outer cable (pull-do not push) while turning the ad-

**Clutch release cable adjustment—GLC**

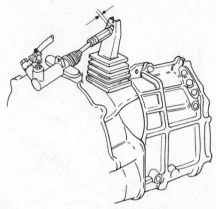

**Clutch fork free-play is measured between arrows**

justing nut until the clearance shown in the illustration is .06-.09 in. Then, tighten the locknut.

### GLC-Front Wheel Drive

The cable adjustment on the front wheel drive models is accomplished by turning an adjustment nut located on the end of the clutch cable at the release bracket mounted on the top of the transaxle case.

Loosen the locknut and turn the adjusting nut until the gap (clearance) between the roller on the cable and the release bracket is between .08 and .12 in., tighten the locknut.

### *RELEASE FORK FREE-PLAY ADJUSTMENT*

1. Unfasten the return spring from the release fork.
2. Loosen the locknut on the release rod.
3. Turn the adjusting nut on the release rod until the proper release fork free-play obtained:
   - RX-3-0.12-0.16 in.
   - RX-4 and Cosmo
   - RX-2-0.16-0.20 in.
4. Carefully tighten the locknut and hook the return spring back on the release fork.

## Driven Disc and Pressure Plate

### *REMOVAL AND INSTALLATION*

CAUTION: *The clutch driven disc contains asbestos, which has been determined to be a cancer causing agent. Never clean clutch surfaces with compressed air! Avoid inhailing any dust from any clutch surface! When cleaning any clutch surfaces, use a commercially available brake cleaning fluid.*

1. Remove the transmission, as detailed above.
2. Attach a brake to the flywheel.
3. Install a clutch arbor to hold the clutch in place.

NOTE: *An old input shaft makes an excellent arbor.*

4. Unfasten the bolts which secure the clutch cover, one turn at a time in sequence, until the clutch spring tension is released. Do not remove the bolts singly.
5. Remove the clutch disc.

NOTE: *Be careful not to get grease or oil on the surface of the clutch disc.*

6. Unhook the return spring from the throwout bearing and remove the bearing.
7. Pull out the release fork until its retaining spring frees itself from the ball stud. Withdraw the fork from the housing.

### Clutch installation is performed in the following order:

1. Clean the flywheel and pressure plate surfaces with fine emery paper. Be sure that there is no oil or grease on them. Grease the eccentric shaft needle bearing.
2. Apply Loctite® on the eccentric shaft threads (RX-2 and RX-3 only). Install the flywheel with its keyway over the key on the eccentric shaft.
3. Apply sealer to both sides of the flywheel lockwasher and position the lockwasher on the eccentric shaft.
4. Install the flywheel locknut and on rotary engine cars, tighten it to 350 ft. lbs. or as tight as possible with an extension not longer than three feet long on the wrench, then bend the tabs of the lockwasher up around it.
5. Use an arbor to center the clutch disc during installation. Install the clutch disc with the long end of its hub facing the transmission.

NOTE: *Use an old input shaft to center the clutch disc, if an arbor is not available.*

6. Align the O-mark on the clutch cover with the reamed hole of the O-mark on the flywheel.
7. Tighten the clutch cover bolts evenly, and in two or three stages, to 13-20 ft. lbs.

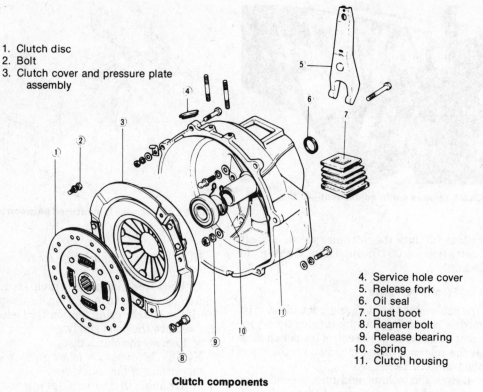

1. Clutch disc
2. Bolt
3. Clutch cover and pressure plate
   assembly

4. Service hole cover
5. Release fork
6. Oil seal
7. Dust boot
8. Reamer bolt
9. Release bearing
10. Spring
11. Clutch housing

**Clutch components**

8. Grease the pivot pin. Insert the release fork through its boot so that its retaining spring contacts the pivot pin.

9. Lightly grease the face of the throwout bearing its clutch housing retainer.

10. Install the throwout bearing and return spring. Check the operation of the release fork and throwout bearing for smoothness.

11. Install the transmission.

## Clutch Master Cylinder

### REMOVAL AND INSTALLATION

1. Unfasten the hydraulic line from the master cylinder outlet.

CAUTION: *Use care not to drip any hydraulic fluid on the car's painted surfaces, as it is an excellent paint remover.*

2. Remove the nuts which secure the master cylinder assembly to the firewall.

3. Withdraw the master cylinder straight out and away from the firewall.

4. Installation is performed in the reverse order of removal. Bleed the hydraulic system as detailed below.

### OVERHAUL

1. Thoroughly clean the outside of the master cylinder.

2. Drain the hydraulic fluid from the cylinder. Unbolt the reservoir from the cylinder body.

3. Remove the boot from the cylinder.

4. Release the wire piston stop with a screwdriver and withdraw the stop washer.

5. Withdraw the piston, piston cups, and return spring from the cylinder bore.

6. Wash all the parts in clean hydraulic (brake) fluid.

7. Examine the piston cups. If they are damaged, softened, or swollen, replace them with new ones.

8. Check the piston and bore for scoring or roughness.

9. Use a wire gauge to check the clearance between the piston and its bore. Replace either the piston or the cylinder if the clearance is greater than 0.006 in.

10. Be sure that the compensating port in the cylinder is not clogged.

**Assembly of the master cylinder is performed in the following order.**

1. Dip the piston and cups in clean hydraulic (brake) fluid.

2. Bolt the reservoir up to the cylinder body.

3. Fit the return spring into the cylinder.

4. Insert the primary cup into the bore so that its flat side is facing the piston.

5. Place the secondary cup on the piston and insert them in the cylinder bore.

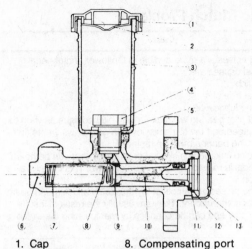

**Removing the clutch release cylinder**

1. Cap
2. Baffle
3. Reservoir
4. Bolt
5. Washer
6. Cylinder
7. Return spring

8. Compensating port
9. Primary cup
10. Piston
11. Stop
12. Stop wire
13. Boot

**Cutaway view of the clutch master cylinder**

6. Install the stop washer and the wire piston stop.

7. Fill the reservoir half-full of hydraulic fluid. Operate the piston with a screwdriver until fluid spurts out of the cylinder outlet.

8. Fit the boot on the cylinder.

## Clutch Release Cylinder

### REMOVAL AND INSTALLATION

1. Raise the vehicle and support with jack stands.

2. Unscrew the hydraulic line from the release cylinder.

3. Unhook the release fork return spring from the cylinder.

4. Unfasten the nuts which secure the release cylinder to the transmission.

5. Installation is performed in the reverse order of removal. Bleed the hydraulic system as detailed below and adjust the release fork free-play as detailed above.

### OVERHAUL

Consult the "Master Cylinder Overhaul" section above for release cylinder overhaul procedures.

### SYSTEM BLEEDING

1. Remove the rubber cap from the bleeder screw on the release cylinder.

2. Place a bleeder tube over the end of the bleeder screw.

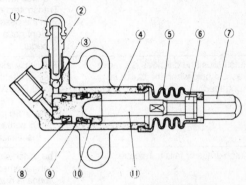

1. Cap
2. Bleed screw
3. Valve
4. Cylinder
5. Boat
6. Locknut

7. Adjusting nut
8. Primary cup
9. Secondary cup
10. Piston
11. Pushrod

**Cutaway view of the clutch release cylinder**

3. Submerge the other end of the tube in a jar half-filled with hydraulic (brake) fluid.

4. Depress the clutch pedal fully and allow it to return slowly.

5. Keep repeating Step 4 while watching the hydraulic fluid in the jar. As soon as the air bubbles disappear, close the bleeder screw.

NOTE: *During the bleeding procedure, the reservoir must be kept at least 3/4 full.*

6. Remove the tube and refit the rubber cap. Fill the reservoir with hydraulic fluid.

## AUTOMATIC TRANSMISSION/ TRANSAXLE

### Identification

On all models, the Vehicle Information Code Plate mounted on the firewall in the engine compartment lists the transmission or transaxle type. On the third line, labeled "Transaxle" or "Transmission" the transaxle/transmission model is listed, preceding a space. The serial number is stamped following the space.

## Troubleshooting Basic Clutch Problems

| Problem | Cause |
|---|---|
| Excessive clutch noise | Throwout bearing noises are more audible at the lower end of pedal travel. The usual causes are:<br>• Riding the clutch<br>• Too little pedal free-play<br>• Lack of bearing lubrication<br>A bad clutch shaft pilot bearing will make a high pitched squeal, when the clutch is disengaged and the transmission is in gear or within the first 2″ of pedal travel. The bearing must be replaced.<br>Noise from the clutch linkage is a clicking or snapping that can be heard or felt as the pedal is moved completely up or down. This usually requires lubrication.<br>Transmitted engine noises are amplified by the clutch housing and heard in the passenger compartment. They are usually the result of insufficient pedal free-play and can be changed by manipulating the clutch pedal. |
| Clutch slips (the car does not move as it should when the clutch is engaged) | This is usually most noticeable when pulling away from a standing start. A severe test is to start the engine, apply the brakes, shift into high gear and SLOWLY release the clutch pedal. A healthy clutch will stall the engine. If it slips it may be due to:<br>• A worn pressure plate or clutch plate<br>• Oil soaked clutch plate<br>• Insufficient pedal free-play |
| Clutch drags or fails to release | The clutch disc and some transmission gears spin briefly after clutch disengagement. Under normal conditions in average temperatures, 3 seconds is maximum spin-time. Failure to release properly can be caused by:<br>• Too light transmission lubricant or low lubricant level<br>• Improperly adjusted clutch linkage |
| Low clutch life | Low clutch life is usually a result of poor driving habits or heavy duty use. Riding the clutch, pulling heavy loads, holding the car on a grade with the clutch instead of the brakes and rapid clutch engagement all contribute to low clutch life. |

# Fluid Pan

## PAN REMOVAL AND INSTALLATION

1. Raise and support the vehicle.
2. Place a drain pan under the transmission pan.
3. Remove the pan attaching bolts (except the two at the front). Loosen the two at the front slightly. Allow the fluid to drain.
4. Remove the pan.
5. Remove and discard the gasket.
6. Install a new pan gasket and install the pan on the transmission.
7. Lower the vehicle and fill the transmission with fluid. Check the transmission operation.

## FILTER SERVICE

1. Remove the transmission oil pan as described above.
2. Remove the attaching bolts and remove the filter assembly. On all models with transaxle, the filter is held in place by four bolts.
3. Install the filter and torque the bolts alternately (diagonally) is several stages to 4–5 ft. lbs.

# Adjustments

## SHIFT LINKAGE ADJUSTMENT

### 1972-75

1. Unfasten the T-joint on the intermediate lever.
2. Place the range selector lever, which is mounted on the side of the transmission case, in Neutral; i.e., so that the slot in the selector shaft is pointing straight up and down.
3. Adjust the console-mounted gear selector lever by turning the T-joint until it indicates Neutral.
4. Reconnect the T-joint. Check the gear selector operation in all other ranges to see that the linkage has no slack.

### 1976-84, Except 626 with Front Wheel Drive

1. Place the transmission selector lever in Neutral.
2. Disconnect the clevis from the lower end of the selector arm.
3. Move the manual lever to the N position.
NOTE: *The N position is the third detent from the back.*

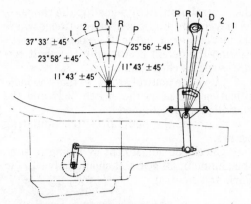

**Transmission linkage adjustment**

**Align the neutral safety switch by inserting a drill through the holes in it**

4. Loosen the two clevis retaining nuts and adjust the clevis so that it freely enters the lever hole.

5. Tighten the retaining nuts.

6. Connect the clevis to the lever and secure with the spring washer, flat washer and retaining clip.

### 323 and 626 w/Front Wheel Drive

1. Engage the parking brake. Remove the shift lever boot. Loosen both locknuts on the cable.

2. Shift the shift level to **N**. Shift the selector on the side of the transaxle to the same position by counting detents.

3. Turn the lower locknut until it just touches the shifter collar. Then, torque the upper locknut to 6-8 ft.lb.

4. Have someone watch the lever on the transaxle. Slowly push the lever toward part until the lever on the transmission just begins to move, and note how fat the shifter has moved. Return the lever to **N** and repeat the procedure going toward **D**. If the distances are the same in both directions, the adjustment is correct. If not, adjust so as to tighten the lower locknut if the shift lever moves too far in the forward direction, or adjust so as to tighten the upper locknut if it moves too far to the rear.

## NEUTRAL SAFETY SWITCH ADJUSTMENT

### RX-2, RX-3

1. Check the shift linkage, as detailed above, before adjusting the neutral safety switch.

2. Remove the nut which secures the gear selector lever and the neutral safety switch attaching bolts.

3. Unfasten the screw which is located underneath the switch body.

4. Place the selector shaft in Neutral by using the gear selector lever.

NOTE: *If the linkage is adjusted properly,*

*the slot in the selector shaft should be vertical.*

5. Move the switch body so that the screw hole in the case aligns with the hole in the internal rotor.

6. Check their alignment by inserting an 0.009 in. diameter pin or a No. 53 drill through the holes.

7. Once the proper alignment is obtained, tighten the switch mounting bolts. Remove the pin or drill and insert the screw back into the hole.

8. Tighten the nut which secures the gear shift selector lever.

9. Check the operation of the neutral safety switch again. If it still is not operating properly, i.e., the car starts in positions other than Park or Neutral or the back-up lights come on in gears other than Reverse, replace the switch.

### RX-4, Cosmo and 808

1. Remove the housing from the shift lever.

2. Adjust the shift lever so that there is 0-0.012 in. clearance between the pin and the guide plate, when the lever is in Neutral.

3. Adjust the neutral safety switch so that the pin hole in the switch body is aligned with the pin hole of the siding plate when the shift lever is in Neutral.

4. Check the adjustment by trying to start the engine in all gears. It should only start in Park or Neutral.

5. Reinstall the housing on the shift lever.

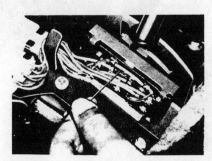

**Adjusting RX-4 and Cosmo neutral safety switch**

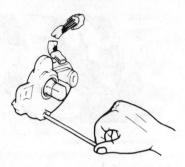

**Adjusting GLC neutral safety switch**

### GLC

NOTE: *Front wheel drive models use a hydraulic switch that must be replaced if faulty, it is non-adjustable.*

1. Adjust shift linkage as described above. Put the selector lever in neutral position (3rd detent from the rear).

2. Remove the transmission manual lever retaining nut and pull the lever off the switch.

3. Loosen (do not remove) the two switch retaining bolts and remove the alignment pin hole screw at the bottom of the switch.

4. Gently rotate the switch back and forth while attempting to insert a .078 in. diameter pin into the alignment pin hole. When alignment is correct the pin will slide through the hole in the internal rotor. Tighten the switch attaching bolts and remove the pin.

5. Reinstall the alignment pin hole screw. Position the manual lever back onto the switch shaft and install the washer and nut.

6. Check the operation of the switch.

#### 626 w/Rear Wheel Drive

1. Place the transmission selector lever in the neutral position.

2. Loosen the neutral switch attaching screws.

3. Position the manual shift lever shaft in

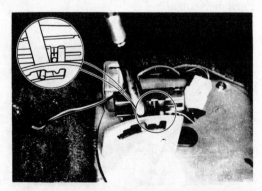

**Adjusting the neutral safety switch—model 626**

the neutral position by adjusting the range select lever. The proper neutral position is where the slot of the manual shaft is positioned vertical and the detent positions in the shaft correctly with a click sound.

4. Move the neutral switch so that the identification marks on the switch body and the sliding plate are aligned.

5. Tighten the neutral switch adjusting screws.

6. Check the adjustment by trying to start the engine in all gears. It should only start in Park and Neutral.

### NEUTRAL START SWITCH ADJUSTMENT

#### Front Wheel Drive Cars

1. Apply the parking brake. Place the gearshift lever in "NEUTRAL" position.

2. Loosen the two mounting screws of the neutral switch so that it can be rotated. Now, rotate it so that the end of the operating lever is directly over the flange on the switch body and the holes in that flange and the outer end of the lever are lined up.

3. Hold the switch securely in place while torquing the mounting screws to 7.5–8.5 ft. lb.

4. Recheck the function of the switch by attempting to start the engine in all selector positions. It should start only in Park and Neutral.

### KICKDOWN SWITCH AND DOWNSHIFT SOLENOID ADJUSTMENT

#### All Except 626

1. Check the accelerator linkage for smooth operation.

2. Turn the ignition on, but do not start the engine.

3. Depress the accelerator pedal fully to the floor. As the pedal nears the end of its travel, a light click should be heard from the downshift solenoid.

4. If the kickdown switch operates too soon, loosen the locknut on the switch shaft. Adjust the shaft so that the accelerator linkage makes contact with it when the pedal is depressed approximately 7/8 of the way to the floor. Tighten the locknut.

5. If no noise comes from the solenoid at all, check the wiring for the solenoid and the switch.

6. If the wiring is in good condition, remove the wire from the solenoid and connect it to a 12V power source. If the solenoid does not click when connected, it is defective and should be replaced.

NOTE: *When the solenoid is removed, about two pints of transmission fluid will leak out; have a container ready to catch it. Remember*

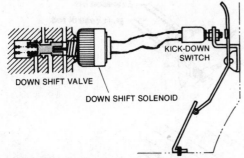

**Kickdown switch and downshift solenoid adjustment**

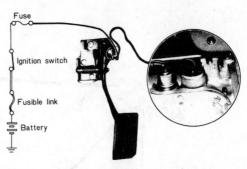

**Kickdown switch adjustment—model 626**

to add more fluid to the transmission after installing the new solenoid.

### 626 with Rear Wheel Drive

1. Disconnect the wiring connectors from the kickdown switch.
2. Screw out the kick-sown switch a few turns.
3. Dully depress the accelerator pedal.
4. Gradually screw in the kick-down switch until you hear a clicking sound then screw it in 1/2 turn more.
5. Tighten the locknut and connect the wiring connectors.

### 323 and 626 with Front Wheel Drive

1. Disconnect the wires from the kickdown solenoid (located above the accelerator pedal) and replace with a continuity tester. Have someone slowly depress the accelerator pedal as you read the tester to check for continuity. Continuity should begin when the accelerator pedal is depressed 7/8 of the way.
2. If the adjustment is incorrect, loosen the locknut and turn the switch clockwise for earlier engagement or counterclockwise for later engagement. Tighten the locknut and reconnect the wires.

### ADJUSTING BRAKE BAND

#### Rear Wheel Drive Models

NOTE: *On all cars but the GLC and 626, this adjustment can be made by removing the cover located on the lower right front of the transmission (three bolts). On the GLC and 626, the transmission pan must be removed-the servo piston stem and locknut are visible at the left front.*

Loosen the locknut and then torque the servo piston stem to 9-11 ft.lb. Then, back off exactly two turns. Hold the stem stationary and tighten the locknut to 11-29 ft.lb.

#### Front Wheel Drive Models

NOTE: *This procedure does not apply to the front wheel drive 323 and 626 as there is no brake band adjustment possible on these models.*

1. Raise the vehicle and support safely.
2. Locate the servo cover and remove from the right side of the transmission case.
3. Loosen locknut and tighten the servo adjusting bolt to 9-11 ft. lbs. torque.
4. Loosen the servo bolt two full turns and tighten the locknut.
5. Install the servo cover and lower vehicle.

## Transmission/Transaxle

### REMOVAL AND INSTALLATION

#### RX-3 and RX3-SP

The automatic transmission is filled with Type F fluid.

1. Remove the heat shroud. Remove the exhaust pipe bracket from the torque converter housing.
2. Detach the exhaust pipe.
CAUTION: *The exhaust system on rotary eninge-equipped Mazdas get considerably hotter than a conventional system; be sure to allow enough time for it to cool.*
3. Remove the driveshaft.
4. Detach the speedometer cable.
5. Remove the control rod.
6. Unfasten the vacuum lines from the vacuum modulator.
7. Unfasten the multiconnector form the downshift solenoid and the neutral safety switch.
8. Disconnect the oil cooler lines.
9. Remove the starter.
10. Matchmark the torque converter and the flex-plate.
11. Working through the starter motor mounting hole, remove the four bolts which secure the torque converter to the flex-plate.
12. Support the transmission.
13. Remove the crossmember.

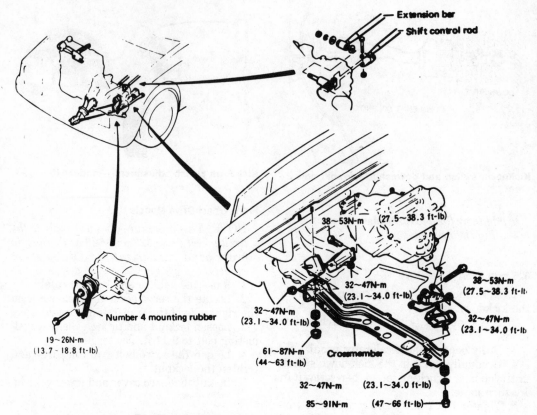

Extension bar

Shift control rod

38~53N-m (27.5~38.3 ft-lb)

38~53N-m (27.5~38.3 ft-lb)

32~47N-m (23.1~34.0 ft-lb)

Number 4 mounting rubber

19~26N-m (13.7~18.8 ft-lb)

32~47N-m (23.1~34.0 ft-lb)

32~47N-m (23.1~34.0 ft-lb)

61~87N-m (44~63 ft-lb)

Crossmember

32~47N-m (23.1~34.0 ft-lb)

85~91N-m (47~66 ft-lb)

**Transaxle mountings, automatic shown-manual similar**

14. Remove the bolts which secure the torque converter housing to the top of the engine.

15. Raise the transmission so that it is level.

16. Use a screwdriver to carefully apply pressure between the torque converter and the flexplate.

17. Slide the transmission rearward and lower it from the car.

CAUTION: *Do not rest the weight of the transmission on the torque converter splines.*

18. Automatic transmission installation is the reverse or removal. There are several points which should be noted, however:

a. Before installing transmission, use a dial indicator to measure flex-plate runout. If runout exceeds 0.020 in., the flex-plate must be replaced.

b. Hand-tighten the four torque converter installation bolts and then lock the flex-plate with a brake. Next, tighten the four bolts evenly, and in several stages, to 29-36 ft. lbs.

c. Check the fluid level again and road test the car.

### RX-4, RX-7 and Cosmo

The transmission is filled with Type F fluid.

1. Remove the converter access hole cover.

Lock the flex-plate by holding the drive pulley lockbolt with a wrench.

2. Matchmark the converter and flex-plate. Unfasten the four converter-to-flex-plate securing bolts.

3. Remove the exhaust pipe.

4. Remove the driveshaft.

5. Remove speedometer cable.

6. Remove all vacuum lines and electrical leads from the transmission.

7. Remove the starter.

8. Remove the bottom cover from the converter housing.

9. Support the transmission and remove the crossmember.

10. Disconnect the oil cooler.

11. Unbolt the converter housing, raise the transmission to a level place and separate it from the flex-plate.

12. Automatic transmission installation is the revere of removal. There are several points which should be noted, however.

a. Before installing the transmission, use a dial indicator to measure flexplate runout. Runout should be around 0.012 in. If runout exceeds 0.020 in. the flex-plate must be replaced.

b. After completing transmission installation, rotate the eccentric shaft to be sure that there is no interference in the transmission.

### 808, 626 and GLC-Rear Wheel Drive

Use only Type F transmission fluid.
1. Drain the transmission.
2. Remove the heat insulator.
3. Disconnect the exhaust pipe.
4. Disconnect the driveshaft at the rear axle flange.
5. Remove the driveshaft.
6. Disconnect the speedometer cable.
7. Disconnect the shift rod.
8. Remove all vacuum hoses.
9. Disconnect all wiring.
10. Disconnect the oil cooler lines.
11. Remove the access cover from the lower end of the converter housing.
12. Matchmark the drive plate and torque converter for realignment and remove the converter bolts.
13. Support the transmission with a jack and remove the crossmember.
14. Remove the converter housing-to-engine bolts.
15. Remove the filler tube.
16. Separate the flex-plate and the converter.
17. Remove the transmission and converter as an assembly.
18. To install the transmission, reverse the removal procedure.

### 323 and 626-Front Wheel Drive

The procedure is identical to that of manual transaxle removal except for a few items. You must disconnect the transmission shift cable instead of the manual transmission shift linkage and disconnect the wires to the inhibitor switch and kickdown solenoid. Also disconnect the vacuum line to the modulator. There are five bolts (instead of four) connecting the engine to the transmission. Also, just before removing the two lower bolts connecting engine and transmission, remove the bolts joining the torque converter and drive plate. To do this, you'll need to turn the engine with a socket on the crankshaft pulley bolt. At installation, torque these bolts to 25-36 ft.lb. Crossmember and transaxle mount nuts are used with two sizes of bolts. Torque the smaller to 32-40 ft. lbs. and the larger to 69-85 ft. lbs.

### GLC-Front Wheel Drive

1. Raise the vehicle and support it safely. Disconnect the negative battery cable.
NOTE: *When removing or installing the transaxle assembly the rear end of the power plant (engine) must be lifted with the aid of a chain.*
2. Disconnect all electrical wiring and connections, control linkages from the transaxle. Mark these units to aid in reassembling.
3. Remove the front wheels. Disconnect the lower ball joints from the steering knuckles. Pull the driveshafts from the differential gears.
NOTE: *A circlip is positioned on the driveshaft ends and engages in a groove, machined in the differential side gears. The driveshafts may have to be forced from the differential housing to release the clip from the groove. Do not apply a sharp impact. Do not allow the driveshaft's free end to drop. Damage may occur to the ball and socket joints and to the rubber boots. Wire the shafts to the vehicle body when released from the differential.*
4. Support the engine with a jack. Remove the crossmember and the mounting bolts retaining the transaxle in place. Remove the unit from the vehicle.
5. Installation is the reverse of removal.
NOTE: *Be sure the rubber mounts are not twisted or distorted and not in contact with the body.*
6. To properly install the driveshafts in the differential side gears, position the open end of the circlip in the up position, and with the driveshaft in a horizontal position, push the driveshafts into the side gears. To be sure the circlip engages the groove, a sound may be heard or attempt to pull the driveshaft from the differential. Reconnect the ball joints at the lower arms.

## DRIVELINE

### Driveshaft and U-Joints

#### REMOVAL AND INSTALLATION

##### RX-3 and GLC-Rear Wheel Drive

1. Raise the rear end of the car and support it using jackstands.
CAUTION: *Be sure that the car is securely supported. Remember, you will be working underneath it.*
2. Matchmark the flanges on the driveshaft and pinion so that they may be installed in their original position.
3. Remove the four bolts which secure the driveshaft to the pinion flange.
4. Lower the back end of the driveshaft and slide the front end out of the transmission.
5. Plug up the hole in the transmission to prevent it from leaking.

## Troubleshooting Basic Automatic Transmission Problems

| Problem | Cause | Solution |
|---|---|---|
| Fluid leakage | • Defective pan gasket | • Replace gasket or tighten pan bolts |
| | • Loose filler tube | • Tighten tube nut |
| | • Loose extension housing to transmission case | • Tighten bolts |
| | • Converter housing area leakage | • Have transmission checked professionally |
| Fluid flows out the oil filler tube | • High fluid level | • Check and correct fluid level |
| | • Breather vent clogged | • Open breather vent |
| | • Clogged oil filter or screen | • Replace filter or clean screen (change fluid also) |
| | • Internal fluid leakage | • Have transmission checked professionally |
| Transmission overheats (this is usually accompanied by a strong burned odor to the fluid) | • Low fluid level | • Check and correct fluid level |
| | • Fluid cooler lines clogged | • Drain and refill transmission. If this doesn't cure the problem, have cooler lines cleared or replaced. |
| | • Heavy pulling or hauling with insufficient cooling | • Install a transmission oil cooler |
| | • Faulty oil pump, internal slippage | • Have transmission checked professionally |
| Buzzing or whining noise | • Low fluid level | • Check and correct fluid level |
| | • Defective torque converter, scored gears | • Have transmission checked professionally |
| No forward or reverse gears or slippage in one or more gears | • Low fluid level | • Check and correct fluid level |
| | • Defective vacuum or linkage controls, internal clutch or band failure | • Have unit checked professionally |
| Delayed or erratic shift | • Low fluid level | • Check and correct fluid level |
| | • Broken vacuum lines | • Repair or replace lines |
| | • Internal malfunction | • Have transmission checked professionally |

NOTE: *Use an old U-joint yoke, or, if none is available, place a plastic bag, secured with rubber bands, over the hole.*

6. Driveshaft installation is performed in the reverse order of removal. Tighten the driveshaft-to-pinion flange bolts to 22 ft. lbs. on RX-3, and 25-27 ft. lbs. on GLC.

### RX-2 and 626 Models

The driveshaft used on RX-2 and 626 models is removed in a manner similar to that outlined for RX-3 and GLC models above. The only difference in the removal procedure is that the center bearing must be unbolted prior to driveshaft removal. Remove the driveshaft and the center bearing as a single unit.

NOTE: *Do not remove the oil seals and the center bearing from the support unless they are defective.*

Installation is performed in the reverse order of removal. Tighten the center bearing support bolts to 14-21 ft. lbs. - RX-2, 27-38 ft. lbs.-626 and the drive-shaft-to-pinion flange bolts to 25-27 ft. lbs.

### RX-4, 808, and Cosmo

Perform this operation only when the exhaust system is cold.

1. Remove the front heat insulator.

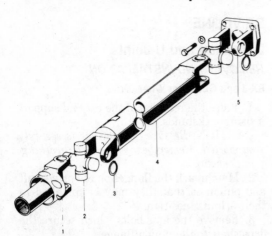

1. Yoke
2. Spider and bearing cup assembly
3. Snap-ring
4. Shaft
5. Yoke

**Components of the RX-3 driveshaft**

## Lockup Torque Converter Service Diagnosis

| Problem | Cause | Solution |
|---|---|---|
| No lockup | • Faulty oil pump<br>• Sticking governor valve<br>• Valve body malfunction<br>   (a) Stuck switch valve<br>   (b) Stuck lockup valve<br>   (c) Stuck fail-safe valve<br>• Failed locking clutch<br>• Leaking turbine hub seal<br>• Faulty input shaft or seal ring | • Replace oil pump<br>• Repair or replace as necessary<br>• Repair or replace valve body or its internal components as necessary<br><br><br>• Replace torque converter<br>• Replace torque converter<br>• Repair or replace as necessary |
| Will not unlock | • Sticking governor valve<br>• Valve body malfunction<br>   (a) Stuck switch valve<br>   (b) Stuck lockup valve<br>   (c) Stuck fail-safe valve | • Repair or replace as necessary<br>• Repair or replace valve body or its internal components as necessary |
| Stays locked up at too low a speed in direct | • Sticking governor valve<br>• Valve body malfunction<br>   (a) Stuck switch valve<br>   (b) Stuck lockup valve<br>   (c) Stuck fail-safe valve | • Repair or replace as necessary<br>• Repair or replace valve body or its internal components as necessary |
| Locks up or drags in low or second | • Faulty oil pump<br>• Valve body malfunction<br>   (a) Stuck switch valve<br>   (b) Stuck fail-safe valve | • Replace oil pump<br>• Repair or replace valve body or its internal components as necessary |
| Sluggish or stalls in reverse | • Faulty oil pump<br>• Plugged cooler, cooler lines or fittings<br>• Valve body malfunction<br>   (a) Stuck switch valve<br>   (b) Faulty input shaft or seal ring | • Replace oil pump as necessary<br>• Flush or replace cooler and flush lines and fittings<br>• Repair or replace valve body or its internal components as necessary |
| Loud chatter during lockup engagement (cold) | • Faulty torque converter<br>• Failed locking clutch<br>• Leaking turbine hub seal | • Replace torque converter<br>• Replace torque converter<br>• Replace torque converter |
| Vibration or shudder during lockup engagement | • Faulty oil pump<br><br>• Valve body malfunction<br><br><br>• Faulty torque converter<br>• Engine needs tune-up | • Repair or replace oil pump as necessary<br>• Repair or replace valve body or its internal components as necessary<br>• Replace torque converter<br>• Tune engine |
| Vibration after lockup engagement | • Faulty torque converter<br>• Exhaust system strikes underbody<br>• Engine needs tune-up<br>• Throttle linkage misadjusted | • Replace torque converter<br>• Align exhaust system<br>• Tune engine<br>• Adjust throttle linkage |
| Vibration when revved in neutral Overheating: oil blows out of dip stick tube or pump seal | • Torque converter out of balance<br>• Plugged cooler, cooler lines or fittings<br>• Stuck switch valve | • Replace torque converter<br>• Flush or replace cooler and flush lines and fittings<br>• Repair switch valve in valve body or replace valve body |
| Shudder after lockup engagement | • Faulty oil pump<br>• Plugged cooler, cooler lines or fittings<br>• Valve body malfunction<br><br><br>• Faulty torque converter<br>• Fail locking clutch<br>• Exhaust system strikes underbody<br>• Engine needs tune-up<br>• Throttle linkage misadjusted | • Replace oil pump<br>• Flush or replace cooler and flush lines and fittings<br>• Repair or replace valve body or its internal components as necessary<br>• Replace torque converter<br>• Replace torque converter<br>• Align exhaust system<br>• Tune engine<br>• Adjust throttle linkage |

# Transmission Fluid Indications

The appearance and odor of the transmission fluid can give valuable clues to the overall condition of the transmission. Always note the appearance of the fluid when you check the fluid level or change the fluid. Rub a small amount of fluid between your fingers to feel for grit and smell the fluid on the dipstick.

| If the fluid appears: | It indicates: |
| --- | --- |
| Clear and red colored | • Normal operation |
| Discolored (extremely dark red or brownish) or smells burned | • Band or clutch pack failure, usually caused by an overheated transmission. Hauling very heavy loads with insufficient power or failure to change the fluid, often result in overheating.<br>Do not confuse this appearance with newer fluids that have a darker red color and a strong odor (though not a burned odor). |
| Foamy or aerated (light in color and full of bubbles) | • The level is too high (gear train is churning oil)<br>• An internal air leak (air is mixing with the fluid). Have the transmission checked professionally. |
| Solid residue in the fluid | • Defective bands, clutch pack or bearings. Bits of band material or metal abrasives are clinging to the dipstick. Have the transmission checked professionally. |
| Varnish coating on the dipstick | • The transmission fluid is overheating |

2. Remove the nuts which secure the downpipe to the thermal reactor flange.

3. Remove the downpipe from the main muffler flange.

4. Matchmark the pinion and driveshaft flanges.

5. Unfasten the center bearing.

6. Remove the driveshaft.

7. Driveshaft installation is the reverse of removal. Tighten the yoke-to-front driveshaft locknut to 116-130 ft. lbs.

## U-JOINT OVERHAUL

Perform this procedure with the driveshaft removed from the car.

1. Matchmark both the yoke and the driveshaft so that they can be returned to their original balancing position during assembly.

2. Remove the bearing snap-rings from the yoke.

3. Use a hammer and a brass drift to drive in one of the bearing cups. Remove the cup which is protruding from the other side of the yoke.

4. Remove the other bearing cups by pressing them from the spider. One the GLC and 626, bearings may be removed by tapping on the base of the yoke with a hammer.

5. Withdraw the spider from the yoke.

6. Examine the spider journals for rusting or wear. Check the bearing for smoothness or pitting.

7. Measure the spider diameter. The standard diameter on RX-2 and RX-3 is 0.5795 in. If the spider wear exceeds 0.0040 in. on RX-2 models or 0.0079 in. on RX-3 models, replace

the spider. On RX-4 the minimum diameter is .6472 in., on 808 and 626 it is .5746 in., and on GLC it is .4996 in. If diameter is too small, replace the spider.

NOTE: *The spider and bearing are replace as a complete assembly only.*

8. Check the seals and rollers for wear or damage.

**Assembly of the U-joint is performed in the following order.**

1. Pack the bearing cups with grease.

2. Fit the rollers into the cups and install the dust seals.

3. Place the spider in the yoke and them fit one of the bearing cups into its bore in the yoke.

4. Press the bearing cup home, while guiding the spider into it, so that a snap-ring can be installed.

5. Press-fit the other bearings into the yoke.

1. Roller bearing (cup)    4. Yoke
2. Spider    5. Driveshaft
3. Oil seal    6. Snap-ring

**Components of the U-joint**

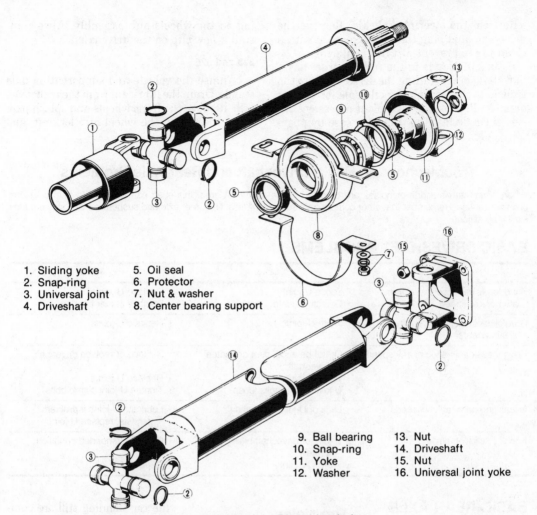

1. Sliding yoke
2. Snap-ring
3. Universal joint
4. Driveshaft
5. Oil seal
6. Protector
7. Nut & washer
8. Center bearing support

9. Ball bearing
10. Snap-ring
11. Yoke
12. Washer
13. Nut
14. Driveshaft
15. Nut
16. Universal joint yoke

**Components of the RX-2 driveshaft**

6. Select a snap-ring to obtain minimum end-play of the spider. Use snap-rings of the same thickness on both sides to center the spider.

NOTE: *Selective fit snap-rings are available in sizes ranging from 0.048 to 0.054 in.*

7. Install the spider/yoke assembly and bearings into the driveshaft in the same manner as the spider was assembled to the yoke.

8. Test the operation of the U-joint assembly. The spider should move freely with no binding.

## Drive Axles
### INSPECTION
#### Front Wheel Drive

1. Loosen the front wheel lugs, raise the car and safely support it on jackstands, Remove the wheels and tires.

2. Check the drive axle inner and outer boots for cracks or damage, for leaking grease or loose bands. Replace or repair if necessary.

3. Turn the drive axle by hand, if the splines or joints are excessively loose, replace or repair as necessary.

4. Examine the drive axle for cracks or twist. Replace if necessary.

### REMOVAL AND INSTALLATION
#### GLC

1. See Step 1 of Inspection. Drain the transaxle fluid after removing the splash shields.

2. Loosen the drive axle locknut at the center of the disc brake hub after raising the lock tab. Apply brake pressure while loosening.

3. Remove the lower ball joint from the steering knuckle (see Chapter 8).

4. Remove the drive axle from the transaxle case by pulling the brake caliper outward with increasing force. While applying outward force, hit the drive axle shaft with a brass hammer, if necessary, to help in removal.

5. Remove the locknut and pull the drive

axle from the steering knuckle. Remove the drive axle and plug the transaxle case with a clean rag to prevent dirt from entering.

6. Installation is in the reverse order of removal. Before installing the drive axle into the transaxle case, check the oil seals for cuts or damage. Replace the oil seals if necessary. Insert the axle into the transaxle case by push-

ing on the wheels hub assembly. Always install a new clip on the driveaxle.

### 323 and 626

1. Raise the vehicle and support it on axle stands. Drain the lubricant from the transaxle.

2. Remove the front wheels and splash pan. Raise the tab on the wheel hub locknut, and

## Troubleshooting Basic Driveshaft and Rear Axle Problems

When abnormal vibrations or noises are detected in the driveshaft area, this chart can be used to help diagnose possible causes. Remember that other components such as wheels, tires, rear axle and suspension can also produce similar conditions.

## BASIC DRIVESHAFT PROBLEMS

| Problem | Cause | Solution |
|---|---|---|
| Shudder as car accelerates from stop or low speed | • Loose U-joint<br>• Defective center bearing | • Replace U-joint<br>• Replace center bearing |
| Loud clunk in driveshaft when shifting gears | • Worn U-joints | • Replace U-joints |
| Roughness or vibration at any speed | • Out-of-balance, bent or dented driveshaft<br>• Worn U-joints<br>• U-joint clamp bolts loose | • Balance or replace driveshaft<br>• Replace U-joints<br>• Tighten U-joint clamp bolts |
| Squeaking noise at low speeds | • Lack of U-joint lubrication | • Lubricate U-joint; if problem persists, replace U-joint |
| Knock or clicking noise | • U-joint or driveshaft hitting frame tunnel<br>• Worn CV joint | • Correct overloaded condition<br>• Replace CV joint |

## BASIC REAR AXLE PROBLEMS

First, determine when the noise is most noticeable.

Drive Noise: Produced under vehicle acceleration.

Coast Noise: Produced while the car coasts with a closed throttle.

Float Noise: Occurs while maintaining constant car speed (just enough to keep speed constant) on a level road.

## Road Noise

Brick or rough surfaced concrete roads produce noises that seem to come from the rear axle. Road noise is usually identical in Drive or Coast and driving on a different type of road will tell whether the road is the problem.

## Tire Noise

Tire noises are often mistaken for rear axle problems. Snow treads or unevenly worn tires produce vibrations seeming to originate elsewhere. **Temporarily** inflating the tires to 40 lbs will significantly alter tire noise, but will have no effect on rear axle noises (which normally cease below about 30 mph).

## Engine/Transmission Noise

Determine at what speed the noise is most pronounced, then stop the car in a quiet place. With the transmission in Neutral, run the engine through speeds corresponding to road speeds where the noise was noticed. Noises produced with

the car standing still are coming from the engine or transmission.

## Front Wheel Bearings

While holding the car speed steady, lightly apply the footbrake; this will often decease bearing noise, as some of the load is taken from the bearing.

## Rear Axle Noises

Eliminating other possible sources can narrow the cause to the rear axle, which normally produces noise from worn gears or bearings. Gear noises tend to peak in a narrow speed range, while bearing noises will usually vary in pitch with engine speeds.

then have someone apply the brakes as you loosen the nut.

3. Remove the tow nuts, bushings, and washers and disconnect the stabilizer bar from the steering knuckle.

4. Remove the clinch bolts and nuts and them pry the lower control arm downward in order to separate the steering knuckle and lower ball joint. Be careful not to damage the dust cover for the ball joint.

**On the left side.**

5. Now, insert a lever (for automatic trans-axles, you'll have to use a chisel) between the driveshaft and transaxle case (don't go in too for, or you will damage the seal). Tap the end of the pry bar or chisel lightly to pull the shaft out of the case just until it unlocks.

6. Remove the driveshaft locknut from the center of the brake rotor. Pull the front hub outward and toward the rear. Disconnect the driveshaft form the wheel hub, if necessary by using a puller. Then pull the driveshaft straight out of the transaxle, supporting the joint on the transaxle side to prevent damage to the seal. Seal the transaxle opening with a clean rag.

**On the right side:**

7. Insert a lever between the cross shaft and outer driveshaft and tap on the outer end of the lever to separate the two shafts just until they unlock.

8. Remove the driveshaft locknut and then pull the front hub outward and toward the rear and disconnect the driveshaft form the front hub. If necessary, use a puller. Then, disconnect the driveshaft from the cross-shaft completely.

9. If it is necessary to remove the cross-shaft, remove the cross-shaft mounting bracket bolts and then remove the shaft and bracket as an assembly, being careful not to disturb the position of differential gears. Cover the opening in the differential case with a clean rag.

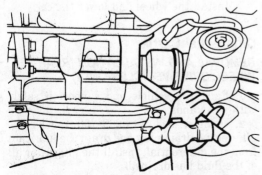

**Levering the cross-shaft and right side driveshaft apart on the 626**

10. Installation is the reverse of removal, but note these points:

a. Check the transaxle oil seal for damage and replace it if necessary.

b. Replace the clips at the inner ends of driveshaft or cross-shaft where they are locked into the differential gears in the transaxle.

c. Install the shafts into the transaxle carefully to avoid damage to the oil seal. Push the joint in on the differential side. Check the differential gears for alignment before attempting to install the shafts. If they are not aligned, turn them with your finger, as necessary.

d. After installation, pull the hub forward to make sure the driveshaft remains locked in the transaxle.

e. Install a new locknut onto the outer end of the driveshaft, adjusting wheel bearings as described in chapter 8. Crimp the tabs over after they are aligned with the groove in he driveshaft.

f. Tighten the stabilizer bar link nut until 1 in. of thread is exposed.

g. Torque the lower control arm to ball joint nut and bolt to 32-40 ft. lbs.

h. Torque the control link for the lower arm and stabilizer bar to 9-13 ft. lbs.

i. Refill the differential with fresh fluid meeting proper specifications.

## CV-JOINT OVERHAUL
### GLC

NOTE: *The joint on the wheel side of the drive axle is non-rebuildable. If worn, the joint and axle must be replaced. The boot may be changed if necessary. Do not interfere with the balancer found on the right axle unless necessary for wheel joint boot replacement. If balancer is removed it must be reinstalled in the same position 14.45 ins. from the front of the wheel joint.*

1. Remove the boot band by raising the locking clip and band with a pair of pliers.

2. Remove the lock clip from the inner edge of the ball joint casting. Remove the casting.

3. Remove the snap-ring from the end of the splines and remove the cage and bearings.

4. Carefully pry the balls from the bearing cage. After the balls are removed turn the cage slightly and remove it from the inner ring.

5. Wash all of the parts in a safe solvent and inspect for wear.

6. A joint kit for the transaxle end and boot kits for both ends are available. The kits are installed in the reverse order of disassembly. Always use the grease supplied with the kits. Tape the spline ends of the shaft when installing the rubber boots.

**323 and 626**

Disassemble the driveshaft as shown in the exploded view. The clip (2) should be removed with an ordinary screwdriver, while the snap ring (4) should be removed with snap ring pliers or a similar tool.

Pull the ball bearings, inner ring and cage out of the shaft while still assembled. Then insert an ordinary screwdriver between the inner ring and cage to gently pry each ball out. Finally, matchmark the cage and inner ring and then turn the cage 30 degrees and pull it off the inner ring.

Assemble in reverse order, being careful to repack bearings in the grease supplied with the kit in a thorough manner.

## REAR AXLE

### Determining Axle Ratio

The axle ratio is obtained by dividing the number of teeth on the drive pinion gear into the larger number of teeth on the ring gear. It is always expressed as a proportion and is a simple expression of gear speed reduction and torque multiplication.

NOTE: *This procedure applies to models with rear wheel drive only*

To find an unknown axle ratio, make a chalk mark on a tire and on the driveshaft. Move the car ahead (or back) slowly for one tire rotation and have an observer note the number of driveshaft rotations. The number of driveshaft rotations if the axle ratio. You can get more accuracy by going more than one tire rotation and dividing the result by the number of tire rotations. This can also be done by jacking up both rear wheels and turning them by hand.

### Axle Shaft, Bearing and Seal
#### REMOVAL AND INSTALLATION

NOTE: *The left and the right rear axle shafts are not interchangeable as the left shaft is shorter than the right. It is, therefore, not a good idea to remove them both at once.*

1. Remove the wheel cover and loosen the lug nuts.
2. Raise the rear of the car and support the axle housing on jackstands.
3. Unfasten the lug nuts and remove the wheel.
4. Remove the brake assembly. (See Chapter 8). On Cosmo, remove the brake disc. Disconnect parking brake cable, if necessary.
5. Unfasten the nuts which secure the brake backing plate and the bearing retainer to the axle housing.
6. Withdraw the axle shaft with a puller.

Measure the depth of the bearing seal

**Axle shaft installation is performed in the following order:**

1. Apply grease to the oil seal lips and then insert the oil seal into the axle housing.
2. On all models but GLC check the axle shaft end-play in the following manner:
    a. Temporarily install the brake backing plate on the axle shaft.
    b. Measure the depth of the bearing seal and then measure the width of the bearing outer race.
    c. The difference between the two measurements is equal to the overall thickness of the adjusting shims required. Shims are available in thicknesses of 0.004 and 0.016 in.
NOTE: *The maximum permissible endplay is 0.004 in.*
3. Remove the backing plate and apply sealer to the rear axle surfaces which contact it. Install the backing plate again.
4. Install the rear axle shaft, bearing retainer, gasket, and shims through the backing plate and into the axle housing. Coat the shims with a small amount of sealer first.
5. Engage the splines on the differential side gear with those on the end of the axle shaft.
6. On Cosmo, install the brake disc. Install the brake assembly and adjust it. Connect parking brake cable and adjust it if necessary. See Chapter 8.
7. Install the wheel and lower the car.

### Differential Carrier
#### REMOVAL AND INSTALLATION (REAR WHEEL DRIVE VEHICLES ONLY)

1. Raise the vehicle and support it safely with jackstands.
2. Using wrench 49 0259 730, remove the differential drain plug and drain the lubricant from the differential. Install the plug after all of the fluid has drained.
3. Remove the axle shafts.
4. Remove the driveshaft.

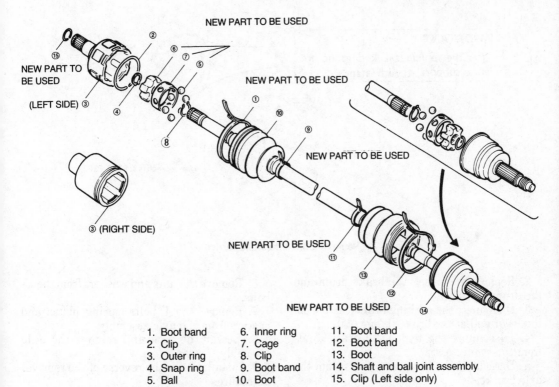

NEW PART TO BE USED

NEW PART TO
BE USED

(LEFT SIDE) ③

③ (RIGHT SIDE)

NEW PART TO BE USED

NEW PART TO BE USED

NEW PART TO BE USED

NEW PART TO BE USED

| 1. Boot band | 6. Inner ring | 11. Boot band |
| 2. Clip | 7. Cage | 12. Boot band |
| 3. Outer ring | 8. Clip | 13. Boot |
| 4. Snap ring | 9. Boot band | 14. Shaft and ball joint assembly |
| 5. Ball | 10. Boot | 15. Clip (Left side only) |

**Exploded view of 626 front wheel drive driveshaft**

5. Remove the carrier-to-differential housing retaining fasteners and remove the carrier assembly from the housing.

6. Clean the carrier and axle housing mating surfaces.

7. If the differential originally used a gasket between the carrier and the differential housing, replace the gasket. If the unit had no gasket, apply a thin film of oil-resistant silicone sealer to the mating surfaces of both the carrier and the housing and allow the sealer to set according to the manufacturer's instructions.

8. Place the carrier assembly onto the housing and install the carrier-to-housing fasteners. Torque the fasteners to 12–17 ft. lb.

9. Install the driveshaft(s) and axle shafts as previously outlined.

10. Install the brake drums and wheels.

11. Fill the differential with the proper amount of SAE 80W–90 fluid (see the Capacities Chart).

## Axle Housing
### REMOVAL AND INSTALLATION

Raise the vehicle on a hoist and support the axle assembly with a suitable lifting devise.

1. Drain the lubricant from the axle housing and remove the driveshaft.

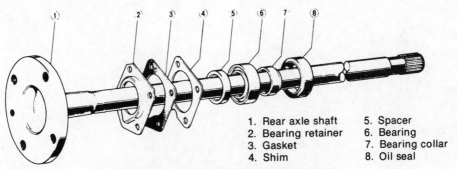

| 1. Rear axle shaft | 5. Spacer |
| 2. Bearing retainer | 6. Bearing |
| 3. Gasket | 7. Bearing collar |
| 4. Shim | 8. Oil seal |

**Components of the rear axle shaft assembly**

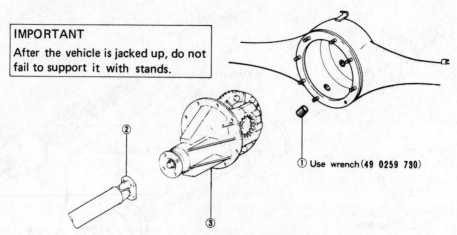

> **IMPORTANT**
> After the vehicle is jacked up, do not
> fail to support it with stands.

① Use wrench (49 0259 730)

**Removing the differential carrier**

2. Remove the wheel, the brake drum and the drum assembly.

3. Disconnect the parking brake cable from the lever and at the brake flange plate.

4. Disconnect the hydraulic brake lines from the connectors.

5. Disconnect the shock absorbers from the axle brackets.

6. Remove the nuts and washers from the U-bolts.

7. Remove the U-bolts, spring plates and spacers from the axle assembly.

8. Lower the jack and remove the axle assembly.

9. Installation is the reverse of the removal procedure.

# Suspension and Steering

# 7

## FRONT SUSPENSION

### MacPherson Struts

*REMOVAL AND INSTALLATION*

1. Remove the wheel cover and loosen the lug nuts.

2. Raise the front of the vehicle and support it with jackstands. Do not jack it or support it by any of the front suspension members. Remove the wheel.

CAUTION: *Be sure that the car is securely supported. Remember, you will be working underneath it.*

3. On rear wheel drive models, remove the caliper and disc as described in Chapter 8.

4. Support the strut from underneath, and then unfasten the nuts which secure the supper shock mount to the top of the wheel arch. Disconnect the brake line from the strut.

5. Remove the two bolts that secure the lower end of the shock to the steering knuckle arm.

6. Remove the shock and coil spring as a complete assembly.

7. Mount the strut (shock/spring) assembly in a vise. Protect the shock tube by placing a piece of soft metal on either side between the tube and vice jaws. Compress the coil spring with a spring compressor.

8. Hold the upper end of the shock piston rod with a pipe wrench and unfasten the locknut.

9. Remove the parts from the top of the shock absorber in the order shown in the appropriate illustration.

CAUTION: *When removing the spring compressor from the coil spring, do so gradually so that spring tension is not released all at once.*

10. Installation of the MacPherson strut is performed in the reverse order of removal. Tighten the nut on the top of the piston rod to 10 ft.lb. on most rear wheel drive models. On GLC front drive and 626 through 1982, torque the piston rod nut to 47–59 ft.lb. On front wheel drive GLC, 1983 and later, torque the piston rod nut to 41–49 ft.lb., the mounting block to suspension tower to 17–21 ft.lb. On 626 front drive models, torque the piston rod nut to 47–59 ft.lb., the mounting block to suspension tower nuts to 16–21 ft.lb., and the lower strut bolts to 69–86 ft.lb.

On 1983 and later front wheel drive models, there is a mark or hole in the mounting block. Be sure it faces the inside of the vehicle when positioning the block.

NOTE: *If a new coil spring is being fitted, match it with an adjusting plate of the correct thickness to obtain equal road clearance on both sides. Do not use more than two adjusting plates on a side.*

### Control Arm

*REMOVAL AND INSTALLATION*

**Except Front Wheel Drive**

1. Perform the first two steps of the MacPherson strut removal procedure.

2. Remove the cotter pin and nut, which secure the tie rod end, from the knuckle arm, then use a puller to separate them.

3. Unfasten the bolts which secure the lower end of the shock absorber to the knuckle arm.

4. Remove the nut then withdraw the rubber bushing and washer which secure the stabilizer bar to the control arm.

5. Unfasten the nut and bolt which secure the control arm to the frame member.

6. Push outward on the strut assembly while removing the end of the control arm from the frame member.

7. Remove the control arm and steering knuckle arm as an assembly.

8. Install the assembly in a vise. Remove its cotter pin and unfasten the ball joint nut; then

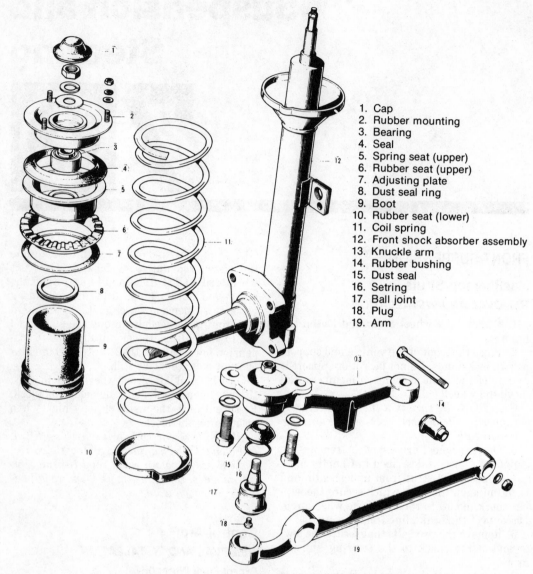

1. Cap
2. Rubber mounting
3. Bearing
4. Seal
5. Spring seat (upper)
6. Rubber seat (upper)
7. Adjusting plate
8. Dust seal ring
9. Boot
10. Rubber seat (lower)
11. Coil spring
12. Front shock absorber assembly
13. Knuckle arm
14. Rubber bushing
15. Dust seal
16. Setring
17. Ball joint
18. Plug
19. Arm

**MacPherson strut front suspension—rear wheel drive models**

separate the knuckle arm from the control arm with a puller.

9. Installation of the control arm is performed in the reverse order of its removal. Torque the control arm-to-crossmember nut and bolt to: 51–65 ft.lb. on the RX-2; 34 ft.lb. on the RX-3; 54–69 ft.lb. on the RX-4 and Cosmo; 29–40 ft.lb. on the GLC 626 and 808.

**Front Wheel Drive GLC to 1982**

1. Loosen the wheel lugs, raise the car and safely support it on jackstands. Remove the front wheel.

2. Remove the through bolt connecting the lower arm to the steering knuckle.

3. Remove the bolts and nuts mounting the control arm to the body (two inner and three outer).

4. Remove the lower control arm. The ball joint can be serviced at this time if necessary.

5. Installation is the reverse order of removal. Mounting Torque:
   • Ball Joint to Steering Knuckle: 32–40 ft.lb.
   • Outer Bolts: 43–54 ft.lb.
   • Inner Bolts: 69–86 ft.lb.

**1983–85 Front Wheel Drive GLC**

1. Support the vehicle front end via the crossmember on axle stands.

2. Remove the two bolts which fasten the ball joint to the lower arm from the arm.

3. Now, remove the two bolts attaching the

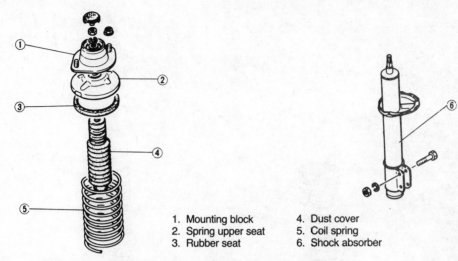

1. Mounting block
2. Spring upper seat
3. Rubber seat
4. Dust cover
5. Coil spring
6. Shock absorber

**Exploded view of 1983 and later GLC front strut**

rear of the lower arm to the body, and the three connecting the front of the lower arm to the body.

4. To install, reverse the removal procedure, torquing the front three bolts mounting the unit to the body to 69–86 ft.lb., and rear body bracket bolts to 43–54 ft.lb., and the knuckle to arm bolts to 32–40 ft.lb.

### 1983–87 Front Wheel Drive 626

1. Support the front of the vehicle via the crossmember on safety stands. Remove the splash shield from the side you'll be working on.

2. Remove the two locknuts, washers, bushings, bolt and spacer that link the stabilizer bar to the lower arm. Keep the parts in order.

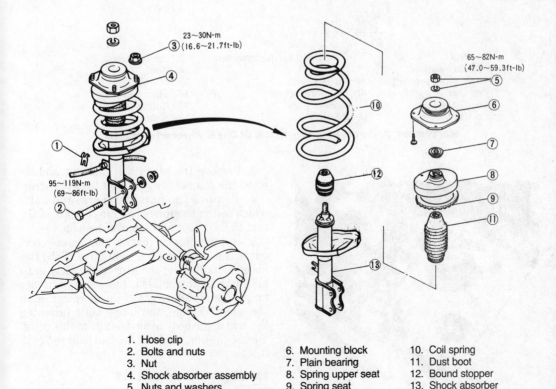

1. Hose clip
2. Bolts and nuts
3. Nut
4. Shock absorber assembly
5. Nuts and washers
6. Mounting block
7. Plain bearing
8. Spring upper seat
9. Spring seat
10. Coil spring
11. Dust boot
12. Bound stopper
13. Shock absorber

**Exploded view of 1983 and later 626 front strut**

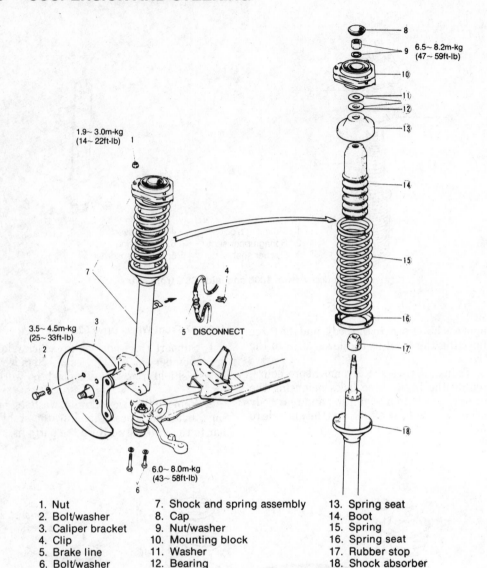

1.9~ 3.0m-kg
(14~ 22ft-lb)

3.5~ 4.5m-kg
(25~ 33ft-lb)

6.5~ 8.2m-kg
(47~ 59ft-lb)

5 DISCONNECT

6.0~ 8.0m-kg
(43~ 58ft-lb)

| | | |
|---|---|---|
| 1. Nut | 7. Shock and spring assembly | 13. Spring seat |
| 2. Bolt/washer | 8. Cap | 14. Boot |
| 3. Caliper bracket | 9. Nut/washer | 15. Spring |
| 4. Clip | 10. Mounting block | 16. Spring seat |
| 5. Brake line | 11. Washer | 17. Rubber stop |
| 6. Bolt/washer | 12. Bearing | 18. Shock absorber |

**MacPherson strut front assembly-typical GLC rear wheel drive models**

**Unfasten the three bolts which secure the upper shock mount to the wheel arch (arrows)**

3. Remove the pinch bolt and nut and remove the stem of the ball joint from the strut.

4. Remove the nuts, washers, and bolts which fasten the inner two hinge joints of the arm to the body, and remove the arm.

5. In installation, reverse the above procedures, but wait for final tightening of the two hinge bolts linking the arm to the body until all parts are assembled, the other parts are torqued, and the weight of the car can rest on the wheel. Torque the hinge bolts fastening the arm to the body to 69–86 ft.lb. at this point. Torque the pinch bolt for the ball joint to 32–39 ft.lb.

### 1986-87 Front Wheel Drive 323

1. Jack up the front of the vehicle and support it with jackstands.

**Removing the control arm**

2. Remove the wheel and splash shield. Remove the nut, bolt, bushings and retainers that secure the stabilizer bar to the lower control arm.

3. Remove the pinch bolt and nut and seperate the ball joint from the steering knuckle.

4. Remove the nuts, washers, and bolts which fasten the inner two hinge joints of the arm to the body, and remove the arm.

5. Installation is the reverse of the removal procedure. Torque the lower arm mounting bolte to 66–86 ft.lb.

## Tension Rod and Stabilizer Bar
### REMOVAL AND INSTALLATION
#### Rear Wheel Drive 626

1. Raise the vehicle and support with jackstands.

2. Remove the tension rod attaching nuts from the suspension arm.

3. Remove the nuts, washers and rubber bushings holding the tension rod to the tension rod bracket and remove the tension rod.

4. Remove the control rod assembly.

5. Remove the stabilizer bar support plate and bushings.

6. Installation is the reverse of removal.

NOTE: *When installing the stabilizer bushing with the support plate, place the open end of the bushing toward the front.*

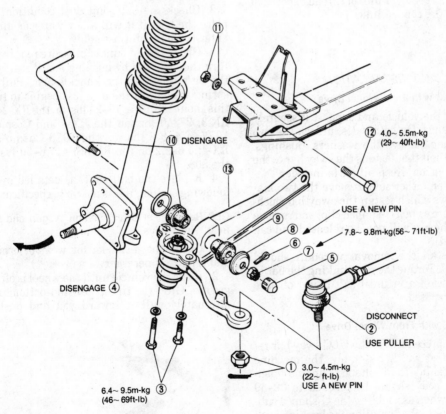

1. Nut/cotter pin
2. Tie rod
3. Bolt/washer
4. Shock absorber
5. Stop
6. Cotter pin
7. Nut
8. Washer
9. Rubber bush
10. Stabilizer bar/washer/rubber bush
11. Nut/washer
12. Bolt
13. Control arm and steering knuckle arm

**Removing the control arm—GLC rear wheel drive models**

**1986–87 323**

1. Raise the vehicle and support with jackstands.

2. Remove the two locknuts, washers, bushings, bolt and spacer that link the stabilizer bar to the lower arm. Keep the parts in order.

3. Remove the nuts, washers, rubber bushings and bracket holding the stabilizer bar to frame and remove the stabilizer bar.

4. Inspect the stabilizer bar for damage such as bends, cracks, or metal deterioration. Inspect the bushings for signs of wear or deterioration and replace as necessary. Install in the reverse of the removal procedure.

5. Mount the bushings so that the seam faces the rear of the chassie.

6. Mount the bracket side of the stabilizer first and temporarily tighten it. After mounting the control link side, tighten to the specified torque with the vehicle in the unloaded condition.

7. Tighten the stabilizer bar bushing and bracket bolts to 23–34 ft.lb.

8. Tighten the bushing to control arm nut so that there is 0.43″ (11mm) of thread exposed at the top of the control link.

## Sway Bar
### REMOVAL AND INSTALLATION
**1983–85 GLC with Front Wheel Drive**

1. Raise the vehicle and support it securely on axle stands. On both sides, unlock the two locknuts and remove the washers, bushings, spacer and bolt that fastens the sway bar to the front suspension. Keep all parts in order.

2. Now, on either side, remove the two machine screws which fasten the sway bar bushing to the body via a U-shaped clip, and remove the clip. The bar will now be released and can be removed.

3. To install, the removal procedure should be reversed. Torque the nuts linking the bar to the suspension arm until ¼″ (6mm) of bare thread is exposed.

**626 and 323 with Front Wheel Drive**

Follow the procedure for the GLC sway bar removal, just above. In assembly, the machine screws fastening the U-shaped clip and bushing to the body should be torqued to 32–39 ft.lb. Also, when assembling the U-shaped rubber bushings to the bar, align the bushing with the line on the bar and install it so the notch faces the rear of the car. Tighten the locknuts on top of the bolt linking the sway bar to the steering knuckle until 1″ (25.4mm) of bare thread is exposed.

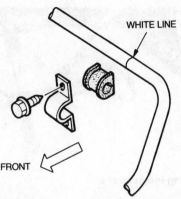

WHITE LINE

FRONT

**626 sway bar bushing installation. Align the bushing with the line on the bar, on either side, notch facing rearward.**

## Ball Joints
### INSPECTION
**All Except Below**

1. Perform Steps 1–5 of the control arm removal procedure.

2. Check the ball joint dust condition. Replace the boot if it will allow water or dirt to enter the ball joint assembly.

3. Check the amount of pressure required to turn the ball stud by hooking a pull scale into the tie rod hole in the knuckle arm. Pull the spring scale until the arm just begins to turn; this should require: 13–24 lbs. on the RX-2 and RX-3; 27–40 lbs. on the RX-4 and Cosmo to 1977; 4.4–8.8 lbs. on the 1978 Cosmo and RX-4; 4.6–9.2 on the RX-3SP; 17.6–30 lbs. on the 808.

4. Replace the ball joint, as detailed in the following section, if it is not up to specification.

**GLC Rear Wheel Drive, Station Wagon and 626 Rear Wheel Drive**

1. Check the just boot for wear or cracks, and replace if necessary.

2. Raise the vehicle until the wheel is off the ground. Grab the tire at top and bottom, and alternately pull it toward you and push it

**Checking the pressure required to turn the ball stud with a spring scale**

away to check for ball joint end play. Wear limit is 0.04″ (1mm). If necessary, replace ball joint and control arm assembly. See control arm removal and installation procedure above. When installing ball joint nut, torque to 43–51 ft.lb. on the GLC and 46–69 ft.lb. on the 626.

### Front Wheel Drive GLC

1. Raise the vehicle and support it securely. Remove the front wheel.

2. Unbolt the ball joint where it connects to the lower arm. Put the hook of a spring scale in the outer bolt hole. Turn the ball joint back and forth several times and then measure the rotating torque on the spring scale. Turn the joint slowly and make sure the scale stays at 90 degrees to the joint lever. Rotating torque should be 6.3–10.9 lbs. Otherwise, replace the ball joint.

### Front Wheel Drive 323 and 626

NOTE: *This procedure is usually done with a Mazda factory tool 49 0180 510B or equivalent. If you can't get this part, a preload attachment, you won't be able to make this test unless you can figure a way to measure the rotating torque of the joint with a torque wrench.*

Raise the vehicle, support it securely, and remove the front wheel. Remove the pinch bolt and nut from the steering knuckle. Install a preload attachment lever onto the ball joint or devise a way to measure rotating torque right at the ballstud with a torque wrench. Pressure at the end of the preload attachment required to turn the ballstud should be 4.4–7.7 lb. Torque at the stud should be 1.45–2.53 lb.

### *REMOVAL AND INSTALLATION*

### All Except GLC and 626

1. Complete the control arm removal procedure as detailed above.

2. Remove the set ring and the dust boot from the ball joint.

3. Clean the ball joint and control arm assembly.

4. Press the ball joint out of the control arm. **Installation of a new ball joint if performed in the following order:**

1. Clean the ball joint mounting bore and coat it with kerosene.

2. Press the ball joint into the control arm. NOTE: *If the pressure required to press the new ball joint into place is less than 3,300 lbs., the bore is worn and the control arm must be replaced.*

3. Attach the ball joint/control arm assembly to the steering knuckle. Tighten the nut to 60 ft.lb. and insert the cotter pin. The 60 ft.lb.

figure has been changed on the 1978 RX-3SP, Cosmo, and RX-4; it is now 43–58 ft.lb. on those models.

4. Install the control arm in the car, as detailed above.

### Rear Drive 626 and GLC

On the GLC and 626 models refer to the Control Arm removal and installation procedure. When installing the ball joint nut torque to 43–51 lbs. on the GLC and 46–69 ft.lb. on the 626.

### Front Wheel Drive GLC

1. Raise the vehicle and support it securely by the front crossmember. Remove the front wheel.

2. Remove the pinch bolt and nut from the bottom of the strut. Pull the ball stud out.

3. Remove the two bolts attaching the joint lever to the lower control arm, and remove the assembly.

4. Install in reverse order. Check and adjust front end alignment, if necessary.

### Front Wheel Drive 323/626

See the procedure above for lower control arm removal and installation. If the ball joint is defective, the control arm and joint are replaced as an assembly.

## Front End Alignment
### *CASTER AND CAMBER*

Caster and camber are preset by the manufacturer. They require adjustment only if the suspension and steering linkage components are damaged, in which case, repair is accomplished by replacing the damaged part except on RX-4 626 (rear drive) and Cosmo.

On these models, the caster and camber may be changed by rotating the shock absorber support. If they can't be brought to within specifications, replace or repair suspension parts as necessary.

To check caster and camber, use one of the alignment machines following its manufacturer's instructions. Compare the results obtained, against the specifications in the Wheel Alignment Specification chart.

### *TOE-IN ADJUSTMENT*

Toe-in is the difference in the distance between the front wheels, as measured at both the front and rear of the front tires.

1. Raise the front of the car so that its front wheels are just clear of the ground.

2. Use a scribing block to mark a line at the center of each tire tread while rotating the wheels by hand.

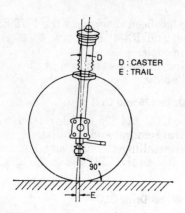

D : CASTER
E : TRAIL

**Caster**

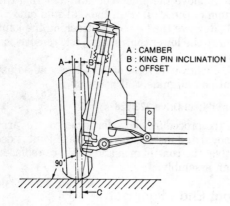

A : CAMBER
B : KING PIN INCLINATION
C : OFFSET

**Camber**

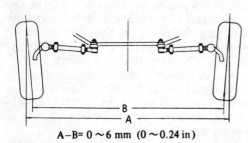

A–B= 0 ~ 6 mm (0 ~ 0.24 in )

**Measuring toe-in**

3. Measure the distance between the marked lines at both their front and rear.
NOTE: *Take both measurements at equal distances from the ground.*
4. The toe-in is equal to the difference between the front and rear measurements (front figure smaller). See chart below.
5. To adjust the toe-in, loosen the tie rod locknuts and turn both tie rods an equal amount until the proper measurement is obtained.

# REAR SUSPENSION

## Springs

### *REMOVAL AND INSTALLATION*

#### RX-3, RX-4, and GLC Wagon

1. Remove the wheel cover and loosen the lug nuts.
2. Raise the back end of the car and support it with jackstands.
CAUTION: *Be sure that the car is securely supported. Remember, you will be working underneath it.*
3. Remove the lug nuts and the wheel.
4. Support the rear axle housing with jackstands.
5. Disconnect the lower part of the shock from the spring clamp. Unfasten the nuts which secure the U-bolt. Withdraw the U-bolt seat, rubber pad, plate, and the U-bolt itself.
6. Unfasten the two bolts and the nut that secure the spring pin to the front end of the rear spring.
7. Pry the spring pin out with a large, flat pry bar inserted between the spring pin and its body bracket.
8. Unfasten the nuts and the bolts which attach the rear shackle to the car's body.
9. Withdraw the rear spring assembly, complete with its shackle.
10. Remove the shackle assembly from the end of the spring.
11. Pull the rubber bushings out from both ends of the spring.
12. Rear spring installations is performed in the reverse order of removal. When installing the rubber bushings, do not lubricate them. Tighten the U-bolt securing nuts to 30 ft.lb. and both the spring pin and the shackle pin to 14 ft.lb.

#### RX-2 Models, GLC, and 626 with Front Wheel Drive

Rear coil spring removal is performed as part of the shock absorber removal operation. See the appropriate section following for the combined procedure.

#### Cosmo

1. Remove the rear wheels.
2. Support the lower arms with a jack.
3. Remove the pivot bolt and nut which secures the rear end of the lower arm to the axle housing.
4. Lower the jack to relieve the spring pressure on the lower arm and remove the spring.
5. If replacing one spring only, a suitable adjusting plate will be necessary to give equal road clearance on each side.
6. Install spring in reverse order of removal, but do not tighten bolts while car is on stands.

## Wheel Alignment Specifications

| Year | Model | Camber Range (deg) | Camber Preferred Setting (deg) | Caster Range (deg) | Caster Preferred Setting (deg) | Toe-in (in.) | Steering Axis Inclination (deg) |
|---|---|---|---|---|---|---|---|
| 1972–74 | RX-2 | ¼P–1¾P | 1P | ½N–1½P | ½P | 0–0.24 | 8¾P |
| 1975 | RX-3 | 1P–2P | 1½P | ½N–1½P | ½P | 0–0.24 | 8 7/10P |
| | RX-4 | 1½P–2½P | 2P | 0–2P | 1P | 0–0.24 | 9½P |
| | 808 | ⅔P–2⅙P | 1⅓P | ½N–1½P | ½P | 0–0.24 | 8¾P |
| 1976 | 808 (1600) | ① | ② | ③–2P | ½P | 0–0.24 | 8½P |
| 1976–77 | 808 (1300) | ④ | ⑤ | ½N–1½P | ½P | 0–0.24 | 8⅔P |
| 1976–78 | RX-3, RX-3SP | ③ | ⑥ | ½N–1½P | ½P | 0–0.24 | 8⅔P |
| | RX-4 | 1P–2P | 1½P | ⑦ | ⑧ | 0–0.24 | 9⅔P ⑨ |
| 1977 | Cosmo | 1½P–3P ⑩ | 2¼P ⑪ | 0–2P | 1P | 0–0.24 | 9¾P |
| 1977–78 | 808 (1600) | ⑫ | ⑬ | ⑭ | ⑮ | 0–0.24 | ⑯ |
| | GLC | — | ⅔P | ⅝P–2⅓P | 1 35/60 | 0–0.24 | 8½P |
| 1978 | Cosmo | 0P–2P | 1P | 1½p–3P ⑰ | 2¼ ⑱ | 0–0.24 | 9¾P |
| 1979–80 | GLC | 15′–1°15′ ⑲ | 45′ ⑳ | 15′–2°25′ ㉑ | 1°45′ ㉓ | 0–0.24 | 8°45′ |
| | 626 | 45′–1°45′ | 1°15′ | 3⅔–4 ㉒ | ㉔ | 0–0.24 | 10°40′ |
| 1981–82 | GLC | — | 50′P | — | 1°25′P | 0.12 out-0.12 in | 12°20′ |
| 1979–82 | 626 | 45′–1°45′ | 1°15′ | 3⅔–4 ㉒ | ㉔ | 0–0.24 | 10°40′ |
| 1983 | GLC Wagon | ¼P–1¼P | ¾P | 51′P–2°21′P | 1°36′P | .24 in | 8°43′ |
| 1983–84 | 626 | −⅙P–+1⅚P | ⅓P | +50′–+2°25′ | 1°40′ | .0–.24 | 12°55′ |
| 1983–84 | GLC | +25′–+1°25′ | +55′ | +1°10′–+1°40′ | 1°55′ | .12 out-.12 in | 12°10′ |
| '85 | GLC | 7/16P–1 7/16P | 15/16P | 1 3/16P–2 11/16P | 1 15/16P | 0–¼ | 12 3/16 |
| '85 | 626 | 3/16N–13/16P | 5/16P | 15/16P–2 7/16P | 1 11/16P | 0–¼ | 12 15/16 |
| '86–'87 | 323 | 1/16P–1½P | 13/16P | 13/16P–2 5/16P | 1 9/16P | 1/32–¼ | 12⅜ |
| '86–'87 | 626 | 3/16N–13/16P ① | 5/16P | 5/16P–2 7/16P | 1 11/16P | 0–¼ ② | 12 15/16 |

① Sedan: ⅚P–2⅓P
coupe: 1P–2½P
wagon: 1P–2⅓P
② Sedan: 1½P
coupe: 1⅚P
wagon: 1⅔P
③ Sedan & wagon: ⅚N–1⅕P
coupe: 1 1/12P–2P
④ Sedan: ⅔P–2⅙P
coupe wagon: 1P–2⅓P
⑤ Sedan: 1⅓P
coupe wagon: 1⅔P
⑥ Sedan & wagon: 1⅔P
coupe: 1½P
⑦ Sedan & hardtop: 0–2P
wagon: ⅓P–1⅓P
⑧ Sedan & hardtop: 1P
wagon: ½P
⑨ Wagon: 9⅓P
⑩ Manual: 1P–2P
⑪ Manual: 1½P
⑫ Sedan & wagon: 1P–2½P
coupe: 1⅓P–2⅚P
⑬ Sedan & wagon: 1⅚P
coupe: 2 1/12P
⑭ Sedan & coupe: 1/12P–2½P
wagon: ¼P–2¼P
⑮ Sedan & coupe: 1 1/12P
wagon: 1¼P
⑯ Sedan & coupe: 8 5/12P
wagon: 8¼P
⑰ Manual: 1 5/60–2 35/60
⑱ Manual: 1⅝
⑲ Station wagon: 30′–1°30′
⑳ Station wagon: 1°
㉑ Station wagon: 1°–2°30′
㉒ Station wagon: 1°45′
㉓ Right side: 2°55′–4°25′
Left side: 2°25′–3°55′
㉔ Right side: 3°45′
Left side: 3°10′

Rear Wheel Drive 626

1. Raise the rear end of the vehicle and support it with jackstands. Place the jackstands under the bracket on the front sides of the lower arms.
2. Remove the rear wheel.
3. Place a jack under the rear axle housing to support it.
4. Remove the shock absorber lower attaching nut and disengage the shock absorber form the rear axle housing.
5. Remove the lateral rod from the right side of the axle housing.
6. Remove the upper link attaching nut from the rear of the axle housing.
7. Remove the lower arm attaching nut from the rear axle housing.
8. Remove the control rod attaching nut and

## Troubleshooting Basic Wheel Problems

| Problem | Cause | Solution |
| --- | --- | --- |
| The car's front end vibrates at high speed | • The wheels are out of balance<br>• Wheels are out of alignment | • Have wheels balanced<br>• Have wheel alignment checked/adjusted |
| Car pulls to either side | • Wheels are out of alignment<br><br>• Unequal tire pressure<br>• Different size tires or wheels | • Have wheel alignment checked/adjusted<br>• Check/adjust tire pressure<br>• Change tires or wheels to same size |
| The car's wheel(s) wobbles | • Loose wheel lug nuts<br>• Wheels out of balance<br>• Damaged wheel<br><br><br>• Wheels are out of alignment<br><br>• Worn or damaged ball joint<br>• Excessive play in the steering linkage (usually due to worn parts)<br>• Defective shock absorber | • Tighten wheel lug nuts<br>• Have tires balanced<br>• Raise car and spin the wheel. If the wheel is bent, it should be replaced<br>• Have wheel alignment checked/adjusted<br>• Check ball joints<br>• Check steering linkage<br><br>• Check shock absorbers |
| Tires wear unevenly or prematurely | • Incorrect wheel size<br><br>• Wheels are out of balance<br>• Wheels are out of alignment | • Check if wheel and tire size are compatible<br>• Have wheels balanced<br>• Have wheel alignment checked/adjusted |

## Troubleshooting Basic Tire Problems

| Problem | Cause | Solution |
| --- | --- | --- |
| The car's front end vibrates at high speeds and the steering wheel shakes | • Wheels out of balance<br>• Front end needs aligning | • Have wheels balanced<br>• Have front end alignment checked |
| The car pulls to one side while cruising | • Unequal tire pressure (car will usually pull to the low side)<br>• Mismatched tires<br><br>• Front end needs aligning | • Check/adjust tire pressure<br><br>• Be sure tires are of the same type and size<br>• Have front end alignment checked |
| Abnormal, excessive or uneven tire wear<br><br>See "How to Read Tire Wear" | • Infrequent tire rotation<br><br>• Improper tire pressure<br><br>• Sudden stops/starts or high speed on curves | • Rotate tires more frequently to equalize wear<br>• Check/adjust pressure<br><br>• Correct driving habits |
| Tire squeals | • Improper tire pressure<br>• Front end needs aligning | • Check/adjust tire pressure<br>• Have front end alignment checked |

remove the bushings, spacer and washers. Disengage the rear stabilizer bar from the control rod if so equipped.

9. Slowly lower the jack to relieve the spring pressure on the lower arm, then remove the spring.

10. Installation is the reverse of removal.

During installation of the coil spring make sure the open end of the spring faces the rear axle housing. Tighten all bolts temporarily then after the vehicle is lowered to the ground torque to specifications. Upper link and lower arm to axle housing, 66 ft.lb., Lateral rod to axle housing, 66 ft.lb.

## NOISE DIAGNOSIS

| The Noise Is | Most Probably Produced By |
|---|---|
| • Identical under Drive or Coast | • Road surface, tires or front wheel bearings |
| • Different depending on road surface | • Road surface or tires |
| • Lower as the car speed is lowered | • Tires |
| • Similar with car standing or moving | • Engine or transmission |
| • A vibration | • Unbalanced tires, rear wheel bearing, unbalanced driveshaft or worn U-joint |
| • A knock or click about every 2 tire revolutions | • Rear wheel bearing |
| • Most pronounced on turns | • Damaged differential gears |
| • A steady low-pitched whirring or scraping, starting at low speeds | • Damaged or worn pinion bearing |
| • A chattering vibration on turns | • Wrong differential lubricant or worn clutch plates (limited slip rear axle) |
| • Noticed only in Drive, Coast or Float conditions | • Worn ring gear and/or pinion gear |

## Troubleshooting Basic Steering and Suspension Problems

| Problem | Cause | Solution |
|---|---|---|
| Hard steering (steering wheel is hard to turn) | • Low or uneven tire pressure | • Inflate tires to correct pressure |
| | • Loose power steering pump drive belt | • Adjust belt |
| | • Low or incorrect power steering fluid | • Add fluid as necessary |
| | • Incorrect front end alignment | • Have front end alignment checked/adjusted |
| | • Defective power steering pump | • Check pump |
| | • Bent or poorly lubricated front end parts | • Lubricate and/or replace defective parts |
| Loose steering (too much play in the steering wheel) | • Loose wheel bearings | • Adjust wheel bearings |
| | • Loose or worn steering linkage | • Replace worn parts |
| | • Faulty shocks | • Replace shocks |
| | • Worn ball joints | • Replace ball joints |
| Car veers or wanders (car pulls to one side with hands off the steering wheel) | • Incorrect tire pressure | • Inflate tires to correct pressure |
| | • Improper front end alignment | • Have front end alignment checked/adjusted |
| | • Loose wheel bearings | • Adjust wheel bearings |
| | • Loose or bent front end components | • Replace worn components |
| | • Faulty shocks | • Replace shocks |
| Wheel oscillation or vibration transmitted through steering wheel | • Improper tire pressures | • Inflate tires to correct pressure |
| | • Tires out of balance | • Have tires balanced |
| | • Loose wheel bearings | • Adjust wheel bearings |
| | • Improper front end alignment | • Have front end alignment checked/adjusted |
| | • Worn or bent front end components | • Replace worn parts |
| Uneven tire wear | • Incorrect tire pressure | • Inflate tires to correct pressure |
| | • Front end out of alignment | • Have front end alignment checked/adjusted |
| | • Tires out of balance | • Have tires balanced |

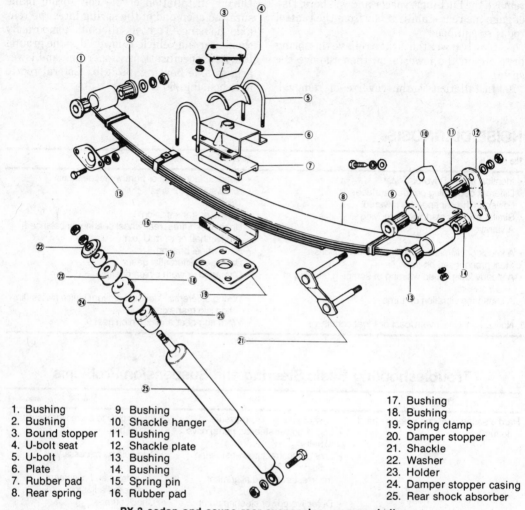

| | | |
|---|---|---|
| 1. Bushing | 9. Bushing | 17. Bushing |
| 2. Bushing | 10. Shackle hanger | 18. Bushing |
| 3. Bound stopper | 11. Bushing | 19. Spring clamp |
| 4. U-bolt seat | 12. Shackle plate | 20. Damper stopper |
| 5. U-bolt | 13. Bushing | 21. Shackle |
| 6. Plate | 14. Bushing | 22. Washer |
| 7. Rubber pad | 15. Spring pin | 23. Holder |
| 8. Rear spring | 16. Rubber pad | 24. Damper stopper casing |
| | | 25. Rear shock absorber |

RX-3 sedan and coupe rear suspension—wagon similar

## Shock Absorbers

### BOUNCE TEST

Each shock absorber can be tested by bouncing the corner of the vehicle until maximum up and down movement is obtained. Release the car. It should stop bouncing in one or two bounces. Compare both front corners or both rear corners but do not compare the front to the rear. If one corner bounces longer than the other it should be inspected for damage and the shock should possibly be replaced.

### REMOVAL AND INSTALLATION

#### RX-3, RX-4, 808 Coupes and Sedans

1. On RX-4, remove the seat. Remove the trim panel from the rear of the luggage compartment.

2. Unfasten the nuts, then remove the washers and rubber bushings from the upper shock absorber mounts.

3. Unfasten the nut and bolt which secures the end of the rear shock to the axle housing.

4. Withdraw the shock from underneath the car.

5. Installation is performed in the reverse order of removal. Tighten the upper shock mount to 15 ft.lb. on all models but the 808. On the 808, tighten the upper nuts until a ¼" (6mm) dimension exists between the top of the shock absorber rod and the top of the rod nut.

#### RX-3, RX-4 and 808 Wagons

1. Raise the back end of the station wagon and support it with jackstands.

CAUTION: *Be sure that the car is securely supported. Remember, you will be working underneath it.*

## Tire Size Comparison Chart

| "Letter" sizes | | | Inch Sizes | Metric-inch Sizes | | |
|---|---|---|---|---|---|---|
| "60 Series" | "70 Series" | "78 Series" | 1965–77 | "60 Series" | "70 Series" | "80 Series" |
| | | | 5.50-12, 5.60-12 | 165/60-12 | 165/70-12 | 155-12 |
| | | Y78-12 | 6.00-12 | | | |
| | | W78-13 | 5.20-13 | 165/60-13 | 145/70-13 | 135-13 |
| | | Y78-13 | 5.60-13 | 175/60-13 | 155/70-13 | 145-13 |
| | | | 6.15-13 | 185/60-13 | 165/70-13 | 155-13, P155/80-13 |
| A60-13 | A70-13 | A78-13 | 6.40-13 | 195/60-13 | 175/70-13 | 165-13 |
| B60-13 | B70-13 | B78-13 | 6.70-13 | 205/60-13 | 185/70-13 | 175-13 |
| | | | 6.90-13 | | | |
| C60-13 | C70-13 | C78-13 | 7.00-13 | 215/60-13 | 195/70-13 | 185-13 |
| D60-13 | D70-13 | D78-13 | 7.25-13 | | | |
| E60-13 | E70-13 | E78-13 | 7.75-13 | | | 195-13 |
| | | | 5.20-14 | 165/60-14 | 145/70-14 | 135-14 |
| | | | 5.60-14 | 175/60-14 | 155/70-14 | 145-14 |
| | | | 5.90-14 | | | |
| A60-14 | A70-14 | A78-14 | 6.15-14 | 185/60-14 | 165/70-14 | 155-14 |
| | B70-14 | B78-14 | 6.45-14 | 195/60-14 | 175/70-14 | 165-14 |
| | C70-14 | C78-14 | 6.95-14 | 205/60-14 | 185/70-14 | 175-14 |
| D60-14 | D70-14 | D78-14 | | | | |
| E60-14 | E70-14 | E78-14 | 7.35-14 | 215/60-14 | 195/70-14 | 185-14 |
| F60-14 | F70-14 | F78-14, F83-14 | 7.75-14 | 225/60-14 | 200/70-14 | 195-14 |
| G60-14 | G70-14 | G77-14, G78-14 | 8.25-14 | 235/60-14 | 205/70-14 | 205-14 |
| H60-14 | H70-14 | H78-14 | 8.55-14 | 245/60-14 | 215/70-14 | 215-14 |
| J60-14 | J70-14 | J78-14 | 8.85-14 | 255/60-14 | 225/70-14 | 225-14 |
| L60-14 | L70-14 | | 9.15-14 | 265/60-14 | 235/70-14 | |
| | A70-15 | A78-15 | 5.60-15 | 185/60-15 | 165/70-15 | 155-15 |
| B60-15 | B70-15 | B78-15 | 6.35-15 | 195/60-15 | 175/70-15 | 165-15 |
| C60-15 | C70-15 | C78-15 | 6.85-15 | 205/60-15 | 185/70-15 | 175-15 |
| | D70-15 | D78-15 | | | | |
| E60-15 | E70-15 | E78-15 | 7.35-15 | 215/60-15 | 195/70-15 | 185-15 |
| F60-15 | F70-15 | F78-15 | 7.75-15 | 225/60-15 | 205/70-15 | 195-15 |
| G60-15 | G70-15 | G78-15 | 8.15-15/8.25-15 | 235/60-15 | 215/70-15 | 205-15 |
| H60-15 | H70-15 | H78-15 | 8.45-15/8.55-15 | 245/60-15 | 225/70-15 | 215-15 |
| J60-15 | J70-15 | J78-15 | 8.85-15/8.90-15 | 255/60-15 | 235/70-15 | 225-15 |
| | K70-15 | | 9.00-15 | 265/60-15 | 245/70-15 | 230-15 |
| L60-15 | L70-15 | L78-15, L84-15 | 9.15-15 | | | 235-15 |
| | M70-15 | M78-15 | | | | 255-15 |
| | | N78-15 | | | | |

Note: Every size tire is not listed and many size comparisons are approximate, based on load ratings. Wider tires than those supplied new with the vehicle, should always be checked for clearance.

2. Remove the locknuts, washers, and rubber bushings from the lower shock absorber mount.

3. Install a compressor on the shock and compress it.

4. Unfasten the bolts which secure the upper shock absorber mounts to the body.

5. Withdraw the shock, with the compressor still attached, from underneath the car.

6. Slowly remove the compressor from the shock.

7. Shock absorber installation is performed in the reverse order of removal. Tighten the upper shock mount to 15 ft.lb., except on the 808. On the 080, tighten the upper nuts until a 1/4" (6mm) dimension exists between the bottom of the shock absorber rod and the bottom of the nuts.

### RX-2 Models

1. Working from inside the luggage compartment, unfasten the nuts which secure the upper end of he shock absorber.

2. Unfasten the nut and bolt at the lower end of the shock absorber.

3. Place a jack underneath the axle housing and raise the car.

4. Place jackstands underneath the frame side rails.

CAUTION: *Be sure that the jackstands are properly placed under the side rails.*

5. Slowly lower the jack to take the load off the springs.

6. Withdraw the shock/coil spring assembly from underneath the car.

7. Mark the shock for identification during

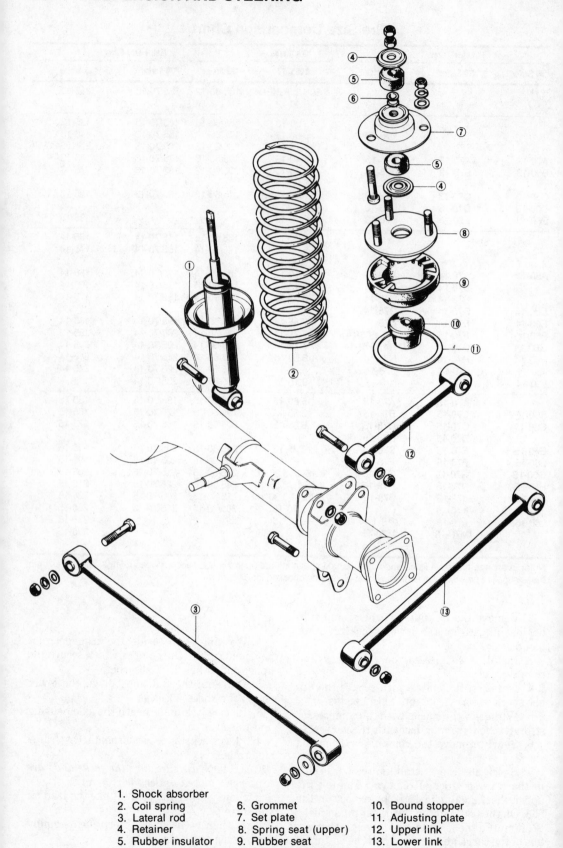

1. Shock absorber
2. Coil spring
3. Lateral rod
4. Retainer
5. Rubber insulator
6. Grommet
7. Set plate
8. Spring seat (upper)
9. Rubber seat
10. Bound stopper
11. Adjusting plate
12. Upper link
13. Lower link

**RX-2 rear suspension assembly**

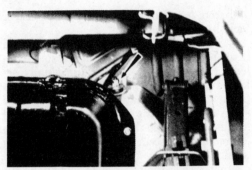

**Arrow show location of upper rear shock mounting nut on RX-3 sedans and coupes**

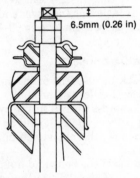

6.5mm (0.26 in)

**Tightening dimension for upper shock mounting nut—808 models**

**Removing the rear shock mounting bracket—RX-3 wagons**

assembly and secure the bottom the shock in a vise.

8. Fit a spring compressor on the spring.

9. Unfasten the locknuts from the upper end of the shock.

10. Remove the washers, bushings, set-plate, spring seat, rubber pad, adjusting plate, and bumper from the top of the shock.

11. Installation of the rear shock is performed in the reverse order of removal. Be sure to mount the shock with its stone guard facing toward the front of the car. Tighten the bolt and nut which secures the lower end of the shock, to 72–86 ft.lb.

NOTE: *If a new coil spring is being fitted, match it with an adjusting plate of the correct thickness to obtain equal road clearance on both sides. There are three different size coil springs available.*

### Rear Wheel Drive GLC

1. Raise the rear of the vehicle and support securely via the frame side rails. Remove the wheels.

2. Remove the upper shock absorber bolt from inside the fender well.

3. Remove the lower shock bolt and nut, and remove the shock.

4. To remove the rear spring, support the lower control arm with a jack. Remove the pivot bolt which connects the lower control arm and rear axle.

5. Very slowly lower the jack until the spring pressure has been relieved, and remove the spring.

6. Install the spring in reverse order of removal, but do not fully tighten the pivot bolt. Then, lower the vehicle until it is at normal ride height and torque the bolt to 47–59 ft.lb.

7. Install the shock absorber in the reverse of the removal procedure.

### Front Wheel Drive GLC

1. Remove the side trim panels form inside the trunk. Loosen and remove the top mounting nuts from the shock absorber assembly.

2. Loosen the rear wheel lugs, raise the car and safely support it on jackstands.

3. Remove the rear wheels. Disconnect the flexible brake hose from the strut.

4. Disconnect the trailing arm from the lower side of the strut: Separate the lateral link and strut by removing the bolt assembly.

5. Remove the strut from the lower unit by removing the two through nuts and bolts.

6. Remove the strut, and brake assembly. Clamp the strut assembly in a vise and loosen the nut at the top of the shock absorber.

CAUTION: *Do not remove the nut at this time.*

7. Compress the coil spring with a compressor tool. Remove the top nut and bracket. Remove the coil spring.

8. Installation is the reverse of removal. After mounting the strut assembly, lower the car to the ground and torque the mountings; Piston rod and mounting block: 41–60 ft.lb. Mounting block and tower mount: 16–20 ft.lb. Lower mounts: 40–50 ft.lb.

### Rear Wheel Drive 626

1. Raise the rear end of the vehicle and place jackstands under the bracket on the the front side of the lower arms.

2. Remove the rear wheel.

3. Remove the bracket attaching nuts from the upper end of the shock absorber.

4. Remove the lower shock absorber retaining nut and remove the shock absorber.

CAUTION: *Do not disassemble the gas sealed type shock absorber as it contains highly compressed gas. Defective shocks should be replaced.*

5. Installation is the reverse of removal. Torque the upper bracket bolts to 28 ft.lb., the lower bracket bolts to 32 ft.lb., and the shock absorber attaching nuts to 53 ft.lb.

### Front Drive 626

1. Jack up the rear of the vehicle and support the crossmember with safety stands.

2. Remove the bolts and nuts attaching the lower end of the strut to the rear suspension arm, and carefully lower the arm. Remove the brake hose clip from the lower end of the strut. Support the strut from underneath.

3. Remove the rear seat and trim. Remove the attaching nut and washer on either side the strut tower. Now, remove the support and remove the strut from the car.

4. Clamp the shock gently in a vise, using soft metal plates on either side to protect the shock tube from distortion. Keep the piston rod of the shock from turning while using a box wrench to carefully loosen the nut on the piston rod only enough for it to reach the top of the threads. The nut must remain securely fastened because the spring pressure is still dangerous.

5. Use two clamps designed for this purpose to compress the spring, one on either side. When the spring is securely compressed so there is no tension on the spring seat, remove the nut, washer, and mounting block and spring seat. Also remove the dust boot, spring,

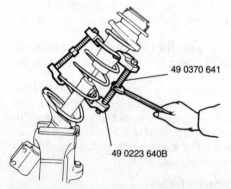

**Compressing the rear spring on 626 with front wheel drive. Use clamps designed for this job only. Mazda numbers are shown—you can use them to shop for an equivalent tool**

and stop. You can now replace the shock or have it rebuilt.

6. To install, reverse the removal procedure. If you're replacing the spring, make sure to release the clamps carefully and gradually before attempting to remove them, and to clamp the new spring adequately for it to be installed safely. Make sure the spring is properly seated top and bottom and that the seat, block, washer, and nut are secure before releasing spring tension.

7. Once the spring tension is held by the nut at the top of the unit, torque it to 47–59 ft.lb. Torque the mounting block installation nuts located behind the rear seat to 17–21 ft.lb., and the bolts fastening the lower end of the strut to the rear suspension arm to 69–86 ft.lb.

### Front Wheel Drive 323

1. Jack up the rear of the vehicle and support it with safety stands.

2. Compress the coil spring by using the coil spring holders 49 0223 640B and 49 0370 641, then remove the nut at the upper end of the piston rod.

3. Remove the bolts and nuts attaching the lower end of the strut to the rear suspension arm, and carefully lower the arm. Remove the brake hose clip from the lower end of the strut. Support the strut from underneath.

4. Remove the nuts from the top of the spring mounting block and remove the shock absorber assembly.

5. Remove the nut and washer that secure the shock absorber to the mounting block and remove the mounting block, spring seat and dust boot. Then remove the bound stopper and the coil spring.

6. Installation is the reverse of the removal procedure. When installing the spring, check that the spring is well seated in the upper and lower seats.

7. When installing the mounting block on the vehicle, make sure that the white point is to the inside of the vehicle.

## STEERING

### Steering Wheel

#### *REMOVAL AND INSTALLATION*

1. Remove the screws which secure the crash pad/horn button assembly to the steering wheel. If there are no mounting screws, pry the pad off, starting at the top. Remove the assembly.

2. Make matchmarks on the steering wheel and steering shaft.

## Troubleshooting the Steering Column

| Problem | Cause | Solution |
|---|---|---|
| Will not lock | • Lockbolt spring broken or defective | • Replace lock bolt spring |
| High effort (required to turn ignition key and lock cylinder) | • Lock cylinder defective<br>• Ignition switch defective<br>• Rack preload spring broken or deformed<br>• Burr on lock sector, lock rack, housing, support or remote rod coupling<br>• Bent sector shaft<br>• Defective lock rack<br>• Remote rod bent, deformed<br>• Ignition switch mounting bracket bent<br>• Distorted coupling slot in lock rack (tilt column) | • Replace lock cylinder<br>• Replace ignition switch<br>• Replace preload spring<br><br>• Remove burr<br><br><br><br>• Replace shaft<br>• Replace lock rack<br>• Replace rod<br>• Straighten or replace<br><br>• Replace lock rack |
| Will stick in "start" | • Remote rod deformed<br>• Ignition switch mounting bracket bent | • Straighten or replace<br>• Straighten or replace |
| Key cannot be removed in "off-lock" | • Ignition switch is not adjusted correctly<br>• Defective lock cylinder | • Adjust switch<br>• Replace lock cylinder |
| Lock cylinder can be removed without depressing retainer | • Lock cylinder with defective retainer<br>• Burr over retainer slot in housing cover or on cylinder retainer | • Replace lock cylinder<br><br>• Remove burr |
| High effort on lock cylinder between "off" and "off-lock" | • Distorted lock rack<br>• Burr on tang of shift gate (automatic column)<br>• Gearshift linkage not adjusted | • Replace lock rack<br>• Remove burr<br><br>• Adjust linkage |
| Noise in column | • One click when in "off-lock" position and the steering wheel is moved (all except automatic column)<br>• Coupling bolts not tightened<br>• Lack of grease on bearings or bearing surfaces<br>• Upper shaft bearing worn or broken<br>• Lower shaft bearing worn or broken<br>• Column not correctly aligned<br>• Coupling pulled apart<br>• Broken coupling lower joint<br><br>• Steering shaft snap ring not seated<br><br>• Shroud loose on shift bowl. Housing loose on jacket—will be noticed with ignition in "off-lock" and when torque is applied to steering wheel. | • Normal—lock bolt is seating<br><br><br><br>• Tighten pinch bolts<br>• Lubricate with chassis grease<br><br>• Replace bearing assembly<br><br>• Replace bearing. Check shaft and replace if scored.<br>• Align column<br>• Replace coupling<br>• Repair or replace joint and align column<br>• Replace ring. Check for proper seating in groove.<br>• Position shroud over lugs on shift bowl. Tighten mounting screws. |
| High steering shaft effort | • Column misaligned<br>• Defective upper or lower bearing<br>• Tight steering shaft universal joint<br>• Flash on I.D. of shift tube at plastic joint (tilt column only)<br>• Upper or lower bearing seized | • Align column<br>• Replace as required<br>• Repair or replace<br>• Replace shift tube<br><br>• Replace bearings |
| Lash in mounted column assembly | • Column mounting bracket bolts loose<br>• Broken weld nuts on column jacket<br>• Column capsule bracket sheared | • Tighten bolts<br><br>• Replace column jacket<br>• Replace bracket assembly |

## Troubleshooting the Steering Column (cont.)

| Problem | Cause | Solution |
|---|---|---|
| Lash in mounted column assembly (cont.) | • Column bracket to column jacket mounting bolts loose | • Tighten to specified torque |
| | • Loose lock shoes in housing (tilt column only) | • Replace shoes |
| | • Loose pivot pins (tilt column only) | • Replace pivot pins and support |
| | • Loose lock shoe pin (tilt column only) | • Replace pin and housing |
| | • Loose support screws (tilt column only) | • Tighten screws |
| Housing loose (tilt column only) | • Excessive clearance between holes in support or housing and pivot pin diameters | • Replace pivot pins and support |
| | • Housing support-screws loose | • Tighten screws |
| Steering wheel loose—every other tilt position (tilt column only) | • Loose fit between lock shoe and lock shoe pivot pin | • Replace lock shoes and pivot pin |
| Steering column not locking in any tilt position (tilt column only) | • Lock shoe seized on pivot pin | • Replace lock shoes and pin |
| | • Lock shoe grooves have burrs or are filled with foreign material | • Clean or replace lock shoes |
| | • Lock shoe springs weak or broken | • Replace springs |
| Noise when tilting column (tilt column only) | • Upper tilt bumpers worn | • Replace tilt bumper |
| | • Tilt spring rubbing in housing | • Lubricate with chassis grease |
| One click when in "off-lock" position and the steering wheel is moved | • Seating of lock bolt | • None. Click is normal characteristic sound produced by lock bolt as it seats. |
| High shift effort (automatic and tilt column only) | • Column not correctly aligned | • Align column |
| | • Lower bearing not aligned correctly | • Assemble correctly |
| | • Lack of grease on seal or lower bearing areas | • Lubricate with chassis grease |
| Improper transmission shifting—automatic and tilt column only | • Sheared shift tube joint | • Replace shift tube |
| | • Improper transmission gearshift linkage adjustment | • Adjust linkage |
| | • Loose lower shift lever | • Replace shift tube |

3. Unfasten the steering wheel hub nut and remove the steering wheel with a puller.

CAUTION: *The steering column is collapsible; pounding on it or applying excessive pressure to it may cause it to deform, in which case the entire column will have to be replaced.*

4. Installation of the steering wheel is performed in the reverse order of removal. Tighten the steering wheel nut to 25 ft.lb.

## Turn Signal Switch

### COMBINATION (TURN SIGNAL) SWITCH REPLACEMENT

#### RX-2, RX-3, 808

1. Remove the steering wheel.
2. Remove the left hand column shroud.
3. Remove the retaining ring (screw on 808) from the combination (turn signal) switch.
4. Withdraw the switch over the steering column.
5. Installation is the reverse of removal.

**Removing the steering column shroud**

#### RX-4 and Cosmo

1. Remove the steering wheel.
2. Loosen the nut which secures the vent knob (left side) and allow the knob assembly to drop away from its mounting bracket.
3. Remove choke knob. Remove the choke retaining nut and separate the choke from the panel.
4. Remove the upper column cover.
5. Disconnect the panel light dimmer switch wiring.
6. Disconnect the exhaust temperature warning light wiring.

7. Loosen, but don't remove the screws at either end of the lower panel cover.

NOTE: *The lift hand screw is located in the hole which was covered by the upper column cover and the right hand screw is above the ashtray opening (ashtray removed).*

8. Pull the upper column cover away from the instrument panel.

9. Disconnect the combination switch connector.

10. Remove the retaining ring from the steering column.

11. Unfasten the combination switch retaining screw and remove the switch.

12. Installation is the reverse of removal.

### GLC, 323 and 626

1. Disconnect the battery. Remove the horn cover cap.

2. Remove the steering wheel attaching nut, and pull off the wheel with a puller.

3. Remove the attaching screws, and remove the right and left steering column covers.

4. Disconnect the connector for the combination switch or, if the ignition switch is being replaced, disconnect connectors for both that and the combination switch.

5. Remove the retaining ring from the steering column (not required on '83 and later 626).

6. Remove the combination retaining screw, and remove the switch.

7. To install, reverse the removal procedure, torquing the steering wheel nut to 22–29 ft.lb.

## Ignition Lock/Switch Assembly
### REMOVAL AND INSTALLATION
#### RX-2, RX-3, 323, 626, 808, GLC

1. Remove the combination switch as described above. Then, withdraw the ignition switch assembly.

2. Install the new switch and tighten the

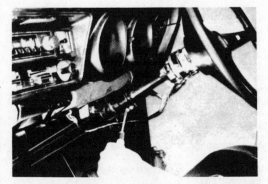

Cut slots in the ignition switch securing bolts and remove them with a screwdriver

mounting bolts. Break their heads off to make the switch difficult for a thief to remove.

3. Reverse the remaining stops of the removal procedure.

#### RX-4 and Cosmo

1. Follow steps under Combination Switch Replacement.

2. Remove the instrument frame brace.

3. Disconnect the switch wires.

4. Remove the switch.

5. Installation is the reverse of removal.

## Tie Rods
### REMOVAL AND INSTALLATION

1. If an alignment machine is not available, measure the length of the tie rod you'll be working on. Remove cotter pin or pins and castellated nut or nuts from one or both ends of the rod, depending upon whether one or both ends requires replacement. Use a puller designed for this purpose to free either or both ends from center link or steering knuckle. If only one end of the rod is to be replaced, loosen the locknut and screw the rod end off the tie rod.

2. To replace, first loosen tie rod locknuts, and then insert rod ends through holes in center link and steering knuckle. If only one end is being replaced, screw the end onto the tie rod and insert pin into center link or steering knuckle. Install nut(s) and torque to 22–33 ft.lb. Install new cotter pins.

3. If an alignment machine is available, adjust toe-in and then torque tie rod locknuts to 51–58 ft.lb. If the car must be taken to a shop for alignment, turn the tie rod so that the length is the same as it was before part(s) were replaced, torque both locknuts and have the toe-in checked as soon as possible.

## Manual Steering Gear
### REMOVAL AND INSTALLATION

1. Raise the vehicle's front end and support it on axle stands. Remove the bolt which secures the universal joint in the steering shaft to the gearbox.

2. Remove the cotter pin from the tie rod end ballstud and loosen the nut. Press the ballstud out of the steering knuckle with a vice-like tool such as MB991113 or equivalent; then remove the nut. Do the same on the other side.

3. Cut the band off the steering joint rubber boot.

4. Remove the left and right tie-rods from the gearbox housing, Remove the bolts that se-

## Troubleshooting the Turn Signal Switch

| Problem | Cause | Solution |
|---|---|---|
| Turn signal will not cancel | • Loose switch mounting screws<br>• Switch or anchor bosses broken<br>• Broken, missing or out of position detent, or cancelling spring | • Tighten screws<br>• Replace switch<br>• Reposition springs or replace switch as required |
| Turn signal difficult to operate | • Turn signal lever loose<br>• Switch yoke broken or distorted<br>• Loose or misplaced springs<br><br>• Foreign parts and/or materials in switch<br>• Switch mounted loosely | • Tighten mounting screws<br>• Replace switch<br>• Reposition springs or replace switch<br>• Remove foreign parts and/or material<br>• Tighten mounting screws |
| Turn signal will not indicate lane change | • Broken lane change pressure pad or spring hanger<br>• Broken, missing or misplaced lane change spring<br>• Jammed wires | • Replace switch<br><br>• Replace or reposition as required<br><br>• Loosen mounting screws, reposition wires and retighten screws |
| Turn signal will not stay in turn position | • Foreign material or loose parts impeding movement of switch yoke<br>• Defective switch | • Remove material and/or parts<br><br>• Replace switch |
| Hazard switch cannot be pulled out | • Foreign material between hazard support cancelling leg and yoke | • Remove foreign material. No foreign material impeding function of hazard switch—replace turn signal switch. |
| No turn signal lights | • Inoperative turn signal flasher<br>• Defective or blown fuse<br>• Loose chassis to column harness connector<br>• Disconnect column to chassis connector. Connect new switch to chassis and operate switch by hand. If vehicle lights now operate normally, signal switch is inoperative<br>• If vehicle lights do not operate, check chassis wiring for opens, grounds, etc. | • Replace turn signal flasher<br>• Replace fuse<br>• Connect securely<br><br>• Replace signal switch<br><br><br><br><br>• Repair chassis wiring as required |
| Instrument panel turn indicator lights on but not flashing | • Burned out or damaged front or rear turn signal bulb<br>• If vehicle lights do not operate, check light sockets for high resistance connections, the chassis wiring for opens, grounds, etc.<br>• Inoperative flasher<br>• Loose chassis to column harness connection<br>• Inoperative turn signal switch<br>• To determine if turn signal switch is defective, substitute new switch into circuit and operate switch by hand. If the vehicle's lights operate normally, signal switch is inoperative. | • Replace bulb<br><br>• Repair chassis wiring as required<br><br><br><br>• Replace flasher<br>• Connect securely<br><br>• Replace turn signal switch<br>• Replace turn signal switch |
| Stop light not on when turn indicated | • Loose column to chassis connection<br>• Disconnect column to chassis connector. Connect new switch into system without removing old. | • Connect securely<br><br>• Replace signal switch |

## Troubleshooting the Turn Signal Switch (cont.)

| Problem | Cause | Solution |
|---|---|---|
| Stop light not on when turn indicated (cont.) | Operate switch by hand. If brake lights work with switch in the turn position, signal switch is defective. | |
| | • If brake lights do not work, check connector to stop light sockets for grounds, opens, etc. | • Repair connector to stop light circuits using service manual as guide |
| Turn indicator panel lights not flashing | • Burned out bulbs<br>• High resistance to ground at bulb socket<br>• Opens, ground in wiring harness from front turn signal bulb socket to indicator lights | • Replace bulbs<br>• Replace socket<br><br>• Locate and repair as required |
| Turn signal lights flash very slowly | • High resistance ground at light sockets<br>• Incorrect capacity turn signal flasher or bulb<br>• If flashing rate is still extremely slow, check chassis wiring harness from the connector to light sockets for high resistance<br>• Loose chassis to column harness connection<br>• Disconnect column to chassis connector. Connect new switch into system without removing old. Operate switch by hand. If flashing occurs at normal rate, the signal switch is defective. | • Repair high resistance grounds at light sockets<br>• Replace turn signal flasher or bulb<br><br>• Locate and repair as required<br><br><br><br>• Connect securely<br><br>• Replace turn signal switch |
| Hazard signal lights will not flash—turn signal functions normally | • Blow fuse<br>• Inoperative hazard warning flasher<br><br>• Loose chassis-to-column harness connection<br>• Disconnect column to chassis connector. Connect new switch into system without removing old. Depress the hazard warning lights. If they now work normally, turn signal switch is defective.<br>• If lights do not flash, check wiring harness "K" lead for open between hazard flasher and connector. If open, fuse block is defective | • Replace fuse<br>• Replace hazard warning flasher in fuse panel<br>• Conect securely<br><br>• Replace turn signal switch<br><br><br><br><br><br>• Repair or replace brown wire or connector as required |

## Troubleshooting the Ignition Switch

| Problem | Cause | Solution |
|---|---|---|
| Ignition switch electrically inoperative | • Loose or defective switch connector<br>• Feed wire open (fusible link)<br>• Defective ignition switch | • Tighten or replace connector<br><br>• Repair or replace<br>• Replace ignition switch |
| Engine will not crank | • Ignition switch not adjusted properly | • Adjust switch |
| Ignition switch wil not actuate mechanically | • Defective ignition switch<br>• Defective lock sector<br>• Defective remote rod | • Replace switch<br>• Replace lock sector<br>• Replace remote rod |
| Ignition switch cannot be adjusted correctly | • Remote rod deformed | • Repair, straighten or replace |

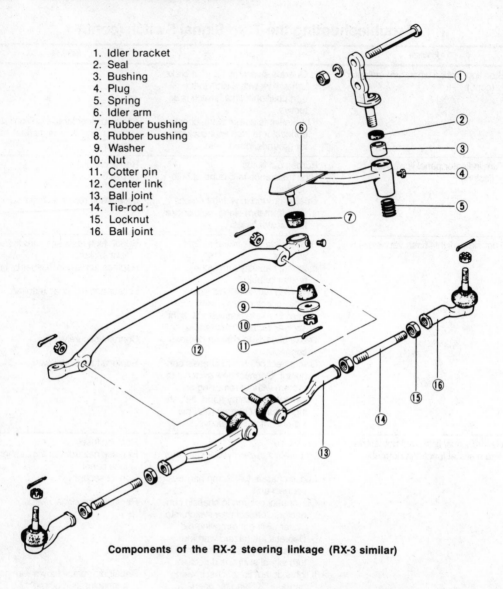

1. Idler bracket
2. Seal
3. Bushing
4. Plug
5. Spring
6. Idler arm
7. Rubber bushing
8. Rubber bushing
9. Washer
10. Nut
11. Cotter pin
12. Center link
13. Ball joint
14. Tie-rod
15. Locknut
16. Ball joint

**Components of the RX-2 steering linkage (RX-3 similar)**

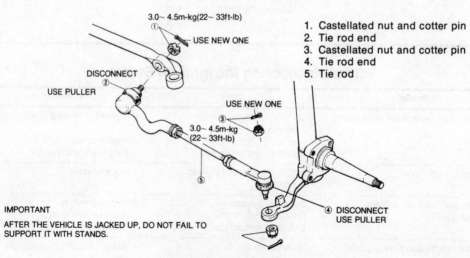

3.0~ 4.5m-kg(22~ 33ft-lb)

USE NEW ONE

DISCONNECT

USE PULLER

USE NEW ONE

3.0~ 4.5m-kg
(22~ 33ft-lb)

1. Castellated nut and cotter pin
2. Tie rod end
3. Castellated nut and cotter pin
4. Tie rod end
5. Tie rod

④ DISCONNECT
USE PULLER

IMPORTANT

AFTER THE VEHICLE IS JACKED UP, DO NOT FAIL TO
SUPPORT IT WITH STANDS.

**Replacing tie rod—GLC**

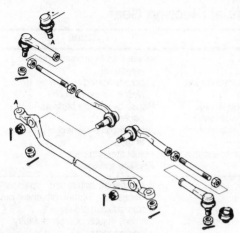

**Replacing tie rod—model 626**

cure the mounting bracket and rubber mountings, and pull the gearbox out of the vehicle. Work slowly to keep the unit from being damaged.

5. Install the unit in reverse order. Make sure the rubber sleeve in which the unit is mounted faces so that the tabs fit in the notch located away from the crossmember. Use a new band for the steering joint rubber boot. Adjust toe-in. Use the following torques in ft. lb.: mounting bracket attaching bolts—43–58 ft. lb.; ballstud nut—17 ft. lb. (then turn farther to align castellations with the cotter pin hole and install a new cotter pin). Turn the steering wheel back and forth to test steering operation.

## Power Steering Gear

### REMOVAL AND INSTALLATION

1. Raise the vehicle and support it on axle stands. Remove the bolt attaching the steering shaft universal joint to the gearbox.

2. Remove the cotter pin from the tie rod end ballstud and then loosen the nut. Press the ballstud out of the steering knuckle with a vice-like tool such as MB991113 or equivalent. Remove the nut and pull the stud out of the knuckle.

3. Place a drain pan under the gearbox and the disconnect the pressure and return hose connectors with a flare nut wrench, and allow the fluid to drain.

4. Unbolt and remove the two bolts in each gearbox mounting clamp with a ratchet and long extension, working from the engine compartment side.

5. Pull the gearbox out the right side of the vehicle, working carefully to keep the unit from being damaged.

6. Install in reverse order, noting the following points: Make sure the rubber mounting

sleeve is positioned so the flat side faces the crossmember and apply adhesive to the rounded side so the slit will not open up when the unit is clamped in place. Torque the gearbox mounting bolts to 43–58 ft. lb. and the ballstud nut to 17 ft. lb. (then turn farther to align castellations with the cotter pin hole and install a new cotter pin).

7. Have someone keep the power steering reservoir filled with Dexron®II automatic transmission fluid as you perform this procedure. Disconnect the high tension wire and use the starter to spin the engine while you turn the steering wheel from stop to stop several times. Lower the vehicle, reconnect the ignition wire and start the engine, letting it idle. Have someone continue to turn the steering wheel from lock to lock continuously until there are no more bubbles in the power steering fluid reservoir and the level remains constant as the wheel is turned back and forth. Stop the procedure. Make sure the fluid reservoir is full. Check for leaks. Adjust the toe-in.

## Power Steering Pump

### REMOVAL & INSTALLATION

1. Raise and support the front end on jackstands.

2. Remove the power steering pump pulley nut.

3. Loosen the drive belt tensioner pulley and remove the belt.

4. Remove the pulley from the pump.

5. Position a drain pan under the pump and disconnect the hoses.

6. Remove the bracket-to-pump bolts and remove the pump from the car.

7. Installation is the reverse of removal. Adjust the belt to give $1/2$ in. deflection along its longest straight run. Bleed the system.

### BLEEDING THE SYSTEM

1. Raise and support the front end on jackstands.

2. Check the fluid level and fill it, if necessary.

3. Start the engine and let it idle. Turn the steering wheel lock-to-lock, several times. Recheck the fluid level.

4. Lower the vehicle to the ground.

5. With the engine idling, turn the wheel lock-to-lock several times again. If noise is heard in the fluid lines, air is present.

6. Put the wheels in the straight ahead position and shut off the engine.

7. Check the fluid level. If it is higher than when you last checked it, air is in the system. Repeat Step 5. Keep repeating Step 5 until no air is present.

## Troubleshooting the Manual Steering Gear

| Problem | Cause | Solution |
|---|---|---|
| Hard or erratic steering | • Incorrect tire pressure | • Inflate tires to recommended pressures |
| | • Insufficient or incorrect lubrication | • Lubricate as required (refer to Maintenance Section) |
| | • Suspension, or steering linkage parts damaged or misaligned | • Repair or replace parts as necessary |
| | • Improper front wheel alignment | • Adjust incorrect wheel alignment angles |
| | • Incorrect steering gear adjustment | • Adjust steering gear |
| | • Sagging springs | • Replace springs |
| Play or looseness in steering | • Steering wheel loose | • Inspect shaft spines and repair as necessary. Tighten attaching nut and stake in place. |
| | • Steering linkage or attaching parts loose or worn | • Tighten, adjust, or replace faulty components |
| | • Pitman arm loose | • Inspect shaft splines and repair as necessary. Tighten attaching nut and stake in place |
| | • Steering gear attaching bolts loose | • Tighten bolts |
| | • Loose or worn wheel bearings | • Adjust or replace bearings |
| | • Steering gear adjustment incorrect or parts badly worn | • Adjust gear or replace defective parts |
| Wheel shimmy or tramp | • Improper tire pressure | • Inflate tires to recommended pressures |
| | • Wheels, tires, or brake rotors out-of-balance or out-of-round | • Inspect and replace or balance parts |
| | • Inoperative, worn, or loose shock absorbers or mounting parts | • Repair or replace shocks or mountings |
| | • Loose or worn steering or suspension parts | • Tighten or replace as necessary |
| | • Loose or worn wheel bearings | • Adjust or replace bearings |
| | • Incorrect steering gear adjustments | • Adjust steering gear |
| | • Incorrect front wheel alignment | • Correct front wheel alignment |
| Tire wear | • Improper tire pressure | • Inflate tires to recommended pressures |
| | • Failure to rotate tires | • Rotate tires |
| | • Brakes grabbing | • Adjust or repair brakes |
| | • Incorrect front wheel alignment | • Align incorrect angles |
| | • Broken or damaged steering and suspension parts | • Repair or replace defective parts |
| | • Wheel runout | • Replace faulty wheel |
| | • Excessive speed on turns | • Make driver aware of conditions |
| Vehicle leads to one side | • Improper tire pressures | • Inflate tires to recommended pressures |
| | • Front tires with uneven tread depth, wear pattern, or different cord design (i.e., one bias ply and one belted or radial tire on front wheels) | • Install tires of same cord construction and reasonably even tread depth, design, and wear pattern |
| | • Incorrect front wheel alignment | • Align incorrect angles |
| | • Brakes dragging | • Adjust or repair brakes |
| | • Pulling due to uneven tire construction | • Replace faulty tire |

## Troubleshooting the Power Steering Gear

| Problem | Cause | Solution |
|---|---|---|
| Hissing noise in steering gear | • There is some noise in all power steering systems. One of the most common is a hissing sound most evident at standstill parking. There is no relationship between this noise and performance of the steering. Hiss may be expected when steering wheel is at end of travel or when slowly turning at standstill. | • Slight hiss is normal and in no way affects steering. Do not replace valve unless hiss is extremely objectionable. A replacement valve will also exhibit slight noise and is not always a cure. Investigate clearance around flexible coupling rivets. Be sure steering shaft and gear are aligned so flexible coupling rotates in a flat plane and is not distorted as shaft rotates. Any metal-to-metal contacts through flexible coupling will transmit valve hiss into passenger compartment through the steering column. |
| Rattle or chuckle noise in steering gear | • Gear loose on frame | • Check gear-to-frame mounting screws. Tighten screws to 88 N·m (65 foot pounds) torque. |
| | • Steering linkage looseness | • Check linkage pivot points for wear. Replace if necessary. |
| | • Pressure hose touching other parts of car | • Adjust hose position. Do not bend tubing by hand. |
| | • Loose pitman shaft over center adjustment<br>**NOTE:** A slight rattle may occur on turns because of increased clearance off the "high point." This is normal and clearance must not be reduced below specified limits to eliminate this slight rattle. | • Adjust to specifications |
| | • Loose pitman arm | • Tighten pitman arm nut to specifications |
| Squawk noise in steering gear when turning or recovering from a turn | • Damper O-ring on valve spool cut | • Replace damper O-ring |
| Poor return of steering wheel to center | • Tires not properly inflated | • Inflate to specified pressure |
| | • Lack of lubrication in linkage and ball joints | • Lube linkage and ball joints |
| | • Lower coupling flange rubbing against steering gear adjuster plug | • Loosen pinch bolt and assemble properly |
| | • Steering gear to column misalignment | • Align steering column |
| | • Improper front wheel alignment | • Check and adjust as necessary |
| | • Steering linkage binding | • Replace pivots |
| | • Ball joints binding | • Replace ball joints |
| | • Steering wheel rubbing against housing | • Align housing |
| | • Tight or frozen steering shaft bearings | • Replace bearings |
| | • Sticking or plugged valve spool | • Remove and clean or replace valve |
| | • Steering gear adjustments over specifications | • Check adjustment with gear out of car. Adjust as required. |
| | • Kink in return hose | • Replace hose |
| Car leads to one side or the other (keep in mind road condition and wind. Test car in both directions on flat road) | • Front end misaligned | • Adjust to specifications |
| | • Unbalanced steering gear valve<br>**NOTE:** If this is cause, steering effort will be very light in direction of lead and normal or heavier in opposite direction | • Replace valve |

## Troubleshooting the Power Steering Gear (cont.)

| Problem | Cause | Solution |
|---|---|---|
| Momentary increase in effort when turning wheel fast to right or left | • Low oil level<br>• Pump belt slipping<br>• High internal leakage | • Add power steering fluid as required<br>• Tighten or replace belt<br>• Check pump pressure. (See pressure test) |
| Steering wheel surges or jerks when turning with engine running especially during parking | • Low oil level<br>• Loose pump belt<br>• Steering linkage hitting engine oil pan at full turn<br>• Insufficient pump pressure<br><br>• Pump flow control valve sticking | • Fill as required<br>• Adjust tension to specification<br>• Correct clearance<br><br>• Check pump pressure. (See pressure test). Replace relief valve if defective.<br>• Inspect for varnish or damage, replace if necessary |
| Excessive wheel kickback or loose steering | • Air in system<br><br><br><br><br>• Steering gear loose on frame<br><br>• Steering linkage joints worn enough to be loose<br>• Worn poppet valve<br>• Loose thrust bearing preload adjustment<br>• Excessive overcenter lash | • Add oil to pump reservoir and bleed by operating steering. Check hose connectors for proper torque and adjust as required.<br>• Tighten attaching screws to specified torque<br>• Replace loose pivots<br><br>• Replace poppet valve<br>• Adjust to specification with gear out of vehicle<br>• Adjust to specification with gear out of car |
| Hard steering or lack of assist | • Loose pump belt<br>• Low oil level<br>**NOTE:** Low oil level will also result in excessive pump noise<br><br>• Steering gear to column misalignment<br>• Lower coupling flange rubbing against steering gear adjuster plug<br>• Tires not properly inflated | • Adjust belt tension to specification<br>• Fill to proper level. If excessively low, check all lines and joints for evidence of external leakage. Tighten loose connectors.<br>• Align steering column<br><br>• Loosen pinch bolt and assemble properly<br><br>• Inflate to recommended pressure |
| Foamy milky power steering fluid, low fluid level and possible low pressure | • Air in the fluid, and loss of fluid due to internal pump leakage causing overflow | • Check for leak and correct. Bleed system. Extremely cold temperatures will cause system aeration should the oil level be low. If oil level is correct and pump still foams, remove pump from vehicle and separate reservoir from housing. Check welsh plug and housing for cracks. If plug is loose or housing is cracked, replace housing. |
| Low pressure due to steering pump | • Flow control valve stuck or inoperative<br>• Pressure plate not flat against cam ring | • Remove burrs or dirt or replace. Flush system.<br>• Correct |
| Low pressure due to steering gear | • Pressure loss in cylinder due to worn piston ring or badly worn housing bore<br>• Leakage at valve rings, valve body-to-worm seal | • Remove gear from car for disassembly and inspection of ring and housing bore<br>• Remove gear from car for disassembly and replace seals |

## Troubleshooting the Power Steering Pump

| Problem | Cause | Solution |
|---|---|---|
| Chirp noise in steering pump | • Loose belt | • Adjust belt tension to specification |
| Belt squeal (particularly noticeable at full wheel travel and stand still parking) | • Loose belt | • Adjust belt tension to specification |
| Growl noise in steering pump | • Excessive back pressure in hoses or steering gear caused by restriction | • Locate restriction and correct. Replace part if necessary. |
| Growl noise in steering pump (particularly noticeable at stand still parking) | • Scored pressure plates, thrust plate or rotor<br>• Extreme wear of cam ring | • Replace parts and flush system<br>• Replace parts |
| Groan noise in steering pump | • Low oil level<br>• Air in the oil. Poor pressure hose connection. | • Fill reservoir to proper level<br>• Tighten connector to specified torque. Bleed system by operating steering from right to left—full turn. |
| Rattle noise in steering pump | • Vanes not installed properly<br>• Vanes sticking in rotor slots | • Install properly<br>• Free up by removing burrs, varnish, or dirt |
| Swish noise in steering pump | • Defective flow control valve | • Replace part |
| Whine noise in steering pump | • Pump shaft bearing scored | • Replace housing and shaft. Flush system. |
| Hard steering or lack of assist | • Loose pump belt<br>• Low oil level in reservoir<br>**NOTE:** Low oil level will also result in excessive pump noise<br><br>• Steering gear to column misalignment<br>• Lower coupling flange rubbing against steering gear adjuster plug<br>• Tires not properly inflated | • Adjust belt tension to specification<br>• Fill to proper level. If excessively low, check all lines and joints for evidence of external leakage. Tighten loose connectors.<br>• Align steering column<br>• Loosen pinch bolt and assemble properly<br><br>• Inflate to recommended pressure |
| Foaming milky power steering fluid, low fluid level and possible low pressure | • Air in the fluid, and loss of fluid due to internal pump leakage causing overflow | • Check for leaks and correct. Bleed system. Extremely cold temperatures will cause system aeriation should the oil level be low. If oil level is correct and pump still foams, remove pump from vehicle and separate reservoir from body. Check welsh plug and body for cracks. If plug is loose or body is cracked, replace body. |
| Low pump pressure | • Flow control valve stuck or inoperative<br>• Pressure plate not flat against cam ring | • Remove burrs or dirt or replace. Flush system.<br>• Correct |
| Momentary increase in effort when turning wheel fast to right or left | • Low oil level in pump<br><br>• Pump belt slipping<br>• High internal leakage | • Add power steering fluid as required<br>• Tighten or replace belt<br>• Check pump pressure. (See pressure test) |
| Steering wheel surges or jerks when turning with engine running especially during parking | • Low oil level<br>• Loose pump belt<br>• Steering linkage hitting engine oil pan at full turn<br>• Insufficient pump pressure | • Fill as required<br>• Adjust tension to specification<br>• Correct clearance<br><br>• Check pump pressure. (See pressure test). Replace flow control valve if defective. |

## Troubleshooting the Power Steering Pump (cont.)

| Problem | Cause | Solution |
|---|---|---|
| Steering wheel surges or jerks when turning with engine running especially during parking (cont.) | • Sticking flow control valve | • Inspect for varnish or damage, replace if necessary |
| Excessive wheel kickback or loose steering | • Air in system | • Add oil to pump reservoir and bleed by operating steering. Check hose connectors for proper torque and adjust as required. |
| Low pump pressure | • Extreme wear of cam ring<br>• Scored pressure plate, thrust plate, or rotor<br>• Vanes not installed properly<br>• Vanes sticking in rotor slots<br><br>• Cracked or broken thrust or pressure plate | • Replace parts. Flush system.<br>• Replace parts. Flush system.<br><br>• Install properly<br>• Freeup by removing burrs, varnish, or dirt<br>• Replace part |

**8**

## BRAKE SYSTEM

### Adjustment

#### FRONT DISC BRAKES

The front disc brakes are self-adjusting by design. As the brake pads and discs wear, fluid pressure compensates for the amount of wear. Because this action causes the fluid level to go down, its level should be checked and replenished as often as is necessary.

#### REAR DRUM BRAKES

##### All Models Except GLC, 323 and 626 with Front Wheel Drive

1. Block the front wheels, raise the car, and support it with jackstands.
   CAUTION: *Be sure that the car is securely supported. Remember, you will be working underneath it.*
2. Release the parking brake completely.
3. Remove the adjusting hole plugs from the backing plate.
4. Engage the adjuster with a screwdriver. Turn the adjuster in the direction of the arrow stamped on the backing plate until the brake shoes are fully expanded, i.e. the wheel will not turn.
5. Pump the brake pedal several times to be sure that the brake shoe contacts the drum evenly.
   NOTE: *If the wheel turns after you remove your foot from the brake pedal, continue turning the adjuster until the wheel will no longer rotate.*
6. Back off on the adjuster about 4–5 notches. The wheel should rotate freely, without dragging. If it does not, turn the adjuster an additional notch.
7. Pump the brake pedal several times and check wheel rotation again.
8. Fit the plug into the adjusting hole and

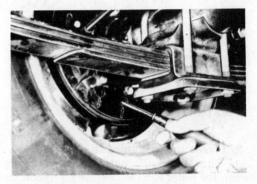

**Adjusting the rear brake shoes**

then repeat the adjusting procedure for the three other rear brake shoes.

##### GLC, 323 and 626 with Front Wheel Drive

NOTE: *Front wheel drive models are equipped with self-adjusting brakes, no external adjustment is possible.*

1. Raise and securely support the vehicle. Make sure parking brake is fully released.
2. Loosen anchor pin locknuts. Hold locknut and turn anchor pin until the wheel locks. Anchor pins on each wheel are turned in opposite directions. On the right side, forward pin turns clockwise, and the rear pin counterclockwise. On the left side, the forward pin turns counterclockwise, the rear pin clockwise. Then turn the anchor pin back until the wheel just turns freely. Hold the adjustment and tighten the locknut.
3. Then turn the anchor pin back until the wheel just turns freely. Hold the adjustment and tighten the locknut.
4. Repeat for the other shoe on the first wheel, and then adjust both shoes on the second wheel.

#### BRAKE PEDAL

##### All Models to 1982

1. Detach the wiring from the brake light switch terminals.

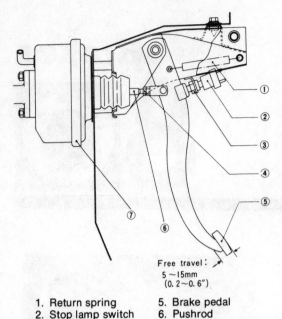

Free travel:
5 ~15mm
(0. 2~0. 6")

1. Return spring
2. Stop lamp switch
3. Locknut
4. Locknut
5. Brake pedal
6. Pushrod
7. Power brake unit

**Brake pedal components**

2. Loosen the locknut on the switch.

3. Turn the switch until the distance between the pedal and the floor is: 7.3" (185mm) for the RX-2, RX-3, RX-4, and 808; 8.58" (218mm) for the Cosmo w/manual trans.; 8.24" (209mm) for the Cosmo w/automatic trans.; 7.48" (190mm) for the rear wheel drive GLC w/ manual trans.; 7.68" (195mm) for the rear wheel drive GLC w/automatic trans.; 8.46" (215mm) for the GLC w/front wheel drive; 8.66" (220mm) for the 626.

4. Tighten the locknut on switch.

5. Loosen the locknut located on the pushrod.

6. Rotate the pushrod until the pedal free travel of 0.2–0.6" (5–15mm) is obtained for all exc. the GLC, 626 and Cosmo; 0.28-0.35" (7–9mm) for the GLC, 626 and Cosmo.

7. Tighten the pushrod locknut.

### 1983 and Later 626

1. Remove the blower duct. Measure the distance from the center of the brake pedal (front surface) to the firewall (behind the insulation). It should be 8.43–8.47" (214–215mm). To adjust, disconnect the stop lamp switch electrical connector, loosen the stop switch locknut, and adjust the pedal height until it is correct.

2. Depress the brake pedal several times. Loosen the operating rod locknut and turn the rod to adjust the pedal play until it is 0.28–0.35" (7–9mm).

3. Tighten both locknuts and reconnect the stop lamp switch electrical connector. Replace the blower duct.

### 1983–85 GLC, and 1986-87 323

1. Remove the cover under the instrument panel. Loosen the brake lamp switch locknut and then turn the switch outward until the pedal does not touch it. Loosen the operating rod locknut and turn the rod to adjust the pedal height to 8.46–8.66" (215–220mm) on the GLC, 8.62–8.82" (219–224mm) on the 323. Measure from the center of the front of the pedal back to the firewall (behind insulation). Lock the position of the operating rod with the locknut.

2. Screw the lamp switch inward until it just touches the pedal lever (add an additional ½ turn for the 323).

3. Check the play in the brake pedal. It should be 0.28–0.35" (7–9mm) on the GLC; 0.16–0.28" (4–7mm) on the 323. If necessary, adjust the play as described in Step 1 above by loosening the locknut and adjusting the operating rod. Tighten the locknut. Replace the cover that goes under the instrument panel.

## HYDRAULIC SYSTEM

## Master Cylinder

### REMOVAL AND INSTALLATION

1. Remove the air cleaner for clearance if necessary.

2. Detach all of the hydraulic lines from the master cylinder. Detach connector for fluid level sensor.
NOTE: *On models which have a fluid reservoir located separately from the master cylinder, remove the lines which run between the two and plug the lines to prevent leakage.*

3. Unfasten the nuts which secure the master cylinder to the power brake unit.

4. Withdraw the master cylinder assembly straight out and away from the power brake unit.
NOTE: *Be careful not to spill brake fluid on the painted surfaces of the car, as it makes an excellent paint remover.*

5. Installation of the master cylinder is performed in the reverse order of its removal. Fill its reservoir and bleed the brake system, as detailed below.

### OVERHAUL

RX-2, RX-3

1. Clean the outside of the master cylinder and drain any brake fluid remaining in it.

2. Remove the fluid reservoir from the top, if so equipped.

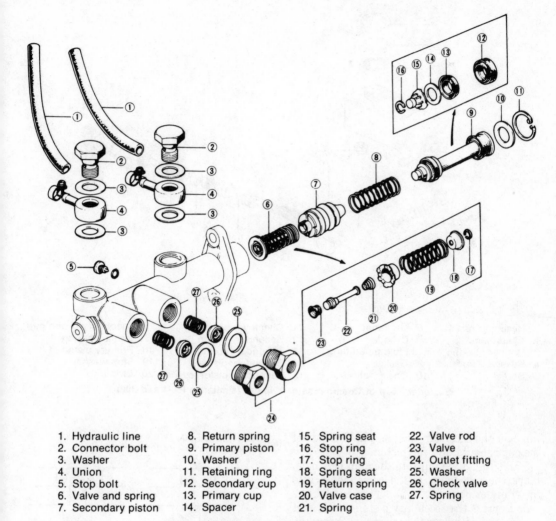

**Master cylinder components—RX-2 and RX-3**

| | |
|---|---|
| 1. Hydraulic line | 8. Return spring |
| 2. Connector bolt | 9. Primary piston |
| 3. Washer | 10. Washer |
| 4. Union | 11. Retaining ring |
| 5. Stop bolt | 12. Secondary cup |
| 6. Valve and spring | 13. Primary cup |
| 7. Secondary piston | 14. Spacer |

| | |
|---|---|
| 15. Spring seat | 22. Valve rod |
| 16. Stop ring | 23. Valve |
| 17. Stop ring | 24. Outlet fitting |
| 18. Spring seat | 25. Washer |
| 19. Return spring | 26. Check valve |
| 20. Valve case | 27. Spring |
| 21. Spring | |

3. Remove the boot from the rear of the cylinder.

4. Depress the primary piston and withdraw the snapring from the rear of the cylinder bore.

5. Withdraw the washers, piston, cups, spacer, seat, and return spring from the cylinder bore.

6. Depress the secondary piston, using a rod, and remove the secondary piston bolt from the outside of the cylinder.

7. Remove the secondary piston assembly from the bore.

NOTE: *Blow out the assembly with compressed air, if necessary.*

8. Unfasten the hydraulic line fittings from the master cylinder outlet.

9. Withdraw the check valves and springs from the outlets.

10. Wash all of the components in clean brake fluid.

CAUTION: *Never use kerosene or gasoline to clean the master cylinder components.*

11. Examine all of the piston cups and replace any that are worn, damaged, or swollen.

12. Check the cylinder bore for roughness or scoring. Check the clearance between the piston and cylinder bore with a feeler gauge. Replace either the piston or the cylinder, if the clearance exceeds 0.006″ (0.15mm).

13. Blow the dirt and the remaining brake fluid out of the cylinder with compressed air.

**Master cylinder assembly is performed in the following order:**

1. Dip all of the components, except for the cylinder, in clean brake fluid.

2. Install the check valve assemblies in the master cylinder outlets.

3. Insert the return spring and the valve components into the cylinder bore.

4. Fit the secondary cup and the primary

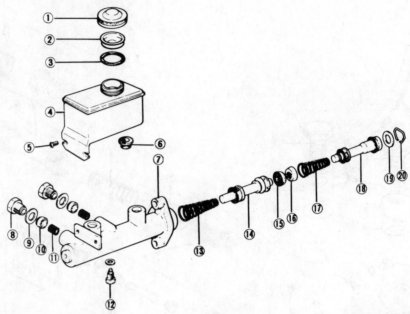

1. Reservoir gap
2. Fluid baffle
3. Rubber packing
4. Reservoir tank
5. Screw
6. Grommet
7. Cylinder
8. Fluid pipe fitting
9. Gasket
10. Check valve
11. Check valve
12. Secondary piston
13. Secondary spring
14. Secondary piston
15. Secondary piston cup
16. Secondary piston cup
17. Primary spring
18. Primary piston
19. Stop washer
20. Stop ring

**Exploded view of Cosmo master cylinder (similar to RX-4 and 808)**

cup over the secondary piston. The flat side of the cups should face the piston.

5. Fit the guide pin into the stop bolt hole. Place the secondary piston components into the cylinder bore.

6. Depress the secondary piston as far as it will go and withdraw the guide pin. Screw the stop bolt into the hole.

7. Place the primary cups on the primary piston with the flat side of the cups facing the piston.

8. Insert the return spring and the primary piston into the bore.

9. Depress the primary piston, then install the stop washer and snapring.

NOTE: *Be sure that the piston cups do not cover up the compensating ports.*

10. Install the dust boot on the end of the cylinder.

### RX-4, 808, Cosmo

1. Clean the outside of the master cylinder with brake fluid and drain the unit thoroughly.

2. Remove connector bolts, unions, and lock-washers from master cylinder inlets.

3. With a screwdriver, remove the piston stop and washer ring, from the cylinder.

4. Remove the primary piston cups, spacer, and spring seat assembly and return spring.

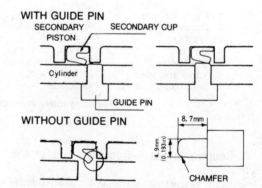

**Using a guide pin to remove the secondary piston—RX-4, Cosmo, GLC, 808**

5. Loosen, but DO NOT REMOVE the secondary piston stop bolt.

6. Push the secondary piston in with the screwdriver, remove the stop bolt, and insert the guide pin in its place. If necessary, you can make a guide pin, reading the dimensions off the illustration.

7. Gradually allow the secondary piston and cups and the return spring to come out of the cylinder. If they will not come out under spring pressure, apply compressed air to the outlet hole.

8. Remove all pipe fittings, gaskets, and check valves and springs from the cylinder.

9. Wash all components in clean brake fluid. NEVER use gasoline or kerosene, as it dissolves rubber parts. Check the cylinder bore for roughness or scoring. Check clearance between piston and cylinder bore wear limit is 0.006″ (0.15mm). If necessary, replace parts. Blow remaining dirt out with compressed air. Replace any piston cups that are worn, torn, or swelled. Make sure compensating ports are open.

10. Dip pistons and cups in clean brake fluid.

11. Install check valves and springs into outlet holes. Install pipe fittings and torque to 43–51 ft.lb.

12. Install primary and secondary cups onto secondary piston.

13. Install the guide pin, and then insert the piston assembly and return spring into the master cylinder. Push the piston in as far as it will go with a screwdriver, hold while remov-

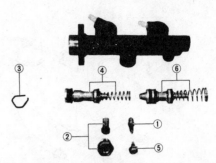

**Exploded view of the 626 master cylinder to 1982**

ing the guide pin and installing the stop bolt and washer and then remove the screwdriver.

14. Install the primary and secondary cups onto the primary piston, and then install the return spring and primary piston assembly. Install stop washer and piston stop ring.

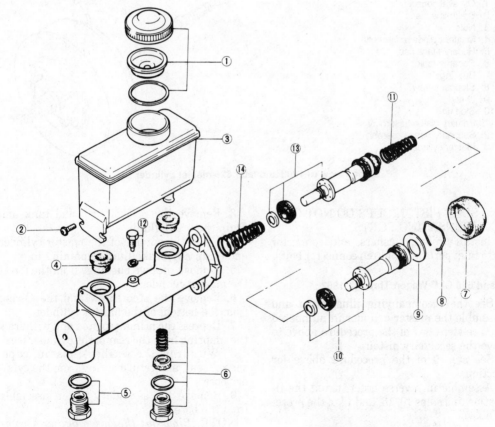

1. Reservoir cap and gasket
2. Screw
3. Fluid reservoir
4. Seal
5. Pipe fitting and packing for front brakes
6. Pipe fitting and packing, check valve and spring, for rear brakes
7. Rubber boot
8. Snap ring
9. Washer
10. Primary piston and cup
11. Primary spring
12. Stop bolt and washer
13. Secondary piston and cup
14. Secondary spring

**Exploded view of the GLC master cylinder to 1982**

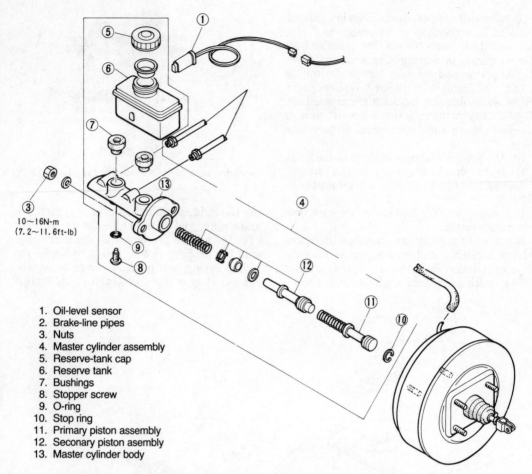

1. Oil-level sensor
2. Brake-line pipes
3. Nuts
4. Master cylinder assembly
5. Reserve-tank cap
6. Reserve tank
7. Bushings
8. Stopper screw
9. O-ring
10. Stop ring
11. Primary piston assembly
12. Seconary piston asembly
13. Master cylinder body

10~16N-m
(7.2~11.6ft-lb)

**Exploded view of 1983 and later 626 master cylinder**

MAKE SURE PISTON CUPS DO NOT COVER COMPENSATING PORTS.

15. Install unions, washers, and connector bolts to inlet ports and tighten connector bolts.

### GLC and 626 GLC Wagon Through 1982

1. See the accompanying illustration and disassemble the master cylinder in numbered order. See steps 6–7 of the procedure above to remove the secondary piston.

2. See step 9 of the procedure above for inspection.

3. Assemble in reverse order, using the illustration and steps 10, 13, and 14 of the procedure above.

### 1983-87 626, 1986-87 323 and 1983–85 GLC

See the accompanying illustration to help in the disassembly and reassembly of the master cylinder.

1. Disconnect the fluid level sensor.

2. Using a line wrench, disconnect the two brake fluid pipes from the master cylinder.

3. Remove the resovoir cap and tank and drain the brake fluid.

4. Clean the outside of the master cylinder and drain any brake fluid remaining in it.

5. Remove the two bushings from the top of the master cylinder

6. Remove the stop screw and the O-ring from the bottom of the master cylinder.

7. Depress the primary piston and withdraw the snapring from the rear of the cylinder bore.

8. Withdraw the washers, piston, cups, spacer, seat, and return spring from the cylinder bore.

9. Remove the secondary piston assembly from the bore.

NOTE: *Blow out the assembly with compressed air, if necessary.*

10. Wash all of the components in clean brake fluid.

CAUTION: *Never use kerosene or gasoline to clean the master cylinder components.*

11. Examine all of the piston cups and replace any that are worn, damaged, or swollen.

12. Check the cylinder bore for roughness or

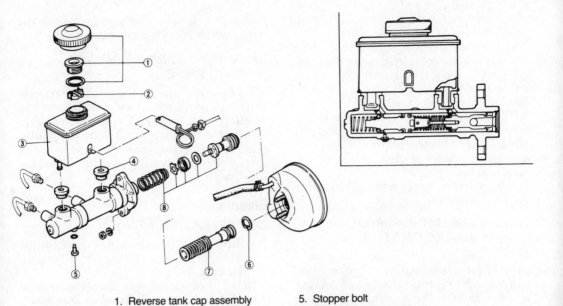

1. Reverse tank cap assembly
2. Float
3. Reserve tank
4. Bushing
5. Stopper bolt
6. Stop ring
7. Primary piston assembly
8. Secondary piston assembly

**Exploded view of 1983 and later GLC master cylinder**

scoring. Check the clearance between the piston and cylinder bore with a feeler gauge. Replace either the piston or the cylinder, if the clearance exceeds 0.006″ (0.15mm).

13. Blow the dirt and the remaining brake fluid out of the cylinder with compressed air.

**Master cylinder assembly is performed in the following order:**

1. Dip all of the components, except for the cylinder, in clean brake fluid.

2. Insert the return spring and the valve components into the cylinder bore.

3. Fit the secondary cup and the primary cup over the secondary piston. The flat side of the cups should face the piston.

4. Place the secondary piston components into the cylinder bore.

5. Using a crosstipped screwdriver depress the secondary piston as far as it will go into the cylinder bore. Screw the stop bolt into the hole.

6. Place the primary cups on the primary piston with the flat side of the cups facing the piston.

7. Insert the return spring and the primary piston into the bore.

8. Depress the primary piston, then install the stop washer and snapring.

NOTE: *Be sure that the piston cups do not cover up the compensating ports.*

Notes regarding proper disassembly, inspection, and reassembly are as follows:

a. Use snapring pliers to remove the stop ring.

b. To remove the secondary piston, blow compressed air gently through the brake line port that's positioned toward the front of the car when the unit is installed.

c. Inspect the cylinder bore and pistons for obvious wear, corrosion, or physical damage. Inspect the springs for obvious damage or for weakness.

d. Inspect the fluid reservoir for warping or cracks.

e. Check clearance between piston and cylinder bore. The limit is 0.006″ (0.15mm).

f. If the cylinder body is defective, replace the entire unit. If the piston is defective, replace the piston assembly. If the reservoir is defective, replace the reservoir, diaphragm and cap as a set. Always replace the secondary piston cups and O-ring and the entire primary piston assembly.

g. In assembly, coat the piston and cups, and cylinder bore with clean brake fluid. Make sure the cups are the proper size for the bore (⅞″ [22mm]). When assembling secondary piston cups, note that, going from the inner end of the piston outward, cups face: inward, and outward.

h. When installing the stop screw, push the primary piston all the way in with a Phillips screwdriver, and make sure the piston passes the stop screw hole. Install and tighten the screw with the piston held in position. Then test the position of the piston by repeatedly forcing it in and releasing it with the screwdriver. It should remain properly positioned inside the master cylinder.

i. Press the secondary piston in by hand after coating all parts with brake fluid, and then install the stop ring with snapring pliers. Adjust the power brake unit pushrod clearance as described below.

NOTE: *The GLC master cylinder has no stop screw. Also, bore size is $^{13}\!/_{16}$" (21mm) on the GLC. Check the outer surface of piston cups and outer cylinder surface for appropriate markings.*

Adjust the power brake unit pushrod clearance as described below.

### POWER BRAKE UNIT PUSHROD CLEARANCE ADJUSTMENT

NOTE: *This procedure is required after re-build of late model master cylinders (1983 and later). It requires the use of a Mazda special tool 49 B002 765 or equivalent because the clearance between the power brake unit pushrod and master cylinder piston cannot be measured when the two are assembled. Since this is a simple adjustment, you might find that, if the tool is expensive, it would actually be cheaper to take the brake unit and rebuilt master cylinder to a qualified mechanic to have it performed.*

1. Set the unit on the end of the master cylinder with the head of the adjusting bolt upward. Make sure both legs rest on the master cylinder mounting flange and then turn the bolt down until it just touches the bottom of the pushrod recess in the piston.

2. Turn the unit upside down and rest the other ends of the legs on the mounting flange on the power brake unit. There should be no vacuum in the unit. If there is any gap between the power brake unit pushrod, loosen the pushrod locknut and turn the pushrod until it just touches the head of the bolt. Tighten the locknut. This will ensure a pushrod to piston clearance of 0.016–0.024" (0.4–0.6mm) on the 626; 0.004–0.020" (0.1–0.5mm) on the GLC; 0.875" (22mm) on the 323.

## Proportioning Valve

### REMOVAL AND INSTALLATION

The proportioning valve regulates the pressure to the rear brakes, reducing it under hard braking, to minimize lockup of the rear wheels. The valve is removed by unfastening the connections, removing the mounting bolts, and removing it. In installation, use the inlet and outlet arrows on the body of the valve to make connections properly from the master cylinder and to the wheels, and note the **F**

marking, indicating the port leading to the front brakes. Bleed the system.

### CENTERING THE BRAKE FAILURE WARNING VALVE

After a partial failure of the brake system, this valve will go off center and will activate the warning light. Simply bleed the system after repairs are complete, make sure the master cylinder reservoir has plenty of fluid in it, and depress the brake pedal several times until the light goes out.

## Bleeding

### DISC BRAKES (FRONT)

1. Remove the bleeder screw cap from the wheel cylinder which is furthest from the master cylinder.

NOTE: *Keep the master cylinder reservoir at least ¾ full during the bleeding operation.*

2. Install a vinyl tube over the bleeder screw. Submerge the other end of the tube in a jar half full of clean brake fluid.

3. Open the bleeder valve. Fully depress the brake pedal and allow it to return slowly.

4. Repeat this operation until air bubbles cease flowing into the jar.

5. Close the valve, remove the tube, and install the cap on the bleeder valve.

### DRUM BRAKES (REAR)

1. Repeat Steps 1–2 of the disc brake bleeding procedure.

2. Depress the brake pedal rapidly several times.

3. Keep the brake pedal depressed and open the bleeder valve. Close the valve without releasing the pedal.

4. Repeat this operation until bubbles cease to appear in the jar.

5. Remove the tube and install the cap on the bleeder valve.

**Bleeding the rear wheel cylinders**

# FRONT DISC BRAKES

## Disc Brake Pads

### INSPECTION

Most models provide an inspection slot in the top of the caliper for checking the pad thickness. However, if the thickness seems marginal, the pads should be removed from the caliper and checked. Models not having an inspection slot will require pad removal to check the thickness of the friction material.

### REMOVAL AND INSTALLATION

#### All models to 1982 and GLC Wagon

NOTE: *Prior to the installation of new brake pads, remove ½ of the brake fluid from both sides of the dual master cylinder reservoir(s). This allows for the displaced fluid when the caliper piston is pushed back into the caliper. Discard the fluid and replace the master cylinder reservoir cover.*

1. Loosen the wheel lugs, raise the front of the car and safely support it on jackstands. Remove the front wheels and tires.

2. On RX-2 (various), RX-3 and 808: These models use a torque plate single piston floating caliper. To remove the brake pads; Pry the pad protector from the top of the caliper. Remove the spring clip from the holes in the two through pins and outer pad. Remove the inner spring clip, note the difference in the shape of the two clips. They must be reinstalled in the same place. Pull the brake pads from the caliper. Note any shims between the pads and the caliper, replace them in the same position when installing new pads. Use a piece of hardwood and a C-clamp to push the caliper piston back into the caliper to provide clearance for the new brake pads.

3. On GLC Rear Wheel Drive, Cosmo and RX-2 (various): These models use a single piston caliper that slides on a mounting bracket

**Removing the brake pads—RX-3 models**

attached to the steering knuckle. To remove the pads; Remove the clips or pins that hold the caliper guide or retaining key in place. Tap out the guide or key. If there is only one key or guide, remember it's position. Lift the caliper from the mounting bracket. Support the caliper with a piece of wire so it is not hanging on the brake hose. Remove the brake pads from the mounting bracket. A support plate is under each pad. They are not interchangeable and must be installed correctly. Use a C-clamp and push the caliper piston back into the caliper.

4. 626 and GLC-Front Wheel Drive: These models use a caliper that floats on guide pins and bushings that are threaded into a mounting bracket. To remove the pads; Disconnect the horseshoe clip retaining the brake hose to the front strut. Remove the caliper guide pins and anti-rattle springs or clips.

NOTE: *Variations in pad retainers, anti-rattle and retaining springs occur from year to year. Work on one side at a time, note the position of each spring, etc. for correct installation.*

5. On 1982 models: remove the upper spring clip (if equipped) and the lower pin bolt which retains the caliper to the mount. Rotate the caliper upward. On other years, remove the mounting pins, lift the caliper up and away from the disc rotor. Support the caliper with wire, do not permit it to hang by the brake hose. All versions slide the outboard pad from the adapter. Remove the inboard pad from the caliper or adapter. Note the location of any shims for reinstallation. Use a C-clamp to push the caliper piston back into the caliper.

6. Pad installation for all models is the reverse of removal. Fill the master cylinder and bleed the brakes after replacing the brake pads.

#### 1983–85 GLC

1. Raise the front of the vehicle, support it with safety stands, and remove the front wheels. Unclip the brake hose at the shock absorber by pressing the lower clip outward with a screwdriver and then forcing the clip downward.

2. Use a screwdriver to release the spring clip at the top of the caliper by forcing it inward and then forward.

3. Pull out the lower slide pin and then hinge the caliper upward and wire it to the strut to hold it in this position.

4. Turn the wheel hub until one of the four indentations lines up with the pads. Then, remove the pad, shim and spring on either side. Remove the springs from the pads.

5. Remove about half the fluid from the

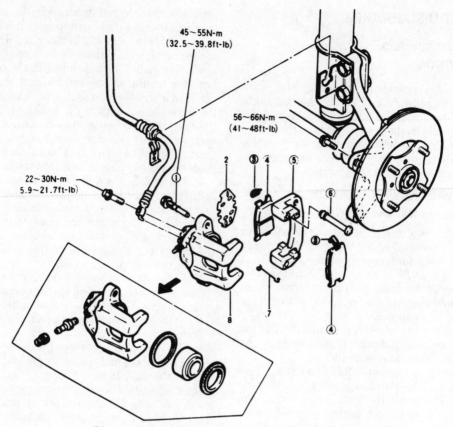

45~55N-m
(32.5~39.8ft-lb)

56~66N-m
(41~48ft-lb)

22~30N-m
5.9~21.7ft-lb)

**Disc brake components GLC front wheel drive model**

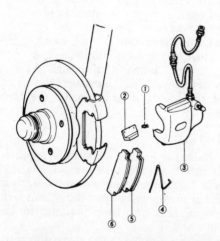

1. Locking clip
2. Stopper plate
3. Caliper
4. Anti-rattle spring
5. Brake shoe
6. Brake shoe

**Front disc brake assembly—GLC rear wheel drive**

master cylinder reservoir. Clean the exposed piston surface. Then, use a C-clamp to depress the caliper piston back into the caliper. This will permit the new, thicker pad to be installed.

6. Install in reverse order, making sure to

transfer the shim and spring to the new pad. If either is warped or fatigued, replace it. Grease the contact surface between the pad mounting support and the caliper assembly, and to both surfaces of the outer and inner shims. Apply grease sparingly.

Also, grease the slide pin and bushing. Bleed the brakes. Make sure to pump the pedal after installation to take up clearance and test for full pedal.

### 1983–87 626 and 1986–87 323

1. Raise the vehicle and support it on axle stands. Remove the front wheels.

2. Remove the two caliper installation bolts and then pull the caliper off the disc. Tie the caliper up to prevent putting tension on the brake hose.

3. Remove the outer pad by using a screwdriver to release the clip. Then, remove the inner pad.

4. Remove about half the brake fluid from the reservoir in the master cylinder. Use a C-clamp to force the piston back into the caliper.

5. Reverse the removal procedure to install. If either or both pads shows excessive wear, re-

Removing the return spring from 1983 and later GLC calipers

place both pads. Before reattaching the caliper, push the sleeve toward the outside of the caliper so the sleeve boot does not get pinned between the caliper and steering knuckle and get torn. Torque the upper installation bolt to 12–18 ft.lb. and the lower installation bolt to 15–21 ft.lb.

## Disc Brake Calipers

### REMOVAL AND INSTALLATION

#### All Models

1. Perform the disc brake pad removal procedure, as detailed above.
2. Detach the hydraulic line from the caliper. Plug the end of the line to prevent the entrance of dirt or the loss of fluid.
3. Unfasten the bolts or pin which secure

the caliper to the support, and remove the caliper.

4. Follow the caliper removal procedure in reverse order for installation. Bleed the hydraulic system after completing installation.

### OVERHAUL

#### All Models

1. Thoroughly clean the outside of the caliper.
2. Remove the dust boot retainer and the boot.
3. Place a piece of hardwood in front of the piston.
4. Gradually apply compressed air through the hydraulic line fitting and withdraw the piston.

NOTE: *If the piston is frozen and cannot be removed from the caliper, tap lightly around it, while air pressure is being applied.*

5. Withdraw the piston and seal from the caliper bore.
6. If necessary, remove the bleeder screw.
7. Wash all of the parts in clean brake fluid. Dry them off with compressed air.

CAUTION: *Do not wash the parts in kerosene or gasoline.*

8. Examine the caliper bore and piston for scores, scratches, or rust. Replace either part, as required. Minor scratches or scoring can be corrected by dressing with crocus cloth. On late model GLC, remove the caliper bushing with a slide pin and inspect it for excess wear or cracks.

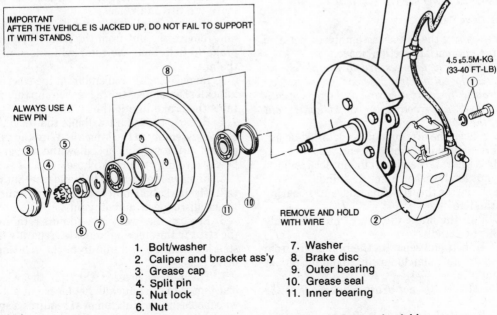

IMPORTANT
AFTER THE VEHICLE IS JACKED UP, DO NOT FAIL TO SUPPORT IT WITH STANDS.

ALWAYS USE A NEW PIN

4.5 ≤5.5M-KG (33-40 FT-LB)

REMOVE AND HOLD WITH WIRE

1. Bolt/washer
2. Caliper and bracket ass'y
3. Grease cap
4. Split pin
5. Nut lock
6. Nut
7. Washer
8. Brake disc
9. Outer bearing
10. Grease seal
11. Inner bearing

**Front brake caliper, disc and bearing assembly—GLC rear wheel drive**

Installing the piston seal retainer on the caliper

Checking the front brake disc runout

NOTE: *Discard the old piston seal and dust boot. Replace them with new ones. Apply clean brake fluid to the piston and bore. Assemble the caliper in the reverse order of disassembly. On late model GLC, apply grease to the dust boot and piston seal according to the directions in the kit. Install the dust boot onto the piston and then install the assembly into the caliper. Apply grease to the slide pin and bushing.*

9. On late model 626, you should also install the dust seal onto the piston and then install the assembly into the caliper. Apply the red grease packed in the seal kit to the piston seal. Apply the orange grease to the dust seal. Also apply the orange grease to the pin outer circumference, the inner surface of the bushing, and the dust boot.

## Brake Disc Rotor

### REMOVAL AND INSTALLATION

#### Rear Drive Car

1. Remove the caliper assembly, as detailed in the appropriate section above.

NOTE: *It is unnecessary to completely remove the caliper from the car. Leave the hydraulic line connected to it and wire the caliper to the underbody of the car so that it is out of the way.*

2. Check the disc runout, as detailed below, before removing it from the car.

3. Withdraw the cotter pin, nut lock, adjusting nut, and washer from the spindle.

4. Take the thrust washer and outer bearing off the hub.

5. Pull the brake disc/wheel hub assembly off of the spindle.

6. Unbolt and separate the brake disc from the hub, after matchmarking them for proper installation.

CAUTION: *Do not drive the disc off of the hub.*

7. Installation of the disc and hub is performed in the reverse order of removal. Adjust the bearing preload, as detailed below.

### INSPECTION

1. Measure the lateral runout of the disc with a dial indicator while the disc is still installed on the spindle.

NOTE: *Be sure that the wheel bearings are adjusted properly before checking runout.*

2. If runout exceeds specification, replace or resurface the disc.

3. Inspect the surface of the disc for scores or pits and resurface it, if necessary.

4. If the disc is resurfaced, its thickness should be no less than the figure shown in the Brake Specifications Chart.

#### Front Wheel Drive GLC through 1982

1. Loosen the lug nuts, raise the front of the car and safely support it on jackstands. Remove the tire and wheel.

2. Raise the staked tab from the hub center nut, remove the nut from the axle. Apply the brake to help hold the rotor while loosening the nut.

3. Remove the tie rod end from the steering knuckle. Disconnect the horseshoe clip that retains the brake line to the strut.

4. Remove the mounting bolts that hold the caliper assembly to the knuckle. Wire the caliper out of the way, do not allow the caliper to be supported by the brake hose.

5. Remove the through bolt and nut that retains the lower ball joint to the steering knuckle and disconnect the ball joint.

6. Remove the two bolts and nuts retaining the strut to the steering knuckle. Separate the steering knuckle and hub from the strut and drive axle.

7. The hub is pressed through the wheel bearings into the knuckle. Replacement of the wheel bearings or hub removal requires a special puller and access to a bench press. Your

dealer or local automotive machine shop can handle the job for you.

8. Remove the inner oil seal and bearing. Remove the wheel hub from the knuckle with a wheel hub puller (Mazda tool 49 F001 726). Remove the outer bearing using a press and Mazda tools 49 F401 368 and 49 F401 365. Drive the outer and inner race from the knuckle with a brass drift and hammer.

9. Install new inner and outer races. Pack the inner and outer bearing and install in knuckle. Use Mazda tool 49 B001 727 tighten the tool nut and measure the preload with a scale connected to the caliper mounting hole on the knuckle. Various spacers are available to increase or decrease the preload. Preload should be 1.7–6.9 in.lb.

10. Install the inner and outer grease seals. Press fit the hub through the bearings into the knuckle. Use 6613.8 lbs. of pressure to install.

11. Installation of the knuckle and hub is in the reverse order or removal. Always use a new axle locknut and tighten it to 116–174 ft.lb. Stake the locknut after tightening. Knuckle to strut mounting; 58–86 ft.lb. Knuckle to ball joint; 33–40 ft.lb. Knuckle to tie rod end; 22–33 ft.lb.

### 1983–85 Front Wheel Drive GLC

NOTE: *This is a complex procedure requiring a number of special tools, especially if inspection reveals bearing work is required. Before proceeding, check on availability of these tools.*

1. Raise the vehicle and support it via the crossmember, using safety stands. Inspect the rotor as described immediately above. Check for wheel bearing play be grasping the tires at top and bottom and attempting to rock them. There should be not noticeable play. Make sure you don't confuse normal play in the ball joint at the bottom of the strut with wheel bearing play. Also, spin the tire and make sure it turns smoothly and that there is no bearing noise. If there is looseness, the hub and knuckle should be disassembled and the bearing preload adjusted, as described below under Wheel Bearings. Remove the wheel and tire.

2. Raise the tab on the driveshaft locknut at the steering knuckle. Have someone apply the brakes while you loosen the nut. Use a puller to separate the tie rod end from the steering knuckle. If the tie rod end is difficult to separate, it may be lightly tapped with a hammer.

3. Raise the claw of the clip fastening the brake line to the strut and separate the line from the strut.

4. Remove the caliper from the strut (see the appropriate procedure above) and hang it up

out of the way. The hydraulic line need not be disconnected.

5. Remove the bolts and nuts fasten the ball joint lever to the lower control arm. Then, remove the bolts and nuts fastening the knuckle to the strut. Remove the knuckle assembly, separating it from the driveshaft. Avoid scratching the oil seal.

6. Now, use a puller to separate the ball joint from the knuckle assembly and mount the assembly in a vise. Use a wheel hub puller Mazda part No. 49 B001 726 or equivalent to remove the hub from the steering knuckle.

7. Matchmark the hub and rotor for reassembly in the same manner, remove the four bolts, and remove the rotor.

8. Install in reverse order. Torque the rotor bolts to 33–39 ft.lb. Make sure the rotor is in the same position, if it is being re-used. Use a press to install the wheel hub to the knuckle. Torque the knuckle to strut bolts to 58–86 ft.lb., the knuckle to ball joint bolts to 33–39 ft.lb., the control arm to ball joint bolts to 69–86 ft.lb., the caliper bolts to 41–48 ft.lb. and the knuckle to tie rod end nut to 22–23 ft.lb. Install a new driveshaft locknut, torque it to 116–174 ft.lb. and then stake it onto the groove in the end of he driveshaft with a dull punch or similar device. Use a new cotter pin on the tie rod end locknut.

### 626 and 323 Front Wheel Drive

1. Raise the vehicle and support it securely by the center crossmember using axle stands. Inspect the disc brake rotor as described above in the procedure for disc removal for rear drive cars. If the disc requires replacement or machining, proceed to inspect the wheel bearing and then remove it.

NOTE: *Step 2 involves inspection of the wheel bearing. While it is good practice to*

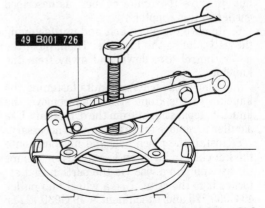

**Removing the wheel hub with a special puller—GLC with front wheel drive**

*make this inspection before removing the wheel hub and rotor, it is a time consuming procedure. If you have not reason to suspect wheel bearing problems and only wish to replace the rotor, skip to Step 3.*

2. Spin the tire to check for roughness in the bearing or unusual noise. Then, remove the tire and remove the brake caliper, as described above. Hang the caliper out of the way without disconnecting the hydraulic line. Finally, mount a dial indicator to the strut and zero it with the wheel hub pushed inward. Then pull the hub outward to check for end play. If it is greater than 0.0079″ (0.2mm), replace the bearing as described in the appropriate procedure below.

Use a screwdriver and hammer to remove the crimp from the driveshaft locknut and have someone apply the brakes while you loosen it. You'll have to temporarily reinstall the caliper to do this. Then, remove the caliper, tighten the nut loosely by hand and use a spring scale to rotate the hub via one of the wheel studs. Angle the scale at 90 degrees to a line through the center of the hub. Measure the starting torque required. Then, reinstall the caliper, torque the driveshaft bolt to 116–124 ft.lb. while someone applies the brakes, remove the caliper, and measure the starting torque. If it is more than 4.4 lb. over the former starting torque, this also indicates that the wheel bearing must be replaced.

3. Use a puller to disconnect the tie rod end from the steering knuckle. You can tap the ball joint lightly with a hammer, if removal is difficult.

4. Remove the locknuts, washer and bushings and disconnect the stabilizer bar from the control arm.

5. If you have not already done so, use a screwdriver and hammer to remove the crimp from the driveshaft locknut. Have someone apply the brakes while you loosen it. Remove the nut. Remove the brake caliper, as described earlier in this chapter.

6. Remove the pinch bolt and nut fastening the ball joint to the knuckle. Then, push the lower control arm down and away from the knuckle.

7. Remove the bolts and nuts fastening the knuckle to the front strut and remove the knuckle, separating it from the driveshaft. Use a puller to remove the driveshaft, if necessary.

8. Install the pinch bolt and nut back onto the knuckle and tighten loosely. Thin, mount the assembly in a vise via the portion that attaches it to the strut. Use a wheel hub puller 49 G030 725 and attachment A 49 G030 727 or equivalent tools to separate the hub and rotor from the knuckle.

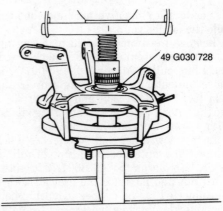

49 G030 728

**Use the attachment shown or equivalent to press the hub and knuckle together on the front drive 626**

9. Matchmark the hub and rotor, remove the attaching bolts, and separate the rotor from the hub.

10. To install, align the mating marks, install the rotor mounting bolts, and torque to 36–43 ft.lb.

11. Position the front hub assembly so it is supported without using the wheel studs, and use an attachment B, Mazda tool No. 49 G030 728 or equivalent and use a press to press fit the knuckle to front hub. Align the support with the center of the spindle. The attachment applies pressure to the inner race of the wheel bearing. The edge of the wheel bearing must contact the wheel hub.

12. Slide the front hub and knuckle onto the driveshaft and then position the knuckle on the lower strut and install the bolts. Torque them to 69–86 ft.lb.

13. Loosen the pinch bolt and nut, install the ball joint into the kncukle, and then torque the pinch bolt to 32–40 ft.lb.

14. Install the brake caliper and torque the upper bolt to 12–18 ft.lb. and lower to 14–22 ft.lb.

15. Install a new driveshaft locknut and torque it to 166–124 ft.lb. Crimp the nut into the groove in the axle with a dull tool until at least a $\frac{1}{16}$″ (1.6mm) indentation is produced.

16. Reconnect the stabilizer bar to the link that fastens it to the lower control arm. Torque the locknuts until 1″ (25.4mm) of threads is exposed. Torque the locknuts to 9–13 ft.lb. against each other.

17. Connect the tie rod end to the knuckle, torque the nut to 22–33 ft.lb. and then tighten it further if necessary to align the castellations in the nut with the cotter pin hole and install a new cotter pin.

18. Install the wheel and lower the vehicle.

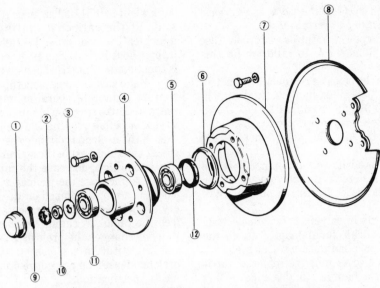

1. Grease cap
2. Nut lock
3. Flat washer
4. Hub
5. Inner bearing
6. Dust ring
7. Brake disc
8. Backing plate
9. Cotter pin
10. Adjusting nut
11. Outer bearing
12. Grease seal

**RX-3 front wheel hub assembly—RX-2 similar**

## Wheel Bearings

NOTE: *See Disc Brake Rotor Removal & Installation, above, for GLC 1981–82 front wheel bearing surface.*

### REMOVAL AND INSTALLATION

**Rear Wheel Drive**

1. Remove the brake disc/hub assembly and separate them, as detailed earlier.

2. Drive the seal out and then remove the inner bearing from the hub.

3. Drive the outer bearing races out with a brass drift applied to the slots provided for this purpose.

4. Clean the inner and outer bearings completely and dry them with compressed air.

CAUTION: *Do not use compressed air to spin the bearings dry.*

5. Clean the spindle and the hub cavity with solvent.

6. Installation is performed in the reverse order or removal. The following point should be noted, however:

   a. Repack the bearings and the hub cavity with lithium grease. Do not over pack them.

   b. Install the wheel hub-to-brake disc bolts to 36 ft.lb. torque.

   c. Adjust the bearing preload, as described below.

NOTE: *Rear wheel bearing service on GLC front wheel drive model is the same as the previous section.*

### PRELOAD ADJUSTMENT

**Rear Wheel Drive**

NOTE: *This operation is performed with the wheel, grease cap, nut lock, and cotter pin removed.*

1. On GLC and 626, torque adjusting nut to 14–18 ft.lb. then rotate the brake disc to seat the bearings. On all other models, rotate the hub/disc assembly while tightening the adjusting nut to seat the bearings.

2. Back off the adjusting nut about $\frac{1}{6}$ of a turn.

3. Hook a spring scale in one of the bolt holes on the hub.

4. Pull the spring scale squarely, until the hub just begins to rotate. The scale reading should be 0.9–2.2 lbs. except on the GLC and 626, GLC reading is 0.33–1.32 lbs. 626 reading is 0.77–1.92 lbs. Tighten the adjusting nut until the proper spring scale reading is obtained.

5. Place the castellated nut lock over the adjusting nut. Align one of the slots on the nut lock with the hole in the spindle and fit a new cotter pin into place.

### REMOVAL, INSTALLATION, AND ADJUSTMENT

**1983–85 GLC**

NOTE: *This procedure requires many special tools. Check on the availability of these before starting. It may be cheaper for you to have some aspects of the work done professionally then to buy certain tools.*

1. Follow Steps 1–7 in the procedure for Disc Brake Rotor Removal & Installation for this model.

2. Arrange the bearing remover (Mazda tool No. 49 F401 365 or equivalent) and attachment B (49 F401 368 or equivalent) as shown and, with a press, remove the outer bearing's inner race. Make sure the hub does not fall and get damaged.

3. Use a brass drift and a hammer to strike the edge of the outer race and remove it. Tap all around the race, forcing it out in small increments.

4. Wash parts in solvent before inspecting. Inspect the knuckle for damage, rust in the bearing bore, or a bad dust cover or seal.

5. If the dust cover must be replaced, tap it in place with a hammer and a pipe of 3.2" (81mm) in diameter. Make sure the dust cover is positioned as shown.

6. Fit the bearing outer race into the knuckle with a brass rod and hammer. Make sure it seats in the knuckle.

7. Check the bearing preload by installing a spacer selector (Mazda tool No. 49 B001 727 or equivalent) in a vise and assembling to it the steering knuckle along with the original spacer. Bearing preload (the torque required to start it turning) should be 1.7–6.9 in.lb. This is

equivalent to 0.5–1.9 lbs. measured by a spring scale at the caliper mounting hole of the knuckle. The tool must be tightened to 145 ft.lb. in 36 ft.lb. increments. As each increment is completed, rotate the bearing to seat it properly, make sure it turns smoothly, and then repeat the tightening operation until 145 ft.lb. is reached. Make sure you again turn the bearing to seat it before reading the preload.

8. If the preload is outside specifications, increase the thickness of the spacer to decrease it if it is too high; decrease the thickness of the spacer to increase the preload if it is too low. There is a mark stamped on the outer periphery of the spacer that represents its thickness (see the table). A change in thickness of one number changes the preload 1.7–3.5 in.lb.

9. Substitute a new spacer, and repeat the preload measuring procedure until the preload meets specification.

10. Apply grease to the lip of a new outer oil seal and gently tap it in with a plastic hammer. Make sure the surface is flush with the knuckle when it's installed.

11. In the same way, but using an appropriate installer (Mazda tool No. is 49 B001 795) install a new inner seal.

12. Fill these areas with lithium grease meeting NGLI No. 2 specification: the spaces between the bearing rollers: the space between inner and outer bearings; the pace between each bearing and the adjacent seal.

13. Using the spacer selector described above

**Checking front wheel bearing preload**

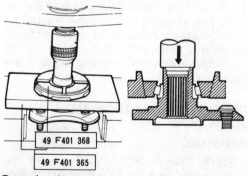

| 49 F401 368 |
| 49 F401 365 |

**Removing the outer front wheel bearing's inner race on 626**

| Stamped mark | Thickness |
|---|---|
| 1 | 6.285 mm (0.2474 in) |
| 2 | 6.325 mm (0.2490 in) |
| 3 | 6.365 mm (0.2506 in) |
| 4 | 6.405 mm (0.2522 in) |
| 5 | 6.445 mm (0.2538 in) |
| 6 | 6.485 mm (0.2554 in) |
| 7 | 6.525 mm (0.2570 in) |
| 8 | 6.565 mm (0.2586 in) |
| 9 | 6.605 mm (0.2602 in) |
| 10 | 6.645 mm (0.2618 in) |
| 11 | 6.685 mm (0.2634 in) |
| 12 | 6.725 mm (0.2650 in) |
| 13 | 6.765 mm (0.2666 in) |
| 14 | 6.805 mm (0.2682 in) |
| 15 | 6.845 mm (0.2698 in) |
| 16 | 6.885 mm (0.2714 in) |
| 17 | 6.925 mm (0.2730 in) |
| 18 | 6.965 mm (0.2746 in) |
| 19 | 7.005 mm (0.2762 in) |
| 20 | 7.045 mm (0.2778 in) |
| 21 | 7.085 mm (0.2794 in) |

**This chart shows the thickness of each spacer used to set wheel bearing preload on the GLC**

and a press, install the wheel hub into the knuckle. This requires as much as 6,613 lbs. pressure.

14. Install the knuckle to the suspension system in reverse of the removal procedure, using a new driveshaft locknut, and observing the following torque figures, all in ft.lb.:

- Rotor to hub bolts: 33–39
- Knuckle to strut bolts: 58–86
- Knuckle to ball joint: 33–39
- Lower arm to ball joint: 69–96
- Knuckle and brake caliper: 41–48
- Driveshaft locknut: 116–174
- Knuckle to tie rod end: 28–32

Make sure to stake over the driveshaft locknut with a dull punch until it is indented into the groove in the shaft at least 0.16" (4mm). Use a new cotter pin for the tie rod end nut.

### 1983–87 626 and 1986–87 323

NOTE: *This procedure requires many special tools. Determine availability before you start work. In some cases it may be less expensive to have certain operations performed by a local repair shop than to purchase appropriate tools. Note also that this bearing's preload is not adjustable, so that if proload does not meet specification the bearing must be replaced.*

1. Follow Steps 1–9 of the procedure for brake rotor removal and installation for this model, above. This includes determining the need to replace the wheel bearing.

2. Remove the snapring from the bearing bore. Mount attachment B (Mazda tool No. 49 G030 728) onto the edge of the inner race of the bearing, mount the knuckle in a vise, and turn the bolt of the wheel hub puller clockwise in order to press the wheel bearing out of the knuckle. Detach the puller from the knuckle.

3. Inspect the knuckle for cracks, heat damage, or rust. The dust cover may be left in place unless it is damaged. If it must be replace, note

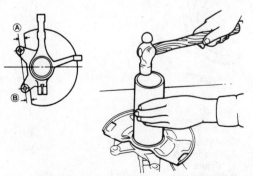

**Position the dust cover on the 626 steering knuckle as shown**

its position before removal. Then, install a new one with a pipe of about 3.4" (81mm) in diameter and a press. Replace the oil seal if it is damaged or worn at the contact surface.

4. Inspect the oil seal for proper position. If it has moved upward, press it back into position. The knuckle should be placed so it is securely supported by its center, i.e., the center of the knuckle should be aligned with the spindle of the press. Then, press in the new bearing with a piece of pipe about 2.6" (66mm) in diameter bearing only on the outer race.

5. Install the snapring.

6. Reinstall the rotor to the hub and press the hub back into the knuckle as described start in Step 10 of the Disc Brake Rotor Removal & Installation procedure for the 626, above. Continue with the remaining steps to install the knuckle back onto the car.

## REAR DISC BRAKES

Rear disc brakes are used on the Cosmo, the 626 and the 323. Basic design of the caliper and pads is identical to that of the front disc brakes on that car; therefore, for pad removal and installation, caliper removal and installation, and caliper overhaul, see applicable procedures for front disc brakes. Rear disc brake disc removal and installation procedure is provided below.

### Brake Discs
#### REMOVAL AND INSTALLATION

1. Securely support the vehicle on stands and remove the wheels. Check the later runout of the disc with a dial indicator. The limit is 0.0039" (0.01mm).

2. Remove the bolts attaching the caliper bracket, and remove the caliper and bracket as an assembly, and wire it to the rear spring.

3. Fully release the parking brake. Remove the disc attaching screws, install them into the tapped holes about 90 degrees from their normal position, and screw them in evenly to force the disc off the axle shaft flange. Remove screws from disc.

4. To install, position the disc, aligning identification marks on axle shaft flange and disc. Install mounting screws. If a new disc is being installed, install it in each of the four possible positions and check lateral runout with a dial indicator. Install the disc in the position in which runout is minimized, and then match mark disc and axle flange.

# REAR DRUM BRAKES

## Brake Drums

### REMOVAL AND INSTALLATION

#### Rear Wheel Drive

1. Remove the wheel disc and loosen the lug nuts.

2. Raise the rear of the car and support it with jackstands.

CAUTION: *Be sure that the car is securely supported. Remember, you will be working underneath it.*

3. Remove the lug nuts and the rear wheel.

4. Be sure that the parking brake is fully released.

5. Remove the bolts which secure the drum to the rear axle shaft flange or center locknut.

NOTE: *If the drum will not come off easily, screw the drum securing bolts into the two tapped holes in the drum. Tighten the bolts evenly in order to force the drum away from the flange.*

6. Rear brake drum installation is performed in the reverse order of removal. Adjust the shoes after installation is completed or prior to installation on GLC (fwd).

### INSPECTION

1. Examine the drum for cracks or overheating spots. Replace the drum if either of these are present.

2. Check the drum for scoring. Light scoring can be corrected with sandpaper.

3. Check the drum with a dial indicator for out of roundness; turn the drum if it is beyond the specifications shown in the Brake Specifications Chart.

4. If the drum must be turned because of excessive scoring or out of roundness, the drum's inside diameter should not exceed the specifications shown in the chart.

• RX-2 models: 7.9135" (201mm)

NOTE: *If one drum is turned, the opposite drum should also be turned to the same size.*

#### Front Wheel Drive 626, 323 and GLC

1. Loosen the rear wheel lugnuts. Raise the vehicle and support it securely. Remove the lugnuts and wheel.

2. Unstake the locknut and remove it. Pull off the drum, being careful to catch the washer and bearings if they fall out of the center of the drum. If it is difficult to remove the drum.

• On GLC, remove the lever stop from the backing plate to increase the brake shoe clearance.

• On 323 and 626, remove the backing plate plug to increase the shoe clearance. If this does not make it easy to remove the drum, loosen the parking brake lever adjustment nut.

3. Reinstall the drum with the washer and bearing in proper position. Install a new locknut and torque it to 18–22 ft.lb. Turn the drum

---

**IMPORTANT**

After the vehicle is jacked up, do not fail to support it with stands.

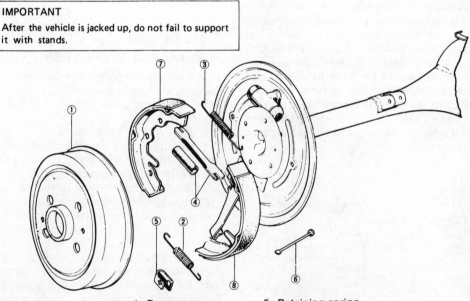

1. Drum
2. Return spring
3. Return spring
4. Parking brake strut
5. Retaining spring
6. Guide pin
7. Brake shoe
8. Brake shoe

**Rear brake assembly—GLC**

three revolutions to seat the bearing. Then loosen the nut and tighten it only finger tight.

4. Use a spring scale on one of the wheel studs to measure the torque required to start the drum rotating. Angle the scale at 90 degrees to a line drawn through the center of the drum and the stud.

5. On 323 and 626, tighten the lock nut until the torque required to start the drum rotating is 15–35 oz. less than that measured above. On GLC, add the pull measured above to the specified preload torque of 0.9–2.2 lb. and turn the locknut in gradually, measuring the starting torque, until the preload figure you've determined is produced. Then, stake the locknut into the groove in the rear spindle with a dull tool until it is indented at least 0.08″ (2mm).

## Brake Shoes

### REMOVAL AND INSTALLATION

**Except Front Wheel Drive GLC**

1. Perform the brake drum removal procedure, as detailed above.

2. Remove the return springs from the upper side of the shoe using a brake spring removal tool.

3. Remove the return springs from the lower side of the shoes in the same manner as Step 2.

4. Remove the shoe retaining spring.

 a. On RX-3, RX-4, 808 and Cosmo models by removing the retaining pin with pliers.

 b. On RX-2, 626 and GLC models by compressing the retaining spring while turning the pin 90 degrees.

5. Withdraw the primary shoes and the parking brake link.

6. Disengage the parking brake lever from the secondary shoes by unfastening its retaining clip.

7. Remove the secondary shoe.

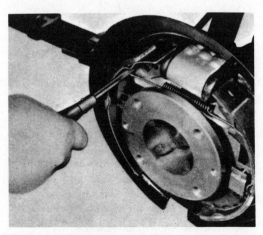

**Shoe return spring removal**

CAUTION: *Be careful not to get oil or grease on the lining material.*

8. Inspect the linings and replace them if they are badly burned or worn 0.039 in beyond the specification for a new lining. See Brake Specification chart.

9. Replace the linings if they are saturated with oil or grease.

**Brake shoe installation is performed in the following manner:**

1. Lubricate the threads of the adjusting screw, the sliding surfaces of the shoes, and the backing plate flanges with a small quantity of grease.

CAUTION: *Be careful not to get grease on the lining surfaces.*

2. Install the eye of the parking brake cable through the parking brake lever which has previously been installed on the secondary shoe and secured with its retaining clip.

3. Fit the link between the shoes.

4. Engage the shoes with the slots in the anchor (adjusting screw) and the wheel cylinder.

5. Fasten the shoes to the backing plate with the retaining springs and pins.

6. Install the shoe return springs with the tool used during removal.

7. Install the drums and adjust the shoes as detailed elsewhere.

NOTE: *If a slight amount of grease has gotten on the shoes during installation, it may be removed by light sanding.*

**Front Wheel Drive GLC**

1. Loosen the rear wheel lugs, raise the rear of the car and support it safely on jackstands. Remove the rear tire and wheel.

2. Remove the rear brake drum. Clean the dirt from the brake components with a dry brush.

3. Disconnect the parking brake cable from the lever at the rear of the brake mounting plate.

4. Remove the lower return spring from between the two brake shoes. Disconnect the upper return spring from the front brake shoe. Remove the clip that holds the front shoe to the mounting plate and remove the front shoe.

5. Disconnect the adjuster spring from the rear brake shoe. Remove the mounting clip and the rear brake shoe.

6. Disconnect the adjuster spring from the rear brake shoe. Remove the mounting clip and the rear brake shoe.

7. Push on the adjuster lever while rotating a screwdriver between and quadrant and the knurled pin to retract the self adjuster.

8. Apply a small amount of grease to the mounting plate brake shoe contact points. In-

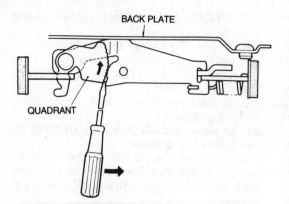

Releasing tension on the self adjuster, 626 with front wheel drive. Insert a screwdriver as shown and turn it to turn the quadrant in the arrowed direction.

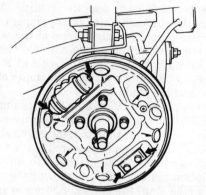

Greasing the 626 backing plate and brake mechanism

stall the shoes, mounting clips and springs in the reverse order of removal.

9. Install the brake drum using a new hub nut (be sure to stake the nut). Connect the parking brake cables. Bleed the brakes if necessary. Pump the pedal several times to adjust the drum to shoe clearance.

### 626 and 323 with Front Wheel Drive

1. Remove the brake drum, as described above. Clean the dirt from the brake components with a dry brush. Do not blow dirt away as the dust may contain asbestos, which you could then inhale.

2. To ease removal of the leading shoe, and installation of the return spring later, insert an ordinary screwdriver into the gap between the quadrant of the automatic adjuster mechanism and twist it in the arrowed direction to release tension.

3. Use brake pliers to remove the return springs. Then, use needle nose pliers to remove the holding pins (from the backing Plate) and clips.

4. Push the bottoms of the shoes outward in order to release them from the anchors and then unhook them at the wheel cylinder. Remove the leading shoe first.

5. Linings must be at least 0.039" (1mm) thick or conform to inspection standards in your state. Replace them regardless of he thickness if there are any signs of peeling or cracks. The brake drum should be turned if there is grooving or cracking. The limit on inner diameter is 7.913" (201mm). Shoes should be replaced as a set on each wheel. Both rear wheels should be done if either side shows excessive wear.

6. Apply grease to the areas shown in the accompanying illustration by both types of arrows.

7. Reverse the removal procedure to install.

Make sure to apply the brakes several times to take up the adjustment before the vehicle is driven.

## Wheel Cylinders

### REMOVAL AND INSTALLATION

1. Remove the brake drums and shoes as detailed above.

2. Disconnect the hydraulic line from the wheel cylinder by unfastening the flare nut on the rear of the backing plate. Use a flare nut wrench.

3. Plug the line to prevent dirt from entering the system or brake fluid from leaking out.

4. Unfasten the nuts which secure the wheel cylinder to the backing plate and remove the cylinder.

5. Installation of the wheel cylinder is performed in the reverse order of removal. Bleed the hydraulic system and adjust the brake shoes after installation is completed.

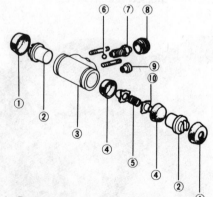

1. Boot
2. Piston
3. Cylinder body
4. Piston cup
5. Return spring
6. Steel ball
7. Bleeder screw
8. Bleeder screw cap
9. Hydraulic line seat
10. Pushrod

**Rear wheel cylinder components—typical**

## Brake Specifications

All measurements given are (in.) unless noted

| Model | Lug Nut Torque (ft. lbs.) | Master Cylinder Bore | Brake Disc | | Brake Drum | | | Minimum Lining Thickness | |
|---|---|---|---|---|---|---|---|---|---|
| | | | Minimum Thickness | Maximum Run-Out | Diameter | Max. Machine O/S | Max. Wear Limit | Front | Rear |
| RX-2 | 65–72 | 0.875 | 0.433 | 0.003 | 7.874 | 7.90 | 7.9135 | 0.276 | 0.039 |
| RX-3 | 65 | 0.875 | 0.394 | 0.003 | 7.874 | 7.90 | 7.9135 | 0.276 | 0.039 |
| RX-4 | 65–72 | 0.875 | 0.433 | 0.004 | 9.0 | 9.025 | 9.0395 | 0.276 | 0.039 |
| B1600 | 65–72 | 0.750 | — | — | 10.236 ③ | 10.276 ④ | — | 0.039 | 0.039 |
| Rotary Pickup | 65–72 | 0.875 | 0.433 | 0.004 | 10.236 | 10.275 | — | 0.276 | 0.039 |
| 808 | 65–72 | 0.8125 | 0.394 | 0.004 | 7.874 | 7.90 | 7.9135 | 0.256 | 0.039 |
| Cosmo | 65–72 | 0.875 | 0.6693 ① | 0.0024 ② | — | — | — | 0.276 | 0.276 |
| GLC (RWD) | 65–72 ⑥ | ¹³⁄₁₆ | 0.4724 | 0.0024 | 7.874 | ⑤ | 7.9135 | 0.276 | 0.039 |
| GLC (FWD) to 1982 | 65–80 | ¹³⁄₁₆ | 0.39 | 0.004 | 7.09 | ⑤ | 7.13 | 0.276 | 0.039 |
| 626 (RWD) | 65–80 | ⁷⁄₈ | 0.4724 | 0.004 | 7.874 | ⑤ | 7.9135 | 0.256 | 0.039 |
| GLC 1983–84 | 65–80 | ¹³⁄₁₆ | 0.39 | 0.004 | 7.09 | — | 7.13 ⑤ | 0.04 | 0.04 |
| 626 (FWD) to 1984 | 65–87 | ⁷⁄₈ | 0.51 | 0.004 | 7.87 | — | 7.91 ⑤ | 0.04 | 0.04 |

① Rear: 0.354
② Rear: 0.004
③ Front: 10.236
④ Front: 10.276
⑤ No machining maximum given—remove minimum amount which smooths surface, then ensure drum inner diameter meets specification
⑥ 65–80—1979–80
NOTE: *Minimum lining thickness is as recommended by the manufacturer. Due to variations in state inspection regulations, the minimum allowable thickness may be different than recommended by the manufacturer.*

## Brake Specifications

(All measurements given are inches unless noted.)

| Year | Model | Lug Nut Torque (ft. lbs.) | Master Cylinder Bore | Brake Rotor | | Brake Drum | | Minimum Lining Thickness | |
|---|---|---|---|---|---|---|---|---|---|
| | | | | Minimum Thickness | Maximum Runout | Inside Diameter | Wear Limit | Front | Rear |
| '85 | GLC | 65–80 | ¹³⁄₁₆ | 0.390 | 0.0040 | 7.090 | 7.130 | 0.118 | 0.040 |
| | 626 | 65–80 | ⁷⁄₈ | 0.550 ① | 0.0040 | 7.8741 | 7.9135 | 0.040 | 0.040 |
| '86–'87 | 323 | 65–87 | 0.8750 | 0.630 ② | 0.0030 | 7.870 | 7.910 | 0.120 | 0.040 |
| | 626 | 65–87 | ⁷⁄₈ | 0.710 ② | 0.0040 | 7.870 | 7.910 | 0.118 | 0.040 |

**NOTE:** Minimum lining thickness is as recommended by the manufacturer. Due to variations in state inspection regulations, the minimum allowable thickness may be different than specified.
① Diesel: 0.710
② Rear disc: 0.350

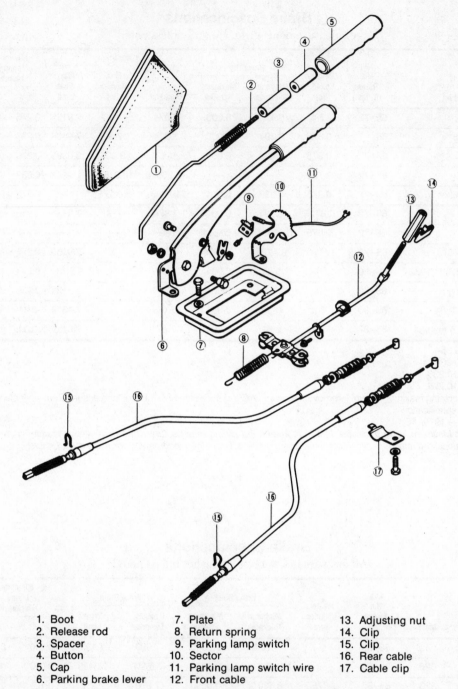

1. Boot
2. Release rod
3. Spacer
4. Button
5. Cap
6. Parking brake lever
7. Plate
8. Return spring
9. Parking lamp switch
10. Sector
11. Parking lamp switch wire
12. Front cable
13. Adjusting nut
14. Clip
15. Clip
16. Rear cable
17. Cable clip

**RX-3 parking brake components—RX-2 similar**

### OVERHAUL

1. Remove the boots at either end of the wheel cylinder.

2. Withdraw the pistons, piston cups, push-rods, filling blocks (GLC, 323 and 626 only), and return spring.

3. Wash all of the components in clean brake fluid.

CAUTION: *Never use kerosene or gasoline to clean wheel cylinder components.*

4. Check the cylinder bore and piston for roughness or scoring. Use a wheel cylinder hone, if necessary.

5. Measure the clearance between the cylinder and the piston with a feeler gauge. If the clearance if greater than 0.006″ (0.15mm), replace either the piston or the cylinder.

# CHILTON'S
# AUTO BODY REPAIR TIPS

**Tools and Materials • Step-by-Step Illustrated Procedures**
**How To Repair Dents, Scratches and Rust Holes**
**Spray Painting and Refinishing Tips**

With a little practice, basic body repair procedures can be mastered by any do-it-yourself mechanic. The step-by-step repairs shown here can be applied to almost any type of auto body repair.

# TOOLS & MATERIALS

You may already have basic tools, such as hammers and electric drills. Other tools unique to body repair — body hammers, grinding attachments, sanding blocks, dent puller, half-round plastic file and plastic spreaders — are relatively inexpensive and can be obtained wherever auto parts or auto body repair parts are sold. Portable air compressors and paint spray guns can be purchased or rented.

## Auto Body Repair Kits

The best and most often used products are available to the do-it-yourselfer in kit form, from major manufacturers of auto body repair products. The same manufacturers also merchandise the individual products for use by pros.

Kits are available to make a wide variety of repairs, including holes, dents and scratches and fiberglass, and offer the advantage of buying the materials you'll need for the job. There is little waste or chance of materials going bad from not being used. Many kits may also contain basic body-working tools such as body files, sanding blocks and spreaders. Check the contents of the kit before buying your tools.

# BODY REPAIR TIPS

## Safety

Many of the products associated with auto body repair and refinishing contain toxic chemicals. Read all labels before opening containers and store them in a safe place and manner.

• Wear eye protection (safety goggles) when using power tools or when performing any operation that involves the removal of any type of material.

• Wear lung protection (disposable mask or respirator) when grinding, sanding or painting.

## Sanding

**1** Sand off paint before using a dent puller. When using a non-adhesive sanding disc, cover the back of the disc with an overlapping layer or two of masking tape and trim the edges. The disc will last considerably longer.

**2** Use the circular motion of the sanding disc to grind *into* the edge of the repair. Grinding or sanding away from the jagged edge will only tear the sandpaper.

**3** Use the palm of your hand flat on the panel to detect high and low spots. Do not use your fingertips. Slide your hand slowly back and forth.

# WORKING WITH BODY FILLER

## Mixing The Filler

**C**leanliness and proper mixing and application are extremely important. Use a clean piece of plastic or glass or a disposable artist's palette to mix body filler.

**1** Allow plenty of time and follow directions. No useful purpose will be served by adding more hardener to make it cure (set-up) faster. Less hardener means more curing time, but the mixture dries harder; more hardener means less curing time but a softer mixture.

**2** Both the hardener and the filler should be thoroughly kneaded or stirred before mixing. Hardener should be a solid paste and dispense like thin toothpaste. Body filler should be smooth, and free of lumps or thick spots.

Getting the proper amount of hardener in the filler is the trickiest part of preparing the filler. Use the same amount of hardener in cold or warm weather. For contour filler (thick coats), a bead of hardener twice the diameter of the filler is about right. There's about a 15% margin on either side, but, if in doubt use less hardener.

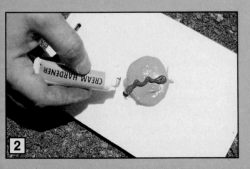

**3** Mix the body filler and hardener by wiping across the mixing surface, picking the mixture up and wiping it again. Colder weather requires longer mixing times. Do not mix in a circular motion; this will trap air bubbles which will become holes in the cured filler.

## Applying The Filler

**1** For best results, filler should not be applied over 1/4″ thick.

Apply the filler in several coats. Build it up to above the level of the repair surface so that it can be sanded or grated down.

The first coat of filler must be pressed on with a firm wiping motion.

Apply the filler in one direction only. Working the filler back and forth will either pull it off the metal or trap air bubbles.

# REPAIRING DENTS

**B**efore you start, take a few minutes to study the damaged area. Try to visualize the shape of the panel before it was damaged. If the damage is on the left fender, look at the right fender and use it as a guide. If there is access to the panel from behind, you can reshape it with a body hammer. If not, you'll have to use a dent puller. Go slowly and work the metal a little at a time. Get the panel as straight as possible before applying filler.

**1** This dent is typical of one that can be pulled out or hammered out from behind. Remove the headlight cover, headlight assembly and turn signal housing.

**2** Drill a series of holes ½ the size of the end of the dent puller along the stress line. Make some trial pulls and assess the results. If necessary, drill more holes and try again. Do not hurry.

**3** If possible, use a body hammer and block to shape the metal back to its original contours. Get the metal back as close to its original shape as possible. Don't depend on body filler to fill dents.

**4** Using an 80-grit grinding disc on an electric drill, grind the paint from the surrounding area down to bare metal. Use a new grinding pad to prevent heat buildup that will warp metal.

**5** The area should look like this when you're finished grinding. Knock the drill holes in and tape over small openings to keep plastic filler out.

**6** Mix the body filler (see Body Repair Tips). Spread the body filler evenly over the entire area (see Body Repair Tips). Be sure to cover the area completely.

**7** Let the body filler dry until the surface can just be scratched with your fingernail. Knock the high spots from the body filler with a body file ("Cheesegrater"). Check frequently with the palm of your hand for high and low spots.

**8** Check to be sure that trim pieces that will be installed later will fit exactly. Sand the area with 40-grit paper.

**9** If you wind up with low spots, you may have to apply another layer of filler.

**10** Knock the high spots off with 40-grit paper. When you are satisfied with the contours of the repair, apply a thin coat of filler to cover pin holes and scratches.

**11** Block sand the area with 40-grit paper to a smooth finish. Pay particular attention to body lines and ridges that must be well-defined.

**12** Sand the area with 400 paper and then finish with a scuff pad. The finished repair is ready for priming and painting (see Painting Tips).

Materials and photos courtesy of Ritt Jones Auto Body, Prospect Park, PA.

# REPAIRING RUST HOLES

There are many ways to repair rust holes. The fiberglass cloth kit shown here is one of the most cost efficient for the owner because it provides a strong repair that resists cracking and moisture and is relatively easy to use. It can be used on large and small holes (with or without backing) and can be applied over contoured areas. Remember, however, that short of replacing an entire panel, no repair is a guarantee that the rust will not return.

**1** Remove any trim that will be in the way. Clean away all loose debris. Cut away all the rusted metal. But be sure to leave enough metal to retain the contour or body shape.

**2** Grind away all traces of rust with a 24-grit grinding disc. Be sure to grind back 3-4 inches from the edge of the hole down to bare metal and be sure all traces of paint, primer and rust are removed.

**3** Block sand the area with 80 or 100 grit sandpaper to get a clear, shiny surface and feathered paint edge. Tap the edges of the hole inward with a ball peen hammer.

**4** If you are going to use release film, cut a piece about 2-3″ larger than the area you have sanded. Place the film over the repair and mark the sanded area on the film. Avoid any unnecessary wrinkling of the film.

**5** Cut 2 pieces of fiberglass matte to match the shape of the repair. One piece should be about 1″ smaller than the sanded area and the second piece should be 1″ smaller than the first. Mix enough filler and hardener to saturate the fiberglass material (see Body Repair Tips).

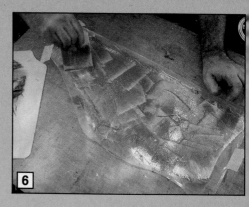

**6** Lay the release sheet on a flat surface and spread an even layer of filler, large enough to cover the repair. Lay the smaller piece of fiberglass cloth in the center of the sheet and spread another layer of filler over the fiberglass cloth. Repeat the operation for the larger piece of cloth.

**7** Place the repair material over the repair area, with the release film facing outward. Use a spreader and work from the center outward to smooth the material, following the body contours. Be sure to remove all air bubbles.

**8** Wait until the repair has dried tack-free and peel off the release sheet. The ideal working temperature is 60°-90° F. Cooler or warmer temperatures or high humidity may require additional curing time. Wait longer, if in doubt.

**9** Sand and feather-edge the entire area. The initial sanding can be done with a sanding disc on an electric drill if care is used. Finish the sanding with a block sander. Low spots can be filled with body filler; this may require several applications.

**10** When the filler can just be scratched with a fingernail, knock the high spots down with a body file and smooth the entire area with 80-grit. Feather the filled areas into the surrounding areas.

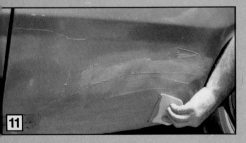

**11** When the area is sanded smooth, mix some topcoat and hardener and apply it directly with a spreader. This will give a smooth finish and prevent the glass matte from showing through the paint.

**12** Block sand the topcoat smooth with finishing sandpaper (200 grit), and 400 grit. The repair is ready for masking, priming and painting (see Painting Tips).

Materials and photos courtesy Marson Corporation, Chelsea, Massachusetts

# PAINTING TIPS

## Preparation

**1** SANDING — Use a 400 or 600 grit wet or dry sandpaper. Wet-sand the area with a 1/4 sheet of sandpaper soaked in clean water. Keep the paper wet while sanding. Sand the area until the repaired area tapers into the original finish.

**2** CLEANING — Wash the area to be painted thoroughly with water and a clean rag. Rinse it thoroughly and wipe the surface dry until you're sure it's completely free of dirt, dust, fingerprints, wax, detergent or other foreign matter.

**3** MASKING — Protect any areas you don't want to overspray by covering them with masking tape and newspaper. Be careful not get fingerprints on the area to be painted.

**4** PRIMING — All exposed metal should be primed before painting. Primer protects the metal and provides an excellent surface for paint adhesion. When the primer is dry, wet-sand the area again with 600 grit wet-sandpaper. Clean the area again after sanding.

## Painting Techniques

**P** aint applied from either a spray gun or a spray can (for small areas) will provide good results. Experiment on an old piece of metal to get the right combination before you begin painting.

**SPRAYING VISCOSITY (SPRAY GUN ONLY)** — Paint should be thinned to spraying viscosity according to the directions on the can. Use only the recommended thinner or reducer and the same amount of reduction regardless of temperature.

**AIR PRESSURE (SPRAY GUN ONLY)** — This is extremely important. Be sure you are using the proper recommended pressure.

**TEMPERATURE** — The surface to be painted should be approximately the same temperature as the surrounding air. Applying warm paint to a cold surface, or vice versa, will completely upset the paint characteristics.

**THICKNESS** — Spray with smooth strokes. In general, the thicker the coat of paint, the longer the drying time. Apply several thin coats about 30 seconds apart. The paint should remain wet long enough to flow out and no longer; heavier coats will only produce sags or wrinkles. Spray a light (fog) coat, followed by heavier color coats.

**DISTANCE** — The ideal spraying distance is 8″-12″ from the gun or can to the surface. Shorter distances will produce ripples, while greater distances will result in orange peel, dry film and poor color match and loss of material due to overspray.

**OVERLAPPING** — The gun or can should be kept at right angles to the surface at all times. Work to a wet edge at an even speed, using a 50% overlap and direct the center of the spray at the lower or nearest edge of the previous stroke.

**RUBBING OUT (BLENDING) FRESH PAINT** — Let the paint dry thoroughly. Runs or imperfections can be sanded out, primed and repainted.

Don't be in too big a hurry to remove the masking. This only produces paint ridges. When the finish has dried for at least a week, apply a small amount of fine grade rubbing compound with a clean, wet cloth. Use lots of water and blend the new paint with the surrounding area.

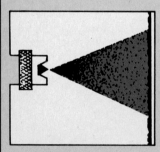

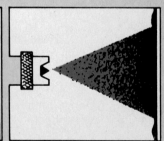

| **WRONG** | **CORRECT** | **WRONG** |
|---|---|---|
| *Thin coat. Stroke too fast, not enough overlap, gun too far away.* | *Medium coat. Proper distance, good stroke, proper overlap.* | *Heavy coat. Stroke too slow, too much overlap, gun too close.* |

6. Examine the piston cups for wear, softening, or swelling; replace them if necessary.

**Assembly is performed as follows:**

1. Apply clean brake fluid to the cylinder bore, pistons, and cups.

2. Fit the steel ball into the bleed hole and install the screw, if they were removed.

3. Insert the parts into the cylinder bore in the reverse order of removal.

NOTE: *Install the piston cups so that their flat side is facing outward.*

4. Fit the boots over both ends of the cylinder.

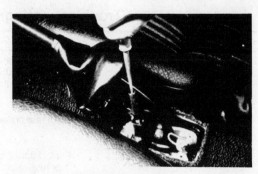

**Adjusting the parking brake**

## PARKING BRAKE

### *ADJUSTMENT*

1. Adjust the rear brake shoes. Note that on Cosmo, rear (parking) brake shoes are adjusted the same way as ordinary rear drum brakes are adjusted.

2. Adjust the front cable with the nut or screw located at the rear of the parking brake handle. The handle should require 3–7 notches for RX-3, RX-4 GLC (rear wheel drive) and Cosmo models, 3–4 notches for 808, 2–3 notches for RX-2 models and 5–7 notches for 626 with rear wheel drive, 7–9 for 626 with front wheel drive, 9–15 for the front wheel drive 323 with rear disc, 7–11 with drums, 3–7 for GLC Wagon, and 5–9 notches for GLC front wheel drive to apply the parking brake.

3. Operate the parking brake several times; check to see that the rear wheels do not drag when it is fully released. Also, make sure the brake warning light lights when the lever is pulled up one notch, but is out when it is fully released.

## Troubleshooting the Brake System

| Problem | Cause | Solution |
|---|---|---|
| Low brake pedal (excessive pedal travel required for braking action.) | • Excessive clearance between rear linings and drums caused by inoperative automatic adjusters | • Make 10 to 15 alternate forward and reverse brake stops to adjust brakes. If brake pedal does not come up, repair or replace adjuster parts as necessary. |
| | • Worn rear brakelining | • Inspect and replace lining if worn beyond minimum thickness specification |
| | • Bent, distorted brakeshoes, front or rear | • Replace brakeshoes in axle sets |
| | • Air in hydraulic system | • Remove air from system. Refer to Brake Bleeding. |
| Low brake pedal (pedal may go to floor with steady pressure applied.) | • Fluid leak in hydraulic system | • Fill master cylinder to fill line; have helper apply brakes and check calipers, wheel cylinders, differential valve tubes, hoses and fittings for leaks. Repair or replace as necessary. |
| | • Air in hydraulic system | • Remove air from system. Refer to Brake Bleeding. |
| | • Incorrect or non-recommended brake fluid (fluid evaporates at below normal temp). | • Flush hydraulic system with clean brake fluid. Refill with correct-type fluid. |
| | • Master cylinder piston seals worn, or master cylinder bore is scored, worn or corroded | • Repair or replace master cylinder |
| Low brake pedal (pedal goes to floor on first application—o.k. on subsequent applications.) | • Disc brake pads sticking on abutment surfaces of anchor plate. Caused by a build-up of dirt, rust, or corrosion on abutment surfaces | • Clean abutment surfaces |
| Fading brake pedal (pedal height decreases with steady pressure applied.) | • Fluid leak in hydraulic system | • Fill master cylinder reservoirs to fill mark, have helper apply brakes, check calipers, wheel cylinders, differential valve, tubes, hoses, and fittings for fluid leaks. Repair or replace parts as necessary. |
| | • Master cylinder piston seals worn, or master cylinder bore is scored, worn or corroded | • Repair or replace master cylinder |
| Decreasing brake pedal travel (pedal travel required for braking action decreases and may be accompanied by a hard pedal.) | • Caliper or wheel cylinder pistons sticking or seized | • Repair or replace the calipers, or wheel cylinders |
| | • Master cylinder compensator ports blocked (preventing fluid return to reservoirs) or pistons sticking or seized in master cylinder bore | • Repair or replace the master cylinder |
| | • Power brake unit binding internally | • Test unit according to the following procedure:<br>(a) Shift transmission into neutral and start engine<br>(b) Increase engine speed to 1500 rpm, close throttle and fully depress brake pedal<br>(c) Slow release brake pedal and stop engine<br>(d) Have helper remove vacuum check valve and hose from power unit. Observe for backward movement of brake pedal.<br>(e) If the pedal moves backward, the power unit has an internal bind—replace power unit |

## Troubleshooting the Brake System (cont.)

| Problem | Cause | Solution |
|---|---|---|
| Spongy brake pedal (pedal has abnormally soft, springy, spongy feel when depressed.) | • Air in hydraulic system<br><br>• Brakeshoes bent or distorted<br>• Brakelining not yet seated with drums and rotors<br>• Rear drum brakes not properly adjusted | • Remove air from system. Refer to Brake Bleeding.<br>• Replace brakeshoes<br>• Burnish brakes<br><br>• Adjust brakes |
| Hard brake pedal (excessive pedal pressure required to stop vehicle. May be accompanied by brake fade.) | • Loose or leaking power brake unit vacuum hose<br>• Incorrect or poor quality brakelining<br>• Bent, broken, distorted brakeshoes<br>• Calipers binding or dragging on mounting pins. Rear brakeshoes dragging on support plate. | • Tighten connections or replace leaking hose<br>• Replace with lining in axle sets<br><br>• Replace brakeshoes<br>• Replace mounting pins and bushings. Clean rust or burrs from rear brake support plate ledges and lubricate ledges with molydisulfide grease.<br>**NOTE:** If ledges are deeply grooved or scored, do not attempt to sand or grind them smooth—replace support plate. |
| | • Caliper, wheel cylinder, or master cylinder pistons sticking or seized<br>• Power brake unit vacuum check valve malfunction | • Repair or replace parts as necessary<br>• Test valve according to the following procedure:<br>(a) Start engine, increase engine speed to 1500 rpm, close throttle and immediately stop engine<br>(b) Wait at least 90 seconds then depress brake pedal<br>(c) If brakes are not vacuum assisted for 2 or more applications, check valve is faulty |
| | • Power brake unit has internal bind | • Test unit according to the following procedure:<br>(a) With engine stopped, apply brakes several times to exhaust all vacuum in system<br>(b) Shift transmission into neutral, depress brake pedal and start engine<br>(c) If pedal height decreases with foot pressure and less pressure is required to hold pedal in applied position, power unit vacuum system is operating normally. Test power unit. If power unit exhibits a bind condition, replace the power unit. |
| | • Master cylinder compensator ports (at bottom of reservoirs) blocked by dirt, scale, rust, or have small burrs (blocked ports prevent fluid return to reservoirs).<br>• Brake hoses, tubes, fittings clogged or restricted<br><br>• Brake fluid contaminated with improper fluids (motor oil, transmission fluid, causing rubber components to swell and stick in bores<br>• Low engine vacuum | • Repair or replace master cylinder<br>**CAUTION:** Do not attempt to clean blocked ports with wire, pencils, or similar implements. Use compressed air only.<br>• Use compressed air to check or unclog parts. Replace any damaged parts.<br>• Replace all rubber components, combination valve and hoses. Flush entire brake system with DOT 3 brake fluid or equivalent.<br><br>• Adjust or repair engine |

## Troubleshooting the Brake System (cont.)

| Problem | Cause | Solution |
|---|---|---|
| Grabbing brakes (severe reaction to brake pedal pressure.) | • Brakelining(s) contaminated by grease or brake fluid | • Determine and correct cause of contamination and replace brakeshoes in axle sets |
| | • Parking brake cables incorrectly adjusted or seized | • Adjust cables. Replace seized cables. |
| | • Incorrect brakelining or lining loose on brakeshoes | • Replace brakeshoes in axle sets |
| | • Caliper anchor plate bolts loose | • Tighten bolts |
| | • Rear brakeshoes binding on support plate ledges | • Clean and lubricate ledges. Replace support plate(s) if ledges are deeply grooved. Do not attempt to smooth ledges by grinding. |
| | • Incorrect or missing power brake reaction disc | • Install correct disc |
| | • Rear brake support plates loose | • Tighten mounting bolts |
| Dragging brakes (slow or incomplete release of brakes) | • Brake pedal binding at pivot | • Loosen and lubricate |
| | • Power brake unit has internal bind | • Inspect for internal bind. Replace unit if internal bind exists. |
| | • Parking brake cables incorrrectly adjusted or seized | • Adjust cables. Replace seized cables. |
| | • Rear brakeshoe return springs weak or broken | • Replace return springs. Replace brakeshoe if necessary in axle sets. |
| | • Automatic adjusters malfunctioning | • Repair or replace adjuster parts as required |
| | • Caliper, wheel cylinder or master cylinder pistons sticking or seized | • Repair or replace parts as necessary |
| | • Master cylinder compensating ports blocked (fluid does not return to reservoirs). | • Use compressed air to clear ports. Do not use wire, pencils, or similar objects to open blocked ports. |
| Vehicle moves to one side when brakes are applied | • Incorrect front tire pressure | • Inflate to recommended cold (reduced load) inflation pressure |
| | • Worn or damaged wheel bearings | • Replace worn or damaged bearings |
| | • Brakelining on one side contaminated | • Determine and correct cause of contamination and replace brakelining in axle sets |
| | • Brakeshoes on one side bent, distorted, or lining loose on shoe | • Replace brakeshoes in axle sets |
| | • Support plate bent or loose on one side | • Tighten or replace support plate |
| | • Brakelining not yet seated with drums or rotors | • Burnish brakelining |
| | • Caliper anchor plate loose on one side | • Tighten anchor plate bolts |
| | • Caliper piston sticking or seized | • Repair or replace caliper |
| | • Brakelinings water soaked | • Drive vehicle with brakes lightly applied to dry linings |
| | • Loose suspension component attaching or mounting bolts | • Tighten suspension bolts. Replace worn suspension components. |
| | • Brake combination valve failure | • Replace combination valve |
| Chatter or shudder when brakes are applied (pedal pulsation and roughness may also occur.) | • Brakeshoes distorted, bent, contaminated, or worn | • Replace brakeshoes in axle sets |
| | • Caliper anchor plate or support plate loose | • Tighten mounting bolts |
| | • Excessive thickness variation of rotor(s) | • Refinish or replace rotors in axle sets |
| Noisy brakes (squealing, clicking, scraping sound when brakes are applied.) | • Bent, broken, distorted brakeshoes | • Replace brakeshoes in axle sets |
| | • Excessive rust on outer edge of rotor braking surface | • Remove rust |

## Troubleshooting the Brake System (cont.)

| Problem | Cause | Solution |
|---|---|---|
| Noisy brakes (squealing, clicking, scraping sound when brakes are applied.) (cont.) | • Brakelining worn out—shoes contacting drum of rotor | • Replace brakeshoes and lining in axle sets. Refinish or replace drums or rotors. |
| | • Broken or loose holdown or return springs | • Replace parts as necessary |
| | • Rough or dry drum brake support plate ledges | • Lubricate support plate ledges |
| | • Cracked, grooved, or scored rotor(s) or drum(s) | • Replace rotor(s) or drum(s). Replace brakeshoes and lining in axle sets if necessary. |
| | • Incorrect brakelining and/or shoes (front or rear). | • Install specified shoe and lining assemblies |
| Pulsating brake pedal | • Out of round drums or excessive lateral runout in disc brake rotor(s) | • Refinish or replace drums, re-index rotors or replace |

# Body and Trim

**9**

## EXTERIOR

### Front Door

#### REMOVAL AND INSTALLATION

**All Models**

1. Support the door securely. Then, using a wax pencil or crayon, make an outline of the hinge where it attaches to the door.

2. Remove the door trim panel, and disconnect the electrical connectors for the power windows, door locks etc. (if equipped). Remove the hinge-to-door attaching bolts.

3. Remove the door.

**To install:**

4. Align the door hinge with the mark previously made on the door.

5. Install the hinge to door attaching bolts.

6. Connect the electrical connections.

7. Tighten the bolts securely and check the door for proper movement.

#### ADJUSTMENT

**Door Latch Striker and Door Alignment**

The door latch striker can be adjusted laterally and vertically as well as fore and aft. The striker should not be adjusted to correct door sag.

**All Models**

1. Loosen the striker attaching screws and move the striker as required.

2. Tighten the attaching screws and check the door for fit. Repeat the procedure if necessary.

The door hinges provide sufficient adjustment latitude to correct most door misalignment conditions. Do not cover up a poor door alignment with the door latch striker adjustment.

1. Loosen the hinge attaching bolts and move the hinge as required.

2. Tighten the attaching bolts and check the door for fit. Repeat the procedure if necessary.

### Door Hinge

#### REMOVAL AND INSTALLATION

**All Models**

1. Support the door.

2. Remove the hinge-to-body attaching bolts.

3. Remove the hinge-to-door attaching bolts and remove the hinge.

4. Position the hinge to the body and door, and install the attaching bolts.

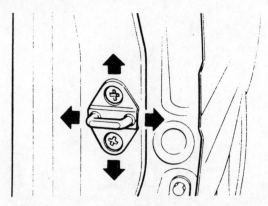

Adjusting the front door striker

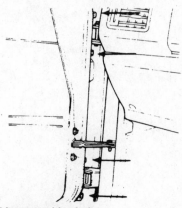

Door hinge attaching bolts

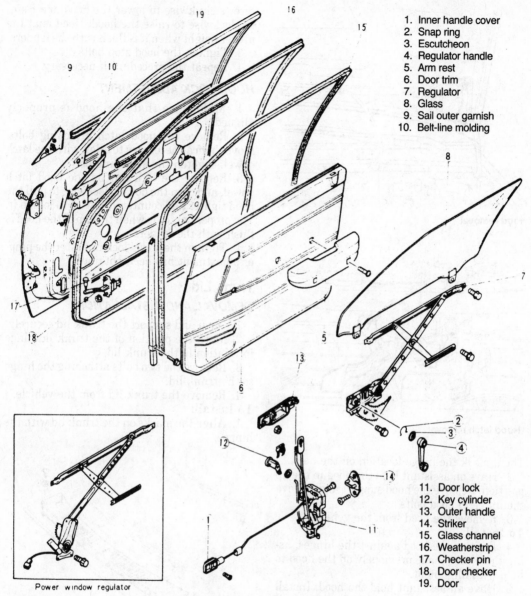

1. Inner handle cover
2. Snap ring
3. Escutcheon
4. Regulator handle
5. Arm rest
6. Door trim
7. Regulator
8. Glass
9. Sail outer garnish
10. Belt-line molding

11. Door lock
12. Key cylinder
13. Outer handle
14. Striker
15. Glass channel
16. Weatherstrip
17. Checker pin
18. Door checker
19. Door

Power window regulator

**Exploded view front door components**

5. Adjust the door as described above and tighten the attaching bolts.

## Door Locks

### REMOVAL AND INSTALLATION

#### All Models

1. Remove the regulator handle, arm rest etc.

2. Remove the trim panel and watershield.

3. Remove the bolts attaching the inner handle and remove the inner handle.

4. Raise the glass fully and disconnect the remote control rod from the lock cylinder.

5. Remove the door lock attaching screw(s) and remove the door lock.

6. Remove the retainer that secures the door lock cylinder to the door inner panel and remove the lock cylinder.

7. Installation is the reverse of the removal procedure.

## Hood

### REMOVAL AND INSTALLATION

#### All Models

NOTE: *You will need an assistant to perform this procedure.*

1. Open the hood and support it securely.

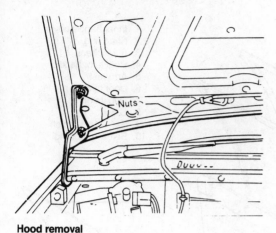

**Hood removal**

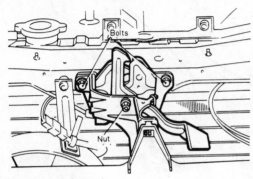

**Hood latch removal**

Then, mark the hinge location on the hood.

2. Have an assistant hold the hood in the up position. Remove the hood support and remove the hinge to hood bolts.

3. Remove the hood from the vehicle.

**To Install:**

4. Position the hood against the hinges, using the marks made previously on the hood to help with alignment.

5. Have an assistant hold the hood. Install the hinge to hood bolts, the hood support and the hood support bolts.

6. Tighten all bolts securely and check the hood for proper alignment.

### ALIGNMENT

The hood is provided with to-and-fro, up-and-down and side-to-side adjustments.

To make the to-and-fro and side-to-side adjustments:

1. Loosen the hood attaching bolts and move the hood to the proper position, then tighten the attaching bolts.

2. Repeat the procedure if necessary.

**To make the up-and-down adjustment(at the rear of the hood):**

1. Loosen the hood stop bolts.

2. Using a screwdriver, turn the hood stop

screws clockwise to lower the hood and counterclockwise to raise the hood. Hood is at the proper height when it is flush with the fenders.

3. Tighten the hood stop bolts.

4. Repeat the procedure if necessary.

### HOOD LOCK ADJUSTMENT

1. Make sure that the hood is properly aligned.

2. Remove the hood latch attaching bolts. Move them as necessary to align with the latch dowel. Tighten the attaching bolts.

3. Remove the lock nut on the hood latch dowel, and turn the dowel clockwise to pull the hood tighter and counterclockwise to loosen it. The proper height is when the top of the hood is flush with the fenders.

4. Tighten the dowel lock nut after the proper adjustment has been obtained.

## Trunk Lid

### REMOVAL AND INSTALLATION

1. Open and support the trunk lid securely.

2. Mark the position of the trunk lid hinge in relation to the trunk lid.

3. Remove the two bolts attaching the hinge to the trunk lid.

4. Remove the trunk lid from the vehicle.

**To Install:**

1. Align the marks on the trunk lid with the hinges.

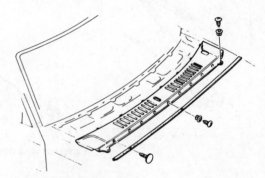

**Cowl plate removal**

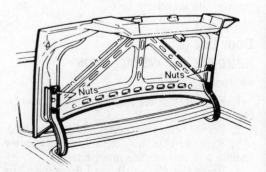

**Trunk lid**

2. Install the hinge-to-trunk lid bolts.

3. Tighten the trunk lid bolts and adjust if necessary.

### ADJUSTMENT

To make the to-and-fro or side-to-side adjustment, loosen the trunk lid attaching bolts and move the trunk lid as necessary. Tighten the trunk lid attaching bolts.

To make the up-and-down adjustment, loosen the hinge-to-hinge support attaching bolts and raise or lower the hinge as necessary. The trunk lid is at the correct height when it is flush with the trunk deck.

## Trunk Lid Lock
### ADJUSTMENT

To adjust the trunk lid lock, loosen the striker attaching bolts, and move the striker as required, then tighten the attaching bolts.

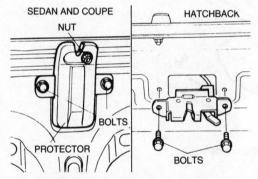

**Trunk and hatchback locks**

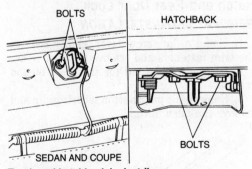

**Trunk and hatchback lock striker**

## Hatch or Rear Door
### REMOVAL AND INSTALLATION

1. Open the rear door fully and disconnect the negative battery cable.

2. Carefully remove the trim fasteners with a flat screwdriver and and remove the door trim.

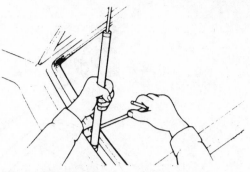

**Stay damper removal**

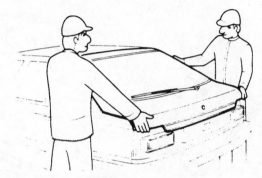

**Removing the hatch door**

3. Disconnect the wiring couplings and the ground wire.

4. Pull out the wiring harness from the rear door.

5. Disconnect the washer hose at the nozzle located on the back door and pull it out of the rear door (if equipped).

6. Support the rear door with a suitable bar. Then remove the ball studs from both the upper and lower ends of the stay dampers. Remove the stay dampers.

CAUTION: *Never disassemble the stay damper as gas is filled in the cylinder. Do not apply an oil or paint onto the piston rod. Be careful not to damage the piston rod. Do not turn the piston rod and the cylinder when the piston rod is extended. When discarding the stay damper, drill a 0.08–0.12" (2–3mm) hole in the bottom of the damper to release the gas. Make sure to protect yourself against any metal particles that may be thrown into the air by the compressed gas during drilling.*

7. Remove the rear door-to-hinge attaching bolts and remove the rear door.

8. Installation is the reverse of the removal procedure.

### ALIGNMENT

1. To align the to-and-fro position of the door, loosen the hinge attaching bolts on both the back door and the body.

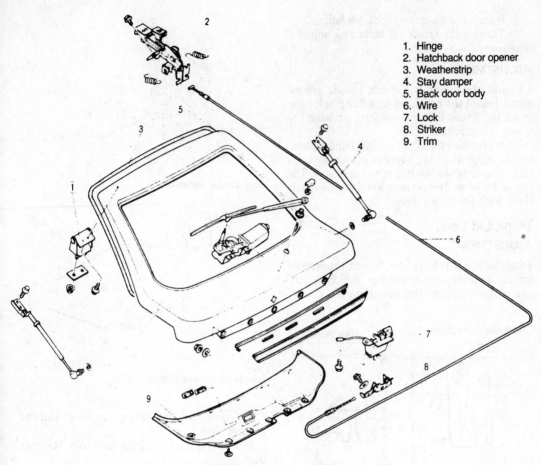

1. Hinge
2. Hatchback door opener
3. Weatherstrip
4. Stay damper
5. Back door body
6. Wire
7. Lock
8. Striker
9. Trim

**Exploded view hatchback door**

2. To adjust the door for the up and down position, loosen the hinge attaching bolts on the back door side, the door lock attaching bolts, and the door striker attaching bolts.

3. Adjust the rear for closing, by moving the door lock and striker.

4. Make all necessary adjustments by moving the rear door in the appropriate directions for the desired adjustments and tighten the attaching bolts.

## Hatch and Rear Door Lock
### REMOVAL AND INSTALLATION

1. Using a flat screwdriver, gently remove the trim fasteners and remove the door trim.

2. Disconnect the rod for the push button release.

3. Remove the push button securing clip and remove the push button.

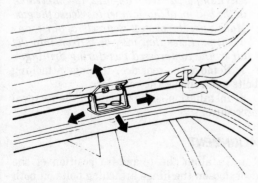

**Adjusting the hatch door hinge**

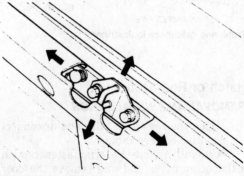

**Adjusting the striker**

1. Interior mirror
2. Sun-visor
3. Front pillar garnish
4. Front header trim
5. Wiper arm
6. Cowl grille

7. Front upper molding
8. Front side molding
9. Molding joint
10. Glass

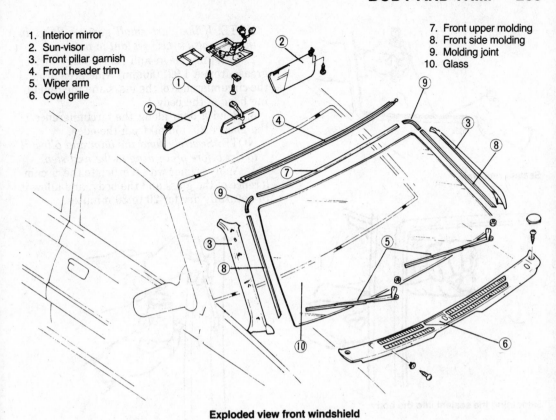

**Exploded view front windshield**

4. Remove the door lock attaching bolts and remove the door lock.

5. Installation is the reverse of the removal procedure.

6. Adjust the door as described above.

## Windshield

NOTE: *Bonded windshields require special tools and procedures. For this reason we recommend that all removal, installation and repair work be referred to a qualified technician.*

### REMOVAL AND INSTALLATION

Special tool set (49 0305 870A) is required to perform this procedure.

1. Remove the rear view mirror, sun visors, front pillar trim, and front header trim.

2. Remove the wiper arms and cowl grille.

3. Remove the front window molding.

4. Remove the glass by separating the glass from the sealant using a commercial power or manually operated remover tool, or use the following procedure.

   a. Use an awl to make a hole in the sealant.

   b. Pass a piece of piano wire, about ⅛″

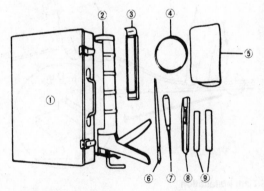

**Windshield removal kit**

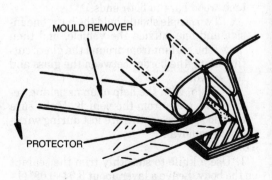

**Windshield moulding removal**

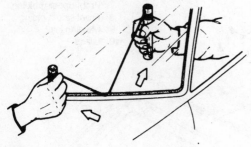

**Sealant removal**

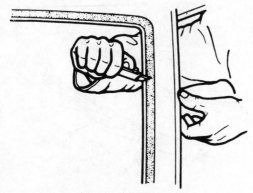

**Smoothing the sealant into the body**

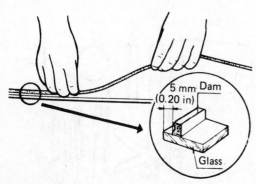

**Dam installation**

(3mm) in diameter, through the hole, and attach wood bars to both ends.

c. Two people should hold the bars, one inside and one outside the vehicle, and then "saw" the sealant from around the glass, cutting along the border between the glass and the sealant.

d. Then, with the help of an assistant, remove the glass from the vehicle. Make sure that no spacers or clips are lost during windshield removal.

**To Install:**

1. Use a knife to smoothly trim the sealant on the body. Leave a layer about 0.04–0.08" (1–2mm) thick.

NOTE: *If there are small gaps or flakes in the sealant use new sealant to patch it.*

2. Carefully clean and remove any dirt or grease from a 1.97" (50mm) wide area around the circumference of the glass and the remaining bond of the body.

3. Bond a dam along the circumference of the glass 0.20" (5mm) from the edge.

NOTE: *Securely bond the dam and allow it to dry before proceeding to the next step.*

4. Apply primer with a brush to the circumference of the glass and the body, and allow it to naturally dry for 20 to 30 minutes.

**Primer application**

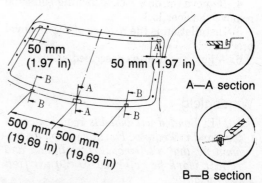

**Positioning of the spacers**

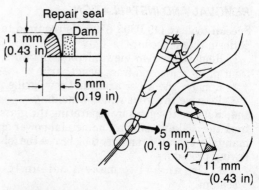

**Application of repair sealer**

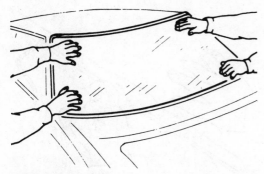

**Windshield installation**

CAUTION: *Be sure not to allow dirt, water, oil, etc. to come in contact with the coated surfaces and do not touch it with your hand.*

5. Install the spacers in the positions shown in the figure. Replace any clips with flaws.

6. When the primer has dried, apply an 0.43″ (11mm) thick bead of repair seal (B001 77 739), 0.20″ (7mm) from the frame of the glass using a sealant gun. Cut the nozzle of the sealant gun to the angle shown in the figure. If necessary, smooth the repair seal to correct any irregularities.

7. Place the windshield into the frame. Fully lower the side windows to prevent any pressure from being exerted on the windshield should the doors be closed suddenly. Keep the door glass open until the repair seal dries to some degree.

| Temperature | Surface hardening time | Time required until car can be put in service |
|---|---|---|
| 5°C (41°F) | Approx. 1.5 hrs | 12 hrs |
| 20°C (68°F) | Approx. 1 hr | 4 hrs |
| 35°C (95°F) | Approx. 10 min. | 2 hrs |

**Sealant hardening chart**

8. Remove any access, or add repair seal where necessary.

9. Check the windshield for water leaks. If a leak is found, wipe off the water and add repair seal (B 001 77 739).

10. After checking for water leakage, mount the pillar garnish, cowl panel, cowl grill, wipers, etc.

11. Attach the front header trim, sun visor, interior mirror, etc.

## Rear Window Glass

### *REMOVAL AND INSTALLATION*

#### All Models Except 323 Hatchback

Use the window tool set (49 0259 865) to remove and install the rear windshield.

NOTE: *This procedure also is used to remove and install the stationary quarter glass on the GLC wagon.*

1. Disconnect the defroster connector, remove the pillar trim, wiper motor and package tray trim (if necessary).

SEDAN AND COUPE

HATCHBACK

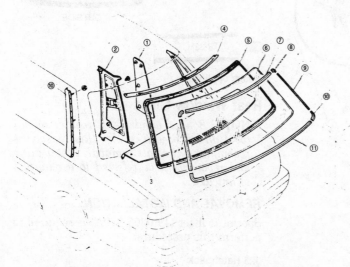

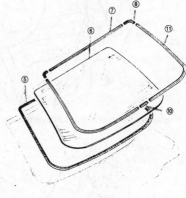

1. Rear pillar garnish
2. Rear pillar trim
3. Package tray trim
4. Rear header trim
5. Weatherstrip
6. Glass
7. Rear upper molding
8. Upper molding joint
9. Rear side molding
10. Lower molding joint
11. Rear lower molding

**Exploded view rear window glass**

2. From inside the vehicle, lift the weatherstrip toward the interior, and remove the glass with the weatherstrip attached.

3. Remove the molding.

**To Install:**

1. Remove any filler remaining on the body surface.

2. Attach the weatherstrip to the glass.

3. Fit string into the weatherstrip on the interior side of the glass, and overlap it about 2.0" (50mm) at the bottom center.

4. Coat the weatherstrip with soapy water so that the weatherstrip will slide easily into the window frame.

5. Align the glass and weatherstrip to the body.

6. While gently tapping around the weatherstrip at the outer side of the glass, pull one end of the string and fit the glass to the body.

7. With the help of an assistant, tap the glass from inside and outside with the palm of your hand. Strike the same place inside and out simultaneously, in order to seat the glass.

8. Install the molding.

9. Put filler TP-33M or equivalent sealant between the body and glass and the weatherstrip.

10. Install the filler as shown in the figure below.

NOTE: *Mask the body with tape so that excess filler can be easily removed.*

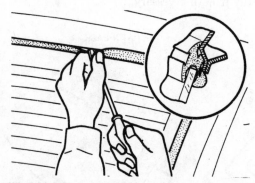

**Windshield and weatherstrip removal**

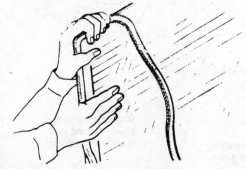

**Attaching the weatherstrip to the glass**

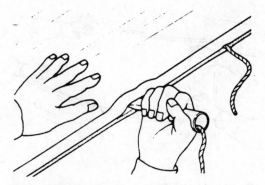

**Fitting string into the weatherstrip**

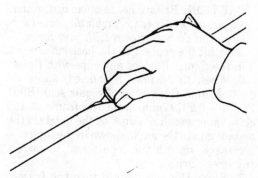

**Applying filler between the body, glass and weatherstrip**

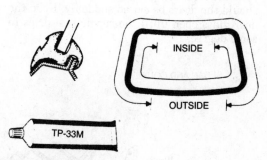

**Sealer application**

## Rear Window Glass

NOTE: *Bonded windshields require special tools and procedures. For this reason we recommend that all removal, installation and repair work be referred to a qualified technician.*

### REMOVAL AND INSTALLATION

Special tool set (49 0305 870A) is required to perform this procedure.

#### 323 Hatchback

1. Remove the wiper arm, wiper motor, back door trim and defogger connector.

2. Remove the rear window molding.

3. Use an awl to make a hole in the sealant.

4. Pass a piece of piano wire, about 1/8"

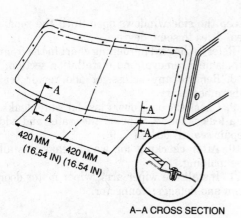

**Placing the rear window spacers**

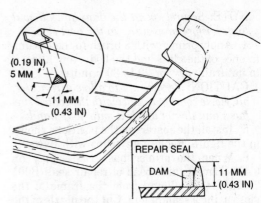

**Applying repair sealant**

(3mm) in diameter, through the hole, and attach wood bars to both ends.

5. Two people should hold the bars, one inside and one outside the vehicle, and then "saw" the sealant from around the glass, cutting along the border between the glass and the sealant.

6. Then, with the help of an assistant, remove the glass from the vehicle. Make sure that no spacers or clips are lost during windshield removal.

**To Install:**

1. Use a knife to smoothly trim the sealant on the body. Leave a layer about 0.04–0.08" (1–2mm) thick.

NOTE: *If there are small gaps or flakes in the sealant use new sealant to patch it.*

2. Carefully clean and remove any dirt or grease from a 1.97" (50mm) wide area around the circumference of the glass and the remaining bond of the body.

3. Bond a dam along the circumference of the glass 0.31" (8mm) from the edge.

1. Screw
2. Lock
3. Hinge cover
4. Screw
5. Glass
6. Weatherstrip

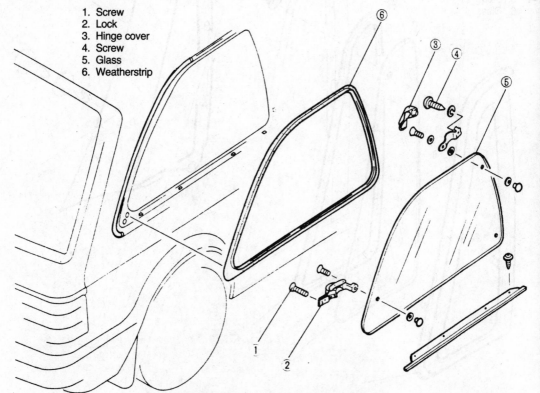

**Quarter window glass, 3 door hatchback**

NOTE: *Securely bond the dam and allow it to dry before proceeding to the next step.*

4. Apply primer with a brush to the circumference of the glass and the body, and allow it to naturally dry for 20 to 30 minutes.

CAUTION: *Be sure not to allow dirt, water, oil, etc. to come in contact with the coated surfaces and do not touch it with your hand.*

5. Install the spacers in the positions shown in the figure. Replace any clips with flaws.

6. When the primer has dried, apply an 0.43" (11mm) thick bead of repair seal (B001 77 739), 0.20" (7mm) from the frame of the glass using a sealant gun. Cut the nozzle of the sealant gun to the angle shown in the figure. If necessary, smooth the repair seal to correct any irregularities.

7. Attach the back door glass to the body. Fully lower the side windows to prevent any pressure from being exerted on the back door glass should the doors be closed suddenly.

Keep the side windows open until the repair seal dries to some degree.

Refer to the seal hardening chart in the front windshield removal and installation section.

8. Remove any access, or add repair seal where necessary.

9. Check the back door glass for water leaks. If a leak is found, wipe off the water and add repair seal (B 001 77 739).

10. After checking for water leaks, install the molding.

11. Install the wiper arm, wiper motor door trim and defogger connector.

## Quarter Window Glass
### *REMOVAL AND INSTALLATION*
#### 3-Door Hatchback

1. Remove the quarter window lock screw and the lock.

1. Rear side trim
2. Nut
3. Pillar trim
4. Seal rubber
5. Stud
6. Glass

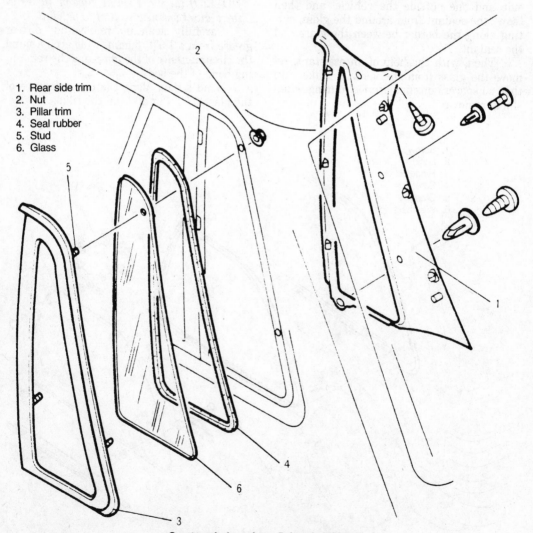

**Quarter window glass, 5 door hatchback**

2. Remove the hinge cover, then remove the screws washers and the window hinge.

3. Remove the quarter glass from the body.

4. Remove the weatherstrip from the glass.

5. Installation is the reverse of the removal procedure.

### 5-Door hatchback

1. Remove the rear side trim.

2. Remove the nut that secures the pillar trim and glass to the vehicle.

3. Remove the pillar trim, glass and rubber seal.

4. Reverse the removal procedure to install.

## INTERIOR

## Door Panels

### REMOVAL AND INSTALLATION

1. Remove the window regulator handle.

2. Remove the arm rest.

3. Remove the door lock knob.

4. Remove the inner door handle cover.

5. Using a flat screwdriver, gently separate the door trim panel clips from the door.

6. Remove the door trim panel.

**To Install:**

1. Place the door trim panel into position on the door.

2. Apply pressure to the trim panel in the areas where the trim panel clips attach to the door.

3. Install the inner door handle cover, door lock knob and the arm rest.

## Door Glass and Regulator

### REMOVAL AND INSTALLATION

1. Lower the window glass and remove the inner handle cover, door lock knob (if necessary), the window regulator handle and the door trim panel.

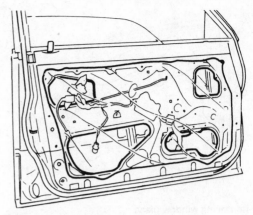

**Door screen removal**

NOTE: *On vehicles with power windows, disconnect the wiring coupling.*

2. Carefully peel off the door screen so that it can be reused.

3. On 1971–83 models remove the six bolts attaching the window regulator to the door.

4. On 1984–87 models replace the window regulator handle and position the door glass so that the door glass installation bolts can be removed from the service hole.

5. Remove the door glass installation bolts.

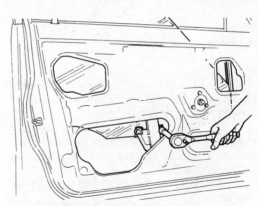

**Removing door glass installation bolts**

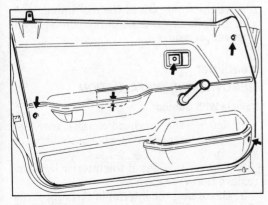

**Door inner cover**

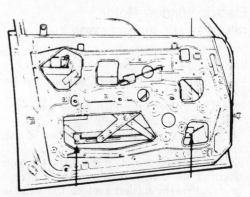

**Window regulator attaching bolts**

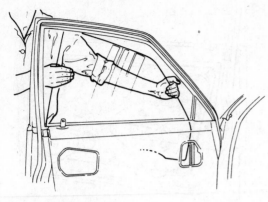

**Removing window glass**

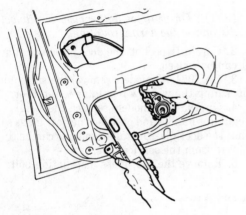

**Removing window regulator**

6. On 1971–83 models, remove the door glass and take out the window regulator through the large access hole.

7. On 1983–87 models, remove the door glass. Remove the regulator installation bolts, and then remove the regulator through the service access hole.

8. Installation is the reverse of the removal procedure.

## Electric Window Motor
### REMOVAL AND INSTALLATION

1. Lower the window glass and remove the inner handle cover, door lock knob (if necessary), the window regulator handle and the door trim panel.

NOTE: *On vehicles with power windows, disconnect the wiring coupling.*

2. Carefully peel off the door screen so that it can be reused.

3. On 1971–83 models remove the six bolts attaching the window regulator to the door.

4. On 1984–87 models replace the window regulator handle and position the door glass so

that the door glass installation bolts can be removed from the service hole.

5. Remove the door glass installation bolts.

6. On 1971–83 models, remove the door glass and take out the window regulator through the large access hole.

7. On 1983–87 models, remove the door glass. Remove the regulator installation bolts, and then remove the regulator through the service access hole.

8. Remove the window motor mounting bolts, then remove the motor from the regulator.

9. Installation is the reverse of the removal procedure.

## Headliner
### REMOVAL AND INSTALLATION

1. Remove the rear view mirror, sun visors, sunvisor holders and the assist grip.

2. Remove the lens of the interior light and remove the screws.

3. Disconnect the interior lamp harness coupler.

4. Remove the hinge cover and the screws, then remove the side glass (3 door hatchback models only) using the procedures found earlier in this section.

5. Remove the weatherstrip.

6. Remove the seaming welt.

7. Remove the front door trim by prying with a flat screwdriver.

8. Remove the center pillar trim.

9. Remove the weatherstrip, fasteners, and then remove the rear pillar trim.

10. Remove the fasteners from the roof lining.

11. Remove the floor lining rear end plate.

NOTE: *On the sedan vehicle, remove the plate while pushing the weatherstrip away from the end plate.*

12. Remove the rear of the roof lining by pulling it free from the corners.

13. Move the roof lining brace rearward and remove the front part of the roof lining.

14. Installation is done in the reverse of the removal procedure.

## Headliner
### REMOVAL AND INSTALLATION
**Vehicle With Sunroof**

1. Remove the overhead console, rear view mirror, sun visors, sunvisor holders and the assist grip.

2. Remove the lens of the interior light and remove the screws.

3. Disconnect the interior lamp harness coupler and remove the interior lamp.

## Sedan

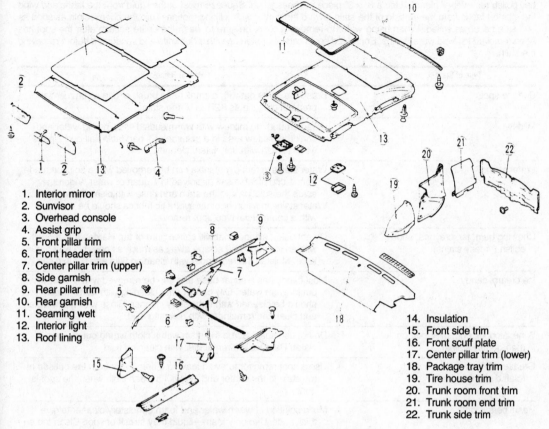

1. Interior mirror
2. Sunvisor
3. Overhead console
4. Assist grip
5. Front pillar trim
6. Front header trim
7. Center pillar trim (upper)
8. Side garnish
9. Rear pillar trim
10. Rear garnish
11. Seaming welt
12. Interior light
13. Roof lining

14. Insulation
15. Front side trim
16. Front scuff plate
17. Center pillar trim (lower)
18. Package tray trim
19. Tire house trim
20. Trunk room front trim
21. Trunk room end trim
22. Trunk side trim

**Exploded view, roof liner and components**

4. Remove the seaming welt from the sunroof opening.

5. Remove the front of the door opening seaming welts.

6. Remove the front pillar trims.

7. Remove the roof lining front lace.

8. Remove the rear of the door opening seaming welts.

9. Remove the rear pillar trim.

10. Remove the roof lining rear lace.

11. Remove the side pillar trim.

12. Remove the attaching screws of the roof lining side lace and remove the side lace.

13. Remove the fasteners at the side of the roof lining and remove the roof lining.

14. Installation is the reverse of the removal procedure.

## How to Remove Stains from Fabric Interior

For rest results, spots and stains should be removed as soon as possible. Never use gasoline, lacquer thinner, acetone, nail polish remover or bleach. Use a 3′ x 3″ piece of cheesecloth. Squeeze most of the liquid from the fabric and wipe the stained fabric from the outside of the stain toward the center with a lifting motion. Turn the cheesecloth as soon as one side becomes soiled. When using water to remove a stain, be sure to wash the entire section after the spot has been removed to avoid water stains. Encrusted spots can be broken up with a dull knife and vacuumed before removing the stain.

| Type of Stain | How to Remove It |
|---|---|
| Surface spots | Brush the spots out with a small hand brush or use a commercial preparation such as K2R to lift the stain. |
| Mildew | Clean around the mildew with warm suds. Rinse in cold water and soak the mildew area in a solution of 1 part table salt and 2 parts water. Wash with upholstery cleaner. |
| Water stains | Water stains in fabric materials can be removed with a solution made from 1 cup of table salt dissolved in 1 quart of water. Vigorously scrub the solution into the stain and rinse with clear water. Water stains in nylon or other synthetic fabrics should be removed with a commercial type spot remover. |
| Chewing gum, tar, crayons, shoe polish (greasy stains) | Do not use a cleaner that will soften gum or tar. Harden the deposit with an ice cube and scrape away as much as possible with a dull knife. Moisten the remainder with cleaning fluid and scrub clean. |
| Ice cream, candy | Most candy has a sugar base and can be removed with a cloth wrung out in warm water. Oily candy, after cleaning with warm water, should be cleaned with upholstery cleaner. Rinse with warm water and clean the remainder with cleaning fluid. |
| Wine, alcohol, egg, milk, soft drink (non-greasy stains) | Do not use soap. Scrub the stain with a cloth wrung out in warm water. Remove the remainder with cleaning fluid. |
| Grease, oil, lipstick, butter and related stains | Use a spot remover to avoid leaving a ring. Work from the outisde of the stain to the center and dry with a clean cloth when the spot is gone. |
| Headliners (cloth) | Mix a solution of warm water and foam upholstery cleaner to give thick suds. Use only foam—liquid may streak or spot. Clean the entire headliner in one operation using a circular motion with a natural sponge. |
| Headliner (vinyl) | Use a vinyl cleaner with a sponge and wipe clean with a dry cloth. |
| Seats and door panels | Mix 1 pint upholstery cleaner in 1 gallon of water. Do not soak the fabric around the buttons. |
| Leather or vinyl fabric | Use a multi-purpose cleaner full strength and a stiff brush. Let stand 2 minutes and scrub thoroughly. Wipe with a clean, soft rag. |
| Nylon or synthetic fabrics | For normal stains, use the same procedures you would for washing cloth upholstery. If the fabric is extremely dirty, use a multi-purpose cleaner full strength with a stiff scrub brush. Scrub thoroughly in all directions and wipe with a cotton towel or soft rag. |

# Mechanic's Data

## General Conversion Table

| Multiply By | To Convert | To | |
|---|---|---|---|
| **LENGTH** | | | |
| 2.54 | Inches | Centimeters | .3937 |
| 25.4 | Inches | Millimeters | .03937 |
| 30.48 | Feet | Centimeters | .0328 |
| .304 | Feet | Meters | 3.28 |
| .914 | Yards | Meters | 1.094 |
| 1.609 | Miles | Kilometers | .621 |
| **VOLUME** | | | |
| .473 | Pints | Liters | 2.11 |
| .946 | Quarts | Liters | 1.06 |
| 3.785 | Gallons | Liters | .264 |
| .016 | Cubic inches | Liters | 61.02 |
| 16.39 | Cubic inches | Cubic cms. | .061 |
| 28.3 | Cubic feet | Liters | .0353 |
| **MASS (Weight)** | | | |
| 28.35 | Ounces | Grams | .035 |
| .4536 | Pounds | Kilograms | 2.20 |
| — | To obtain | From | Multiply by |

| Multiply By | To Convert | To | |
|---|---|---|---|
| **AREA** | | | |
| .645 | Square inches | Square cms. | .155 |
| .836 | Square yds. | Square meters | 1.196 |
| **FORCE** | | | |
| 4.448 | Pounds | Newtons | .225 |
| .138 | Ft./lbs. | Kilogram/meters | 7.23 |
| 1.36 | Ft./lbs. | Newton-meters | .737 |
| .112 | In./lbs. | Newton-meters | 8.844 |
| **PRESSURE** | | | |
| .068 | Psi | Atmospheres | 14.7 |
| 6.89 | Psi | Kilopascals | .145 |
| **OTHER** | | | |
| 1.104 | Horsepower (DIN) | Horsepower (SAE) | .9861 |
| .746 | Horsepower (SAE) | Kilowatts (KW) | 1.34 |
| 1.60 | Mph | Km/h | .625 |
| .425 | Mpg | Km/1 | 2.35 |
| — | To obtain | From | Multiply by |

## Tap Drill Sizes

### National Coarse or U.S.S.

| Screw & Tap Size | Threads Per Inch | Use Drill Number |
|---|---|---|
| No.  5 | 40 | 39 |
| No.  6 | 32 | 36 |
| No.  8 | 32 | 29 |
| No. 10 | 24 | 25 |
| No. 12 | 24 | 17 |
| 1/4 | 20 | 8 |
| 5/16 | 18 | F |
| 3/8 | 16 | 5/16 |
| 7/16 | 14 | U |
| 1/2 | 13 | 27/64 |
| 9/16 | 12 | 31/64 |
| 5/8 | 11 | 17/32 |
| 3/4 | 10 | 21/32 |
| 7/8 | 9 | 49/64 |

### National Coarse or U.S.S.

| Screw & Tap Size | Threads Per Inch | Use Drill Number |
|---|---|---|
| 1 | 8 | 7/8 |
| 1 1/8 | 7 | 63/64 |
| 1 1/4 | 7 | 1 7/64 |
| 1 1/2 | 6 | 1 11/32 |

### National Fine or S.A.E.

| Screw & Tap Size | Threads Per Inch | Use Drill Number |
|---|---|---|
| No.  5 | 44 | 37 |
| No.  6 | 40 | 33 |
| No.  8 | 36 | 29 |
| No. 10 | 32 | 21 |

### National Fine or S.A.E.

| Screw & Tap Size | Threads Per Inch | Use Drill Number |
|---|---|---|
| No. 12 | 28 | 15 |
| 1/4 | 28 | 3 |
| 6/16 | 24 | 1 |
| 3/8 | 24 | Q |
| 7/16 | 20 | W |
| 1/2 | 20 | 29/64 |
| 9/16 | 18 | 33/64 |
| 5/8 | 18 | 37/64 |
| 3/4 | 16 | 11/16 |
| 7/8 | 14 | 13/16 |
| 1 1/8 | 12 | 1 3/64 |
| 1 1/4 | 12 | 1 11/64 |
| 1 1/2 | 12 | 1 27/64 |

**AIR/FUEL RATIO**: The ratio of air to gasoline by weight in the fuel mixture drawn into the engine.

**AIR INJECTION**: One method of reducing harmful exhaust emissions by injecting air into each of the exhaust ports of an engine. The fresh air entering the hot exhaust manifold causes any remaining fuel to be burned before it can exit the tailpipe.

**ALTERNATOR**: A device used for converting mechanical energy into electrical energy.

**AMMETER**: An instrument, calibrated in amperes, used to measure the flow of an electrical current in a circuit. Ammeters are always connected in series with the circuit being tested.

**AMPERE**: The rate of flow of electrical current present when one volt of electrical pressure is applied against one ohm of electrical resistance.

**ANALOG COMPUTER**: Any microprocessor that uses similar (analogous) electrical signals to make its calculations.

**ARMATURE**: A laminated, soft iron core wrapped by a wire that converts electrical energy to mechanical energy as in a motor or relay. When rotated in a magnetic field, it changes mechanical energy into electrical energy as in a generator.

**ATMOSPHERIC PRESSURE**: The pressure on the Earth's surface caused by the weight of the air in the atmosphere. At sea level, this pressure is 14.7 psi at 32°F (101 kPa at 0°C).

**ATOMIZATION**: The breaking down of a liquid into a fine mist that can be suspended in air.

**AXIAL PLAY**: Movement parallel to a shaft or bearing bore.

**BACKFIRE**: The sudden combustion of gases in the intake or exhaust system that results in a loud explosion.

**BACKLASH**: The clearance or play between two parts, such as meshed gears.

**BACKPRESSURE**: Restrictions in the exhaust system that slow the exit of exhaust gases from the combustion chamber.

**BAKELITE**: A heat resistant, plastic insulator material commonly used in printed circuit boards and transistorized components.

**BALL BEARING**: A bearing made up of hardened inner and outer races between which hardened steel ball roll.

**BALLAST RESISTOR**: A resistor in the primary ignition circuit that lowers voltage after the engine is started to reduce wear on ignition components.

**BEARING**: A friction reducing, supportive device usually located between a stationary part and a moving part.

**BIMETAL TEMPERATURE SENSOR**: Any sensor or switch made of two dissimilar types of metal that bend when heated or cooled due to the different expansion rates of the alloys. These types of sensors usually function as an on/off switch.

**BLOWBY**: Combustion gases, composed of water vapor and unburned fuel, that leak past the piston rings into the crankcase during normal engine operation. These gases are removed by the PCV system to prevent the buildup of harmful acids in the crankcase.

**BRAKE PAD**: A brake shoe and lining assembly used with disc brakes.

**BRAKE SHOE**: The backing for the brake lining. The term is, however, usually applied to the assembly of the brake backing and lining.

**BUSHING**: A liner, usually removable, for a bearing; an anti-friction liner used in place of a bearing.

**BYPASS**: System used to bypass ballast resistor during engine cranking to increase voltage supplied to the coil.

**CALIPER**: A hydraulically activated device in a disc brake system, which is mounted straddling the brake rotor (disc). The caliper contains at least one piston and two brake pads. Hydraulic pressure on the piston(s) forces the pads against the rotor.

**CAMSHAFT**: A shaft in the engine on which are the lobes (cams) which operate the valves. The camshaft is driven by the crankshaft, via a belt, chain or gears, at one half the crankshaft speed.

**CAPACITOR**: A device which stores an electrical charge.

**CARBON MONOXIDE (CO)**: a colorless, odorless gas given off as a normal byproduct of combustion. It is poisonous and extremely dangerous in confined areas, building up slowly to toxic levels without warning if adequate ventilation is not available.

**CARBURETOR**: A device, usually mounted on the intake manifold of an engine, which mixes the air and fuel in the proper proportion to allow even combustion.

**CATALYTIC CONVERTER**: A device installed in the exhaust system, like a muffler, that converts harmful byproducts of combustion into carbon dioxide and water vapor by means of a heat-producing chemical reaction.

**CENTRIFUGAL ADVANCE**: A mechanical method of advancing the spark timing by using flyweights in the distributor that react to centrifugal force generated by the distributor shaft rotation.

**CHECK VALVE**: Any one-way valve installed to permit the flow of air, fuel or vacuum in one direction only.

**CHOKE**: A device, usually a moveable valve, placed in the intake path of a carburetor to restrict the flow of air.

**CIRCUIT**: Any unbroken path through which an electrical current can flow. Also used to describe fuel flow in some instances.

**CIRCUIT BREAKER**: A switch which protects an electrical circuit from overload by opening the circuit when the current flow exceeds a predetermined level. Some circuit breakers must be reset manually, while other reset automatically

**COIL (IGNITION)**: A transformer in the ignition circuit which steps of the voltage provided to the spark plugs.

**COMBINATION MANIFOLD**: An assembly which includes both the intake and exhaust manifolds in one casting.

**COMBINATION VALVE**: A device used in some fuel systems that routes fuel vapors to a charcoal storage canister instead of venting them into the atmosphere. The valve relieves fuel tank pressure and allows fresh air into the tank as fuel level drops to prevent a vapor lock situation.

**COMPRESSION RATIO**: The comparison of the total volume of the cylinder and combustion chamber with the piston at BDC and the piston at TDC.

**CONDENSER**: 1. An electrical device which acts to store an electrical charge, preventing voltage surges.
2. A radiator-like device in the air conditioning system in which refrigerant gas condenses into a liquid, giving off heat.

**CONDUCTOR**: Any material through which an electrical current can be transmitted easily.

**CONTINUITY**: Continuous or complete circuit. Can be checked with an ohmmeter.

**COUNTERSHAFT**: An intermediate shaft which is rotated by a mainshaft and transmits, in turn, that rotation to a working part.

**CRANKCASE**: The lower part of an engine in which the crankshaft and related parts operate.

**CRANKSHAFT**: The main driving shaft of an engine which receives reciprocating motion from the pistons and converts it to rotary motion.

**CYLINDER**: In an engine, the round hole in the engine block in which the piston(s) ride.

**CYLINDER BLOCK**: The main structural member of an engine in which is found the cylinders, crankshaft and other principal parts.

**CYLINDER HEAD**: The detachable portion of the engine, fastened, usually, to the top of the cylinder block, containing all or most of the combustion chambers. On overhead valve engines, it contains the valves and their operating parts. On overhead cam engines, it contains the camshaft as well.

**DEAD CENTER**: The extreme top or bottom of the piston stroke.

**DETONATION**: An unwanted explosion of the air fuel mixture in the combustion chamber caused by excess heat and compression, advanced timing, or an overly lean mixture. Also referred to as "ping".

**DIAPHRAGM**: A thin, flexible wall separating two cavities, such as in a vacuum advance unit.

**DIESELING**: A condition in which hot spots in the combustion chamber cause the engine to run on after the key is turned off.

**DIFFERENTIAL**: A geared assembly which allows the transmission of motion between drive axles, giving one axle the ability to turn faster than the other.

**DIODE**: An electrical device that will allow current to flow in one direction only.

**DISC BRAKE**: A hydraulic braking assembly consisting of a brake disc, or rotor, mounted on an axle, and a caliper assembly containing, usually two brake pads which are activated by hydraulic pressure. The pads are forced against the sides of the disc, creating friction which slows the vehicle.

**DISTRIBUTOR**: A mechanically driven device on an engine which is responsible for electrically firing the spark plug at a predetermined point of the piston stroke.

**DOWEL PIN**: A pin, inserted in mating holes in two different parts allowing those parts to maintain a fixed relationship.

**DRUM BRAKE**: A braking system which consists of two brake shoes and one or two wheel cylinders, mounted on a fixed backing plate, and a brake drum, mounted on an axle, which revolves around the assembly. Hydraulic action applied to the wheel cylinders forces the shoes outward against the drum, creating friction and slowing the vehicle.

**DWELL**: The rate, measured in degrees of shaft rotation, at which an electrical circuit cycles on and off.

**ELECTRONIC CONTROL UNIT (ECU)**: Ignition module, module, amplifier or igniter. See Module for definition.

**ELECTRONIC IGNITION**: A system in which the timing and firing of the spark plugs is controlled by an electronic control unit, usually called a module. These systems have not points or condenser.

**ENDPLAY**: The measured amount of axial movement in a shaft.

**ENGINE**: A device that converts heat into mechanical energy.

**EXHAUST MANIFOLD**: A set of cast passages or pipes which conduct exhaust gases from the engine.

**FEELER GAUGE**: A blade, usually metal, of precisely predetermined thickness, used to measure the clearance between two parts. These blades usually are available in sets of assorted thicknesses.

**F-Head**: An engine configuration in which the intake valves are in the cylinder head, while the camshaft and exhaust valves are located in the cylinder block. The camshaft operates the intake valves via lifters and pushrods, while it operates the exhaust valves directly.

**FIRING ORDER**: The order in which combustion occurs in the cylinders of an engine. Also the order in which spark is distributed to the plugs by the distributor.

**FLATHEAD**: An engine configuration in which the camshaft and all the valves are located in the cylinder block.

**FLOODING**: The presence of too much fuel in the intake manifold and combustion chamber which prevents the air/fuel mixture from firing, thereby causing a no-start situation.

**FLYWHEEL**: A disc shaped part bolted to the rear end of the crankshaft. Around the outer perimeter is affixed the ring gear. The starter drive engages the ring gear, turning the flywheel, which rotates the crankshaft, imparting the initial starting motion to the engine.

**FOOT POUND (ft.lb. or sometimes, ft. lbs.)**: The amount of energy or work needed to raise an item weighing one pound, a distance of one foot.

**FUSE**: A protective device in a circuit which prevents circuit overload by breaking the circuit when a specific amperage is present. The device is constructed around a strip or wire of a lower amperage rating than the circuit it is designed to protect. When an amperage higher than that stamped on the fuse is present in the circuit, the strip or wire melts, opening the circuit.

**GEAR RATIO**: The ratio between the number of teeth on meshing gears.

**GENERATOR**: A device which converts mechanical energy into electrical energy.

**HEAT RANGE**: The measure of a spark plug's ability to dissipate heat from its firing end. The higher the heat range, the hotter the plug fires.

**HUB**: The center part of a wheel or gear.

**HYDROCARBON (HC)**: Any chemical compound made up of hydrogen and carbon. A major pollutant formed by the engine as a byproduct of combustion.

**HYDROMETER**: An instrument used to measure the specific gravity of a solution.

**INCH POUND (in.lb. or sometimes, in. lbs.)**: One twelfth of a foot pound.

**INDUCTION**: A means of transferring electrical energy in the form of a magnetic field. Principle used in the ignition coil to increase voltage.

**INJECTION PUMP**: A device, usually mechanically operated, which meters and delivers fuel under pressure to the fuel injector.

**INJECTOR**: A device which receives metered fuel under relatively low pressure and is activated to inject the fuel into the engine under relatively high pressure at a predetermined time.

**INPUT SHAFT**: The shaft to which torque is applied, usually carrying the driving gear or gears.

**INTAKE MANIFOLD**: A casting of passages or pipes used to conduct air or a fuel/air mixture to the cylinders.

**JOURNAL**: The bearing surface within which a shaft operates.

**KEY**: A small block usually fitted in a notch between a shaft and a hub to prevent slippage of the two parts.

**MANIFOLD**: A casting of passages or set of pipes which connect the cylinders to an inlet or outlet source.

**MANIFOLD VACUUM**: Low pressure in an engine intake manifold formed just below the throttle plates. Manifold vacuum is highest at idle and drops under acceleration.

**MASTER CYLINDER**: The primary fluid pressurizing device in a hydraulic system. In automotive use, it is found in brake and hydraulic clutch systems and is pedal activated, either directly or, in a power brake system, through the power booster.

**MODULE**: Electronic control unit, amplifier or igniter of solid state or integrated design which controls the current flow in the ignition primary circuit based on input from the pick-up coil. When the module opens the primary circuit, the high secondary voltage is induced in the coil.

**NEEDLE BEARING**: A bearing which consists of a number (usually a large number) of long, thin rollers.

**OHM**: ($\Omega$) The unit used to measure the resistance of conductor to electrical flow. One ohm is the amount of resistance that limits current flow to one ampere in a circuit with one volt of pressure.

**OHMMETER**: An instrument used for measuring the resistance, in ohms, in an electrical circuit.

**OUTPUT SHAFT**: The shaft which transmits torque from a device, such as a transmission.

**OVERDRIVE**: A gear assembly which produces more shaft revolutions than that transmitted to it.

**OVERHEAD CAMSHAFT (OHC)**: An engine configuration in which the camshaft is mounted on top of the cylinder head and operates the valve either directly or by means of rocker arms.

**OVERHEAD VALVE (OHV)**: An engine configuration in which all of the valves are located in the cylinder head and the camshaft is located in the cylinder block. The camshaft operates the valves via lifters and pushrods.

**OXIDES OF NITROGEN (NOx)**: Chemical compounds of nitrogen produced as a byproduct of combustion. They combine with hydrocarbons to produce smog.

**OXYGEN SENSOR**: Used with the feedback system to sense the presence of oxygen in the exhaust gas and signal the computer which can reference the voltage signal to an air/fuel ratio.

**PINION**: The smaller of two meshing gears.

**PISTON RING**: An open ended ring which fits into a groove on the outer diameter of the piston. Its chief function is to form a seal between the piston and cylinder wall. Most automotive pistons have three rings: two for compression sealing; one for oil sealing.

**PRELOAD**: A predetermined load placed on a bearing during assembly or by adjustment.

**PRIMARY CIRCUIT**: Is the low voltage side of the ignition system which consists of the ignition switch, ballast resistor or resistance wire, bypass, coil, electronic control unit and pick-up coil as well as the connecting wires and harnesses.

**PRESS FIT**: The mating of two parts under pressure, due to the inner diameter of one being smaller than the outer diameter of the other, or vice versa; an interference fit.

**RACE**: The surface on the inner or outer ring of a bearing on which the balls, needles or rollers move.

**REGULATOR**: A device which maintains the amperage and/or voltage levels of a circuit at predetermined values.

**RELAY**: A switch which automatically opens and/or closes a circuit.

**RESISTANCE**: The opposition to the flow of current through a circuit or electrical device, and is measured in ohms. Resistance is equal to the voltage divided by the amperage.

**RESISTOR**: A device, usually made of wire, which offers a preset amount of resistance in an electrical circuit.

**RING GEAR**: The name given to a ring-shaped gear attached to a differential case, or affixed to a flywheel or as part a planetary gear set.

**ROLLER BEARING**: A bearing made up of hardened inner and outer races between which hardened steel rollers move.

**ROTOR**: 1. The disc-shaped part of a disc brake assembly, upon which the brake pads bear; also called, brake disc.
2. The device mounted atop the distributor shaft, which passes current to the distributor cap tower contacts.

**SECONDARY CIRCUIT**: The high voltage side of the ignition system, usually above 20,000 volts. The secondary includes the ignition coil, coil wire, distributor cap and rotor, spark plug wires and spark plugs.

**SENDING UNIT**: A mechanical, electrical, hydraulic or electromagnetic device which transmits information to a gauge.

**SENSOR**: Any device designed to measure engine operating conditions or ambient pressures and temperatures. Usually electronic in nature and designed to send a voltage signal to an on-board computer, some sensors may operate as a simple on/off switch or they may provide a variable voltage signal (like a potentiometer) as conditions or measured parameters change.

**SHIM**: Spacers of precise, predetermined thickness used between parts to establish a proper working relationship.

**SLAVE CYLINDER**: In automotive use, a device in the hydraulic clutch system which is activated by hydraulic force, disengaging the clutch.

**SOLENOID**: A coil used to produce a magnetic field, the effect of which is produce work.

**SPARK PLUG**: A device screwed into the combustion chamber of a spark ignition engine. The basic construction is a conductive core inside of a ceramic insulator, mounted in an outer conductive base. An electrical charge from the spark plug wire travels along the conductive core and jumps a preset air gap to a grounding point or points at the end of the conductive base. The resultant spark ignites the fuel/air mixture in the combustion chamber.

**SPLINES**: Ridges machined or cast onto the outer diameter of a shaft or inner diameter of a bore to enable parts to mate without rotation.

**TACHOMETER**: A device used to measure the rotary speed of an engine, shaft, gear, etc., usually in rotations per minute.

**THERMOSTAT**: A valve, located in the cooling system of an engine, which is closed when cold and opens gradually in response to engine heating, controlling the temperature of the coolant and rate of coolant flow.

**TOP DEAD CENTER** (TDC): The point at which the piston reaches the top of its travel on the compression stroke.

**TORQUE**: The twisting force applied to an object.

**TORQUE CONVERTER**: A turbine used to transmit power from a driving member to a driven member via hydraulic action, providing changes in drive ratio and torque. In automotive use, it links the driveplate at the rear of the engine to the automatic transmission.

**TRANSDUCER**: A device used to change a force into an electrical signal.

**TRANSISTOR**: A semi-conductor component which can be actuated by a small voltage to perform an electrical switching function.

**TUNE-UP**: A regular maintenance function, usually associated with the replacement and adjustment of parts and components in the electrical and fuel systems of a vehicle for the purpose of attaining optimum performance.

**TURBOCHARGER**: An exhaust driven pump which compresses intake air and forces it into the combustion chambers at higher than atmospheric pressures. The increased air pressure allows more fuel to be burned and results in increased horsepower being produced.

**VACUUM ADVANCE**: A device which advances the ignition timing in response to increased engine vacuum.

**VACUUM GAUGE**: An instrument used to measure the presence of vacuum in a chamber.

**VALVE**: A device which control the pressure, direction of flow or rate of flow of a liquid or gas.

**VALVE CLEARANCE**: The measured gap between the end of the valve stem and the rocker arm, cam lobe or follower that activates the valve.

**VISCOSITY**: The rating of a liquid's internal resistance to flow.

**VOLTMETER**: An instrument used for measuring electrical force in units called volts. Voltmeters are always connected parallel with the circuit being tested.

**WHEEL CYLINDER**: Found in the automotive drum brake assembly, it is a device, actuated by hydraulic pressure, which, through internal pistons, pushes the brake shoes outward against the drums.

A: Ampere

AC: Alternating current

A/C: Air conditioning

A-h: Ampere hour

AT: Automatic transmission

ATDC: After top dead center

$\mu$A: Microampere

bbl: Barrel

BDC: Bottom dead center

bhp: Brake horsepower

BTDC: Before top dead center

BTU: British thermal unit

C: Celsius (Centigrade)

CCA: Cold cranking amps

cd: Candela

$cm^2$: Square centimeter

$cm^3$, cc: Cubic centimeter

CO: Carbon monoxide

$CO_2$: Carbon dioxide

cu.in., $in^3$: Cubic inch

CV: Constant velocity

Cyl.: Cylinder

DC: Direct current

ECM: Electronic control module

EFE: Early fuel evaporation

EFI: Electronic fuel injection

EGR: Exhaust gas recirculation

Exh.: Exhaust

F: Fahrenheit

F: Farad

pF: Picofarad

$\mu$F: Microfarad

FI: Fuel injection

ft.lb., ft. lb., ft. lbs.: foot pound(s)

gal: Gallon

g: Gram

HC: Hydrocarbon

HEI: High energy ignition

HO: High output

hp: Horsepower

Hyd.: Hydraulic

Hz: Hertz

ID: Inside diameter

in.lb.; in. lb.; in. lbs: inch pound(s)

Int.: Intake

K: Kelvin

kg: Kilogram

kHz: Kilohertz

km: Kilometer

km/h: Kilometers per hour

k$\Omega$: Kilohm

kPa: Kilopascal

kV: Kilovolt

kW: Kilowatt

l: Liter

l/s: Liters per second

m: Meter

mA: Milliampere

mg: Milligram

mHz: Megahertz

mm: Millimeter

mm$^2$: Square millimeter

m$^3$: Cubic meter

MΩ: Megohm

m/s: Meters per second

MT: Manual transmission

mV: Millivolt

μm: Micrometer

N: Newton

N-m: Newton meter

NOx: Nitrous oxide

OD: Outside diameter

OHC: Over head camshaft

OHV: Over head valve

Ω: Ohm

PCV: Positive crankcase ventilation

psi: Pounds per square inch

pts: Pints

qts: Quarts

rpm: Rotations per minute

rps: Rotations per second

R-12: A refrigerant gas (Freon)

SAE: Society of Automotive Engineers

SO$_2$: Sulfur dioxide

T: Ton

t: Megagram

TBI: Throttle Body Injection

TPS: Throttle Position Sensor

V: 1. Volt; 2. Venturi

μV: Microvolt

W: Watt

∝: Infinity

<: Less than

>: Greater than

# Index